"Charles Haddon Spurgeon was, by common consent, the greatest preacher of Victorian England. His vivid, witty sermons—published weekly—enjoyed an enormous circulation in many parts of the world. In this book, Thomas Breimaier, a tutor in the theological college Spurgeon founded, examines the content of Spurgeon's sermons in the context of the preacher's whole career, clearly establishing that the cross was their central theme and conversion their overriding aim."

David Bebbington, emeritus professor of history, University of Stirling, Scotland

"C. H. Spurgeon was the most popular and effective preacher of the Victorian age. Thomas Breimaier's scholarly but accessible study of Spurgeon's use of the Bible shows clearly that a focus on the cross of Christ and an appeal to his hearers to turn to Christ in faith were the consistent hallmarks of his preaching and writing. Breimaier has broken new ground through this book. It will become an indispensable addition to scholarship on this eminent but too often caricatured Victorian."

Brian Stanley, professor of World Christianity, University of Edinburgh School of Divinity

"I am happy to recommend this rich, judicious study of Charles Spurgeon's preaching and theology. Every student and admirer of Spurgeon will want to read this book."

Thomas S. Kidd, Vardaman Distinguished Professor of History, Baylor University

"While Spurgeon has often loomed large in certain segments of Christianity and popular piety, academic studies of his thought remain rather scant. This erudite work of historical theology will leave readers with a better understanding of Spurgeon's theology of Scripture and of his interpretive commitments, methods, and aims."

Matthew Y. Emerson, professor of religion and dean, Hobbs College of Theology and Ministry, Oklahoma Baptist University

"In *Tethered to the Cross*, Thomas Breimaier has done a marvelous job crafting a superb academic study of Spurgeon that is very accessible to a broad readership. Readers will finish its pages and be surprised to find that they not only thoroughly know Spurgeon's biography, but that they also have been deeply informed by his theology and the nineteenth-century historical context in which he lived. Noteworthy throughout the book is the way Breimaier illuminates Spurgeon's interpretation of Scripture, showing us how the great preacher connected all of Scripture with the grand evangelical themes of conversion and the cross of Christ."

Robert W. Caldwell III, Southwestern Baptist Theological Seminary, author of *Theologies of the American Revivalists*

"Just when we thought that the 'Spurgeonic canon' was closed, Tom Breimaier has produced this definitive study, which inspires as it informs."

Alistair Begg, Parkside Church, Cleveland, Ohio

"I am delighted to commend this scholarly study of the approach of C. H. Spurgeon to his work as a minister. Spurgeon was often termed the 'Prince of Preachers,' but his preaching and its hermeneutical underpinning have not previously been analyzed with the care shown by Thomas Breimaier in *Tethered to the Cross*. Based on thorough research, Breimaier argues convincingly that Spurgeon in his sermons and his writings saw the cross of Christ as central. He shows that Spurgeon's passionate commitment was to biblical preaching as the communication of the gospel. The way these themes are explored here both informs and inspires."

Ian Randall, research associate, Cambridge Centre for Christianity Worldwide

"This is an exceptional work by a talented, gifted, Christian scholar. The life and ministry of Charles Haddon Spurgeon is rightly understood as a rich treasure store bequeathed to the global church. *Tethered to the Cross* is an absolute must-have for anyone wishing to be enriched by the timeless truths of the gospel woven throughout the life and preaching of the Prince of Preachers."

Philip McCormack, principal of Spurgeon's College, London

TETHERED TO THE CROSS

The Life and Preaching of

THOMAS BREIMAIER

Academic

An imprint of InterVarsity Press
Downers Grove, Illinois

InterVarsity Press
P.O. Box 1400, Downers Grove, IL 60515-1426
ivpress.com
email@ivpress.com

*InterVarsity Press® is the book-publishing division of InterVarsity Christian Fellowship/USA®, a movement
of students and faculty active on campus at hundreds of universities, colleges, and schools of nursing
in the United States of America, and a member movement of the International Fellowship of Evangelical Students.
For information about local and regional activities, visit intervarsity.org.*

*All Scripture quotations, unless otherwise indicated, are taken from are taken from the Holy Bible,
King James Version.*

Cover design and image composite: David Fassett
Interior design: Jeanna Wiggins
*Images: Portrait of Charles Spurgeon © duncan1890 / DigitalVision Vectors / Getty Images
        grunge background © in-future / iStock / Getty Images Plus*

ISBN 978-0-8308-5330-4 (print)
ISBN 978-0-8308-5331-1 (digital)

Printed in the United States of America ∞

Library of Congress Cataloging-in-Publication Data
A catalog record for this book is available from the Library of Congress.

P	25	24	23	22	21	20	19	18	17	16	15	14	13	12	11	10	9	8	7	6	5	4	3	2	1
Y	37	36	35	34	33	32	31	30	29	28	27	26	25	24	23	22	21	20							

To Holly Edmisten Amacher, in whose classroom

I first discovered the world of history.

CONTENTS

FOREWORD

Timothy Larsen

A TRULY GREAT PREACHER IS MARKED by a combination of faith and fire—*faith* in two senses. The first is the faith was once delivered unto the saints. The sermons of great preachers are messages of substance. They are not merely frothy concoctions of sentiment and anecdote, but rather they find their center of gravity in the purity of doctrine, in the profundity of Scripture, and in the power of the gospel. The second is *faith* in the sense of personal conviction. This living faith is also fuel for the fire. Great preachers have convictions that are contagious. They speak existentially to the whole person, unleashing deep emotions and galvanizing the heart, the intellect, and the will. They move their hearers, and not merely in an ephemeral and superficial way. Deep calleth unto deep. The hearer feels located, as if the preacher is speaking specifically to him or to her. The messenger provokes a response in the listener.

In the context of specific ages, nations, or denominations, a few figures will emerge preeminent, widely hailed as fitting the above portrait of a great preacher. In the early church, John Chrysostom was one. His very name, Chrysostom (the golden-mouthed), was really an honorary title in tribute to his power in the pulpit. In the twelfth century, I would not have wanted to try to hold out with a bad conscience against an authoritative proclamation from Bernard of Clairvaux—nor in the fourteenth century against a piercing oration from Catherine of Siena. In the eighteenth century, even a penny-pinching Deist such as Benjamin Franklin found himself throwing all his money into the offering plate when George Whitefield made the appeal. Would that Franklin had also joined the myriads who gave their lives to Christ when Whitefield delivered a sermon! The nineteenth century was a sermonic age that produced a company of great preachers. Even just in the single city of London many worthy voices were raised in the cause of Christ whose ministries resounded to other countries and down the decades well beyond their deaths. I have been a Victorian scholar my whole career, but if I was transported back in time to Victorian London, I would skip the chance to see Queen Victoria and opt instead to go hear Catherine Booth, the mother of the Salvation Army, preach with fiery conviction the gospel of Jesus Christ.

Greatest, of course, is a silly category. The kingdom of God is not a listicle. When Stanley Hauerwas was named "America's Best Theologian" by *Time* magazine, he had the grace and wisdom to reply, "Best is not a theological category." We make no more invidious a claim than that Charles Haddon Spurgeon is numbered among the great preachers. And Spurgeon himself, desiring no solitary perch of preeminence, would have been the first to add, "And may their tribe increase." Every great preacher from the past whose words we can read or whom we can learn about is a gift to us today. We do not need to choose. They are a great cloud of witnesses, and they all belong to us. The memory of the righteous is a blessing.

Still, Spurgeon's ministry was so extraordinary according to so many metrics that authors shy away from making the superlative claims that stare them in the face. No one I have read has ever said that Spurgeon, in his day, was the pastor of the largest Christian congregation in the entire world. If he was not, however, who was? If he was not the Christian author with more words in print than any other, then who was? If his sermons did not circulate more widely than anyone else's, then whose did? If he was not the most popular preacher of the nineteenth century, then who was? Again, these claims do not matter in themselves. They are, in truth, as we have already intimated, a little unseemly when discussing servants of Jesus Christ. The point is simply that it was so incalculably vast that it is easier to underestimate than overestimate the reach and significance of Spurgeon's ministry.

You could be buried alive in books about Spurgeon. His giant reputation has created an entire publishing phenomenon focusing on just one man.

The first book about Spurgeon was published when he was just twenty-two years old! By the time he was twenty-three, the first full biography had already appeared. At his death at the early age of fifty-seven, biographies of Spurgeon started appearing at the rate of one per month. Just one of these, *The Life and Work of Charles Haddon Spurgeon* by G. Holden Pike, was six volumes long.

Still, Spurgeon has been scandalously neglected by scholars. It is hard to think of anyone with his level of fame and reputation who has been so thoroughly ignored. There are literally only a handful of scholarly books on Spurgeon. For a long, long time, Patricia Kruppa's *Charles Haddon Spurgeon: A Preacher's Progress*, published in 1982 but essentially her 1968 PhD dissertation, held the field alone. It was a flawed study, but as the only scholarly one, it was also essential. (And there is still such a dearth of academic studies on Spurgeon that it has been recently reissued by a new publisher without even being revised or updated.) Today, however, people have the privilege of reading Tom Nettles's wonderful and worthy book, *Living by Revealed Truth: The Life and Pastoral Theology of Charles Haddon Spurgeon* (2013). If you want to read a biography of Spurgeon, start with it. Nettles did his research well, but he chose to write a book that tilted toward the preferences of the popular market rather than attending to the needs and concerns of scholars. Perhaps the best academic study of Spurgeon hitherto has been Peter J. Morden, *"Communion with Christ and His People": The Spirituality of C. H. Spurgeon* (2010).

Thomas Breimaier's *Tethered to the Cross: The Life and Preaching of Charles H. Spurgeon* is the most important scholarly study of Spurgeon that has ever been written. It is the very best place to start for anyone who wants to study Spurgeon. It is extremely well researched and highly judicious. You can trust that the claims are well grounded and right. It is also a joy to read.

Before turning to the central themes of *Tethered to the Cross*, it is worth mentioning a few unexpected delights that one encounters along the way—almost by the bye, but not quite. I myself have done research and written scholarly chapters on Spurgeon, and for what it is worth, these were new delights for me that either Breimaier has uncovered or I had somehow hitherto missed. One is Spurgeon's poignant and profound sermon "Accidents, Not Punishments." His text was Luke 13:1-5. People were shaken by recent deaths in a train collision, and Spurgeon preached against the assumption that these people were being punished because of their exceptional sinfulness. When David Livingstone died deep in the interior of Africa, they found a copy of that sermon among his possessions. He had marked it "very good."

I was also struck by Spurgeon's refusal to take up even seemingly Christian or scriptural concerns that he felt would deflect him from his fundamental task of preaching the gospel. On the issue of a young earth, he simply retorted, "I do not know, and I do not care, much about the question." Likewise he refused to join the rage among conservative Christians for eschatological theories and end-times speculation. On the imagery in the book of Revelation, Spurgeon declared, "I confess I am not sent to decipher the Apocalyptic symbols, my errant is humbler but equally useful, I am sent to bring souls to Jesus Christ."

I was also pleased to learn about the amazing Lavinia Bartlett, a woman in Spurgeon's congregation who matched him in her zeal for souls and in the converting power of her Bible teaching. Spurgeon's own magazine, *The Sword and the Trowel*, recommended that male preachers sit under Bartlett's ministry in order to learn how to be more effective. Stories were told of souls whose hearts had remained hard even under Spurgeon's ministry but had been cracked open for Christ to enter in through Bartlett's teaching. Likewise I was riveted by the account of an African American preacher and former slave from Virginia, Thomas L. Johnson, who trained at Spurgeon's seminary, the Pastors' College, before going on to a fruitful ministry. Echoing Paul's letter to Philemon, Spurgeon sent him out into a racist world with this reference: "He is a beloved brother in the Lord and should be received as such." And I was staggered to learn that there came a point at which the majority of all the Baptist ministers in England and Wales had been trained by Spurgeon in his Pastors' College. Not only did Spurgeon apparently have the largest congregation in the world, but the second largest congregation in London (and, for all I know, the world) was one founded by his disciple and former student, Archibald Brown—the East End Tabernacle. (After Spurgeon's death, Brown would eventually succeed Spurgeon at the Metropolitan Tabernacle.)

Whatever you think of Spurgeon—even if you dislike him—if you want to study him, this book is *essential* for you. If you love Spurgeon, however, you will love this book. Breimaier has gone straight to the secret of Spurgeon's power. Charles Haddon Spurgeon preached Christ and him crucified. Spurgeon's aim was not simply to preach the Bible. It was to preach the gospel, through the Scriptures, by the power of the Holy Spirit. The gospel kept his eyes steadfastly fixed upon the cross. With the power of the cross of Christ to convert people ever before him, the whole Bible was open to him. He ransacked the Old Testament from cover to cover for treasures new and old. The New Testament ever brought forth its daily bread. Breimaier shows convincingly that Spurgeon would find an evangelistic message in texts where even other prominent conservative evangelical preachers did not. To lose sight of this reality, he insisted, is to forget your own story of salvation: "By the Word of the Lord you were brought to the cross, and comforted by the atonement." This book is about Spurgeon's long obedience in the same direction. He lived the advice he gave to aspiring ministers: "First and above all things, keep to plain evangelical doctrines; whatever else you do or do not preach, be sure incessantly to bring forth the soul-saving truth of Christ and him crucified."

ACKNOWLEDGMENTS

THIS BOOK BEGAN AS MY DOCTORAL THESIS at New College, University of Edinburgh, and as such it could not have gotten off the ground without the wise and helpful support of my supervisors, Stewart J. Brown and Ian J. Shaw. Their feedback has been instrumental in developing and shaping its content.

I am grateful for the kind reception that I received during visits to several libraries and archives. I was able to visit and explore the collection of books at Midwestern Baptist Theological Seminary's Spurgeon Library prior to its official opening. Christian George, the former director, not only facilitated my visit but also introduced me to Ronni Kurtz and Brian Albert, who were both helpful in tracking down particular resources. Additionally, Judy Powles and Annabel Haycraft at Spurgeon's College provided access to resources from the College's Heritage Room. Finally, through the help of the Reverend Iain H. Murray and Sam Cunnington, the Edinburgh office of the Banner of Truth Trust graciously granted me access to their full set of *The Sword and the Trowel*. Additionally, I am very grateful for the hospitality of several families who provided accommodation for me—namely, Tim and Shelagh Prime, Phil and Andrea Doggart, Ken and Joyce Smith, and Tim and Bernice Sigler.

I might not have gotten started on this path if it were not for the guidance of several key lecturers who pointed me toward further study in Christian history and theology. I am grateful for the instruction I received from, among others, Timothy Larsen, Gregg Quiggle, Michael McDuffee, Tim M. Sigler, and Trevor J. Burke.

I've been fortunate to have known several pastors and former pastors who provided guidance and encouragement to me over the years. My sincere thanks go to Mike Willmer, Matt Round, Liam Garvie, Paul Rees,

Andy Prime, Martin Smith, Euan Dodds, Sam Orr, Peter Grainger, Jonty Allcock, Phil Tinker, Alex Lyell, the late Derek Prime, and finally, Alistair Begg, who first introduced me to the preaching of C. H. Spurgeon.

Several fellow students had a hand in shaping the ideas in this book, and I am grateful for conversations with a robust cast of characters including: Andrew Kaiser, Kengo Akiyama, Andrew Kelley, Steven Stiles, Josh Coutts, Brad Penner, Andrew Kloes, Brent Brodie, Liam Sutherland, Eric Beck, Jaime Wright, Hannah Clardy, Will Kelly, David Kirkpatrick, Ryan Tafilowski, JT Turner, Elijah Hixson, Simeon Burke, Amy Plender, Andrew Ong, Russell Newton, Takayuki Yagi, Joe Linnhoff, Cam Clausing, and Patrick Brown.

Throughout the process of writing this book, a core group of friends have remained a constant source of support and encouragement. Among them are Ashish and Narissa Varma, Trevor and Heather Tarpinian, Phil and Alyssa EuBank, Glenn Wickline, Sarah Cross, Jonathan and Sonia Weaver, Alex and Selassi Spence, Russell and Becky Newton, Ian and Becky Cameron, Tze Hung Seeto, and James Doc.

The team at IVP Academic did a great job from beginning to end. David McNutt is an excellent editor and has been a helpful guide along the publication process. I'm also grateful for Emily Varner's feedback as copyeditor, which aided in sharpening the finished product.

My parents, Mark and Jo Ann Breimaier, encouraged me to read, study, and follow lines of inquiry throughout my life, and it was through their influence that I first encountered the pages of the Bible and the message of hope within.

Finally, my deepest gratitude goes to my wife, Hannah, who has kindly and patiently put up with me talking about Spurgeon and theological hermeneutics longer than any spouse should.

INTRODUCTION

The Cross in the Tabernacle

WHILE STILL IN HIS TWENTIES, Charles Haddon Spurgeon became a familiar name for many English evangelicals. His preaching was a topic of debate in newspapers and magazines within a year of his arrival in London. His critics included the English novelist George Eliot, who reluctantly acknowledged that Spurgeon "has the gift of a fine voice, very flexible and various; he is admirably fluent and clear in his language," though she held little regard for his theology, which she branded as the "the most superficial, grocer's back-parlour view of Calvinistic Christianity."[1] His popularity extended beyond the upper working and lower middle classes, and in time his admirers would include the earl of Shaftesbury, American President James Garfield, and Prime Minister William Gladstone. By his fortieth birthday, he oversaw a magazine, a college for pastors, a vocational evening school, almshouses, two orphanages, and the largest congregation in the English-speaking world.

Spurgeon's sermons were the centerpiece of his ministry. He preached over three thousand messages during his tenure at the Metropolitan Tabernacle. Along with his publishers, Passmore and Alabaster, Spurgeon revolutionized the process of sermon distribution. The sermons were recorded by stenographers on Sundays and were quickly typeset, edited by Spurgeon, and sold for a penny each in London the following week. When the transatlantic telegraph cable was successfully installed, newspapers in Chicago and Boston published sermons that had been preached in the

---

[1] Ernest A. Payne, "Gleanings from the Correspondence of George Eliot," *Baptist Quarterly* 27 (1958): 180.

Metropolitan Tabernacle the previous week.[2] Spurgeon's sermons were reprinted in periodicals throughout the world, as translations appeared in over thirty languages, including German, Russian, Arabic, and Urdu. By the time of his death, over fifty-six million copies of Spurgeon's sermons had been sold.[3] These sermons found a wide variety of usage, from the pulpits of Russian churches to the pocket of the African explorer David Livingstone.[4]

Spurgeon's engagement with the Bible was responsible for his considerable fame in the Victorian world. His preaching drew listeners from a variety of social backgrounds, and it produced numerous conversions to Christianity. Recently published transcripts of membership interviews that had been conducted in the nineteenth century by elders of Spurgeon's church provide helpful context, introducing congregants such as John Charles Samuel, a man who self-identified as a former "infidel, blasphemer, tavern lounger, and mocker of religion," who was drawn by the popularity of Spurgeon's oratory and visited the New Park Street Chapel on several occasions.[5] Recalling his experience of hearing the famous preacher, Samuel wrote that Spurgeon "looked at me a good deal as if he knew I was an infidel. I felt he was preaching only to me."[6] A New Park Street Chapel elder's notes on the conversion of a man named John Fletcher recorded that Fletcher "looked everywhere for comfort but the right places. But at last he was constrained to look only to Christ, and now sincerely believes he has found mercy through the Saviour's blood and

---

[2]The transmission process omitted some of Spurgeon's sermon content, and he was unhappy with the result, writing that "in the process of transmission, the eggs were broken, and the very life of them was crushed." C. H. Spurgeon, *C. H. Spurgeon's Autobiography, Compiled from His Diary, Letters, and Records, by His Wife and His Private Secretary*, vol. 4, *1878–1892* (Chicago: Fleming H. Revell, 1900), 110-11.

[3]Robert H. Ellison, *The Victorian Pulpit: Spoken and Written Sermons in Nineteenth-Century Britain* (Selinsgrove, PA: Susquehanna University Press, 1998), 47.

[4]Mark Hopkins, *Nonconformity's Romantic Generation: Evangelical and Liberal Theologies in Victorian England* (Milton Keynes, UK: Paternoster, 2004), 155. Spurgeon's material remained popular in Russia into the years of the Soviet Union. See Alexander Popov, "The Evangelical Christians-Baptists in the Soviet Union as a Hermeneutical Community" (PhD thesis, International Baptist Theological Seminary, 2010), 94.

[5]Hannah Wyncoll, ed., *Wonders of Grace: Original Testimonies of Converts During Spurgeon's Early Years* (London: Wakeman Trust, 2016), 22-26.

[6]Wyncoll, *Wonders of Grace*, 24-25.

trusts alone in Jesus."[7] Another interviewee, Rose Edwards, said that in Spurgeon's preaching she "saw the love of Christ as she never saw it before," and that the "sermon convinced her of the very great guilt of her sins and led her to cry for mercy and forgiveness."[8] Accounts of conversions generated by Spurgeon's preaching often emphasized common themes, which included a sense of the preacher speaking directly to them and an overwhelming conviction generated by reflection upon Christ's crucifixion.[9]

In referring to his method of biblical interpretation, Spurgeon was said to insist, "I take my text and make a beeline to the cross." The quotation, which certainly resonates with Spurgeon's general approach to Scripture, is problematic in that I have not found it within Spurgeon's sermons or books.[10] However, Spurgeon's beeline reference does appear in a variety of books on preaching, and also, without citation, in Lewis Drummond's biography of Spurgeon, published in 1992.[11] The earliest reference to the quotation appears in a sermon by the Southern Baptist pastor W. A. Criswell (1909–2002), though Criswell did not identify his original source.[12] The quotation, wherever it first appeared, is valuable in raising the larger question of how Spurgeon approached the biblical text. Did he make a "beeline" to the cross in every sermon? Did he have a unified approach to biblical interpretation?

The primary goal of this book is to identify and analyze C. H. Spurgeon's approach to biblical hermeneutics. It will argue that Spurgeon, one of the most renowned preachers of his era, viewed the entire Bible through the lens of the cross of Christ, with an aim to bring about the conversion of sinners.[13] This approach led him to interpret texts throughout the Bible in

---

[7]Wyncoll, *Wonders of Grace*, 33.

[8]Wyncoll, *Wonders of Grace*, 38.

[9]For a helpful introduction to crucicentrism and conversionism in the context of Victorian evangelicalism, see David W. Bebbington, *The Dominance of Evangelicalism: The Age of Spurgeon and Moody* (Downers Grove, IL: InterVarsity Press, 2005), 24-33.

[10]This topic has even produced a popular recent blog post. See Christian George, "6 Quotes Spurgeon Didn't Say," The Spurgeon Center, August 8, 2017, www.spurgeon.org/resource-library /blog-entries/6-quotes-spurgeon-didnt-say.

[11]Lewis A. Drummond, *Spurgeon: Prince of Preachers* (Grand Rapids, MI: Kregel Publications, 1992), 223.

[12]W. A. Criswell, "Nothing but Jesus (1 Corinthians 2:1-2)," sermon given March 27, 1955, www .wacriswell.com/sermons/1955/nothing-but-jesus/.

[13]This follows Spurgeon's language in an 1887 sermon where he proclaimed, "Everything is seen in its reality when you look through the glass, the ruby glass of the atoning sacrifice. Use

a similar manner, resulting in sermons, articles, and instruction that favored cross-centered language, aimed at the conversion of unbelievers. These themes of crucicentrism and conversionism are drawn in part from the historian David Bebbington's seminal work, *Evangelicalism in Modern Britain*.[14] In it, Bebbington argues that evangelicals are characterized by the presence of four key theological emphases: *activism, biblicism, crucicentrism,* and *conversionism*.[15] It should be noted that while Spurgeon's teaching and extant ministries exemplified all four of Bebbington's categories, this work will focus primarily on the particular role that crucicentrism and conversionism played in his biblical interpretation. For Spurgeon, all of these points were interconnected, and as such many sermons included a focus upon the cross and the need for conversion, as well as an emphasis that those in the congregation who were already converted should deepen their knowledge of the Bible and actively engage in personal evangelism. Further, it will be noted that Spurgeon's engagement with the Bible varied according to a number of factors, most notably the nature of his audience. As such, while the primary focus of this project will remain on the overarching themes of crucicentrism and conversionism throughout Spurgeon's preached and written material, at certain points it will be noted that he was not restricted to these themes and varied his content and presentation in light of his intended audience.

THREE STUDIES OF NINETEENTH-CENTURY PREACHING AND CHARLES H. SPURGEON

This book stands on the shoulders of a number of volumes that have helped to inform and shape contemporary understanding of Victorian biblical interpretation, preaching in the nineteenth century, and C. H. Spurgeon

---

this telescope of the cross, and you shall see far and clear; look at sinners through the cross; look at saints through the cross; look at sin through the cross; look at the world's joys and sorrows through the cross; look at heaven and hell through the cross." C. H. Spurgeon, "The Blood of Sprinkling and the Children," sermon no. 1988, given October 23, 1887, from Exodus 12:21-27, *The Metropolitan Tabernacle Pulpit*, vol. 33 (London: Passmore & Alabaster, 1887), 585.

[14]David W. Bebbington, *Evangelicalism in Modern Britain: A History from the 1730s to the 1980s* (London: Routledge, 2005).

[15]Bebbington, *Evangelicalism in Modern Britain*, 2-3.

himself. With regard to the first category, as Benjamin Jowett remarked in 1860, "the path of the critical Interpreter of Scripture is almost always a thorny one in England."[16] Perhaps the most significant movement within nineteenth-century biblical studies was the forward march of higher criticism. This had its roots in seventeenth- and early eighteenth-century English and Irish Deist thought, but by the mid-nineteenth century had become associated with German scholarship, primarily as conducted at the universities of Göttingen and Tübingen. The focus of higher criticism, broadly speaking, was to pursue the original meaning of an ancient text within its historical context. These scholars began to ask historical questions of the Bible and developed theories that challenged, among other things, the traditional authorship of texts and the historical accuracy of biblical descriptions.[17]

British Christians witnessed a significant shift in the nature of biblical scholarship as German works of higher criticism began to appear. Several authors have offered helpful accounts of the theological developments. Hans Frei provides an overview of developments in biblical interpretation over two centuries in his classic work, *The Eclipse of Biblical Narrative*.[18] In his profiles of F. D. Maurice and William Robertson Smith, the biblical scholar J. W. Rogerson explores the controversial work of these two advocates of modern biblical criticism in Britain.[19] Rogerson also contributed to a general introduction to Christian biblical interpretation, with a section devoted to higher criticism in the nineteenth century.[20] Finally, his monograph titled *Old Testament Criticism in the Nineteenth Century* evaluates biblical interpretation in both Germany and England in the light of

---

[16]Benjamin Jowett, "On the Interpretation of Scripture," in *Essays and Reviews*, ed. John William Parker (London: John W. Parker and Son, 1860), 376.

[17]For a general introduction to higher criticism, see John Barton, *The Cambridge Companion to Biblical Interpretation* (Cambridge: Cambridge University Press, 2009), 9-20.

[18]Hans W. Frei, *The Eclipse of Biblical Narrative: A Study in Eighteenth and Nineteenth Century Hermeneutics*, rev. ed. (New Haven, CT: Yale University Press, 1980).

[19]J. W. Rogerson, *The Bible and Criticism in Victorian Britain: Profiles of F. D. Maurice and William Robertson Smith*, Journal for the Study of the Old Testament Supplement Series 201 (Sheffield, UK: Sheffield Academic Press, 1995).

[20]J. W. Rogerson, Christopher Rowland, and Barnabas Lindars, *The Study and Use of the Bible*, vol. 2, *The History of Christian Theology* (Basingstoke, Hants, UK: Marshall Pickering, 1988), 318-79.

theological and sociopolitical developments.[21] For broader engagement with the history of Old Testament interpretation, works from Rudolf Smend and Henning Graf Reventlow are valuable, particularly with regard to nineteenth-century German scholarship.[22] There are also several relevant studies pertaining to New Testament higher criticism in Britain. Stephen Neill's *The Interpretation of the New Testament: 1861–1986* highlights key methodological shifts within New Testament faculties in both Germany and Britain.[23] David M. Thompson offers a similar survey in his *Cambridge Theology in the Nineteenth Century*, the scope of which extends to scholars of both Old and New Testaments as well as influential clergy.[24]

Additional studies survey wider themes in British responses to higher criticism. Tod Jones's study of the Broad-Church movement provides biographical sketches of several important figures in Victorian biblical studies, particularly in his chapter "Cambridge Apostles and Prophets."[25] Taking a literary approach, George Landow's *Victorian Types, Victorian Shadows* provides a thorough investigation of the role of typology in the arts, examining how Christians from various denominational affiliations in part rooted their biblical interpretation in "divinely intended anticipations of Christ and His dispensation in the laws, events, and people of the Old Testament."[26]

While the historical accounts of the changing reception of the Bible among intellectuals have been valuable, it is also important to consider the popular understanding of the Bible in the Victorian period. Recent years have seen several notable publications on the topic of the Bible in

---

[21]J. W. Rogerson, *Old Testament Criticism in the Nineteenth Century: England and Germany* (London: SPCK, 1984), 147-253.

[22]Rudolf Smend, *From Astruc to Zimmerli*, trans. Margaret Kohl (Tübingen: Mohr Siebeck, 2007); Henning Graf Reventlow, *History of Biblical Interpretation*, trans. Leo G. Perdue, vol. 4, *From the Enlightenment to the Twentieth Century* (Atlanta: Society of Biblical Literature, 2010).

[23]Stephen Neill and N. T. Wright, *The Interpretation of the New Testament, 1861–1986*, 2nd ed. (Oxford: Oxford University Press, 1988), 1-64.

[24]David M. Thompson, *Cambridge Theology in the Nineteenth Century* (Aldershot: Ashgate, 2008).

[25]Tod E. Jones, *The Broad Church: A Biography of a Movement* (Lanham, MD: Lexington Books, 2003), 129-206.

[26]George P. Landow, *Victorian Types, Victorian Shadows: Biblical Typology in Victorian Literature, Art, and Thought* (Boston: Routledge & Kegan Paul, 1980), 3. For the section on Victorian biblical interpretation, see 15-63.

nineteenth-century popular culture. Colin Kidd and R. S. Sugirtharajah have written helpful volumes on the role of race and imperialism in the church's use of the Bible.[27] Willis Glover's book on evangelical Non-conformists and higher criticism, though dated, remains a significant text on the topic, and as such it is referenced in even the most recent scholarship.[28] Glover argues that many evangelicals were initially suspicious of higher criticism because of its roots in "Germanism," which functionally ruled it as both Hegelian and rationalistic.[29] Perhaps the most thorough account to date has been Timothy Larsen's *A People of One Book*, which studies the role that the Bible played in the lives and thought of a diverse cast of historical figures, including C. H. Spurgeon.[30] Central to Larsen's study is the argument that the Bible played a significant role in public and private life of nineteenth-century England, saturating the thought and writings of those both inside and outside the church. Larsen's analysis of Spurgeon offers a comprehensive account of the preacher in his context, though his assessments of Spurgeon's "holy earnestness" to see conversions produced through the preaching of the Bible would have been strengthened by an analysis of Spurgeon's frequent references to Christ's crucifixion, a theme that wove its way through the bulk of his sermons, addresses, printed books, and lectures.[31]

In addition to the preceding volumes on Victorian biblical interpretation, there have been a number of helpful volumes surveying preaching in the era. Commenting on what he viewed to be the most important facet of preaching, the Roman Catholic convert and priest John Henry Newman (1801–1890) remarked that "talent, logic, learning, words, manner, voice, action, all are required for the perfection of a preacher; but 'one thing is necessary'—an intense perception and appreciation of the end for which

---

[27]Colin Kidd, *The Forging of Races: Race and Scripture in the Protestant Atlantic World, 1600–2000* (Cambridge: Cambridge University Press, 2006); R. S. Sugirtharajah, *The Bible and Empire: Postcolonial Explorations* (Cambridge: Cambridge University Press, 2005).

[28]Willis Borders Glover, *Evangelical Nonconformists and Higher Criticism in the Nineteenth Century* (London: Independent Press, 1954).

[29]Glover, *Evangelical Nonconformists*, 39-40.

[30]Timothy Larsen, *A People of One Book: The Bible and the Victorians* (Oxford: Oxford University Press, 2011).

[31]Larsen, *People of One Book*, 258-59.

he preaches, and that is, to be the minister of some definite spiritual good to those who hear him."[32] Middle-class Victorians, who heard on average two different sermons every week, had unprecedented opportunity to attend sermons in a variety of contexts, from local churches to street corners and assembly halls.[33] Those who did not travel to church could read sermons that were transcribed, printed, and sold, some within a week of their first airing. As J. N. Ian Dickson comments, "Sermons and their method of delivery, in an age and religious climate fascinated by both, have a story to tell us about the past."[34]

Studies of preaching in the Victorian church began to appear in the early part of the twentieth century, among them a two-volume *History of Preaching* written by Edwin Dargan.[35] Dargan's work, though dated, provides a good overview of key preachers in the nineteenth century; however, his assessments often focused on the lives of the preachers rather than the content of their preaching. More recently, *The Oxford Handbook of the British Sermon* provides a number of chapters dealing with the intricacies of sermons in the nineteenth century, from John Wolffe's discussion of funeral sermons to Keith Francis and Robert J. Surridge's chapter on evangelical sermons on the apocalypse.[36] Other noteworthy introductions to preaching in the Victorian era include Robert Ellison's *A New History of the Sermon: The Nineteenth Century* and the sixth volume of Hughes Oliphant Old's series on preaching, subtitled *The Modern Age*.[37] Ellison's *New History* is wide-ranging in subject, extending to an analysis of sermons outside the Christian tradition in both Britain and the United States. This approach is not without drawbacks, as several significant preachers from both nations

---

[32]John Henry Newman, *The Idea of a University* (London: Basil Montagu Pickering, 1873), 408.

[33]Hughes Oliphant Old, *The Reading and Preaching of the Scriptures in the Worship of the Christian Church* (Grand Rapids, MI: Eerdmans, 1998), 348; Landow, *Victorian Types*, 15.

[34]J. N. Ian Dickson, *Beyond Religious Discourse: Sermons, Preaching, and Evangelical Protestants in Nineteenth-Century Irish Society* (Milton Keynes, UK: Paternoster, 2007), 1.

[35]Edwin Charles Dargan, *A History of Preaching*, vol. 2, *From the Close of the Reformation Period to the End of the Nineteenth Century, 1572–1900* (London: Hodder & Stoughton, 1912), 470-578.

[36]Keith A. Francis and William Gibson, *The Oxford Handbook of the British Sermon, 1689–1901* (Oxford: Oxford University Press, 2012).

[37]Robert H. Ellison, *A New History of the Sermon: The Nineteenth Century* (Leiden: Brill, 2010); Old, *Reading and Preaching of the Scriptures*, 347-443.

are excluded or minimized in the pursuit of the broader spectrum.[38] One final monograph on preaching worth noting is Ian Dickson's *Beyond Religious Discourse*, which analyzes evangelical sermons in nineteenth-century Ireland.[39] While geographically removed from Spurgeon's London, Dickson's analysis of evangelicalism and preaching in Ireland makes valuable contributions to a wider understanding of nineteenth-century preaching.

Finally, several books and chapters on Victorian preaching feature discussions of Spurgeon himself. *The View from the Pulpit*, edited by P. T. Phillips, explores the pulpit ministry of Christian ministers from a number of theological camps, including R. J. Helmstadter's treatment of C. H. Spurgeon and social work in London.[40] While Helmstadter rightly observes that "salvation was overwhelmingly the dominant theme" of Spurgeon's ministry, his chapter focuses primarily on Spurgeon's activism. Andrew Tate offers a literary study of Spurgeon's conversion account—with insights into the influence of Spurgeon's conversion upon his preaching— though he does not engage with enough of Spurgeon's sermons and other printed material to comprehensively develop his argument.[41] Robert Ellison's *The Victorian Pulpit* offers a unique approach to the categorization of sermons on what he describes as an orality-literacy spectrum, locating sermon content on a range between oral and literary uses of language.[42] Ellison's work, criticized by some for being too narrow in scope, nevertheless provides a valuable analysis of Spurgeon's preaching in one of his three case studies.[43] He argues that Spurgeon is representative of the "orality" side of the rhetorical pendulum, constructing sermons that bore

---

[38]Spurgeon, though acknowledged as influential, receives surprisingly few references throughout the volume.

[39]Dickson, *Beyond Religious Discourse*.

[40]R. J. Helmstadter, "Spurgeon in Outcast London," in *The View from the Pulpit: Victorian Ministers and Society*, ed. P. T. Phillips (Toronto: Macmillan, 1978), 161-85.

[41]Andrew Tate, "Evangelical Certainties: Charles Spurgeon and the Sermon as Crisis Literature," in *Reinventing Christianity: Nineteenth-Century Contexts*, ed. Linda Woodhead (Aldershot: Ashgate, 2001), 27-36.

[42]Ellison, *Victorian Pulpit*.

[43]See, for instance: Mary Wilson Carpenter, "[Review of] The Victorian Pulpit: Spoken and Written Sermons in Nineteenth-Century Britain," *Victorian Studies* 43, no. 2 (2001): 305-6. While Carpenter raises good points on Ellison's small pool of case studies, his analysis of Spurgeon's preaching remains the best literary study on his sermons.

more in common with classical oratory than the more prosaic offerings of preachers such as John Henry Newman.

These studies are particularly helpful in assessing Victorian preaching from historical, literary, and occasionally theological vantages, though few have combined all three of these components in the study of an individual preacher to identify his or her method of biblical interpretation.[44] As hermeneutics play a central part in the construction of sermons, further investigation into a preacher's approach to biblical interpretation could provide an additional voice to this collection of studies and would contribute helpfully to further studies in the history of biblical interpretation and preaching.

STUDIES OF SPURGEON

Having surveyed the landscape of volumes discussing biblical interpretation and preaching in the nineteenth century, we turn to books written on Spurgeon himself. As early as 1856, when Spurgeon was only twenty-two years old, an American pastor named Elias Lyman Magoon published a selection of Spurgeon's sermons in the United States.[45] Magoon's introduction includes a brief biographical sketch of Spurgeon, which concludes that before long his sermons would be read "from the Eastern Atlantic to the Great Pacific of the west."[46] A more formal biography of the "boy preacher" was published in London the following year.[47] Spurgeon was the subject of newspaper articles, caricatures, and biographies throughout his lifetime, and written work evaluating his life and ministry continues through the present day. Due to the large amount of material written on Spurgeon, the comments below will be limited to the literature most pertinent to the present study.

---

[44]An eighteenth-century example would be Douglas A. Sweeney, *Edwards the Exegete: Biblical Interpretation and Anglo-Protestant Culture on the Edge of the Enlightenment* (Oxford: Oxford University Press, 2016).

[45]Elias Lyman Magoon, *"The Modern Whitfield": Sermons of the Rev. C. H. Spurgeon of London, with an Introduction and Sketch of His Life* (New York: Sheldon, Blakeman, & Co., 1856).

[46]Magoon, *"Modern Whitfield,"* xxxvi.

[47]George J. Stevenson, *Sketch of the Life and Ministry of the Rev. C. H. Spurgeon: From Original Documents Including Anecdotes and Incidents of Travel, Biographical Notices of Former Pastors, Historical Sketch of Park Street Chapel, and an Outline of Mr. Spurgeon's Articles of Faith* (New York: Sheldon, Blakeman, 1857).

While a number of biographical sketches continued to appear throughout Spurgeon's early ministry, perhaps the most influential early biography came in 1881 from his friend George C. Needham.[48] Additionally, Spurgeon's widow, Susannah, and one of his private secretaries, Joseph Harrald, worked to complete a four-volume edition of his autobiography, which served as a basis for many of the biographies that would follow.[49] In the two years following Spurgeon's death in January 1892, a large number of biographies were published, averaging one per month.[50] These early biographies contain a fairly narrow range of assessments of Spurgeon from admiration to outright hagiography, and as such they must be consulted carefully and critically. Several remain worthy of engagement due to their authors' friendship with and proximity to their subject. For instance, G. Holden Pike, another personal secretary, authored a six-volume biography that offers an exhaustive and generally positive view of his friend's life.[51] In addition to the biographical material, eyewitness accounts of services at the Metropolitan Tabernacle are numerous and provide informative first-hand accounts of his preaching. C. Maurice Davies's *Unorthodox London*, published in 1876, is a collection of reflections on visits to a number of London houses of worship, a journey that records the religious world "from the North Pole of Nonconformity to the most torrid regions of Romanism."[52] Davies, a doctor of divinity and former fellow of the University of Durham, provides a theologically informed perspective on both the Metropolitan Tabernacle and Spurgeon himself, situating them in the context of dozens of other church congregations.

A generation later, more critical accounts of Spurgeon appeared. Lewis Brastow's 1904 work *Representative Modern Preachers* refers to

---

[48]George C. Needham, *The Life and Labors of Charles H. Spurgeon, the Faithful Preacher, the Devoted Pastor, the Noble Philanthropist, the Beloved College President, and the Voluminous Writer, Author, Etc., Etc.* (Boston: D. L. Guernsey, 1881).

[49]C. H. Spurgeon, *Autobiography: Compiled from His Diary, Letters, and Records by His Wife and His Private Secretary*, 4 vols. (London: Passmore & Alabaster, 1899–1900).

[50]Arnold A. Dallimore, *Spurgeon: A New Biography* (Edinburgh: Banner of Truth Trust, 1985), ix.

[51]G. Holden Pike, *The Life and Work of Charles Haddon Spurgeon*, 6 vols. (London: Cassell & Company, 1892).

[52]C. Maurice Davies, *Unorthodox London, or, Phases of Religious Life in the Metropolis* (London: Tinsley Bros., 1876), 1.

Spurgeon's "dogmatic provincialism, exegetical crudeness, and intolerance of the modern world," though he also identifies Spurgeon as a "homiletic prodigy" and ranks him with such respected orators as Horace Bushnell, John Henry Newman, and Thomas Guthrie.[53] Brastow, an American Congregationalist minister who eventually served as the dean of Yale Divinity School, tends to focus more on Spurgeon's oratorical flair than the content of his sermons. Later biographies by W. Y. Fullerton and J. C. Carlile offer slightly more comprehensive assessments of their subject.[54]

The mid-twentieth century also produced several works on Spurgeon designed as both historical investigation and instruction for contemporary ministers. Iain H. Murray, a conservative evangelical Presbyterian, portrays Spurgeon's works as valuable if not necessary reading for evangelical Calvinists of all denominations.[55] Through Murray's initiative, the Banner of Truth Trust republished several works of Spurgeon that had long been out of print. Ernest W. Bacon's biography *Spurgeon: Heir of the Puritans* highlights many of the traditional episodes of Spurgeon's life and work, and his biography is the first to focus specifically on lines of continuity from the seventeenth-century Puritan divines to Spurgeon.[56] Engagement with Spurgeon was not limited to English literature, as evidenced by the German Lutheran theologian Helmut Thielicke's *Encounter with Spurgeon*.[57] Thielicke's endorsement of Spurgeon goes so far as his recommendation that his readers "sell all you have (not least of all some of your stock of current sermonic literature) and buy Spurgeon," and then follows his introductory remarks with a German translation of Spurgeon's *Lectures to my*

---

[53]Lewis Orsmond Brastow, *Representative Modern Preachers* (New York: Macmillan, 1904), 383.

[54]W. Y. Fullerton, *C. H. Spurgeon: A Biography* (London: Williams and Norgate, 1920); J. C. Carlile, *C. H. Spurgeon: An Interpretive Biography* (London: Religious Tract Society and the Kingsgate Press, 1934), 132-51. It should be noted that both Fullerton and Carlile were heavily influenced by Spurgeon in their respective pastoral work. This is particularly true in the case of Fullerton, who counted Spurgeon as a friend and mentor.

[55]Iain H. Murray, *The Forgotten Spurgeon* (London: Banner of Truth Trust, 1966); Iain H. Murray, *Spurgeon v. Hyper-Calvinism: The Battle for Gospel Preaching* (Edinburgh: The Banner of Truth Trust, 2002).

[56]Ernest W. Bacon, *Spurgeon: Heir of the Puritans* (London: Allen & Unwin, 1967).

[57]C. H. Spurgeon and Helmut Thielicke, *Encounter with Spurgeon* (London: James Clarke, 1963).

Students.[58] In addition to Thielicke's work, Michael Nicholls, David Bebbington, and Ian M. Randall have each provided further investigation of both the Pastors' College and Spurgeon's work as an educator.[59]

Some biographies in more recent years, such as those from Arnold Dallimore and Lewis Drummond, have avoided the hagiographic tone and offered more balanced appraisals than those provided by the earlier biographers.[60] Dallimore's work, which intended to provide a theologically oriented assessment of Spurgeon, succeeds only partially in achieving its author's goal. Having written the book to appeal to a wide-ranging audience, the Baptist pastor Dallimore's investigation of Spurgeon's theology is often limited to brief descriptions of his positions at significant moments within his career, such as the Downgrade Controversy. Lewis Drummond's biography, released to coincide with centenary of Spurgeon's death in 1992, unfortunately contains a number of errors, including a reference to Spurgeon preaching at the commemoration service of John Bunyan's tomb in 1801, thirty-three years prior to Spurgeon's birth.[61] The most recent major biographical study was written by Tom Nettles, who sympathizes with Spurgeon's theology and praxis yet provides a fairly comprehensive overview of much of the available primary source material, including a strong engagement with Spurgeon's magazine, *The Sword and the Trowel.*[62]

The first critical biography of Spurgeon was the Columbia University doctoral thesis of 1968 by Patricia Kruppa, titled *Charles Haddon Spurgeon:*

---

[58]Spurgeon and Thielicke, *Encounter with Spurgeon*, 45.

[59]David W. Bebbington, "Spurgeon and British Evangelical Theological Education," in *Theological Education in the Evangelical Tradition*, ed. D. G. Hart and R. Albert Mohler (Grand Rapids, MI: Baker, 1996), 217-34; Mike Nicholls, *Lights to the World: A History of Spurgeon's College 1856–1992* (Harpenden, UK: Nuprint, 1994); Ian M. Randall, *A School of the Prophets: 150 Years of Spurgeon's College* (London: Spurgeon's College, 2005); Ian M. Randall, "Charles Haddon Spurgeon, the Pastor's College and the Downgrade Controversy," in *Discipline and Diversity*, ed. Kate Cooper and Jeremy Gregory, Studies in Church History, vol. 43 (Suffolk, UK: The Boydell Press, 2007), 366-76; Ian M. Randall, "The World Is Our Parish: Spurgeon's College and World Mission, 1856–1892," in *Baptists and Mission: Papers from the Fourth International Conference on Baptist Studies*, ed. Ian M. Randall and Anthony R. Cross, Studies in Baptist History and Thought 29 (Milton Keynes, UK: Paternoster, 2007), 64-77.

[60]Dallimore, *Spurgeon: A New Biography*; Drummond, *Spurgeon: Prince of Preachers*.

[61]Drummond, *Spurgeon: Prince of Preachers*, 346.

[62]Tom Nettles, *Living by Revealed Truth: The Life and Pastoral Theology of Charles Haddon Spurgeon* (Ross-shire, UK: Christian Focus, 2013).

A Preacher's Progress, which has been published several times, most recently in 2017.[63] Kruppa's interaction with primary sources, including a
significant number of periodicals, remains unmatched among the current
biographies. In some areas, however, her assessment requires further
analysis, such as her statement that Spurgeon "measured everything he
read against the yardstick of a verbally inspired Bible and the pronounce-
ments of the Puritans, and in consequence, found little to approve of in the
theological writing of his own time."[64] While Spurgeon certainly held biblical inspiration and Puritan theology in a high regard, he found much to
value in a wide range of scholarship, as is duly attested in his *Commenting
and Commentaries*.[65] Furthermore, the tension in which Kruppa's thesis
holds her subject as both "representative Victorian" and "intellectual
captive of the past" is problematic. Mark Hopkins is correct in pointing out
that Kruppa "cannot have it both ways."[66] Hopkins's *Nonconformity's Romantic Generation*, though primarily focused on the Downgrade Controversy, offers critical engagement with Spurgeon's theological positions, particularly in the latter years of his work.[67] Additionally, Peter Morden's
"Communion with Christ and His People" provides a compelling perspective
on Spurgeon and spirituality, along with theological observations on Spurgeon's positions with regard to conversion, baptism, prayer, and suffering.[68]
A particular strength of Morden's writing is his familiarity with the archival
material at Spurgeon's College in London, where he also served as a lecturer
and administrator.

Doctoral dissertations and theses from the late twentieth century to the
present indicate that Spurgeon studies are alive and well on both sides of
the Atlantic. Jeremy Thornton's University of Cambridge thesis of 1974

---

[63]Patricia S. Kruppa, *Charles Haddon Spurgeon: A Preacher's Progress*, Routledge Library Editions:
19th Century Religion (London: Taylor and Francis, 2017).

[64]Kruppa, *Charles Haddon Spurgeon*, 242.

[65]C. H. Spurgeon, *Lectures to My Students*, vol. 4, *Commenting and Commentaries: Lectures
Addressed to the Students of the Pastors' College, Metropolitan Tabernacle* (New York: Sheldon, 1876).

[66]Kruppa, *Charles Haddon Spurgeon*, 18; Hopkins, *Nonconformity's Romantic Generation*, 11.

[67]Hopkins, *Nonconformity's Romantic Generation*.

[68]Peter J. Morden, *"Communion with Christ and His People": The Spirituality of C.H. Spurgeon*
(Oxford: Regent's Park College, 2010).

explores Spurgeon's soteriology, or doctrine of salvation. Thornton surveys a variety of Spurgeon's preached and written material and argues that Spurgeon "adhered strongly to a defined body of truth, that lay at the heart of his ministry."[69] He then expands his argument by evaluating Spurgeon's Calvinism in comparison to the Calvinism of both the Puritans and a number of contemporary figures. Timothy McCoy's Southern Baptist Theological Seminary dissertation of 1989 surveys Spurgeon as an evangelist, with a helpful analysis of the theological dimensions to his evangelism.[70] McCoy's work, in which he seeks to follow in the tradition of Bacon's *Spurgeon: Heir of the Puritans*, draws lines of continuity from Spurgeon's doctrine of salvation to his methodology of evangelism. John David Talbert's Southwestern Baptist Theological Seminary dissertation, also of 1989, surveys Christology broadly throughout Spurgeon's preaching, with particular focus on Spurgeon's engagement with Old Testament texts.[71] Talbert's investigation of the role of Christology in Spurgeon's sermons is helpful; as he restricts his investigation to the Old Testament, however, he does not provide a sufficiently comprehensive evaluation of Spurgeon's biblical interpretation. A noteworthy recent doctoral thesis is Christian T. George's St. Andrews University thesis of 2011 on Spurgeon and Christology, which provides a balanced view of Spurgeon as both a pastor and a theological figure.[72] In discussions of Spurgeon and biblical interpretation, George seeks to classify Spurgeon's hermeneutics in the language of Alexandrian and medieval allegory.[73] He rightly suggests that for Spurgeon, "any technique used to preach the immediacy of salvation was acceptable

---

[69]Jeremy Thornton, "The Soteriology of C. H. Spurgeon: Its Biblical and Historical Roots and Its Place in His Preaching" (PhD thesis, University of Cambridge, 1974), 5.

[70]Timothy A. McCoy, "The Evangelistic Ministry of C. H. Spurgeon: Implications for a Contemporary Model for Pastoral Evangelism" (PhD diss., The Southern Baptist Theological Seminary, 1989), 108-96; Nicholls offers a similar investigation; see Mike Nicholls, *C. H. Spurgeon: The Pastor Evangelist* (Didcot, UK: Baptist Historical Society, 1992).

[71]John David Talbert, "Charles Haddon Spurgeon's Christological Homiletics: A Critical Evaluation of Selected Sermons from Old Testament Texts" (PhD diss., Southwestern Baptist Theological Seminary, 1989).

[72]Christian T. George, "Jesus Christ, The 'Prince of Pilgrims': A Critical Analysis of the Ontological, Functional, and Exegetical Christologies in the Sermons, Writings, and Lectures of Charles Haddon Spurgeon (1834–1892)" (PhD thesis, University of St. Andrews, 2011).

[73]Sidney Greidanus makes a similar argument. See Sidney Greidanus, *Preaching Christ from the Old Testament* (Grand Rapids, MI: Eerdmans, 1999), 151-62.

hermeneutically."[74] Though George interacts with Spurgeon's hermeneutics, his primary objective is an exploration of Spurgeon's Christology.

Duncan Ferguson's article on Spurgeon's hermeneutics correctly identifies the role of both Puritan and Baptist traditions in his methodology, as well as Spurgeon's christocentric focus, yet in his analysis Ferguson minimizes the extent to which Spurgeon's crucicentrism and conversionism were present in his biblical interpretation.[75] Furthermore, Ferguson's conclusion that Spurgeon has a "complete resistance to historical scrutiny" is surprising, given that while he references the introduction to *Commenting and Commentaries*, he neglected to mention the latter survey portion of the book, in which Spurgeon grants positive reviews to a number of commentaries written from a critical perspective.[76] Several more recent articles or book chapters offer correctives to this perspective. Peter Morden's chapter on Spurgeon and the Bible in his *Communion with Christ and His People* suggests that Spurgeon's perspective on the Bible is the product of a matrix of religion, culture, and temperament.[77] Timothy Larsen's first work on Spurgeon analyzes his posthumously published commentary on the Sermon on the Mount alongside decades of sermonic material on the address.[78] Larsen's second and more exhaustive engagement with Spurgeon and the Bible provides good engagement the subject, though in writing broadly about Spurgeon's biblical engagement he has not fully explored Spurgeon's hermeneutical method.[79] Thus, while there is a significant amount of scholarship on Spurgeon, there is no sustained study of his approach to biblical interpretation. As Spurgeon was known primarily for his use of the Bible in both pulpit and print, further investigation of his interpretation will provide helpful context to the broader ministry of the Victorian "Prince of Preachers."

---

[74]George, "'Prince of Pilgrims,'" 144.
[75]Duncan S. Ferguson, "The Bible and Protestant Orthodoxy: The Hermeneutics of Charles Spurgeon," *Journal of the Evangelical Theological Society* 25, no. 4 (December 1, 1982): 455-66.
[76]Ferguson, "Bible and Protestant Orthodoxy," 465.
[77]Morden, *"Communion with Christ,"* 106-36.
[78]Timothy Larsen, "Charles Haddon Spurgeon," in *The Sermon on the Mount Through the Centuries: From the Early Church to John Paul II* (Grand Rapids, MI: Brazos Press, 2007), 181-205.
[79]Larsen, *People of One Book*, 247-76.

WORDS AND WORKS BY SPURGEON

Considering the total content of his sermons in addition to his printed volumes, commentaries, and magazine, Spurgeon may well have been one of the most prolific English-language authors of his lifetime, having published an estimated eighteen million words.[80] The bulk of this figure comes from Spurgeon's published sermons, the first of which appeared in *The New Park Street Pulpit*, which covered the first six years of Spurgeon's pastorate in London.[81] This collection of sermons was followed by the expansive *Metropolitan Tabernacle Pulpit*, which added an additional fifty-seven volumes.[82] Additionally, Spurgeon wrote a multi-volume commentary on the Psalms titled *The Treasury of David*, as well as a commentary on the book of Matthew titled *The Gospel of the Kingdom*, which was published after his death.[83] Finally, his magazine, *The Sword and the Trowel*, maintained a monthly publication beginning in January 1865.[84] Along with these documents, the archives in the Heritage Room at Spurgeon's College in London contain a number of significant primary sources, including letters and information pertaining to the organization and work of the college from its founding to the present day. Spurgeon's personal library, formerly housed at William Jewell College in Liberty, Missouri, has recently been acquired by the Midwestern Baptist Theological Seminary in Kansas City, Missouri, and is now part of the Seminary's Spurgeon Library.

OUTLINE OF THE BOOK

What follows are six chapters, each exploring a different facet of Spurgeon's crucicentric and conversionistic approach to the biblical text. While the

---

[80]George, "'Prince of Pilgrims,'" 2. For the sake of comparison, the approximate word count of the collected writings of Charles Dickens is four million words.

[81]C. H. Spurgeon, *The New Park Street Pulpit: Sermons Preached by C. H. Spurgeon*, vols. 1-6 (London: Passmore & Alabaster, 1855–1861).

[82]C. H. Spurgeon, *The Metropolitan Tabernacle Pulpit: Sermons Preached and Revised by C. H. Spurgeon*, vols. 7-63 (London: Passmore & Alabaster, 1861–1917).

[83]C. H. Spurgeon, *The Treasury of David*, 7 vols. (London: Marshall Brothers, 1869–1885); C. H. Spurgeon, *The Gospel of the Kingdom: A Commentary on the Book of Matthew* (London: Passmore & Alabaster, 1893).

[84]C. H. Spurgeon, ed., *The Sword and the Trowel*, vols. 1-28 (London: Passmore & Alabaster, 1865–1892). The magazine continued for a number of years following Spurgeon's death, though as this project focuses on Spurgeon's interpretation, it will primarily consult the years when he was active as the magazine's editor.

structure of the chapters is thematic, they follow a broad chronology, beginning with Spurgeon's youth in rural England and culminating in his work as an educator in his Pastors' College.

Chapter one explores Spurgeon's childhood and early theological education, noting the strong influences of village Nonconformity and Puritanism present throughout his youth. The chapter centers on Spurgeon's conversion, which occurred during a sermon from a village preacher at a Primitive Methodist church in Colchester. The sermon, which was little more than a fervent appeal for conversion, was loosely drawn from an Old Testament text, though the words of the preacher on the morning in early 1850 were almost completely focused on the crucifixion of Christ and the conversion of his listeners. The chapter discusses this narrative account as well as Spurgeon's early pastoral ministry in the Cambridgeshire village of Waterbeach.

Chapter two focuses on Spurgeon's biblical interpretation during the first twenty years of his ministry in London. The chapter considers Spurgeon's use of the Bible outside of his preaching, discussing several key moments within his ministry. Discussions include an early controversy with a high Calvinist minister in London who objected to the free offer of the gospel, which was a vital theme in Spurgeon's crucicentric and conversionistic interpretation. The chapter also discusses Spurgeon's publishing during the early years of his ministry, which included the establishment of his magazine, *The Sword and the Trowel*. Finally, the chapter analyzes several of Spurgeon's speeches, focusing particularly on speeches and addresses in which he discussed the nature and proper use of the Bible.

Chapter three considers Spurgeon's engagement with the Old Testament. It opens with a brief survey of developments in critical biblical studies during the eighteenth and nineteenth centuries to provide some context for Spurgeon's treatment of the Bible. The chapter then proceeds to argue that the cross and conversion were central to Spurgeon's approach to Old Testament texts, and these priorities occasionally led him to take circuitous routes to arrive at crucicentric and conversionistic conclusions. The chapter also includes detailed analysis of Spurgeon's engagement with Old Testament scholarship, noting that although he read widely, he would only endorse commentaries that upheld traditional Christian positions on the historicity of the Bible.

Chapter four continues the approach of chapter three, providing a critical analysis of Spurgeon's engagement with New Testament texts. In keeping with the structure of the previous chapter, the discussion of Spurgeon's interpretation provides a brief overview of developments in New Testament scholarship and discusses Spurgeon's assessment of a wide range of commentaries. Although the New Testament does include a significant amount of material that could be considered both crucicentric and conversionistic, the chapter argues that Spurgeon drew crucicentric and conversionist readings from a variety of texts, including texts where he appeared to bypass a straightforward interpretation in favor of an evangelistic one.

Chapter five surveys Spurgeon's ministries outside the pulpit during the latter years of his ministry. The chapter will continue a critical engagement with Spurgeon's magazine, *The Sword and the Trowel*, analyzing articles and book reviews that provide broader context for Spurgeon's assessment of trends in scholarship and how they could be of use to further his crucicentric and conversionistic approach to hermeneutics. In addition to its evaluation of Spurgeon's later publications, the chapter will also briefly assess Spurgeon's perspectives on the Bible amid the Downgrade Controversy, a significant conflict within the Baptist Union of Great Britain and Ireland in 1887 and 1888.

Chapter six, the final chapter, focuses on Spurgeon's work in the realm of education. The chapter will address several of Spurgeon's educational endeavors, from courses for women to evening classes for workers, culminating in an analysis of Spurgeon's Pastors' College, which trained hundreds of Baptist ministers during his lifetime. In addition to a brief survey of the college's history, including observations on the academic staff and students, the chapter analyzes surviving records of student instruction pertaining to biblical studies and preaching, noting parallels to Spurgeon's crucicentric and conversionistic priorities in his own ministry.

In this book I attempt to provide the first sustained investigation of Spurgeon's hermeneutics and in doing so demonstrate that the cross and conversion were central to any understanding of his approach to biblical texts. In the chapters that follow, Spurgeon's interpretation of Scripture will be studied in the context of his conversion and early ministry, publications, addresses, sermons, and instruction to students. In addition to providing a thorough account of an important facet of Spurgeon's work through its exploration of the "Prince of Preachers," the study will help to inform broader studies of the history of preaching and biblical interpretation in the Victorian era.

ECHOES OF ESSEX

Theological Education from Stambourne to Waterbeach

> *Even as a boy he knew his Bible; and at an age when most of us were but boys, he began to preach the gospel, and, from the first, with such remarkable knowledge of the Word of God, and facility and felicity in its presentation as turned the eyes of all men to the boy-preacher of London. . . . And when that boy-preacher startled all London by the marvel of his preaching, and still more by the marvel of his praying; it was the result of early and long study of the Word on the one hand, and communion with God in the closet on the other.*
>
> A. T. PIERSON

BORN IN 1834 IN KELVEDON, ESSEX, Charles Haddon Spurgeon was the first of eight surviving children of John and Eliza Spurgeon.[1] Shortly after Charles's birth, the family relocated to Colchester, where John Spurgeon worked as a clerk for a coal firm while also serving as an itinerant Congregational preacher. The Spurgeons sent eighteen-month-old Charles to live in Stambourne with his paternal grandparents, James and Sarah. Later, Charles Spurgeon would idealize rural England, and he professed

---

A. T. Pierson, "A Thoroughly Furnished Life," quoted in Anonymous, *From the Pulpit to the Palm-Branch: A Memorial of C. H. Spurgeon. Sequel to the Sketch of His Life,* titled *"From the Usher's Desk to the Tabernacle Pulpit." Including the Official Report of the Services in Connection with His Funeral* (New York: A. C. Armstrong and Son, 1892), 256.

[1]The most comprehensive genealogy of the Spurgeon family can be found in William Miller Higgs, *The Spurgeon Family: Being an Account of the Descent and Family of Charles Haddon Spurgeon, with Notes on the Family in General, Particularly the Essex Branch, from 1465 (5 Edward IV) to 1905 (4 Edward VII)* (London: Elliot Stock, 1906).

to a "sentiment of reverence" for Stambourne.[2] The town, which had at one time been called the "headquarters of Protestant resistance," boasted a long history of Nonconformity.[3] James Spurgeon stood firmly within this tradition. The Spurgeons' Congregational church in Stambourne boasted a significant library, much of which came from the collection of a previous minister, Henry Havers.[4] This library was important for the young Charles, whom David Bebbington has described as "bookish."[5] Learning to read while in the care of his grandparents, he was a voracious reader.[6] Indeed, Patricia Kruppa's observation that Spurgeon's "first playthings were books" is a fitting description.[7]

While Puritan works such as Bunyan's *Pilgrim's Progress* were key influences, the Bible was central. Late in his life, he wrote, "Before my conversion, I was accustomed to read the Scriptures to admire their grandeur, to feel the charm of their history, and wonder at the majesty of their language, but I altogether missed the Lord's intent therein."[8] The Lord's intent, according to Spurgeon, was the "inner meaning" within the biblical text, one that drove him toward a crucified Christ and "His great atoning sacrifice."[9] Standing firmly within the Puritan tradition, Spurgeon learned as a child to view the Holy Spirit as essential for biblical interpretation, believing that

---

[2]C. H. Spurgeon, *C. H. Spurgeon's Autobiography, Compiled from His Diary, Letters, and Records, by His Wife and His Private Secretary*, vol. 1, *1834–1854* (Cincinnati: Curts & Jennings, 1898), 29.

[3]Patricia S. Kruppa, *Charles Haddon Spurgeon: A Preacher's Progress*, Routledge Library Editions: 19th Century Religion (London: Taylor and Francis, 2017), 19.

[4]Spurgeon's personal library included many of these volumes, and much of it was made available to students at the Pastors' College. Spurgeon's sons arranged to sell the library collection to William Jewell College, a Baptist college in Liberty, Missouri. The collection was most recently acquired by Midwestern Baptist Theological Seminary, in Kansas City, Missouri, where it is on permanent display in the seminary's Spurgeon Library.

[5]David W. Bebbington, *The Dominance of Evangelicalism: The Age of Spurgeon and Moody* (Downers Grove, IL: InterVarsity Press, 2005), 38.

[6]George J. Stevenson, *Sketch of the Life and Ministry of the Rev. C. H. Spurgeon: From Original Documents Including Anecdotes and Incidents of Travel, Biographical Notices of Former Pastors, Historical Sketch of Park Street Chapel, and an Outline of Mr. Spurgeon's Articles of Faith* (New York: Sheldon, Blakeman, 1857), 26; J. C. Carlile, *C. H. Spurgeon: An Interpretive Biography* (London: Religious Tract Society and the Kingsgate Press, 1934), 55-57; Tom Nettles, *Living by Revealed Truth: The Life and Pastoral Theology of Charles Haddon Spurgeon* (Ross-shire, UK: Christian Focus, 2013), 23-27.

[7]Kruppa, *Charles Haddon Spurgeon: A Preacher's Progress*, 27.

[8]Spurgeon, *Autobiography*, 1:164.

[9]Spurgeon, *Autobiography*, 1:164.

it was only through the Spirit's quickening that "the inner meaning shone forth with wondrous glory."[10]

Spurgeon experienced a religious conversion in 1850, when he was fifteen years old. Electing to worship in a Primitive Methodist Chapel in Colchester rather than taking a longer walk through a snowstorm, Spurgeon listened to a lay minister's sermon on Isaiah 45:22, "Look unto me, and be ye saved, all the ends of the earth." This verse took on special meaning for Spurgeon, and it appeared frequently in his preached and written work in the years that followed. Furthermore, the method that the preacher employed, namely a crucicentric and conversionistic reading of a single verse, provided a model that Spurgeon himself would eventually follow. Newly converted and filled with a passion for souls, Spurgeon set out to preach a similar simple gospel message. He began by passing out gospel tracts in Cambridgeshire and teaching a Sunday school for boys. This work eventually gave way to preaching, which would eventually pave the way for his first pastorate in a small Baptist church in the rural village of Waterbeach.

This chapter will investigate the extent to which Spurgeon's early life shaped his interpretation of the Bible and the development of the particular method with which he approached the biblical text: through the lenses of crucicentrism and conversionism. In his published sermons, which would eventually number over three thousand, there are echoes of both Puritan voices and of a simple Primitive Methodist sermon that he heard in 1850. Spurgeon's early years were saturated with biblical passages, in written and preached form, and the various theological traditions he experienced in his youth culminated in him crafting a thoroughly crucicentric and conversionistic interpretation of the Bible. These traditions included rural Nonconformity, Primitive Methodism, the Established Church, and finally, the Particular Baptist denomination. This chapter will analyze significant moments from Spurgeon's formative years—moments that exemplify his early interaction with the Bible, from his rural childhood to his first pastorate—and evaluate their contribution to his theology and biblical interpretation.

---

[10]Spurgeon, *Autobiography*, 1:164.

STAMBOURNE AND THE EMBERS OF PURITANISM: SPURGEON'S PASTORAL HERITAGE

Spurgeon frequently referred to his youth in rural England in his published works.[11] His idealization of life in rural English countryside was portrayed in one of his final books, the autobiographical *Memories of Stambourne*.[12] Gratitude for his family's religious devotion found expression when he proclaimed to the congregation at the Metropolitan Tabernacle that "it is one of the highest privileges that God has ever been pleased to grant to me that I can rejoice in a father and a grandfather who trained me in the fear of God; and I congratulate every young person who has such a pedigree."[13]

Charles's grandfather James Spurgeon (1776–1864) was the pastor of the local Independent congregation.[14] James had studied at the Hoxton Independent College, a Dissenting academy in London, and had taken up his pastorate in Stambourne in 1810.[15] During James's time as a student, the college was run by a Scottish minister, the Rev. Robert Simpson (1764–1817), who was described as a man who was "in every particular Calvinistic" and "well read in Greek and Latin, but in Hebrew greatly excelled."[16] The *Evangelical Magazine* recorded that Hoxton students' examinations included reading "in Chaldee, part of Daniel; and in Greek, part of the 3rd Olynthiad of Demosthenes. . . . Third-year men read in Hebrew four chapters of Isaiah, in Greek, part of Book I of the *Illiad*; in Latin, part of Tacitus's *Life of Agricola*."[17] Charles Spurgeon's friend, assistant, and eventual biographer, G. H. Pike, regarded James as "one of the last representatives of Old Dissent" and observed that "his faith was old-fashioned

---

[11]Spurgeon, *Autobiography*, 1:13-44.

[12]C. H. Spurgeon and Benjamin Beddow, *Memories of Stambourne: With Personal Remarks, Recollections, and Reflections* (London: Passmore & Alabaster, 1892).

[13]C. H. Spurgeon, "Four Choice Sentences," sermon no. 1630, given February 3, 1881, from Genesis 28:15, *The Metropolitan Tabernacle Pulpit*, vol. 27 (London: Passmore & Alabaster, 1881), 646.

[14]Charles Spurgeon's brother was also named James (1837–1899).

[15]Spurgeon and Beddow, *Memories of Stambourne*, 78. For further information on Hoxton Independent College, which would eventually merge with several other colleges to become New College, London, see Herbert McLachlan, *English Education Under the Test Acts: Being the History of the Nonconformist Academics 1662–1820* (Manchester: Manchester University Press, 1931), 236-41.

[16]McLachlan, *English Education Under the Test Acts*, 238.

[17]Quoted in McLachlan, *English Education Under the Test Acts*, 240.

in its childlike simplicity."[18] Pike may indeed be correct in his assessment of James Spurgeon as representative of an older generation of ministers; however, the Baptist historian Peter Morden cautions that Pike may have been "overpainting" in his attempts to present Charles as a representative of a Puritan tradition.[19]

While thoroughly committed to the Independent church, James was remembered by his grandson as having a cordial relationship with the local established church parish minister, James Hopkins.[20] James Spurgeon also served as an inspiration for the character John Ploughman, a pseudonymous character created by his grandson. The John Ploughman books, which contained a combination of rural anecdotes and Christian devotional material, were among Spurgeon's most popular works.[21] Holding fast to conservative evangelical Independency throughout his entire life, James's last recorded words to his grandson were indicative of his commitment to the legacy of Puritanism. He said, "I have grown in experience; but from the first day until now, I have had no new doctrines to teach my hearers. I have had to make no confessions of error on vital points, but have been held fast to the doctrines of grace, and can now say that I love them better than ever."[22] Charles was deeply influenced by his grandfather's hesitancy toward "new doctrine" and would later refer to it from his own pulpit as "old heresy with a fresh coat of varnish."[23]

John Spurgeon (1810–1902), Charles's father, was also a preacher, though unlike his father and son, much of his ministry was spent as an itinerant. During Charles's youth, John worked as a clerk in a coal mining office in Colchester while traveling nine miles on Sundays to preach to an

---

[18]G. Holden Pike, *The Life and Work of Charles Haddon Spurgeon* (London: Cassell, 1892), 15.

[19]Peter J. Morden, *"Communion with Christ and His People": The Spirituality of C. H. Spurgeon* (Oxford: Regent's Park College, 2010), 22.

[20]Spurgeon, *Autobiography*, 1:10.

[21]C. H. Spurgeon, *John Ploughman's Talk; or, Plain Advice for Plain People* (Philadelphia: H. Altemus, 1896); C. H. Spurgeon, *John Ploughman's Pictures; or, More of His Plain Talk for Plain People* (Philadelphia: H. Altemus, 1896).

[22]Spurgeon and Beddow, *Memories of Stambourne*, 79.

[23]C. H. Spurgeon, "A Sermon to the Lord's Little Children," sermon no. 1711, given March 18, 1883, from John 2:12 & 1 John 2:13 (RV), *The Metropolitan Tabernacle Pulpit*, vol. 29 (London: Passmore & Alabaster, 1883), 166.

independent congregation in Tollesbury. He also ministered for a time in London at the Fetter Lane Congregational Chapel, in 1868.[24] James Allen's biography of Charles Spurgeon suggests that John was additionally involved with an Independent church in Cranbrook, Kent.[25] Allen's book contains a quotation from John in which he laments the burden that the itinerant nature of his ministry placed upon his family. He wrote, "I have been away from home a great deal, trying to build up weak congregations, and felt that I was neglecting the religious training of my own children while I toiled for the good of others."[26] In the same statement, John praised his wife for her dedication to their children in his absence.

Sources related to John Spurgeon are rather scarce and largely limited to incidental references in his son's magazine, *The Sword and the Trowel*.[27] The surviving material suggests that in some respects John's influence upon Charles may best be seen in their work together as ministers. For instance, in his later years John worked alongside his son in supporting the nondenominational Stockwell Orphanage, which was established in 1867. The orphanage provided shelter for over two hundred boys, eventually adding a girls' wing in 1879. While it is not clear whether John had permanent employment as a minister in his later years, there is some evidence to suggest that he continued preaching. In 1877, Charles placed a small advertisement in *The Sword and the Trowel* to recommend his father as an ideal candidate for an Independent congregation looking for "an old-fashioned gospel minister, and an experienced pastor."[28] In addition to working among his son's parachurch ministries, John also occasionally preached at the Metropolitan Tabernacle in Charles's absence.

---

[24]"A Relic of Old Days," *The Quiver* 28, no. 301 (January 1893): 750.

[25]James T. Allen, *The Essex Lad Who Became the Prince of Preachers* (London: Pickering & Inglis, 1893), 8.

[26]Allen, *Essex Lad*, 8.

[27]John Spurgeon's preaching has been preserved in a small number of instances. The first was a prayer given on the occasion of the laying of the Metropolitan Tabernacle cornerstone, and the second was a short speech given during the American evangelist Dwight L. Moody's visit to the Tabernacle in June 1884. See, respectively, the accounts in "The Ceremony of Laying the First Stone of the New Tabernacle," sermon no. 268, given August 16, 1859, *The New Park Street Pulpit*, vol. 5 (London: Passmore & Alabaster, 1859), 356; and C. H. Spurgeon, *Mr. Spurgeon's Jubilee Services: A Memorial Volume* (London: Passmore & Alabaster, 1884), 13.

[28]*The Sword and the Trowel* 13 (1877): 97.

It should not be overlooked that the women in the family also had a significant influence on the young Spurgeon. His father's sister, Ann Spurgeon, helped to care for the young Charles at Stambourne and maintained a keen interest in her nephew's education and ministry in subsequent years.[29] Spurgeon once observed that his future biographers would find no "difficulty in accounting for the position that God has given me. I can tell you of two reasons why I am what I am: My mother, and the truth of my message."[30] In a letter following his conversion, Charles referred to his mother Eliza as the "great means in God's hand of rendering me what I hope I am."[31] Later, in an 1884 sermon called "The Joy of Holy Households," Spurgeon recalled "when my father was absent preaching the gospel, my mother always filled his place at the family altar. . . . We could not have a house without prayer; that would be heathenish or atheistical."[32]

The pastoral work of both the elder Spurgeons ingrained the significance of preaching upon Charles from a young age. James Spurgeon provided a working model of friendly discourse with ministers of differing theological traditions, and both elder Spurgeons were strong proponents of a Puritan theology that would remain central to Charles's identity throughout his ministry.

FROM THE MANSE LIBRARY TO CAMBRIDGESHIRE: SPURGEON'S EARLY EDUCATION

As a child, Spurgeon was known for his love of books, and his appetite for reading would be emphasized by most of his biographers. In one of the first biographical entries about Spurgeon, the American Baptist pastor Elias Lyman Magoon wrote that Spurgeon "began the assiduous study of books at an early period, and evidently has ever since been a comprehensive

---

[29]George J. Stevenson, *Pastor C. H. Spurgeon: His Life and Work to His Forty Third Birthday* (London: Passmore & Alabaster, 1877), 17.

[30]Carlile, *C. H. Spurgeon: An Interpretive Biography*, 24.

[31]Spurgeon to Eliza Spurgeon, May 1, 1850, in *The Letters of Charles Haddon Spurgeon*, collected and collated by his son Charles Spurgeon (London: Marshall Brothers, 1923), 22.

[32]C. H. Spurgeon, "The Joy of Holy Households," sermon no. 2539, given June 19, 1884, from Psalm 118:15-16, *The Metropolitan Tabernacle Pulpit*, vol. 43 (London: Passmore & Alabaster, 1897), 581.

reader of whatever he deems of practical use."[33] Magoon also noted that Spurgeon acquired knowledge from both books and his studies in Maidstone and Cambridge, writing that he "accumulated no small amount of literary treasure; but his best acquisitions were secured in the early and accurate knowledge of human nature, which, through juvenile discipline in diversified life, Providence caused him to possess."[34] Spurgeon later highlighted *An Alarme to Unconverted Sinners* by Joseph Alleine (1634–1668) and *A Call to the Unconverted to Turn and Live* by Richard Baxter (1615–1691) as key texts from his youth.[35]

In addition to the Puritan divines, the young Spurgeon began to read the Bible in a variety of contexts, including times of family prayer. His formative years were spent in households that valued interaction with both the biblical text and contemporary theological developments. In a moment of reflection near the end of his life, Spurgeon highlighted the significance of his early biblical engagement, writing that "I can bear witness that children *can* understand the Scriptures; for I am sure that, when but a child, I could have discussed many a knotty point of controversial theology, having heard both sides of the question freely stated among my father's circle of friends."[36] As a pastor, Spurgeon consistently promoted the benefits of biblical and theological instruction for children of all ages, and this extended to providing Christian reading material aimed specifically at young readers. He published a volume titled *Come Ye Children,* which functioned as an instructive aid for parents and Sunday school teachers as they began to teach the Bible to children.[37] Spurgeon's introduction to this particular book is telling in its emphasis on what he deemed to be the most important facet of biblical instruction, namely that "Christian children mainly need to be taught the doctrine, precept, and life of the gospel: they

[33]Elias Lyman Magoon, *"The Modern Whitfield": Sermons of the Rev. C. H. Spurgeon of London, with an Introduction and Sketch of His Life* (New York: Sheldon, Blakeman, 1856), vi. Magoon's work, which intended to introduce the twenty-two-year-old preacher to American audiences, contained a series of his early sermons at the New Park Street Chapel.

[34]Magoon, *"Modern Whitfield,"* vii.

[35]Spurgeon, *Autobiography,* 1:80.

[36]Spurgeon, *Autobiography,* 1:70.

[37]C. H. Spurgeon, *"Come, Ye Children": A Book for Parents and Teachers on the Christian Training of Children* (London: Passmore & Alabaster, 1897).

require to have Divine truth put before them clearly and forcibly."[38] For Spurgeon, conversionistic interpretation of the Bible was not only a matter for Sunday preaching but also for family devotional reading.

While the influence of Spurgeon's relatives and his personal reading were the primary factors in his theological development, Spurgeon also benefitted considerably from time spent at several schools. He attended the Stockwell School in Colchester beginning in 1844 and subsequently enrolled at St. Augustine's Agricultural College in 1848, along with his brother James Archer Spurgeon. His time at St. Augustine's was brief; he stayed there for one year before taking up a position as an usher, assisting the headmaster at the Newmarket Academy in Cambridgeshire. His duties at Newmarket included working as a tutor and organizing a student missionary society.[39]

While Spurgeon's reflections on his education express gratitude toward his instructors, he reserved the most praise in his autobiography for a woman named Mary King, who worked as a cook at the Newmarket Academy. Spurgeon suggested that he learned "more from her than I should have learned from any six doctors of divinity of the sort we have nowadays. . . . The cook at Newmarket was a godly experienced woman, from whom I learned far more than I did from the minister of the chapel we attended."[40] According to J. D. Everett, an instructor at the Newmarket school, King was a "member of the Bethesda Strict Baptist Church . . . a staunch Calvinist, logical, clear-headed, and had a wonderful knowledge of the Bible. . . . He [Spurgeon] told me, in his own terse fashion, that it was 'cook' who had taught him his theology."[41] This account indicates the extent to which Spurgeon valued lay interpretation of the Bible and also his penchant for hyperbole, even as a student. A few years after his conversion, Spurgeon published a volume titled *The Saint and His Saviour*. While the book was largely focused upon what Spurgeon deemed the various stages of an individual's understanding of and relationship with Christ, he took a

---

[38]Spurgeon, *"Come, Ye Children,"* 8.
[39]Spurgeon, *Autobiography*, 1:55.
[40]Spurgeon, *Autobiography*, 1:53.
[41]Spurgeon, *Autobiography*, 1:54.

moment in a chapter on conversion to highlight the influence of Mary King, writing that he owes "his eternal obligations to an old cook, who was despised as an Antinomian, but who in her kitchen taught him many of the deep things of God, and removed many a doubt from his youthful mind."[42]

EARLY THEOLOGICAL DEVELOPMENT

While Spurgeon's achievements as a preacher are unquestioned, most biographers and historians have not rated him as a theologian.[43] In recent years, however, a few scholars have begun to investigate the theological dimensions of Spurgeon's ministry. Mark Hopkins, for instance, highlights Spurgeon's contributions as a "preacher and mystic."[44] Recent writings by Tom Nettles and Christian George have recognized theological elements in Spurgeon's ministry but have stopped short of labeling Spurgeon as a theologian.[45] Furthermore, several recent works have analyzed Spurgeon's interaction with Victorian scholarship. Christian George's recent doctoral thesis, for instance, has provided a close analysis of Spurgeon's engagement with languages, indicating that he had a "mastery" of Greek and Hebrew, along with "adequate proficiencies" in Latin and French, and a "limited but attempted understanding of German."[46] He was also, as we have seen, a voracious reader. Although he never attended university and his formal education ended in his teenage years, Spurgeon's sermons would eventually achieve a popular influence far greater than that of many theologians of his day.

As a fifteen-year-old student, he composed a sixteen-chapter thesis against Roman Catholicism, combatively titled *Antichrist and Her Brood;*

---

[42]C. H. Spurgeon, *The Saint and His Savior: The Progress of the Soul in the Knowledge of Jesus* (New York: Sheldon, Blakeman, 1858), 126.

[43]Perhaps the sole exception from recent scholarship is Mike Nicholls's statement that Spurgeon is a "forthright theologian." Mike Nicholls, *C. H. Spurgeon: The Pastor Evangelist* (Didcot, UK: Baptist Historical Society, 1992), 147.

[44]Mark Hopkins, *Nonconformity's Romantic Generation: Evangelical and Liberal Theologies in Victorian England* (Milton Keynes, UK: Paternoster, 2004), 151.

[45]Nettles, *Living by Revealed Truth*; Christian T. George, "Jesus Christ, The 'Prince of Pilgrims': A Critical Analysis of the Ontological, Functional, and Exegetical Christologies in the Sermons, Writings, and Lectures of Charles Haddon Spurgeon (1834–1892)" (PhD thesis, University of St. Andrews, 2011).

[46]George has also included a substantial list identifying instances where Spurgeon engages with foreign languages in his sermons. George, "'Prince of Pilgrims,'" 37.

or, Popery Unmasked.[47] Although the essay was never published, a surviving chapter, reproduced in Spurgeon's *Autobiography*, provides a window into his early view of the Bible.[48] The adolescent Spurgeon strongly criticized Catholicism for contributing to the "spiritual ignorance" of its followers. By spiritual ignorance, he meant a lack of engagement with the Bible that was an impediment to conversion, writing that the "greatest spiritual darkness is to be ignorant of the only way of salvation as it is revealed alone in the Scriptures. The Church which withholds the Bible from its members, or takes away from them the genuine word of God, is guilty of bringing the most dreadful famine upon the minds of men."[49] Standing firmly within Protestant tradition, he maintained that vernacular translations of the Bible were of vital importance. He suggested that many Roman Catholic priests were unfamiliar with the biblical text and therefore could not adequately convey the central message of the Bible, namely that of salvation through Christ's crucifixion and resurrection. "Every Christian knows, experimentally," he continued, "that the Bible is the Word of God. When a sinner becomes seriously concerned about his character, state, and prospects, if he reads the Bible, he finds at first that it is all against him. By the holy law of God he is convicted and condemned; and he is conscious of a power and dignity in the Word of condemnation."[50]

In assessing this work, it is worth considering how well this young village Nonconformist understood contemporary Roman Catholic doctrine. Most of his cited references were from Reformation and Puritan-era books, and many of his critiques appear to be directed at late medieval Catholicism. In one of his more forceful statements, he wrote that "in the Bible, the Almighty addresses us as by a voice from Heaven: 'Look unto Me,

---

[47]Spurgeon originally entered the essay, written in November and December 1849, into a competition for a monetary prize. While Spurgeon's offering did not secure the prize, in the subsequent year he received a letter from a Congregationalist minister named George Smith, who offered him an award of £3 as an incentive for the young writer to continue on in his studies. This letter is included in the copy of the essay located in the Heritage Room at Spurgeon's College in London. Box A2.06. A facsimile of both the letter from George Smith and the essay's third chapter is also included in Spurgeon, *Autobiography*, 1:57-66.

[48]Spurgeon, *Autobiography*, 1:60-66.

[49]Spurgeon, *Autobiography*, 1:61.

[50]Spurgeon, *Autobiography*, 1:64.

and be ye saved, all the ends of the earth.' The Church of Rome stands by, and presumes to decide who shall and who shall not hear these words of the Almighty Saviour."[51] The scholarly foundations, in short, were respectable but dated, reflecting the sources that he might have found in his father or grandfather's libraries but not showing much knowledge of contemporary Catholic thought and practice. Spurgeon tellingly suggested that the Catholic priests' withholding of the Bible hindered the conversion of their flocks. Curiously, Spurgeon's biblical reference in this chapter was Isaiah 45:22, a text that would play a prominent role in his conversion just two months later.

SPURGEON'S CONVERSION NARRATIVE

Spurgeon's conversion, which occurred on a January morning in 1850, represents both a turning point in his life and, most significantly for this study, a key encounter with the Bible that further solidified his resolve to connect engagement with Scripture with a message of transformation rooted in the Christian gospel. Narrative accounts of Spurgeon's conversion are numerous, ranging from a brief mention in an early biography written by George Stevenson, to a sustained monologue in Spurgeon's lengthy *Autobiography*.[52] These accounts established a paradigm in which conversion, as Spurgeon experienced it, was not only a pivotal moment in his religious life but an idealized pattern that he attempted to recreate and establish as normative in his own ministry.

One of the hallmarks of nineteenth-century evangelicalism was the emphasis on a particular moment of conviction and repentance leading to an individual's profession of faith, known more commonly then and now as "conversion."[53] Conversion itself is helpfully defined by the church historian Jerald Brauer as a "profound, overwhelming, totally transforming experience in which a person believes that he has experienced death and rebirth

---

[51]Spurgeon, *Autobiography*, 1:63.

[52]See, among others, Stevenson, *Sketch of the Life*, 39-40; Spurgeon, *Autobiography*, 1:97-114; W. Y. Fullerton, *C. H. Spurgeon: A Biography* (London: Williams and Norgate, 1920), 18-32; Morden, *"Communion with Christ,"* 47-76; Kruppa, *Charles Haddon Spurgeon: A Preacher's Progress*, 40-49.

[53]David W. Bebbington, *Evangelicalism in Modern Britain: A History from the 1730s to the 1980s* (London: Routledge, 2005), 5-10.

through the powerful working of the Spirit of God."[54] Narratives of conversion, made popular in England during the Puritan era, illustrated clear lines of demarcation between one's former self and a newly converted identity.[55] Such narratives marked an individual's spiritual progress against an established and systematic *ordo salutis*, or order of salvation. In his introduction to an edited volume of Bunyan's *Grace Abounding to the Chief of Sinners*, Roger Sharrock identifies five stages of conversion utilized by many Puritan ministers, namely:

(1) early providential mercies and opportunities,

(2) unregenerate life: sin and resistance to the Gospel,

(3) conversion (often initiated by an "awakening" sermon),

(4) vocation to preach the Gospel, and

(5) an account of the course of ministry.[56]

Spurgeon, who was well-steeped in Puritan theological writing and devotional practices, crafted an extensive autobiographical account that could fit within these five stages.

Despite the devout influences of his childhood homes, Spurgeon did not have a conversion experience while living with his family, though it was a frequent topic in the correspondence he exchanged with his parents during his time at boarding school.[57] His memoirs suggest that his lack of conversion had worried him throughout much of his youth. Much of this wrestling involved direct engagement with the biblical text. Battling what he described as a period of prolonged depression, Spurgeon records, "When I was for many a month in this state, I used to read the Bible through,

[54]Jerald C. Brauer, "Conversion: From Puritanism to Revivalism," *The Journal of Religion* 58, no. 3 (July 1978): 230.

[55]D. Bruce Hindmarsh, *The Evangelical Conversion Narrative: Spiritual Autobiography in Early Modern England* (Oxford: Oxford University Press, 2005), 33-60; Patricia Caldwell, *The Puritan Conversion Narrative: The Beginnings of American Expression* (Cambridge: Cambridge University Press, 1983); Lewis R. Rambo, *Understanding Religious Conversion* (New Haven: Yale University Press, 1993).

[56]John Bunyan, *Grace Abounding to the Chief of Sinners*, ed. Roger Sharrock (Oxford: Oxford University Press, 1962), xxix.

[57]Spurgeon's family did provide books on the subject of conversion. Included among them were Bunyan's *Grace Abounding*, Richard Baxter's *Call to the Unconverted*, and John Angell James's *The Anxious Enquirer*. See Spurgeon, *Autobiography*, 1:80.

and the threatenings were all printed in capitals, but the promises were in such small type I could not for a long time make them out. . . . I did not believe they were mine."[58] Other journal entries from this time period included descriptions of feeling "like a dog under the table, not allowed to eat of the children's food." Despite extensive reading on the subject of conversion, Spurgeon wrote that he "panted and longed" to understand how to be saved.[59] Spurgeon's reflections here are emblematic of his Puritan-inflected upbringing, in that the Holy Spirit was required to illuminate the text to men and women.[60]

When he introduced the subject of his conversion in his *Autobiography*, Spurgeon kept the Bible central, writing that "the revealed Word awakened me; but it was the preached Word that saved me."[61] Spurgeon's *Autobiography* records January 6, 1850, as the date when he was converted.[62] Opting on a snowy morning to worship in a Primitive Methodist chapel rather than endure his walk any longer, Spurgeon encountered a small congregation where a "thin looking man, a shoemaker or tailor, or something of that sort, went up to the pulpit to preach." The text was Isaiah 45:22, "Look unto me, and be ye saved, all the ends of the earth," an Old Testament prophetic text. Spurgeon's portrayal of the preacher's manner and language is not particularly favorable; he goes so far as to suggest that the uneducated man was "really stupid" and "did not pronounce the words rightly."[63] He also suggests that the preacher's delivery was in keeping with his apparent lack of education. Emphasizing the speaker's thick accent, Spurgeon summarized portions of his sermon in colorful vernacular:

> Many on ye are lookin' to yourselves, but it's no use lookin' there. You'll never find any comfort in yourselves. Some look to God the Father. No, look to

---

[58]Spurgeon, *Autobiography*, 1:85.

[59]Spurgeon, *Autobiography*, 1:105.

[60]This follows, for instance, the argument of the noteworthy Puritan John Owen. See, particularly, John Owen, *The Reason of Faith or, An Answer unto That Enquiry, Wherefore We Believe the Scripture to Be the Word of God?* (Glasgow: W. Falconer, 1801), 133-39.

[61]Spurgeon, *Autobiography*, 1:104; Much of Spurgeon's autobiographical account of his conversion coincides with an earlier publication from the late 1870s. See C. H. Spurgeon, *How Spurgeon Found Christ* (London: James E. Hawkins, n.d.).

[62]Spurgeon, *Autobiography*, 1:104-8.

[63]Spurgeon, *Autobiography*, 1:105.

Him by-and-by. Jesus Christ says, "Look unto *Me*." Some on ye say, "We
must wait for the Spirit's workin'." You have no business with that just now.
Look to *Christ*. The text says. "Look unto *Me*."[64]

The sermon continued on in a strongly crucicentric vein, as the lay minister
exhorted his listeners to "look unto Me; I am sweatin' great drops of blood.
Look unto Me; I am hangin' on the cross. Look unto Me; I am dead and
buried. Look unto Me; I rise again. Look unto Me; I ascend to Heaven.
Look unto Me; I am sittin' at the Father's right hand. O poor sinner, look
unto Me!"[65] As Spurgeon's narrative continues, the preacher turned and
addressed him directly, having seen his discomfort, and narrowed his
message, suggesting that the young man looked "very miserable." According to Spurgeon, this sermon "was a good blow, struck right home. . . .
I looked until I could almost have looked my eyes away, and at that moment
I saw the sun; and I could have risen that instant, and sung with the most
enthusiastic of them, of the precious blood of Christ, and the simple faith
which looks alone to Him."[66] Summarizing his experience, Spurgeon wrote
"my gratitude most of all is due to God, not for books, but for the preached
Word,—and that too addressed to me by a poor, uneducated man. A man
who had never received any training for the ministry, and probably will
never be heard of in this life."[67]

While this narrative from Spurgeon's *Autobiography* has been recounted
in virtually all subsequent biographies, some scholars have observed that
Spurgeon's account of the Primitive Methodist service, written many years
later, may not have been accurate, at least with regard to several details.
Timothy McCoy offers compelling evidence that the sermon actually took
place a week later than Spurgeon's date, on January 13, 1850, and that the
preacher in question was likely a Methodist minister named Robert
Eaglen.[68] Moreover, Spurgeon's narrative account of his conversion

---

[64]Spurgeon, *Autobiography*, 1:106.
[65]Spurgeon, *Autobiography*, 1:106.
[66]Spurgeon, *Autobiography*, 1:106.
[67]Spurgeon, *Autobiography*, 1:104.
[68]Timothy A. McCoy, "The Evangelistic Ministry of C. H. Spurgeon: Implications for a Contemporary Model for Pastoral Evangelism" (PhD diss., The Southern Baptist Theological Seminary,

developed over time, taking on greater detail in later years. This is problematic in that in one of his earliest accounts of his conversion, Spurgeon said that he remembered very few of the details of the events on the January morning. Preaching to the congregation at the New Park Street Chapel, he suggested that he did not know "the man who uttered the words that were the means of relieving my heart: 'Look unto me and be ye saved, all the ends of the earth.' I do not recollect what he said in the sermon, and I am sure I do not care to know. I found Jesus there and then, and that was enough for me."[69] Peter Morden has argued that Spurgeon's retelling of his conversion narrative developed over time, with specific details added or subtracted "until the carefully fashioned, dramatised account of the event in *How Spurgeon Found Christ* was published."[70] Spurgeon's own framing of his conversion became, in the words of Morden, "packaged and marketed as an aid to evangelism."[71]

While some of the discrepancies regarding the finer details of Spurgeon's conversion may remain unanswered, several elements of Spurgeon's accounts do remain consistent in all of his retellings of the event. Among them are Spurgeon's insistence on the relative unimportance of the preacher and his identity, on the importance of a thoroughly crucicentric interpretation of Isaiah 45, and on the Holy Spirit acting as the unseen agent of his conversion.[72] This sermon, which deeply struck Spurgeon, was on one level rather different from the lengthy and eloquent sermons that he himself would later preach. However, there are also some elements that would make their way into his pulpit addresses. First, it focused tightly on one

---

1989), 323-50. See also Nicholls, *C. H. Spurgeon: The Pastor Evangelist*, 4-5; Morden, "*Communion with Christ*," 50-51.

[69]C. H. Spurgeon, "Healing for the Wounded," sermon no. 53, given November 11, 1855, from Psalm 147:3, *The New Park Street Pulpit*, vol. 1 (London: Passmore & Alabaster, 1855), 407.

[70]Morden, "*Communion with Christ*," 52.

[71]Morden, "*Communion with Christ*," 53.

[72]Spurgeon, in an 1888 sermon, suggested that members of his congregation did not need to know the specific date of their conversion. According to Spurgeon, the conversion date "does not matter at all. It is a pleasant thing for a person to know his birthday; but when persons are not sure of the exact date of their birth, they do not, therefore, infer that they are not alive. If a person does not know *when* he was converted, that is no proof that he is not converted." C. H. Spurgeon, "Number Two-Thousand; or, Healing by the Stripes of Jesus," sermon no. 2000, given January 1, 1888, from Isaiah 53:5, *The Metropolitan Tabernacle Pulpit*, vol. 33 (London: Passmore & Alabaster, 1888), 718.

isolated verse. Worship services at Spurgeon's Tabernacle were focused around the sermons, and sermons themselves usually came from a single verse.[73] Second, and more significant, this sermon appears to have ignored the immediate context of the verse in favor of an interpretation that was directly crucicentric. Crucicentrism, often coupled with a strong appeal toward conversion, constituted the evangelistic aim of many of Spurgeon's sermons. Thus, Peter Morden is right to observe that for Spurgeon "the cross of Christ was the fulcrum around which a right understanding of salvation must revolve."[74]

A reference appearing in an early biography affirms Spurgeon's evangelistic impetus. In a section directly following an abridged account of his conversion, Spurgeon was quoted as saying, "I now think I am bound never to preach a sermon without preaching to sinners. I do think that a minister who can preach a sermon without addressing sinners does not know how to preach."[75] David Bebbington has observed that the atoning death of Christ on the cross and the continuing work of the Holy Spirit were "the motor of Spurgeon's ministry."[76]

EARLY MINISTRY OPPORTUNITIES: SUNDAY SCHOOL AND BEYOND

Following his baptism, Spurgeon increased his involvement in church work, establishing a Sunday school that met in the vestry of the Independent chapel in Newmarket.[77] Though he initially intended to take on a group of day pupils and work as an educator, he also developed his abilities as a Sunday school teacher and eventually worked to help train other Sunday school teachers to be more effective communicators.[78] He viewed

---

[73]That is not to say that the verse was always treated in isolation, as there was a separate, shorter section of the service that provided an exposition of the sermon text. These brief expositions provided broader biblical context surrounding the verse upon which Spurgeon would later preach. The expositions appear more frequently in the later editions of the *Metropolitan Tabernacle Pulpit*.

[74]Morden, *"Communion with Christ,"* 57.

[75]Stevenson, *Pastor C. H. Spurgeon*, 20.

[76]Morden, *"Communion with Christ,"* xi.

[77]Stevenson, *Pastor C. H. Spurgeon*, 24.

[78]Spurgeon took out an advert in a Cambridge newspaper indicating that he "intends to take on six or seven young gentlemen as day pupils. He will endeavour to the utmost to impart a good

the work of Sunday school teachers as "helping in this great warfare against the enemy" and credited his lessons to the children in Cambridge as preparing him for his future ministry.[79] Spurgeon went so far as to write that "he who teaches class in a Sabbath-school has earned a good degree. I had rather receive the title of S.S.T. than M.A., B.A., or any other honour that was ever conferred by men."[80]

In his earliest ministry, the evangelical tenets of crucicentrism and conversionism had already begun to take shape in Spurgeon's teaching. Reflecting on his Sunday school work, he lamented the untimely death of one of his students, who had forsaken the interventions of his family and teachers and "drank himself to death at one debauch."[81] Reflecting on his last meeting with the student before his death, he noted the consequences of "not pointing dying sinners to a living Christ, and inviting them to trust in His precious blood."[82] "I daily feel," he added,

> that the atmosphere of earth has as much a tendency to harden my heart as to harden plaster which is newly spread upon the wall; and unless I am baptized anew with the Spirit of God, and constantly stand at the foot of the cross, reading the curse of sin in the crimson hieroglyphics of my Saviour's dying agonies, I shall become as steeled an insensible as many professors already are.[83]

Spurgeon's success as a Sunday school teacher eventually led to invitations for him to train and support other adult Sunday school teachers. Tom Nettles has noted that while Spurgeon was initially uncomfortable with the idea of addressing older Sunday school teachers, his instruction was well-received by them and the meetings eventually became "like a small chapel."[84] In the autumn of 1850, Spurgeon was invited to join the Lay Preacher's

---

commercial education." See Ebenezer Smith, *Two Centuries of Grace: Being a Brief History of the Baptist Church, Waterbeach. An Address at the Centenary Meeting* (Cambridge: Cambridge University Press, 1903), 14.

[79]Spurgeon, *Autobiography*, 1:181.
[80]Spurgeon, *Autobiography*, 1:181.
[81]Spurgeon, *Autobiography*, 1:183.
[82]Spurgeon, *Autobiography*, 1:183.
[83]Spurgeon, *Autobiography*, 1:184.
[84]Nettles, *Living by Revealed Truth*, 58.

Association, despite his young age and rather recent conversion. The association was established to provide support for rural churches in the form of itinerant preachers, and Spurgeon was recommended in part through his connection with the St. Andrew's Street Chapel in Cambridge.[85] His itinerant preaching ministry began with a sermon in Teversham, a village approximately one mile east of Cambridge, and it expanded significantly in the subsequent year.[86] During 1851, he preached nearly two dozen sermons in churches throughout the area, including a small congregation meeting in Waterbeach Chapel.[87]

In an entry in his *Autobiography*, he recorded, "I was for three years a Cambridge man, though I never entered the University. I could not have obtained a degree, because I was a Nonconformist; and moreover, it was a better thing for me to pursue my studies under an admirable scholar and tender friend, and to preach at the same time."[88] As he observed,

> I had, however, a better College course, for, when I first began to preach, this was my usual way of working. I was up in the morning early, praying and reading the Word; all the day, I was either teaching my scholars or studying theology as much as I could; then, at five in the evening, I became a travelling preacher, and went into the villages around Cambridge, to tell out what I had learned. My quiet meditation during the walk helped me to digest what I had read, and the rehearsal of my lesson in public, by preaching it to the people, fixed it on my memory. . . . I never learned so much, or learned it so thoroughly, as when I used to tell out, simply and earnestly, what I had first received into my own mind and heart.[89]

During his first pastorate, Spurgeon briefly considered enrolling at Stepney Academy, a training institution for Baptist ministers located at the time in

---

[85]Stevenson, *Pastor C. H. Spurgeon*, 25.

[86]Spurgeon provided an extended account of this experience in Spurgeon, *Autobiography*, 1:199-201.

[87]The introductory volume to the recently published *Lost Sermons of C. H. Spurgeon* includes a detailed timeline, which notes the dates and corresponding texts of Spurgeon's sermons throughout this period. See Christian T. George, ed., *The Lost Sermons of C. H. Spurgeon*, vol. 1 (Nashville: B&H Academic, 2016), xxxvii-xxxviii.

[88]Spurgeon, *Autobiography*, 1:204. The tutor Spurgeon references in this passage is likely Edwin Sennit Leeding (1813–1890), who first instructed him as a day pupil in Colchester before he set up his own school in Cambridge, where Spurgeon worked as an assistant.

[89]Spurgeon, *Autobiography*, 1:204.

London. Joseph Angus, the President at Stepney, arranged to meet Spurgeon in February 1854. However, when Spurgeon arrived at the meeting place, the maid sent him to the wrong room and the meeting did not take place.[90] Spurgeon later interpreted the missed opportunity as divine providence, as he was invited to take up the pastorate at the New Park Street Chapel in London later that year.[91]

WATERBEACH CHAPEL: SPURGEON'S
EARLY SERMONS AND FIRST PASTORATE

Spurgeon preached at Waterbeach Chapel for the first time on October 3, 1851, and by the end of the month, he was invited to become the church's pastor. Waterbeach, a small village located a few miles north of Cambridge, had a growing population that peaked at near fifteen hundred in the middle of the nineteenth century.[92] Spurgeon quickly became so popular that Ebenezer Smith, a member of Waterbeach Chapel, later recalled that in a single week early on in his pastorate, Spurgeon received fifty-two separate invitations for home visits on a single Sunday.[93] As Spurgeon was still living in Cambridge at the time, he often lodged with the Smith family on Saturday evenings. Writing of one particularly influential sermon, Smith recollected,

> On another occasion he could not sleep on the Saturday night, and early in the morning ere the light had dawned he awoke me. The perspiration was streaming from his forehead, he told me he had seen a vision of Hell. He described the last things, the Judgment, the wailing, the torments and the shriek of the lost, until I grew frightened. The next morning he preached his marvelous sermon on the Final Conflagration, one of the most awful sermons that was ever heard from a Christian pulpit. Men and women

---

[90]This account appears in most biographies of Spurgeon, perhaps most recently in Nettles, *Living by Revealed Truth*, 63-64.

[91]Charles's brother, James Archer Spurgeon, studied at Stepney and eventually received two honorary doctor of divinity degrees. He would go on to assist his brother in the administration of the Pastors' College in London, a key training facility for Baptist ministers.

[92]For further demographic information, see A. P. M. Wright and C. P. Lewis, "Waterbeach: Introduction," in *A History of the County of Cambridge and the Isle of Ely*, vol. 9, *Chesterton, Northstowe, and Papworth Hundreds*, ed. A. P. M. Wright and C. P. Lewis (London: Victoria Country History, 1989), 237-43.

[93]Smith, *Two Centuries of Grace*, 14.

swayed in agony, it was a mental torture unknown in our churches to-day. It seemed as though he shook his audience over the Pit until the smoke of God's wrath filled their eyes and made them weep, and entered their throats until they gasped for mercy. It was not done for effect. The power lay in the fact that it was real to the preacher. He had lived through a nightmare of a terrible experience and it was being used to a holy purpose. He was deeply in earnest and men knew it. He never preached a religion he had simply learned, but a truth that had been cut into his soul by a deep and rich experience.[94]

The sermon as Smith described it corresponds to an unpublished sermon titled "The Great Conflagration."[95] In this early sermon Spurgeon emphasized his belief that the future judgment of humanity was "plainly literal" and that "this fire will melt but not annihilate the globe. Elements . . . shall melt and the whole map shall be in a blazing state. This molten earth shall then become a new earth and a new heaven shall be its canopy."[96] Spurgeon made a number of biblical references throughout the body of the sermon, many of them examples of divine fire acting as an agent of destruction. He closed with an appeal for conversion, inviting his listeners to consider "the dreadful doom of the ungodly to be consumed in this fire . . . [and] to pity and pray for them and labor for their conversion. Father, help. Help through Jesus."[97]

The surviving records of Spurgeon's early sermons are largely comprised of his sermon notes, which are contained in nine notebooks that span the years 1851 to 1854. The notebooks, which are stored in the Heritage Room of Spurgeon's College in London, are currently being published as *The Lost Sermons of C. H. Spurgeon.*[98] The notebooks contain a varied collection of

---

[94]Smith, *Two Centuries of Grace*, 15-16.

[95]C. H. Spurgeon, "The Great Conflagration." This sermon, drawn from 2 Peter 3:10-11, is contained within the fifth notebook of Spurgeon's early sermons and is currently unpublished. I am grateful to Christian George for sharing a copy of this sermon with me in advance of its publication.

[96]Spurgeon, "Great Conflagration."

[97]Spurgeon, "Great Conflagration."

[98]The editor, Christian T. George, is careful to say that "Spurgeon's sermons were never actually 'lost' to history. But they were lost to publishing history." Christian T. George, ed. *The Lost Sermons of C. H. Spurgeon*, vol. 1 (Nashville: B&H Academic, 2016), 23. Beginning with volume four, the collection will be edited by Jason Duesing. Other works that reference the early sermons include Kruppa, *Charles Haddon Spurgeon: A Preacher's Progress*, 62; Morden, *"Communion with Christ,"* 51.

sermon notes and manuscripts, which suggest among other things that
Spurgeon varied his manner of preparing sermons during his early years
as a pastor.[99] While many of the notes are fragmentary, they are the best
source for the themes and content of his earliest sermons.

Furthermore, the *Lost Sermons* are helpful in identifying Spurgeon's
earliest influences with regard to theology and biblical interpretation.
Christian George, the series' first editor, notes that in his youth Spurgeon
borrowed liberally from a diverse group of preachers and authors, including "John Gill, Philip Doddridge, Richard Baxter, John Bunyan,
Charles Simeon, George Whitefield . . . and others."[100] For instance,
Spurgeon's first sermon, simply titled "Adoption," closely followed an
outline from the Baptist theologian and preacher John Gill (1697–1771).[101]
In some instances, Spurgeon directly referred to texts from which he
borrowed, as in the case of a later sermon drawn from the printed
sermons of the noteworthy evangelical Anglican minister Charles
Simeon (1759–1836), whose published sermons and outlines were widely
used throughout the century.[102] It is not possible to know whether
Spurgeon acknowledged these references from the pulpit, and he only
noted some of the references throughout the notebook. What is important for the present study is that the young Spurgeon came under a
diverse and not easily predictable set of influences: he drew inspiration
from long-dead Puritans as well as contemporary authors and from
Methodists and Anglicans as well as Baptists. From his earliest sermons,
Spurgeon saw the value of consulting a variety of sources in his sermon

---

[99]The *Lost Sermons* collection has only currently released the first three volumes, with nine
planned volumes to eventually follow.

[100]George, *Lost Sermons of C. H. Spurgeon*, 1:26.

[101]C. H. Spurgeon, "Adoption," sermon no. 1, given April 13, April 20, July 15, 1851, from Ephesians
1:5, *The Lost Sermons of C. H. Spurgeon*, ed. Christian T. George, vol. 1 (Nashville: B&H Academic, 2016), 66-75. Gill and Spurgeon both presided as pastors at the New Park Street Chapel.
Gill preached there from 1720 until his death in 1771.

[102]C. H. Spurgeon, "Regeneration, Its Causes and Effects," sermon no. 46, from 1 Peter 1:3-5,
n.d., *The Lost Sermons of C. H. Spurgeon*, ed. Christian T. George, vol. 1 (Nashville: B&H Academic, 2016), 292-97. Near the top of the sermon's first page, Spurgeon wrote "Simeon 42,"
which George has identified as a reference to the forty-second sermon in Charles Simeon's
collected volume, *Helps to Composition*, a sermon titled "Regeneration Considered in Its
Causes and Benefits."

preparation, and he would continue to read widely throughout his life. Noting this, George highlights an aside that Spurgeon made in an 1863 sermon where he commented,

> The man who never reads will never be read; he who never quotes will never be quoted. He who will not use the thoughts of other men's brains, proves that he has no brains of his own. Brethren, what is true of ministers is true of all our people. *You* need to read. Renounce as much as you will all light literature, but study as much as possible sound theological works, especially the Puritanic writers, and expositions of the Bible.[103]

The full set of *Lost Sermons* notebooks contains over four hundred sermons and fragments, which provide helpful information regarding Spurgeon's text selection and content outlines.[104] For instance, in the first volume, nearly a third of the sermons were preached from three books: the Gospel of Matthew, Psalms, and Proverbs. Spurgeon's early interest in the former two books he maintained throughout his life, and he would eventually write commentaries on both of them.[105] George, referring to an entry in the *New Park Street Pulpit* series, notes that Spurgeon had hoped eventually to publish his earliest sermons.[106] While Spurgeon never published his earliest sermons, he did publish a series of sermon notes.[107]

The volumes of *Lost Sermons* illustrate the presence of crucicentric language from the outset of his ministry. The title page to the first volume featured a set of drawings by the young preacher, including a crudely sketched cross on a hill with a crown floating above it.[108] One of the most overt references to the crucifixion of Christ was in an undated sermon

---

[103]George, *Lost Sermons of C. H. Spurgeon*, 1:26; C. H. Spurgeon, "Paul—His Cloak and His Books," sermon no. 542, given November 29, 1863, from 2 Timothy 4:13, *The Metropolitan Tabernacle Pulpit*, vol. 9 (London: Passmore & Alabaster, 1863), 668.

[104]Christian George has noted eighteen sermons throughout the notebooks that were unfinished. See George, *Lost Sermons of C. H. Spurgeon*, 1:33.

[105]See C. H. Spurgeon, *The Treasury of David*, vol. 1, *Psalms 1-26* (London: Marshall Brothers, 1869); C. H. Spurgeon, *The Gospel of the Kingdom: A Commentary on the Book of Matthew* (London: Passmore & Alabaster, 1893).

[106]George, *Lost Sermons of C. H. Spurgeon*, 1:46.

[107]C. H. Spurgeon, *My Sermon Notes: A Selection from Outlines of Discourses Delivered at the Metropolitan Tabernacle*, vol. 1 (New York: Funk & Wagnalls, 1891), v.

[108]George, *Lost Sermons of C. H. Spurgeon*, 1:60.

called "Gethsemane's Sorrow."[109] In it, Spurgeon discussed "the Shock given to his unsullied purity by his standing in the room of sinners and bearing their guilt away."[110] Spurgeon suggested that Christ's foreknowledge of the events of the cross would "increase the pain," noting that Christ knew the suffering he would experience from "Herod and his mighty men, the crown of thorns, the horrid flagellation . . . the cry 'crucify him.' His going through the streets, fainting, nailing to the cross, forsaken of his God, his death."[111] His conclusion, captured only in outline form, records that Spurgeon emphasized that the reason for the cross was "to satisfy justice and save sinners."[112]

Spurgeon's early sermons also included what he conceived as cruci-centric messages drawn from the Old Testament. In a sermon drawn from Psalm 22, his notes connect the psalmist's lament with the experience of Christ on the cross:

> He cites instances of God's deliverance of others but remembers the opinions men had of him (5, 6). He sees the wagging of the heads (7, 8). He appeals to God's former love (9, 10). He cries (11). Tell of his enemies (12, 13). He sweat. He fainted. His bones were dislocated by the fixing of the cross in its place. Heart fails. Inflammation comes over him. Thirst, clamminess of the mouth. He is near death. He tells his crucifixion (16). His emaciation and the impudent gaze (17). His garment parted (18).[113]

Psalm 22, one of the most christological of the Old Testament psalms, was referred to by Christ himself during his crucifixion in the Gospel accounts of Matthew and Mark. Spurgeon's final comments were drawn from the last words of the psalm, which read, "He has done it." From this statement, Spurgeon suggested that in the death of Christ, "all is fulfilled, law magnified, justice paid covenant fulfilled. It is finished."[114] George

---

[109]C. H. Spurgeon, "Gethsemane's Sorrow," sermon no. 63, from Matthew 26:38, n.d., *The Lost Sermons of C. H. Spurgeon*, ed. Christian T. George, vol. 1 (Nashville: B&H Academic, 2016), 392-96.

[110]Spurgeon, "Gethsemane's Sorrow," 392.

[111]Spurgeon, "Gethsemane's Sorrow," 392.

[112]Spurgeon, "Gethsemane's Sorrow," 392.

[113]C. H. Spurgeon, "The Church and Its Boast," sermon no. 75, from Psalm 22:31, n.d., *The Lost Sermons of C. H. Spurgeon*, ed. Christian T. George, vol. 1 (Nashville: B&H Academic, 2016), 462.

[114]Spurgeon, "Church and Its Boast," 462.

helpfully notes that Spurgeon's sermon structure borrowed heavily from a book on Psalm 22 written by a nineteenth-century Anglican minister named John Stevenson.[115] Stevenson interpreted Psalm 22 in a cruci-centric fashion and finished the section on the final verse of the Psalm with a series of references to Christ drawn from New Testament references.[116] Spurgeon's sermon shared Stevenson's evangelistic impetus, and his further sermons on the psalm continued in a similar vein.[117] Spurgeon's sermon on Psalm 22 delivered in 1872 expanded on these themes, suggesting that the psalm was

> full of sacrificial suffering. If you desire to comprehend its real meaning you must hear it from the dying lips of the incarnate God. It is through the cross that the nations shall fear and tremble and turn to God. . . . I do not look for the triumph of the church to her treasuries, nor to her institutions of learning, nor even her zeal, or to the popular ability of her preachers: I look to the cross.[118]

Spurgeon's early preaching style looked back to his conversion, and also foreshadowed the structure and aim of his later sermons. There is a clear focus on Christ's crucifixion and appeals for his listeners' conversion.[119] Even Spurgeon's artwork scattered throughout the early sermon notebooks bears this theme. The front page of the first sermon notebook contained a drawing of an angel holding a trumpet, alongside several biblical references.[120] Two are particularly noteworthy for the present study. The first, written in large letters across the center, read, "Skeletons I-LXVII and only skeletons without the Holy Ghost." This statement, surely a reference to

---

[115]George, *Lost Sermons of C. H. Spurgeon*, 1:465. See John Stevenson, *Christ on the Cross: An Exposition of the Twenty-Second Psalm* (London: J. H. Jackson, Islington Green, 1845).

[116]Stevenson, *Christ on the Cross*, 412.

[117]See, for instance, C. H. Spurgeon, "Good News for Seekers," sermon no. 1312, given September 3, 1876, from Psalm 22:26, *The Metropolitan Tabernacle Pulpit*, vol. 22 (London: Passmore & Alabaster, 1876), 493-504; C. H. Spurgeon, "The Triumph of Christianity," sermon no. 1047, given April 21, 1872, from Psalm 22:27, *The Metropolitan Tabernacle Pulpit*, vol. 18 (London: Passmore & Alabaster, 1872), 229-40.

[118]Spurgeon, "Triumph of Christianity," 238.

[119]Several sermons include references to individuals in the various Cambridgeshire churches who were converted after hearing a particular address.

[120]George, *Lost Sermons of C. H. Spurgeon*, 1:60.

Ezekiel 37, highlights the extent to which Spurgeon viewed the Holy Spirit as a necessary agent of illumination behind a preached sermon.[121] The second inscription was a small annotation written next to the bell of the angel's trumpet, which simply read, "Jesus Christ and him crucified."[122] These crucicentric and conversionistic themes continued to develop as Spurgeon perfected his sermon delivery. By the time he began preaching in London, Spurgeon consulted the sermons and outlines of other preachers far less, opting to rely on his own material and interpretive methodology. The early London sermons, many of which contained evocative imagery of the cross and fervent appeals for conversion, helped to establish him as one of the most well-known preachers in the world.

CONCLUSIONS

Charles Spurgeon's early life experiences were instrumental in the development of his method of biblical interpretation. His father and grandfather preached weekly sermons, and his home throughout his childhood and adolescence was filled with biblical language and imagery.[123] While Spurgeon's theology was distilled in the context of Independent Nonconformity, his thought was matured in a Puritan cask through engagement with his grandfather's library. He experienced different Christian traditions throughout his student years, and some of his most pivotal theological developments took place outside the confines of the village Nonconformity in which he was raised. In the Primitive Methodist church and its itinerant preacher, Spurgeon found not only the moment of his conversion but also a model for preaching that he would carry into his own pulpit. Spurgeon's theology was in some ways representative of an intersection between several different traditions. Though he settled in a Baptist church after his conversion and is best known for his ministry in that tradition, several

---

[121]For further elaboration on Spurgeon and pneumatology, see Zachary W. Eswine, "The Role of the Holy Spirit in the Preaching Theory and Practice of Charles Haddon Spurgeon" (PhD diss., Regent University, 2003).

[122]George, *Lost Sermons of C. H. Spurgeon*, 1:60.

[123]Spurgeon's youth would fit largely within the "Evangelical sentimentalism" described by Joseph Stubenrauch in his recent volume. See Joseph Stubenrauch, *The Evangelical Age of Ingenuity in Industrial Britain* (Oxford: Oxford University Press, 2016), 58-98.

significant turning points in Spurgeon's theological development happened within a variety of Protestant traditions.

The emphases that Spurgeon placed upon crucicentric and conversion-istic sermons were present in the earliest years of his ministry. When Spurgeon reflected on his early days at Waterbeach while writing his *Autobiography*, he noted the village's reputation for "noxious liquor" and "all manner of riot and iniquity." He believed that the village was transformed, largely as a result of preaching the cross and conversion, so that "the little thatched chapel was crammed, the biggest vagabonds of the village were weeping floods of tears, and those who had been the curse of the parish became its blessing."[124] Further describing the changes within the village, he observed that "where there had been robberies and villainies of every kind, all round the neighbourhood, there were none, because the men who used to do the mischief were themselves in the house of God, rejoicing to hear of Jesus crucified."[125]

Though Spurgeon narrated this history of his ministry with a degree of pride and sentimentality, he was careful to ascribe the ultimate responsi-bility of the village's transformation to a divine source, testifying "to the praise of God's grace, that it pleased the Lord to work wonders in our midst."[126] Thus Spurgeon's experiences as a youth, his early encounters with the Bible and theological texts, and especially his conversion at age fifteen formed the basis for the crucicentric, conversionistic biblical interpretation that would become central to his subsequent pastoral work. In the fol-lowing chapter, we will see his commitment to this hermeneutic solidify in and through his early ministry in London.

---

[124]Spurgeon, *Autobiography*, 1:228.
[125]Spurgeon, *Autobiography*, 1:228.
[126]Spurgeon, *Autobiography*, 1:228.

THE BIBLE OUTSIDE
THE PULPIT

Spurgeon's Early Years in Ministry

> *I like to read my Bible so as never to have to blink when I approach a text.*
> *I like to have a theology which enables me to read it right through from beginning*
> *to end, and to say, "I am as pleased with that text as I am with the other."*

C. H. SPURGEON

AS WE HAVE SEEN, Spurgeon's experience as a youth, particularly his conversion, shaped his approach to both the Bible and preaching. As he transitioned from a rural congregation to ministry in central London, his approach to the biblical text retained the cross-centered approach as he actively sought the conversion of individuals in his audience. In 1854, Charles Spurgeon took up the pastorate at the New Park Street Chapel in Southwark, a historic London congregation whose former pastors included such noteworthy figures as Benjamin Keach (1640–1704), John Gill (1697–1771), and John Rippon (1751–1836). His early ministry occurred alongside larger revivals that spread throughout Britain and North America during the latter 1850s and early 1860s. After two years of preaching, Spurgeon's congregation had become so large that it had to move to larger rented spaces such as Exeter Hall and Surrey Gardens

C. H. Spurgeon, "General and Yet Particular," sermon no. 566, given April 24, 1864, from John 17:2, *The Metropolitan Tabernacle Pulpit*, vol. 10 (London: Passmore & Alabaster, 1864), 237.

Music Hall. The congregation met in rented space until 1861, when construction was finished on a massive new building located at Elephant and Castle, a prominent location within Southwark. With the new location came a new name, the Metropolitan Tabernacle.

Spurgeon's exhortative and emotive preaching style brought him considerable attention in local periodicals. The biographer H. L. Wayland noted that among Spurgeon's admirers was James Garfield, the American Civil War general who would later become the twentieth president of the United States. Garfield's recollections of his attendance at the Metropolitan Tabernacle began with his admission that he "did not intend to listen to Spurgeon as to some *lusus naturae*, but to try to discover what manner of man he was, and what was the secret of his power."[1] Reflecting on Spurgeon's sermon, Garfield's first comment was that "he evidently proceeded upon the assumption that the Bible, all the Bible, in its very words, phrases, and sentences, is the word of God; and that a microscopic examination of it will reveal ever-opening beauties and blessings."[2] Garfield was also impressed with his delivery:

> He has the word-painting power quite at his command, but uses it sparingly. I could see those nervous motions of the hands and feet which all forcible speakers make when preparing to speak; and also in the speaking, the sympathy between his body and his thoughts which controlled his gestures, and produced those little touches of theatrical power, which are so effective in a speaker.[3]

Not all visitors to the Tabernacle shared Garfield's enthusiasm for the young preacher. Spurgeon had not occupied his post for long before he became the target of public criticism.[4] In 1855, a letter written under the pseudonym "Iconoclast" was submitted to the *Essex Standard*, offering a critique of Spurgeon's work in London. The article suggested that in his sermons "all the most solemn mysteries of our holy religion are by him

---

[1]Quoted in Herman Lincoln Wayland, *Charles H. Spurgeon: His Faith and Works* (Philadelphia: American Baptist Publication Society, 1892), 56.

[2]Wayland, *Charles H. Spurgeon: His Faith and Works*, 57.

[3]Wayland, *Charles H. Spurgeon: His Faith and Works*, 58.

[4]See Tom Nettles, *Living by Revealed Truth: The Life and Pastoral Theology of Charles Haddon Spurgeon* (Ross-shire, UK: Christian Focus, 2013), 70-83.

rudely, roughly, and impiously handled. Mystery is vulgarized, sanctity profaned, common sense outraged, and decency disgusted."[5] An article in the *Illustrated Times* in 1856 contained even stronger language:

> His doctrine is not new; on the contrary, it is nothing more than old Calvinism revived in its most uncompromising form. He is not an orator, scholar, nor man of genius; and he is the very worst reasoner we ever heard. But he is lively—says strange, odd, daring things, which keep the attention brisk, amuse the hearers, and give them something to talk about. Some have compared him to a great preacher of the last century, and say that he is "a second Whitfield [sic]"; but this is rubbish. Whitfield was a fervid orator, a man of genius, a scholar, and a polished gentleman; but Mr. Spurgeon is neither of these. . . . His congregations are made up, not of those "outcasts" who "go nowhere," but of middle-class regular chapel-goers who, wearied with the dulness of their own places of worship, come here for excitement.[6]

In this chapter we will examine Spurgeon's ministry from his move to London to the middle of his career, in the early 1870s. While he was best known for his sermons, during this time period Spurgeon greatly expanded his ministries. He established a college for pastors, two orphanages, and a magazine, all of this while heading the largest Protestant congregation in Britain. In the sections that follow, we will discuss Spurgeon's biblical interpretation in this time period, focusing primarily on sources connected to Spurgeon's broader ministries outside the pulpit of the Metropolitan Tabernacle. These sources will include surviving records of a conflict between Spurgeon and a fellow Baptist pastor and the establishment and early use of his magazine, *The Sword and the Trowel,* as well as the development of his devotional books and his theological addresses on the nature and use of the Bible. Throughout these varied investigations, we will argue that a central theme connecting a majority of Spurgeon's engagement with the Bible emerges, namely the crucicentric and conversionistic emphasis that he placed upon biblical interpretation and instruction.

---

[5]Iconoclast (anonymous), letter to the editor, *Essex Standard* (April 18, 1855), quoted in C. H. Spurgeon, *C. H. Spurgeon's Autobiography, Compiled from His Diary, Letters, and Records, by His Wife and His Private Secretary,* vol. 2, *1854–1860* (Chicago: Fleming H. Revell, 1899), 47.
[6]"The Rev. Charles H. Spurgeon," *Illustrated Times* (October 11, 1856), 7.

THE BIBLE AND THEOLOGICAL DEBATE:
SPURGEON AND HIGH CALVINISM

Within months of his arrival in London, Spurgeon began attracting large crowds of listeners, which in turn led to several articles about him. Many portrayed him as a sensationalist who operated with brash disregard to more conventional and refined methods of preaching. An article reprinted in the London-based *Morning Chronicle* presented both Spurgeon and the New Park Street Chapel alongside a series of tourist attractions, noting that the crowds, "being tired of the hippopotamus, and bored with the stupidity of the Ring and Rotten-row Society dropped in, on Sundays to hear Mr. Spurgeon. An extra amount of steam was put on, fresh spice was added to tickle society's jaded palate."[7] The *Chronicle* suggested that the secret of Spurgeon's success as a preacher was "his profuse command of illustration, and the knack that he has of throwing personal individuality into his sermons."[8] The extent to which Spurgeon used dramatic language amounted to "vulgar irreverence" in the author's estimation, which culminated in the observation that "more than once, last night, the countenance of his audiences wore a broad grin, provoked by the witticism of the preacher. This is a novelty in pulpit eloquence, and few, we hope, will call it an improvement."[9]

While Spurgeon's dynamic preaching style made him a novelty for some observers, others were quick to critique the *content* of his sermons rather than his pulpit manner. Spurgeon's memoirs record that the earliest critiques of his preaching came from fellow Baptists. In a letter to his father in December 1853, Spurgeon wrote, "The London people are rather higher in Calvinism than I am; but I have succeeded in bringing one church to my own views, and will trust, with Divine assistance, to do the same with another. I am a Calvinist; I love what someone called 'glorious Calvinism'; but

---

[7]"Spurgeonism in Belfast," *Morning Chronicle* (London, August 20, 1858). The Ring and Rotten-row were promenade paths that were popular places for wealthy Londoners to take leisurely carriage drives away from the traffic and congestion of the city roads. The hippopotamus, named Obaysch, was a gift from the viceroy of Egypt and had proven to be a popular attraction, sometimes drawing in hundreds of visitors per day.

[8]"Spurgeonism in Belfast."

[9]"Spurgeonism in Belfast."

'Hyperism' is too hot-spiced for my palate."[10] The "hyperism" that Spurgeon mentions in his letter is a reference to high Calvinism, which was a minority doctrinal position by the mid-nineteenth century, one that nevertheless found adherents among both Nonconformists and ministers within the Established Church. In the years that would follow, the young minister would face open and direct challenges to a central tenet of his pastoral ministry, namely his emphasis in sermons on the atonement and the free offer of the gospel, which were the application of his crucicentric and conversionistic biblical interpretation.

High Calvinists held to a restrictive position with regard to evangelism.[11] Ian J. Shaw explains that in high Calvinism the doctrine of "irresistible grace is stressed so that the elect become passive in their regeneration and conversion. . . . High Calvinists are unable to make the free offer of the gospel: faith is not the duty of unbelievers."[12] For high Calvinists, it was theologically contradictory to preach a sermon that contained a free offer of the gospel. As we have seen in the previous chapter, Spurgeon spent a significant portion of his youth reading Calvinistic books from a variety of traditions. Peter Morden rightly connects Spurgeon's conversion to his evangelistic zeal, writing that "Spurgeon the pastor threw himself into a ministry of calling others to look to Christ as he had done."[13] Though Calvinism was a badge he wore proudly, due to Spurgeon's evangelistic preaching style and his practice of open communion, he is best described as an evangelical Calvinist.[14] Robert Shindler, an early biographer, wrote, "Mr. Spurgeon, with all his strong attachment to truths which relate to

---

[10]Spurgeon to John Spurgeon, December 1853, in *Letters of Charles Haddon Spurgeon*, ed. Iain H. Murray (Edinburgh: Banner of Truth Trust, 1992), 41-42.

[11]Ian J. Shaw suggests that "high Calvinist" is preferable to the frequently used term "hyper Calvinist," which was "rejected by most to whom it applied." Ian J. Shaw, *High Calvinists in Action: Calvinism and the City, Manchester and London, c. 1810–1860* (Oxford: Oxford University Press, 2002), 11.

[12]Shaw, *High Calvinists in Action*, 11. For further discussion, see Peter Toon, *The Emergence of Hyper-Calvinism in English Nonconformity, 1689–1765* (London: Olive Tree, 1967).

[13]Peter J. Morden, *"Communion with Christ and His People": The Spirituality of C. H. Spurgeon* (Oxford: Regent's Park College, 2010), 62.

[14]Evangelical Calvinism is a position that lies between high Calvinism, which we have discussed, and moderate Calvinism, which did not accept the doctrine of limited atonement. Though Spurgeon's ministry was defined in part by his free offer of the gospel, he also held to the five points of Calvinism, as articulated at the Synod of Dordt.

divine sovereignty—and he has ever been bold and unflinching in his proc-lamation of them—has always presented the other side, the call of the gospel to all who hear it."[15] Spurgeon's evangelical Calvinist position is evident in a brief section of the March 1868 edition of *The Sword and the Trowel,* where he defended the tension in which he held aspects of election and free will, writing,

> If we honestly desire to gain the heights of divine truth, we shall find many zigzags in the road: here our face will front divine sovereignty with all its lofty grandeur, and anon we shall turn in the opposite direction, towards the frowning peaks of human responsibility. What matters it if we appear to be inconsistent, so long as we keep to the highway of Scripture, which is our only safe road to knowledge![16]

Spurgeon himself would go on to encourage pastors to build their appeals for conversion upon a foundation of doctrinal content. Addressing students later in his ministry, he wrote,

> Some enthusiasts would seem to have imbibed the notion that, as soon as a minister addresses the unconverted, he should deliberately contradict his usual doctrinal discourses, because it is supposed that there will be no conversions if he preaches the whole counsel of God. . . . He who sent us to win souls neither permits us to invent falsehoods, nor to suppress truth. His work can be done without such suspicious methods.[17]

This reference is quite telling for Spurgeon, who saw no difficulty preaching both crucicentric and conversionistic sermons from the "whole counsel" of the Bible and could direct his congregation to a free offer of the gospel from virtually any biblical text.

It is worth briefly noting that one of the former pastors of the New Park Street Chapel, Rev. John Gill, was associated with high Calvinism, though historical surveys of Gill's theology have provided a range of interpretations of his soteriology, or doctrine of salvation, there is not a clear

---

[15] Robert Shindler, *From the Usher's Desk to the Tabernacle Pulpit: The Life and Labors of Charles Haddon Spurgeon* (New York: A. C. Armstrong and Son, 1892), 36.

[16] *The Sword and the Trowel* 4 (1868): 38.

[17] C. H. Spurgeon, *The Soul Winner: How to Lead Sinners to the Saviour* (Chicago: Fleming H. Revell, 1895), 16.

consensus.[18] Spurgeon himself offered varying estimations of Gill. In his *Commenting and Commentaries*, a resource intended for young pastors, Spurgeon wrote that "amid the decadence of his own rigid system, and the disrepute of even more moderate Calvinism, Gill's laurels as an expositor are still green. His ultraism is discarded, but his learning is respected: the world and the church take leave to question his dogmatism, but they both bow before his erudition."[19] In his *Autobiography* years later, however, Spurgeon defended Gill, writing that the

> system of theology with which many identify his name has chilled many churches to their very soul, for it has led them to omit the free invitations of the gospel, and to deny that it is the duty of sinners to believe in Jesus but for this, Dr. Gill must not be altogether held responsible, for a candid reader of his Commentary will soon perceive in it expressions altogether out of accord with such a narrow system.[20]

This reference indicates the degree to which Spurgeon supported the free offer of the gospel and also his decidedly frosty view of high Calvinist doctrine.

Ironically, Spurgeon himself was identified as a high Calvinist in at least one newspaper editorial. James Grant, in the February 19, 1855, editorial of the *Morning Advertiser*, wrote that the "boyish preacher" filled the large hall "capable of containing from 4,000 to 5,000 persons. . . . His doctrines are of the Hyper-Calvinist school."[21] Grant is not the only writer to suggest that the young Spurgeon was influenced by high Calvinism. Mark Hopkins

---

[18]Curt D. Daniel, "Hyper-Calvinism and John Gill" (PhD thesis, University of Edinburgh, 1983); David Mark Rathel, "Was John Gill a Hyper-Calvinist? Determining Gill's Theological Identity," *Baptist Quarterly* 48, no. 1 (2017): 47-59; Jonathan White, "A Theological and Historical Examination of John Gill's Soteriology in Relation to Eighteenth-Century Hyper-Calvinism" (PhD diss., The Southern Baptist Theological Seminary, 2010). Each of these accounts deals extensively with Gill's soteriology. Daniel and Rathel argue that Gill was likely a high Calvinist, while White maintains that the term should not apply to Gill.

[19]C. H. Spurgeon, *Lectures to My Students*, vol. 4, *Commenting and Commentaries; Lectures Addressed to the Students of the Pastors' College, Metropolitan Tabernacle* (New York: Sheldon, 1876), 22.

[20]C. H. Spurgeon, *C. H. Spurgeon's Autobiography, Compiled from His Diary, Letters, and Records, by His Wife and His Private Secretary*, vol. 1, *1834–1854* (Cincinnati: Curts & Jennings, 1898), 310.

[21]James Grant, "The Rev. Mr. Spurgeon," *Morning Advertiser* (February 19, 1855), quoted in Spurgeon, *Autobiography*, 2:64.

suggests that Spurgeon may have been "fettered" with regard to offering a free invitation of the gospel.[22] Peter Morden offers a critique of Hopkins's position, contending that there remains far more evidence of Spurgeon's free offers of the gospel than any hesitancy on the matter.[23]

In the mid-1850s, the Baptist James Wells (1803–1872) offered an appraisal of Spurgeon's ministry. Far more conservative than Spurgeon, Wells relegated both the evangelical and moderate Calvinistic positions "to Paul's dung heap."[24] Wells came from the Strict Baptist tradition and had maintained a sizeable congregation at the Surrey Tabernacle in Southwark prior to Spurgeon's arrival, yet the quick rise of Spurgeon's popularity led the *Lambeth Gazette* to proclaim in 1855 that "the Rev. C. H. Spurgeon is now the star of Southwark. Mr. Wells (commonly known by the curious *sobriquet* of 'Wheelbarrow Wells'), of the Borough Road, has, for some years past, had the run in this line, but he has, at last, got a rival well in his 'tip,' and likely to prove the favourite for a long time."[25] An article referenced by Spurgeon's biographer G. Holden Pike may shed some light on the "wheelbarrow" reference. In it, the unnamed author writes that "James Wells is sent of God to bring His people out of bondage . . . this is his peculiar work; and where is there a man that can knock down a 'duty-faith' fabric and wheel away the rubbish like him?"[26] The term *duty-faith* refers to the doctrinal position that upon hearing the gospel message, it was the duty of the listener to respond with faith and belief. *Duty-faith* was a term used by high Calvinists to describe those who opposed their view and was met with a variety of responses from those whom it was meant to characterize. George Rogers (1799–1892), Spurgeon's friend and the principal of the Pastors' College, wrote an article in *The Sword and the Trowel* that intended to

---

[22]Mark Hopkins, *Nonconformity's Romantic Generation: Evangelical and Liberal Theologies in Victorian England* (Milton Keynes, UK: Paternoster, 2004), 140.

[23]Morden, "Communion with Christ," 62-68.

[24]Quoted in Iain H. Murray, *Spurgeon v. Hyper-Calvinism: The Battle for Gospel Preaching* (Edinburgh: The Banner of Truth Trust, 2002), 56; For further discussion on James Wells's ministry, see Shaw, *High Calvinists in Action*, 240-77.

[25]*Lambeth Gazette* (September 1, 1855), quoted in Spurgeon, *Autobiography*, 2:56. Italics original. Strict Baptists restrict communion to church members baptized as believers.

[26]"Letter to the Editor," *Earthen Vessel* (September 1857), quoted in G. Holden Pike, *The Life and Work of Charles Haddon Spurgeon* (London: Cassell, 1892), 281.

smooth over tensions between Calvinistic Baptists. Rogers addressed the high Calvinists in his conclusion, writing, "Let them consider whether their jealousy for the sovereignty of God on the one hand, does not militate against his equity on the other. Our aim, we hope, is one, and that, whether we strive together or in opposition to each other, it is for the faith of the gospel. May the Spirit of truth lead us into all truth!"[27] The high Calvinists opposed the free offer of the gospel to sinners, which was the practice of all Arminians and most Calvinists, both moderate and evangelical.[28] *Earthen Vessel*, a Baptist newspaper that had ties to high Calvinist ministers and often featured contributions by Wells, offered the following critique of duty-faith in an article that contained three key points: "1. Duty-faith dishonours God. To preach that it is man's duty to believe savingly in Christ is absurd. A babe in grace knows better. . . . 2. Duty-faith points the sinner to himself for a remedy against sin. . . . 3. Duty-faith is calculated to mislead and deceive."[29]

Wells critiqued Spurgeon in a series of pseudonymous letters to the *Earthen Vessel*, beginning with one from "Job" in January 1855. Wells's letter began in a largely complimentary tone, with his introduction stating that he had "no personal antipathy to Mr. Spurgeon" before suggesting that his comments were warranted because "his ministry is a public matter, and therefore open to public opinion."[30] Wells added that Spurgeon "appears to be a well-disposed person—kind, benevolent, courteous, full of goodwill to his fellow creatures . . . a kind of person whom it would almost seem a cruelty to dislike. The same may be, with equal truth, said both of Dr. Pusey and Cardinal Wiseman."[31] Wells's tone sharpened in his next paragraph, where he alluded to existing records of Spurgeon's conversion and then followed these accounts by saying, "I have—*most solemnly have—my doubts*

---

[27] *The Sword and the Trowel* 2 (1866): 12.
[28] See Shaw, *High Calvinists in Action*, 17-18.
[29] *Earthen Vessel* (September 1857), 208, quoted in Murray, *Spurgeon v. Hyper-Calvinism*, 61.
[30] Spurgeon, *Autobiography*, 2:37.
[31] Spurgeon, *Autobiography*, 2:37. The comparison drawn to Edward Bouverie Pusey (1800–1882), a Hebrew language scholar and leader in the Oxford Movement as well as Nicholas Wiseman (1802–1865), a cardinal in the Roman Catholic Church who had recently been appointed the first archbishop of Westminster would have been a largely unfavorable one in Spurgeon's estimation, as well as that of many Baptist readers.

as to the Divine reality of his conversion. I do not say—it is not for me to say—that he is not a regenerated man; but this I do know, that there are conversions which are not of God."[32] Referencing a contentious passage in Hebrews 6, Wells suggested that a minister "may be intellectually enlightened, he may taste of the Heavenly gift, and be made partaker of the Holy Ghost, *professionally*, and taste of the good Word of God, and not yet be regenerated, and therefore not beyond the danger of falling away, even from that portion of truth which such do hold."[33] He went on to list a series of five objections to Spurgeon's ministry, in which he claimed among other points that Spurgeon's pastoral work

> is the most awfully deceptive. . . . It passes by the essentials of the work of the Holy Ghost, and sets people by shoals down for Christians who are not Christians by the quickening and indwelling power of the Holy Ghost. Hence, freewillers, *intellectual* Calvinists, high and low, are delighted with him, together with the philosophic and classic-taste Christian![34]

This last comment highlights Wells's adherence to high Calvinism, as he suggested that Spurgeon's approach to evangelistic preaching was inherently deceptive. He intensified this point in a subsequent paragraph when he suggested that "some people, who perhaps would care to hear only such an intellectually, or rather rhetorically-gifted man as is Mr. Spurgeon, but then they have this advantage at the cost of being *fatally deluded*."[35]

While these letters constructed a scathing review of his preaching, there is no evidence that Spurgeon contacted the *Earthen Vessel* with any rebuttal. Iain Murray is helpful in noting that while Spurgeon did not respond directly to Wells's publications, there were numerous other venues in which he criticized high Calvinism broadly.[36] Perhaps the only surviving mention of controversy with Wells appears in a letter that Spurgeon sent to his fiancée, Susannah Thompson. He wrote, "I find that much stir has been made by 'Job's' letter, and hosts of unknown persons have risen up on my

---

[32]Spurgeon, *Autobiography*, 2:38.
[33]Spurgeon, *Autobiography*, 2:38.
[34]Spurgeon, *Autobiography*, 2:39.
[35]Spurgeon, *Autobiography*, 2:39.
[36]Murray, *Spurgeon v. Hyper-Calvinism*, 59-87.

behalf. It seems very likely that King James [i.e., Wells] will shake his little throne by lifting his hand against one of the Lord's little ones."[37] Spurgeon's opposition to high Calvinism is evident throughout his sermons and printed work. One of the earliest examples is a sermon on the subject of faith at the New Park Street Chapel. In this sermon, he distanced himself from high Calvinist positions because he viewed them as too inward-looking and rigid. He addressed high Calvinists directly, saying, "Some of you, my hearers, and a great many that are not my hearers, are miserable little cramped souls; you have learned a cast-iron creed, and you will never move out of it."[38] Sharpening his approach, he continued, "I do not think I differ from any of my hyper-calvinistic brethren in what I do believe; but I differ from them in what they do not believe. I do not believe any less than they do, but I believe a little more, and think, as we grow, we shall have our belief increased."[39] Finally, he sought to make common faith the basis for greater unity and charity among Christians. Using particularly strong language, he said that he often prayed that God would help the more isolationist Calvinists "to believe that there may be Christian Wesleyans; that there are good [Established] Church people; and not only that Particular Baptists are very good sort of people, but that there are some of God's elect everywhere. I am sure I pray for all bigots, that they may have a little wider heart."[40]

Spurgeon's most significant critique of high Calvinism was with regard to the free offer of the gospel, particularly in the context of sermons. His crucicentric and conversionistic sermons often included an appeal that any unconverted listeners might take the opportunity to believe in Christ. He emphasized this in an 1863 sermon where he observed, "In our own day certain preachers assure us that a man must be regenerated before we may bid him believe in Jesus Christ; some degree of a work of grace in the heart being, in their judgment, the only warrant to believe. This is also

---

[37]Spurgeon to Susannah Thompson, January 1855, in Spurgeon, *Autobiography*, 2:18.
[38]Spurgeon, "The Necessity of Increased Faith," sermon no. 32, given July 1, 1855, from Luke 17:5, *The New Park Street Pulpit*, vol. 1 (London: Passmore & Alabaster, 1855), 249.
[39]Spurgeon, "Necessity of Increased Faith," 249.
[40]Spurgeon, "Necessity of Increased Faith," 250.

false. It takes away a gospel for sinners and offers us a gospel for saints."[41] Thus Spurgeon's altercation with the high Calvinists occurred principally on the basis of his crucicentric and conversionistic engagement with the text, engagement that led him to a particular emphasis on the free offer of the gospel.

The controversy between Spurgeon and Wells appears to have ended in the 1860s. Wells stopped mentioning Spurgeon directly in his *Earthen Vessel* articles, and Spurgeon appears to have worked to reconcile their differences. When Wells became gravely ill in 1871, Spurgeon sent him a letter of encouragement. In its closing remarks, the letter read, "May your sick chamber be the very gate of heaven to your soul, the presence of the Lord filling the house with glory. Do not think of acknowledging this; but if you are able to have it read to you I hope someone will be so good as briefly to tell me how you are."[42] In this early theological controversy in his pastoral ministry, Spurgeon emerged unshaken from his dual commitment to preach the Bible with a strong emphasis on the cross and conversion, and to place the free offer of the gospel at the center not only of his sermons but also of his ministries as a whole.

THE BIBLE AND THE MAGAZINE:
THE SWORD AND THE TROWEL

Following his first Sunday as pastor of the New Park Street Chapel, Spurgeon was accompanied on his walk home by Joseph Passmore, in whom he would not only find a lifelong friend but also a publisher.[43] In the following year, Passmore approached Spurgeon with a plan to publish his weekly sermons. Spurgeon agreed, though the publication did not begin until 1855.[44] Passmore and his business partner, James Alabaster, would go on to publish the bulk of Spurgeon's sermons, along with most of his other

---

[41]C. H. Spurgeon, "The Warrant of Faith," sermon no. 531, given September 20, 1863, from 1 John 3:23, *The Metropolitan Tabernacle Pulpit*, vol. 9 (London: Passmore & Alabaster, 1863), 531.

[42]Spurgeon to Rev. James Wells, March 1871, in Murray, *Letters of Charles Haddon Spurgeon*, 74.

[43]Spurgeon, *Autobiography*, 1:319.

[44]For further discussion on Spurgeon's publications, see Nettles, *Living by Revealed Truth*, 397-400. This comes from a broader chapter titled "Personal Theory and Preferences in the Production of Godly Literature."

titles. Although Spurgeon's sermons preached at both the New Park Street Chapel and the Metropolitan Tabernacle established his ministry in London, it was through printed works that he became known throughout the world. While his sermons drew tremendous crowds, occasionally numbering over twenty thousand, Spurgeon reached far larger audiences through his published sermons.

In addition to his printed sermons, there are a number of additional resources that provide helpful information regarding Spurgeon's biblical interpretation. These include Spurgeon's two biblical commentaries: a multi-volume set on the Psalms called *The Treasury of David* and the posthumously published commentary on Matthew, *The Gospel of the Kingdom*.[45] The most sizable collection of material is found in *The Sword and the Trowel*, a magazine that he founded in 1865. In addition to his claim that the magazine would serve as a "supplement to our weekly sermon," he suggested in his introductory remarks to the first volume that it would "give us an opportunity of urging the claims of Christ's cause, of advocating the revival of godliness, of denouncing error, of bearing witness for truth, and of encouraging the labourers in the Lord's vineyard."[46] Spurgeon set out to accomplish this task by providing a collection of articles, sermons, and book reviews.[47]

In his preface to the first issue of *The Sword and the Trowel*, Spurgeon referred to the biblical passage that inspired the magazine's name, Nehemiah 4:17-18, which read, "They which builded on the wall, and they that bare burdens, with those that laded, every one with one of his hands wrought in the work, and with the other hand held a weapon. For the builders, every one had his sword girded by his side, and so builded. And he that sounded the trumpet was by me." This theme was captured in the magazine's subheading, "A Record of Combat with Sin & Labour for the

---

[45]C. H. Spurgeon, *The Treasury of David*, 7 vols. (London: Marshall Brothers, 1869–1885); C. H. Spurgeon, *The Gospel of the Kingdom: A Commentary on the Book of Matthew* (London: Passmore & Alabaster, 1893). For further discussion of these commentaries, see chapters three and four of this book.

[46]*The Sword and the Trowel* 1 (1865): 5.

[47]As the majority of the publications of *The Sword and the Trowel* occurred in the latter half of Spurgeon's ministry, discussion of the later editions of the magazine will occur in chapter five.

Lord." On the first anniversary of the magazine's publication, Spurgeon boasted that it had already seen positive results, writing that "foes have felt the sword far more than they would care to confess, and friends have seen the work of the trowel on the walls of Zion to their joy and rejoicing."[48] In addition to the publication of sermons, the magazine contained numerous engagements with biblical material, from reprinted sermons and reviews of biblical commentaries to articles and evangelistic tracts.

An early example of Spurgeon's engagement with biblical scholarship was his review of *Ecce Homo* in *The Sword and the Trowel*. The book, which was first published anonymously in 1865, promised "those who feel dissatisfied with the current conceptions of Christ" an opportunity to "reconsider the whole subject from the beginning."[49] The volume's preface maintained that "he whom we call Christ bore no such name, but was simply, as St. Luke describes him, a young man of promise, popular with those who knew him and appearing to enjoy the Divine favour."[50] The author was eventually revealed to be John Robert Seeley (1834–1895), the son of a prominent evangelical publisher, who became a leading Broad-Church thinker and Regius professor of modern history at Cambridge University.

While many evangelicals loudly attacked *Ecce Homo*, Spurgeon believed that the controversy surrounding the book was likely fueling broader interest in it: "Reading men are constantly asking one another, 'Have you read "Ecce Homo," and what do you think of it?'"[51] With regard to the book's authorship, Spurgeon was evidently unaware of Seeley's involvement and instead guessed that "one of our Broad-churchmen has been muddling his brains with the works of Renan and other blasphemers, and has in addition drank deep of German rationalism."[52] Spurgeon's review began with

---

[48] *The Sword and the Trowel* 1 (1865): 2.

[49] Anonymous, *Ecce Homo: A Survey of the Life and Work of Jesus Christ* (London: Macmillan, 1866), xxi. *Ecce Homo*, or "behold the man," is a reference to the Latin words recorded from Pontius Pilate in the Vulgate's translation of John 19:5.

[50] Anonymous, *Ecce Homo*, xxi.

[51] *The Sword and the Trowel* 2 (1866): 308.

[52] *The Sword and the Trowel* 2 (1866): 309. Here Spurgeon is referencing the French Semitic linguist Joseph Ernest Renan (1823–1892), whose controversial *Life of Jesus*, originally published in 1863, followed higher-critical methodology and included particularly anti-Semitic commentary with regard to Christ's Jewish ancestry.

his concern regarding potential theological implications of *Ecce Homo*'s emphasis on Christ's human nature,

> The writer, be he who he may, is no blasphemer of the Lord Jesus, but a warm admirer of the self-denying love of the Man of Sorrows; he sees in him a marvellous revelation of moral truth and power, and believes the great principles of Christianity to be eternal truth. He is a Christian from the point of morals; but, theologically, he will not commit himself; he subscribes to the ethics of the prophet of Nazareth, but counts it to be a part of those ethics to hold his mind free to believe whatever enthusiasm may suggest to it. . . . Miracles are not denied, nor is even the Deity of Christ impugned, but there is an evident shirking of the supernatural, and an attempt to explain the whole of "the wonders of the cross" upon a theory as little as possible objectionable to the sceptic. As we have said before, our author has a sincere admiration for *Christ*, as he always calls him, and makes his example the flame at which holiness is kindled, but he has nothing to say for his deity, his atonement, or any of those verities which are the soul and marrow of the revelation of Jesus.[53]

The *Ecce Homo* review is noteworthy for several reasons. First, it was among Spurgeon's earliest published engagements with biblical scholarship. Though *The Sword and the Trowel* was by this point in its second year of publication and Spurgeon regularly included book reviews in the magazine from its inception, this particular review is substantially longer than his usual format.[54] Furthermore, Spurgeon typically offered limited citations, if any, in his book reviews, whereas in this review he cited several paragraph-long block quotations from the text, in an attempt to provide context for his comments. Additionally, though he expressed his misgivings over some of the book's theological implications, particularly with regard to the presentation of the atonement, he identified several points at which he was in agreement with the author, including phrases such as "the following portrait of Jesus with the woman taken in adultery is equally

---

[53] *The Sword and the Trowel* 2 (1866): 310-11.
[54] Chapters three and four of this book will address Spurgeon's reviews of biblical commentaries more exhaustively. Those reviews most often consisted of two or three paragraphs, whereas the review of *Ecce Homo* covered nearly ten pages.

vivid and original, and possibly we may add accurate" and "when dealing with 'the Society,' by which the author means the church, he gives us the following passage, which has in it a weighty truth."[55]

This review offers a glimpse of both critical scrutiny and charity that was not always present in later book reviews in *The Sword and the Trowel*. The central section of his review is largely positive, and only in the final paragraphs does Spurgeon began to offer extended, strong criticism:

> Many such flowers there are in this basket, but amid them the asp is hidden as we have already shown, and therefore the flowers themselves wither in our sight. . . . We felt indignant at what seemed to us a gratuitous imputation, till we came to sundry infamously cold-blooded remarks upon war, capital punishment, and the infernal *auto da fé* of the Spanish Inquisition, which when contrasted with the author's account of our Lord's rejection of all physical force, and his eulogies of our Lord's humanity of character, led us to think that the imputation may not have been ill founded after all. We are loath to think more harshly than is necessary of those from we differ, but we cannot do less than express our suspicion.[56]

It is noteworthy that Spurgeon's final and major point of disagreement with the volume was not primarily with regard to its Christology or view of the atonement, but rather its endorsement of capital punishment and warfare as acceptable positions for Christians to hold. In his conclusion, he suggested that discerning readers could "possibly read to profit" but "those who have no vocation in the realm of speculation" should avoid the book.[57]

The Sword and the Trowel offered Spurgeon a canvas upon which he could present a wider audience with a diverse range of content, from evangelistic tracts and job notices to essays and book reviews. One reprinted article of particular relevance for the present study was a translation from the Welsh Nonconformist preacher Christmas Evans (1766–1838) titled "Preaching Christ Crucified." Evans's final paragraph offered an approach that Spurgeon would mirror throughout his own ministry, particularly as he wrote, "I am

---

[55] *The Sword and the Trowel* 2 (1866): 313-14.
[56] *The Sword and the Trowel* 2 (1866): 316.
[57] *The Sword and the Trowel* 2 (1866): 313.

not for urging my brethren to refrain from preaching the 'unnumbered lines' of Biblical truth, but exhort them to follow every line right up to the centre, to Christ crucified; who is the great fountain of life, fire, and force."[58] Thus the content of Spurgeon's magazine—from the collection of articles and reviews to his selection of reprinted sermons—often served to feature and expound upon the cross of Christ and the conversion of the unrepentant. The magazine allowed Spurgeon to engage with both classic and contemporary discussion on Christology, yet its pages also afforded him the opportunity to encourage his readers to study the Bible for themselves and to take action in evangelistic efforts. As such, the magazine modeled the evangelical characteristics and positions of its founder.

THE BIBLE AT HOME:
SPURGEON'S DEVOTIONAL WRITINGS

While *The Sword and the Trowel* and Spurgeon's printed sermons remain central to a study of his use of the Bible, his devotional books should not be overlooked. These volumes provide a helpful example of Spurgeon's attempt to guide lay Christians in private biblical study. He was certainly not alone in this effort. Perhaps the most noteworthy pastoral aid came from the Scottish minister Robert Murray M'Cheyne (1813–1843), who prior to his early death produced a guide and calendar titled "Daily Bread," through which individuals could follow an orderly schedule and read through the Bible in a year.[59] M'Cheyne's reading plan, though concise and orderly, lacked any exposition, theological reflection, or guidance through the biblical text, something that Spurgeon would seek to provide across his various devotional writings.

The first mention of these devotional volumes appeared in the November 1865 edition of *The Sword and the Trowel*, where Spurgeon hinted at the publication of a new written work, a devotional collection intended for a broad audience. He wrote,

---

[58] *The Sword and the Trowel* 2 (1866): 121.

[59] M'Cheyne's reading plan was included in most editions of the memoirs published by his friend and fellow minister Andrew A. Bonar. See Andrew A. Bonar, *Memoir and Remains of the Rev. Robert Murray M'Cheyne* (Edinburgh: William Oliphant, 1878), 560-69.

I have almost completed a volume of Readings for every morning in the year, which will (D.V.) be ready by the New Year. By this I hope to commune with thousands of families all over the world every morning at the family altar. . . . I have written much of it out of my own experience of the Lord's sustaining hand in trouble, sickness, and depression of spirit, and therefore hope it may meet the cases of the Lord's tried people.[60]

This volume was published as *Morning by Morning*, a devotional book containing short reflections upon single verses from the Bible. Joseph Angus (1816–1902), the principal of Regent's Park College and a former pastor of the New Park Street Chapel, wrote a short review of Spurgeon's devotional for the February 1866 edition of *The Sword and the Trowel*. In it he praised Spurgeon's efforts, writing that the devotional "is in short the old-fashioned Puritan teaching, which must be *in substance* the teaching of all who would do Christ's work on earth, however the form or language may change."[61] At the close of his review, Angus wrote that "all who love a full-orbed gospel, vigorous, varied thought, and a racy style, will appreciate this volume, which is to be followed, we are glad to see, by a similar one for *Evening Reading*. May God speed them both!"[62] In addition to the second daily devotional mentioned by Angus, *Evening by Evening*, Spurgeon published *The Interpreter, or, Scripture for Family Worship*. *The Interpreter* was the most expensive single book that Spurgeon published, which may explain the suggestion in advertisements that it would be a "grand wedding present."[63] In contrast to Spurgeon's other devotional books, this one offered almost no commentary, many days' readings contained just a sentence or two of editorial summary. A final devotional volume, *The Chequebook of the Bank of Faith*, was published in 1888, just four years before Spurgeon's death. Written near the end of his life, *The Chequebook*

---

[60] *The Sword and the Trowel* 1 (1865): 156.

[61] *The Sword and the Trowel* 2 (1866): 30.

[62] *The Sword and the Trowel* 2 (1866): 31.

[63] An 1882 advertisement from Passmore & Alabaster listed the cloth edition at twenty-five shillings, while the Persian and Turkish leather editions cost thirty-two and forty-two shillings, respectively. A volume of Spurgeon's sermons, by contrast, would cost between six and eight shillings. Among other advertising references, see *Golden Hours: A Monthly Magazine for Family and General Reading* 15 (June 1882): 11.

was not intended to supersede the previous volumes. In his introduction, Spurgeon was clear to distinguish its content as "gathered from a more varied range of topics . . . all the more profitable because they deal with doctrine, experience, practice, and everything else."[64] This final devotional focused primarily on the promises from God to men and women throughout the biblical canon and was meant to be an encouragement to dismayed Christians rather than a steady diet. Spurgeon made this clear, writing that the book "is a sweetmeat of promise only, and it must not interfere with the fuller meals: nay, rather, I hope it will excite a desire for them."[65] These devotionals followed the general format of Spurgeon's sermons, though the reflections were kept to one typescript page of reading per day. Each day began with one verse—or, occasionally, a portion of one verse—followed by Spurgeon's reflections. Particularly in the context of devotional writing, it is apparent that Spurgeon was not primarily concerned with locating the biblical passages within their immediate context. Rather, the devotionals were structured around topical themes related to some portion of the verse.

Spurgeon's use of the biblical text in his devotional books often echoed the crucicentric and conversionistic tone of his sermons. For instance, the entry for February 5 in *The Chequebook* came from Exodus 12:13, which read, "When I see the blood, I will pass over you." Spurgeon bypassed the immediate context of the passage, namely that lamb's blood smeared on the doorposts of the Israelites homes would spare their firstborn children from God's punishment upon the Egyptians. Instead, he presented the verse solely in terms of Christ's atoning death on the cross, writing that Christians rest "in calm security. We have God's Sacrifice and God's Word to create in us a sense of perfect security. He will, he must, pass over us, because he spared not our glorious Substitute. Justice joins hands with love to provide everlasting salvation for all the blood-besprinkled ones."[66] *Morning by Morning* contained similarly

---

[64]C. H. Spurgeon, *The Chequebook of the Bank of Faith: Being Precious Promises Arranged for Daily Use with Brief Comments* (New York: American Tract Society, 1893), viii.

[65]Spurgeon, *Chequebook*, viii.

[66]Spurgeon, *Chequebook*. Reading for February 5.

crucicentric renderings, with direct appeals for his readers' conversion as he wrote of Christ, "We see the great Scapegoat led away by the appointed officers of justice. Beloved, can you feel assured that He carried *your* sin? As you look to the cross upon His shoulders, does it represent *your* sin?"[67] In another devotional entry, Spurgeon addressed individuals who, like him at a young age, were consumed with a sense of dread over whether they were elected to receive salvation from God. His solution, drawn directly from his own conversion narrative, was that they should "look unto Jesus." Addressing the readers directly, he asked, "Do you feel yourself to be a lost, guilty sinner? Go straight-way to the cross of Christ, and tell Jesus so . . . hide in His wounds, and you shall know your election."[68] In an entry in *Evening by Evening*, Spurgeon suggested that devotional Bible reading should be the fuel for evangelism, and that his readers should proclaim "Christ, and nothing but Christ," using the apostle Paul as a model, on the basis that he "lifted up the cross, and extolled the Son of God who bled thereon. Follow his example in all your personal efforts to spread the glad tidings of salvation, and let 'Christ and Him crucified' be your ever recurring theme."[69]

The structural framework of Spurgeon's devotional books indicates his desire to equip Christians to engage in multiple, sustained reflections on the Bible throughout each day. As Timothy Larsen has observed,

> It may be supposed that the ideal was that one would read a chapter of Scripture and the entry from *Morning by Morning* in private at dawn before reading the daily portion from *The Interpreter* as a family before breakfast, sometime during the unsettling turmoil of the day one would pause to read an entry from *The Cheque Book*, and then one would read from the relevant section of *The Interpreter* with the household at dusk before retiring to read privately another chapter as well as the entry from *Evening by Evening*.[70]

---

[67]C. H. Spurgeon, *Morning by Morning* (New York: Robert Carter and Brothers, 1865), 94. Reading for April 3.

[68]Spurgeon, *Morning by Morning*, 199. Reading for July 17.

[69]C. H. Spurgeon, *Evening by Evening* (New York: Sheldon, 1869), 62. Reading for March 2.

[70]Timothy Larsen, *A People of One Book: The Bible and the Victorians* (Oxford: Oxford University Press, 2011), 265.

This amount of Bible reading, ambitious though it may seem, suggests that Spurgeon expected his readers to allocate significant portions of their daily schedule for both personal and family devotions. It is unclear whether his readers routinely engaged with the full breadth of his devotional material on a daily basis, but it is at the very least indicative of what Spurgeon considered ideal spiritual nourishment for Christians. Larsen maintains that there is significance in the amount of time Spurgeon dedicated to the production of these volumes given his busy schedule, writing that "a major motivation was undoubtedly his strong assumption that Christians ought to be reading the Bible daily and his sense of duty as a pastor to assist them in their pursuit of this task."[71] Spurgeon was perhaps more emphatic than Larsen's description, he emphasized daily biblical study to the point that he insisted that "I should like to see all the good books themselves burnt, as well as the bad books of Ephesus, if they keep men from reading Holy Scripture for themselves. Here is the well of purest Gospel undefiled: it springs up in this precious volume with freshness and sweetness unequalled."[72] In addition to devotional entries that called his readers to seek out conversion, Spurgeon also directed readers who were already Christians to "cling to that cross which took thy sin away" and suggested that in doing so, they might "be not contented with this unspeakable blessing for thyself alone, but publish abroad the story of the cross. Holy gladness and holy boldness will make you a good preacher, and all the world will be a pulpit for you to preach in."[73] Thus Spurgeon's devotional material indicates that he viewed crucicentric and conversionistic interpretation as normative not only for preachers but for lay Bible readers as well.

THE BIBLE DISTRIBUTED: SPURGEON'S SPEECHES AT THE BRITISH AND FOREIGN BIBLE SOCIETY

In May 1864 and again in May 1875, Spurgeon addressed the annual meeting of the British and Foreign Bible Society. He used these occasions

---

[71]Larsen, *People of One Book*, 265.

[72]C. H. Spurgeon, "The Secret Food and the Public Name," sermon no. 1079, on Jeremiah 15:16, n.d., *The Metropolitan Tabernacle Pulpit*, vol. 18 (London: Passmore & Alabaster, 1872), 616.

[73]Spurgeon, *Morning by Morning*, 227. Reading for August 14.

to provide lengthy discussions of the nature of the Bible, offering candid thoughts on how Christian men and women should regard and use the Bible. These addresses offer insights into Spurgeon's perceptions of the Bible outside the usual sermon context. Furthermore, they also reveal Spurgeon's perspective with regard to the defense of the Bible in the wake of some conclusions of higher critical scholarship, which some evangelicals regarded as a threat to biblical reliability. As Glover summarizes, for evangelicals the Bible "was not merely a source book for the early history of their religion, but a Bible that was the authoritative and infallible Word of God."[74] This was certainly the case for Spurgeon, who bristled at the thought of Christians mistrusting their Bibles.[75] Spurgeon's crucicentric and conversionistic preaching depended upon a Bible that was both authoritative and infallible, and as such it is necessary to examine instances where he discusses both the use and defense of the Bible.

Known colloquially as the "Bible Society," the British and Foreign Bible Society began in 1804 with the recognition that there were few affordable translations of the Bible in the Welsh language, though their aim expanded rather ambitiously to provide families throughout the world with copies of the Bible translated into their native language. Headquartered in London, its leadership in the early years represented a variety of Protestant traditions.[76] By 1864, the Bible Society had produced millions of translated editions of the Bible that were circulated throughout and beyond the British Empire. As they were funded by voluntary contributions, they depended on noteworthy figures such as Spurgeon to assist with fundraising.

---

[74]Willis Borders Glover, *Evangelical Nonconformists and Higher Criticism in the Nineteenth Century* (London: Independent Press, 1954), 16.

[75]See, for instance, his discussion of Bible translation, where he displays concern that multiple English translations could cause the laity to distrust particular translations. Spurgeon, *Lectures to My Students*, 4:57.

[76]For further discussion on the Bible Society, see Stephen Batalden, Kathleen Cann, and John Dean, eds., *Sowing the Word: The Cultural Impact of the British and Foreign Bible Society, 1804–2004* (Sheffield, UK: Sheffield Phoenix Press, 2006); Leslie Howsam, *Cheap Bibles: Nineteenth-Century Publishing and the British and Foreign Bible Society*, Cambridge Studies in Publishing and Printing History (Cambridge: Cambridge University Press, 1991); Stewart J. Brown, *Providence and Empire: Religion, Politics, and Society in the United Kingdom, 1815–1914* (Harlow: Pearson Longman, 2008), 33-34.

In his introduction to the first address, Spurgeon reflected that the church's use of the Bible in the present day should be characterized by "the application of divine truth on a larger scale, labouring to bring it home to the masses, and to make them read as well as to possess it, and to understand it as well to regard it as the divine Word."[77] He set this aim in contrast to those who felt obligated to engage directly with critical commentators, particularly as he said,

> I do not undertake the task of refuting objections. . . . I don't think that is my particular work, and I believe that ninety-nine out of every hundred Christians are not called for the defence of the Gospel against infidel objectors, so much as the pressing of that Gospel home to men's hearts, casting light upon the eyes that have been in darkness, that they may behold its glory and rejoice therein.[78]

In a turn that may have been startling to his audience, he continued, "Now, the Word of God is nothing but a dead letter till the Spirit of God, with omnipotent arm, grasp it, and then it cuts to the dividing asunder of soul and spirit, and is a discerner of the thoughts and intents of the heart."[79] Pressing further, he said, "Merely to circulate the Bible will not prove its virtues. . . . We may scatter Bibles by millions, and reduce the price to twopence, or nothing, but we have done nothing but add to men's responsibility, unless we pray earnestly that God will lead men to study it, and by His Spirit bless it to their conversion, their edification, their sanctification in righteousness."[80] For Spurgeon, the Bible was the primary vehicle through which God spoke to people, and as such he urged his listeners to endeavor "to bring the Scriptures home to people's hearts."[81] His suggested plan included recommended Sunday School training, midweek "Bible-reading parties," and courses where men and women could meet to discuss

---

[77]C. H. Spurgeon, *Speeches at Home and Abroad*, ed. G. Holden Pike (London: Passmore & Alabaster, 1878), 9. This volume of speeches was collected by Spurgeon's friend G. Holden Pike, whose preface states that "Mr. Spurgeon himself is not responsible for the present publication, having neither suggested, nor had any hand in, the compilation of this volume."

[78]Spurgeon, *Speeches at Home and Abroad*, 9.

[79]Spurgeon, *Speeches at Home and Abroad*, 9.

[80]Spurgeon, *Speeches at Home and Abroad*, 10.

[81]Spurgeon, *Speeches at Home and Abroad*, 11.

the more difficult portions of the biblical text. While Spurgeon valued commentaries and owned a library full of them, he insisted that "many a text that will not open to a commentary will open to prayer. . . . When we draw near to God, feeling that Holy Scripture is His incarnate truth, and we want to get beyond that mere veil . . . then Scripture becomes a real power to us, then it gives us a force which will make our efforts tell upon the world at large."[82]

In the conclusion of the first address, Spurgeon suggested that his listeners commit each day to "teach something scriptural to somebody. Every day a line, and then what a poem will your life's psalm be! Every day a soul, and, oh, what soul-winners you will be! Every day a seed, and then what a harvest shall you have!"[83] While on the surface Spurgeon does not seem especially crucicentric in this address, the theme is present when considered against his broader statements on personal evangelism. He makes the case explicitly in a later address to his students, suggesting that soul winners keep "to the simple story of the cross," teaching that "to be saved, nothing is wanted but a simple trust in the crucified Redeemer."[84] As such, Spurgeon's charge to his listeners to read the Bible so that they might use it for evangelistic ends was foundationally connected to the priority he assigned to crucicentric and conversionistic interpretation.

The second speech to the Bible Society came eleven years and one day later and began with Spurgeon's recollection of his previous address to the society, when he described the collective mood in the room as "dreadfully dreary . . . not long after the famous attack of Colenso."[85] Spurgeon was referring here to John William Colenso (1814–1883), the Anglican bishop of Natal, who published a commentary on the Pentateuch that adopted higher critical methodology and questioned the historicity of much of the narrative.[86] As we have noted, higher criticism had roots in

---

[82]Spurgeon, *Speeches at Home and Abroad*, 13.

[83]Spurgeon, *Speeches at Home and Abroad*, 14.

[84]Spurgeon, *Soul Winner*, 240.

[85]C. H. Spurgeon, "The Bible (Part Second)," in Pike, *Speeches at Home and Abroad*, 16.

[86]See John William Colenso, *The Pentateuch and Book of Joshua Critically Examined* (London: Longman, Green, Longman, Roberts & Green, 1862). In addition to his theological acumen,

seventeenth- and early eighteenth-century English and Irish Deist thought, but by the mid-nineteenth century it had become especially synonymous with German scholarship, primarily at major universities such as Göttingen and Tübingen.[87] These scholars were asking pointed historical questions of the biblical text. They interpreted the biblical text against both recent archeological discoveries and contemporary methods of historical research, and they developed theories that challenged, among other things, the traditional authorship of texts and the historicity of the events within the text.[88] While Colenso's commentary was not the first use of higher criticism published in Britain, Larsen suggests that it was the "first thoroughgoing, indigenous attempt at modern biblical criticism that brought the young discipline to the general attention of British society."[89] Colenso's work received a significant amount of criticism, and many evangelicals spoke out against it.[90] For his part, Spurgeon only made one reference to Colenso from the pulpit in the time surrounding the controversy, one that included his usual wit:

> What a deal of writing there has been lately about and against Dr. Colenso! You need not think of reading the replies to his books, for most of them would be the best means of sending people to sleep that have ever been invented; and after all, they don't answer the man; most of them leave the objections untouched, for there is a speciousness in the objection which is not

---

Colenso was also a trained mathematician, and a significant portion of his doubt in the historical veracity of the Pentateuch came from his estimation that the population figures of the Israelites throughout the wilderness period must have numbered over two million people, a figure that he thought highly improbable.

[87]Colenso, who was based in South Africa, would have had limited knowledge of the developing controversies in Britain, and was working largely from his own resources. See Brown, *Providence and Empire*, 239.

[88]For a general introduction to higher criticism, see John Barton, *The Cambridge Companion to Biblical Interpretation* (Cambridge: Cambridge University Press, 2009), 9-20.

[89]Timothy Larsen, "Biblical Criticism and the Desire for Reform: Bishop Colenso on the Pentateuch," in *Contested Christianity: The Political and Social Context of Victorian Theology* (Waco, TX: Baylor University Press, 2004), 60.

[90]For further work on the Colenso controversy, see Larsen, "Biblical Criticism and the Desire for Reform: Bishop Colenso on the Pentateuch"; Gerald Parsons, "Released from the Thraldom of Mere Bibliolatry: Biblical Criticism in the Sermons of Bishop Colenso," *Modern Believing* 52, no. 2 (2011): 22-29; and Parsons, "Preaching the Broad Church Gospel: The Natal Sermons of Bishop John William Colenso," in *The Oxford Handbook of the British Sermon 1689-1901*, ed. Keith A. Francis and Gerald Parsons (Oxford: Oxford University Press, 2012), 463-79.

easily got over. I think we should be doing much better if, instead of running after this heathenish bishop, we should be running after poor sinners; if, instead of writing books of argument, and entering into discussions, we keep on each, in our sphere, endeavouring to convert souls, imploring the Spirit of God to come down upon us, and make us spiritual fathers in Israel.[91]

These comments reflect the extent to which Spurgeon believed that the primary importance of the Bible was to promote conversion. While he believed that the Bible was an informative and authoritative guide in all areas of life, the conversion of sinners remained the priority in both his own preaching ministry and his instruction to others.

According to Spurgeon, the proclamation of the Bible and the conversions produced by it would bring about a cultural transformation. Speaking to the Bible Society, Spurgeon used an anecdote about a past trip to the Colosseum in Rome, suggesting that the ruins "tell what desolations he hath made in the earth, how he breaketh the bow and cutteth the spear in sunder."[92] He continued on with a measure of bravado, proclaiming that "the time has gone for defending the Bible against anybody, whoever he may be—whether he happens to be a bishop, or to come from the opposite side. Wherever he may happen to come from, let him come! The Bible has been so often defended, and the defences are so admirable, that any more outworks would almost seem to be superfluous."[93] Defending the Bible, Spurgeon proclaimed, was like defending a lion. Rather than try to defend it themselves, he suggested that his listeners simply "open the door and let the lion out; he will take care of himself."[94] The Bible may, as Spurgeon indicated, defend itself; however, he did not believe that the Bible interpreted itself. This second address concluded with an exhortation to his listeners to read the Bible to children, saying, "This is the thing; read the book yourself, and get the meaning of it; then talk it out again to the children; they will receive it so much better. We want subscribers to the

---

[91]C. H. Spurgeon, "Simple but Sound," sermon no. 2955, given in 1863 from John 9:25, *The Metropolitan Tabernacle Pulpit*, vol. 51 (London: Passmore & Alabaster, 1905), 472-73.

[92]Spurgeon, "Bible (Part Second)," 16. He is referencing Psalm 46:9.

[93]Spurgeon, "Bible (Part Second)," 17.

[94]Spurgeon, "Bible (Part Second)," 17.

Bible Society, but we want readers of the Bible and expounders of it far more, so that even the little ones may understand the law of the Lord."[95]

While Spurgeon offered reflections on the nature of the Bible throughout his sermons, these speeches provide evidence of how he believed that the average Christian should view and use the Bible.[96] Both Bible Society addresses presented a similar theme: "Do not complain about there being error in the world—proclaim the Truth."[97] He also displayed an optimistic confidence that opposition to the Bible, both in the form of critical scholarship and emerging atheistic thought, was best addressed not by engagement with the critical scholarship but by consistent teaching of the Bible. For Spurgeon, effectiveness in teaching the Bible was not primarily rooted in learning and scholarly reflection but in dependence on the Holy Spirit to guide the believer to the true meaning of the text. In a sense, these addresses do not emphasize the evangelical tenets of crucicentrism and conversionism to the same extent as many of his sermons and other written material; however, this is almost certainly due to his audience. Spurgeon likely did not feel the need to make a direct, evangelistic appeal to a room populated with wealthy Christian donors who were associated with the British and Foreign Bible Society. In these engagements with the biblical text we can see something else, namely Spurgeon's candid reflections with regard to biblicism and activism. Thus, Spurgeon's exhortation to the Bible Society was that his audience should be actively engaged in communicating the Bible's message and following the Holy Spirit's guidance to produce conversions.

CONCLUSIONS

As we have seen, Spurgeon's transition from his rural pastorate to London was not without difficulty. This was reflected particularly in the controversy

---

[95]Spurgeon, "Bible (Part Second)," 22.

[96]Among other sermons, see Spurgeon, "The Talking Book," sermon no. 1017, given October 22, 1871, from Proverbs 6:22, *The Metropolitan Tabernacle Pulpit*, vol. 17 (London: Passmore & Alabaster, 1871), 589-600; "The Bible Tried and Proved," sermon no. 2084, given May 5, 1889, from Psalm 12:6, *The Metropolitan Tabernacle Pulpit*, vol. 35 (London: Passmore & Alabaster, 1889), 253-64.

[97]Spurgeon, "Bible (Part Second)," 21.

raised by James Wells in the pages of the *Earthen Vessel*. Though Spurgeon was proud to identify himself as a Calvinist and exhorted the doctrines of Calvinistic theology in both his sermons and his writings, the free offer of the gospel remained central to all of his ministries. This was evident in the controversy with Wells, where it became clear that Spurgeon's convictions with regard to the cross and conversion defined both his reading of the biblical text and the content of his sermons.

Spurgeon's connections in the London publishing world enabled him to establish a magazine that provided a venue for reprinted sermons, book reviews, and articles, many of which focused upon matters of biblical interpretation. *The Sword and the Trowel* was not an academic journal and did not feature the measured, critical voices of the theological periodicals that would appear later in the nineteenth century. Still, it had a broad popular appeal, and it remains a valuable resource in assessing matters of particular theological importance for Spurgeon and his closest associates. We noted this in Spurgeon's extended review of *Ecce Homo*, in which he attempted to provide a balanced, critical review of a controversial publication. His review indicates that though he did not receive a higher education, he could engage written material with which he disagreed in a manner that was both charitable and critical. As we have seen, Spurgeon endeavored to use the magazine in a manner that reflected its name, and as such he used its pages as both a defensive sword against what he perceived to be erroneous or fraudulent teaching and as a constructive trowel with which he could promote his preferred biblical interpretation, with a due emphasis on the atonement and conversion, to aid in the global expansion of the church.

We have noted the development of Spurgeon's popular devotional books. Spurgeon, like most of his contemporary evangelical ministers, was emphatic about the necessity of daily Bible reading as a means of ensuring regular communion with God, but he also recognized that many men and women would benefit from an accessible guide in their Bible reading. Each of his devotional works sought to provide a window into the world of the biblical text, with every text viewed as the direct Word of God, and many of his individual textual comments directed the reader to consider work of

Christ on the cross. In constructing his devotional material in this way, Spurgeon encouraged his readers to adopt the same interpretive lens that he used in viewing a biblical text; that is, to view the Bible as highlighting the priorities of crucicentrism and conversionism.

Finally, we have noted that Spurgeon's two recorded addresses to the British and Foreign Bible Society provided clear examples of Spurgeon's theological presuppositions of the nature of the biblical text. In these lectures, Spurgeon downplayed the apparent threat of higher critical biblical scholarship while speaking warmly of the efforts of the Bible Society. His ultimate instruction to his listeners was that they should read and teach from the Bible themselves, with an aim to produce conversions. Thus, Spurgeon's early ministry outside the pulpit reflects his broader concerns regarding a crucicentric, conversionistic focus on biblical interpretation. In the following chapter we will analyze Spurgeon's interpretation of Old Testament texts, exploring the degree to which the cross and conversion remained central in his interpretation.

THE CROSS AND CONVERSION IN SPURGEON'S OLD TESTAMENT INTERPRETATION

We have most certainly departed from the usual mode of preaching,
but we do not feel bound to offer even half a word of apology
for so doing, since we believe ourselves to be free to use any manner
of speech which is calculated to impress the truth upon our hearers.

C. H. SPURGEON

THE NINETEENTH CENTURY REPRESENTS a crossroads between pre-modern biblical interpretation and the advent of biblical higher criticism. As Hans Frei observes, "Modern biblical interpretation began its quest in continuity as well as rebellion."[1] This shift in interpretation reverberated throughout the lecture halls of the universities and subsequently echoed from the pulpits of Europe. Spurgeon's ministry, as we have seen, was deeply rooted in past expressions of Christian theology while simultaneously engaging Britain as it moved toward the height of its global

---

C. H. Spurgeon, "Preface," *The New Park Street Pulpit*, vol. 1 (London: Passmore & Alabaster, 1855), v.

[1] Hans W. Frei, *The Eclipse of Biblical Narrative: A Study in Eighteenth and Nineteenth Century Hermeneutics*, rev. ed. (New Haven, CT: Yale University Press, 1980), 1.

influence. Spurgeon was in many ways representative of the rebellion and continuity that Frei uses to characterize the period. While he revolutionized the process of sermon publication and distribution, he also remained enamored of the Christianity of the Reformers and Puritans.[2] This does not necessarily suggest, as Patricia Kruppa has argued, that he was "an intellectual captive of the past"; however, it does indicate a degree of complexity in Spurgeon's preaching. Robert Ellison, who has written extensively on nineteenth-century preaching, suggests that the purpose of sermons "was not to bring a congregation to assent to a theological theory or set of propositions, but rather to persuade—indeed, to compel—men and women to embark upon a spiritual course of action."[3] The exegetical exploration of texts, and the theological language in which they were presented, were not the end goal of the sermon but rather the means by which the listeners were brought to the end goal. For Spurgeon, the particular course of action was quite simple. His confidence in his approach is perhaps best exemplified in a lengthy and often repeated quotation from a book on evangelism called *The Soul Winner*. In it, he wrote,

> You remember the story of the old minister who heard a sermon by a young man, and when he was asked by the preacher what he thought of it he was rather slow to answer, but at last he said, "If I must tell you, I did not like it at all; there was no Christ in your sermon." "No," answered the young man, "because I did not see that Christ was in the text." "Oh!" said the old minister, "but do you not know that from every little town and village and tiny hamlet in England there is a road leading to London? Whenever I get hold of a text, I say to myself, 'There is a road from here to Jesus Christ, and I mean to keep on His track till I get to Him.'" "Well," said the young man, "but suppose you are preaching from a text that says nothing about Christ?" "Then I will go over hedge and ditch but what I will get at Him." So must we do, brethren; we must have Christ in all our discourses, whatever else is in or not in them.

---

[2]Ian J. Shaw observes that Spurgeon did not himself introduce the weekly printed sermon; this was already in place through the ministry of Nonconformist minister Joseph Irons (1785–1852). Ian J. Shaw, *High Calvinists in Action: Calvinism and the City, Manchester and London, c. 1810–1860* (Oxford: Oxford University Press, 2002), 263.

[3]Robert H. Ellison, *The Victorian Pulpit: Spoken and Written Sermons in Nineteenth-Century Britain* (Selinsgrove, PA: Susquehanna University Press, 1998), 19.

There ought to be enough of the gospel in every sermon to save a soul. Take care that it is so when you are called to preach before Her Majesty the Queen, and if you have to preach to charwomen or chairmen, still always take care that there is the real gospel in every sermon.[4]

In this reference, Spurgeon illustrated his main priority with regard to biblical interpretation, namely that all sermons should include direct reference to Christ and conversion, whether or not those topics were present in the passage he was preaching.[5] This priority occasionally led Spurgeon to interpret texts in a manner that bypassed the immediate context in favor of an approach that achieved his goal of preaching a crucified Christ and a free offer of the gospel.[6] Spurgeon's sermons represent the bulk of his printed work, and they also provide a key vantage point for his biblical interpretation. As his sermons were typically printed, published, and distributed within a week of their first appearance, they provide timely insights into the mood of the church and the mind of the pastor.

A high number of Spurgeon's Old Testament sermons feature crucicentric language, as a brief statistical investigation will show. In surveys of his sermons, drawn from the historical (Numbers), wisdom (Ecclesiastes), and prophetic (Amos) genres, Spurgeon's crucicentric language is rather frequent. Out of twenty-five sermons in Numbers, nineteen had *direct* references to variations of the words *cross*, *crucifixion*, or *Calvary*, while another three sermons had *indirect* reference to the cross, typified by language related to Jesus Christ and sacrifice, statements such as "the blood of Christ" or other references to Christ's physical sacrifice. In total, 88 percent of Spurgeon's sermons from Numbers bore crucicentric references. In Ecclesiastes, the figures are higher. Out of eleven sermons, seven were

---

[4]C. H. Spurgeon, *The Soul Winner: How to Lead Sinners to the Saviour* (Chicago: Fleming H. Revell, 1895), 99-100.

[5]Spurgeon was not speaking hyperbolically with regard to preaching to royalty. During a preaching tour of Holland in 1863, the queen of Holland asked for an audience with Spurgeon. He recorded that in their meeting he had resolved to "talk of nothing but Christ," and noted that he "left that very amiable lady, not having shunned to declare to her the whole counsel of God." C. H. Spurgeon, *C. H. Spurgeon's Autobiography, Compiled from His Diary, Letters, and Records, by His Wife and His Private Secretary*, vol. 1, *1834-1854* (Cincinnati: Curt & Jennings, 1898), 81.

[6]Sidney Greidanus makes a similar criticism. See Sidney Greidanus, *Preaching Christ from the Old Testament* (Grand Rapids, MI: Eerdmans, 1999), 160-62.

directly crucicentric, and three were indirectly crucicentric, totaling 91 percent. His sermons from the prophet Amos are higher still, out of sixteen sermons, only one did not feature direct or indirect language of the cross.[7] These statistics, drawn from multiple genres, indicate a clear pattern of crucicentrism in Spurgeon's approach to the Old Testament.

In the following sections we will briefly summarize developments within the field of Old Testament scholarship during the nineteenth century. From there we will investigate Spurgeon's theological positions concerning the Bible and briefly highlight the Old Testament scholarship that he preferred. Finally, we will analyze Spurgeon's sermons, examining his interpretation from different biblical genres, namely historical, wisdom, and prophetic literature. Throughout the chapter, we will note the degree to which crucicentrism and conversionism shaped Spurgeon's engagement with the biblical text, irrespective of genre.

DEVELOPMENTS IN MODERN
OLD TESTAMENT STUDIES

As Timothy Larsen has argued in his monograph *A People of One Book*, the Bible held a "dominant presence in Victorian life."[8] Larsen's work identifies the Victorian era as a time when the Bible loomed large in the literary, political, and social lives of men and women from all levels of society and from varied religious beliefs.[9] The nineteenth century also represents a significant turning point in biblical scholarship, first on the Continent and subsequently in Britain. Accounts of this historical development are numerous and include valuable works by John Rogerson, Henning Graf Reventlow, and Hans Frei.[10] In this section, we will briefly discuss major

---

[7]The sole outlying sermon was a topical overview of baptism. See C. H. Spurgeon, "Communing with Christ. A Baptizing Sermon," sermon no. 2668, given 1858 from Amos 3:3, *The Metropolitan Tabernacle Pulpit*, vol. 46 (London: Passmore & Alabaster, 1900), 145-52.

[8]Timothy Larsen, *A People of One Book: The Bible and the Victorians* (Oxford: Oxford University Press, 2011), 1.

[9]Larsen includes chapters on agnostics, particularly T. H. Huxley (1825–1895); as well as atheists, represented by Charles Bradlaugh (1833–1891) and Annie Besant (1847–1933).

[10]John Barton, *The Cambridge Companion to Biblical Interpretation* (Cambridge: Cambridge University Press, 2009); Martin J. Buss, *Biblical Form Criticism in Its Context*, Journal for the Study of the Old Testament Supplement Series 274 (Sheffield, UK: Sheffield Academic Press, 1999); Eldon Epp, "Critical Editions and the Development of Text-Critical Methods, Part 2:

works that established critical Old Testament scholarship and subsequent volumes that led to its introduction in British universities.

Critical scholarly engagement with the Old Testament began in the mid-eighteenth century, when scholars began to apply to the biblical text the archaeological, historical, and linguistic methods that were already being used to interpret other ancient documents. Jean Astruc (1684–1766), a French professor of medicine, anonymously published a book titled "Conjectures on the original documents that Moses appears to have used in composing the Book of Genesis. With remarks that support or throw light upon these conjectures."[11] As the title indicates, Astruc posited that the book of Genesis was not composed of one uniform manuscript, but that the author gathered together a series of historical documents to form the final book. A generation after Astruc's publication, the German theologian and Orientalist Johann Gottfried Eichhorn (1752–1827), a professor at Jena University and later at the University of Göttingen, published his *Introduction to the Old Testament*. Astruc, though employing critical methodology, had ultimately attempted to use his new method to defend the traditional position, namely linking Moses

---

From Lachmann (1831) to the Present," in *The New Cambridge History of the Bible*, ed. John Riches, vol. 4, *From 1750 to the Present* (Cambridge: Cambridge University Press, 2015), 13-48; Frei, *Eclipse of the Biblical Narrative*; Scott Mandelbrote and Michael Ledger-Lomas, eds., *Dissent and the Bible in Britain, c. 1650–1950* (Oxford: Oxford University Press, 2013); Henning Graf Reventlow, "The Role of the Old Testament in the German Liberal Protestant Theology of the Nineteenth Century," in *Biblical Studies and the Shifting of Paradigms, 1850-1914*, ed. Henning Graf Reventlow and William Farmer, Journal for the Study of the Old Testament Supplement Series 192 (Sheffield, UK: Sheffield Academic Press, 1995); J. W. Rogerson, *The Bible and Criticism in Victorian Britain: Profiles of F. D. Maurice and William Robertson Smith*, Journal for the Study of the Old Testament Supplement Series 201 (Sheffield, UK: Sheffield Academic Press, 1995); J. W. Rogerson, Christopher Rowland, and Barnabas Lindars, *The Study and Use of the Bible*, vol. 2, *The History of Christian Theology* (Basingstoke, Hants, UK: Marshall Pickering, 1988); Rudolf Smend, *From Astruc to Zimmerli*, trans. Margaret Kohl (Tübingen: Mohr Siebeck, 2007); Henry Wansbrough, *The Use and Abuse of the Bible: A Brief History of Biblical Interpretation* (London: T&T Clark, 2010).

[11]Originally published as Jean Astruc, *Conjectures sur les mémoires originaux dont il paroit que Moyse s'est servi pour composer le Livre de la Genese: Avec des Remarques, qui appuient ou qui éclaircissent ces Conjectures* (Bruxelles: Chez Fricx, 1753). For further investigation of Astruc and his contribution to critical scholarship, see Jan Christian Gertz, "Jean Astruc and Source Criticism in the Book of Genesis," in *Sacred Conjectures: The Context and Legacy of Robert Lowth and Jean Astruc*, ed. John Jarick (London: T&T Clark, 2007), 190-203; Smend, *From Astruc to Zimmerli*, 1-14.

with the authorship of Genesis. By the end of his scholarly career, Eichhorn had concluded that Moses was not the author of the Pentateuch.[12]

Perhaps the most significant development within Old Testament biblical scholarship in the nineteenth century was the development of the documentary hypothesis, most often connected with Julius Wellhausen (1844–1918). Writing over a century later, the University of Göttingen Old Testament professor Rudolf Smend remarked of Wellhausen that "no Old Testament scholar has been read with so much admiration, and none has been so bitterly opposed."[13] While Wellhausen's body of work is often heralded as the dawn of the documentary hypothesis, it was heavily influenced by the prior work of Wilhelm de Wette (1780–1849).[14] Wellhausen admitted this, remarking of de Wette that "you can find everything I have done in the Old Testament in him."[15] Wellhausen's seminal *Prolegomena zur Geschichte Israels* was first published in Berlin in 1878 with an English translation following in 1885, which included an introduction by the Scottish Free Church minister and professor W. Robertson Smith.[16] The documentary hypothesis, which posited that the Pentateuch was not the product of a single author but was rather drawn from four dominant Israelite traditions, was put on display in Wellhausen's *Geschichte Israels*.[17] Higher criticism, which began as a tentative academic investigation by Astruc, was consolidated, at least in German scholarship, in the writings of Wellhausen and his followers. The German universities, particularly the faculties of Göttingen and Tübingen, led a revolution in the world of biblical studies. Momentum in the development of higher critical method led to the formation of Göttingen's *Religionsgeschichtliche Schule*, that is, the history of religions

---

[12]Henning Graf Reventlow, *History of Biblical Interpretation*, vol. 4, *From the Enlightenment to the Twentieth Century*, trans. Leo G. Perdue (Atlanta: Society of Biblical Literature, 2010), 292.

[13]Smend, *From Astruc to Zimmerli*, 91.

[14]Smend, *From Astruc to Zimmerli*, 43-56.

[15]Smend, *From Astruc to Zimmerli*, 43.

[16]Julius Wellhausen, *Geschichte Israels* (Berlin: G. Reimer, 1878); *Prolegomena to the History of Israel: With a Reprint of the Article Israel from the Encyclopedia Britannica*, trans. J. Sutherland Black and Allan Menzies (Edinburgh: A&C Black, 1885).

[17]The four dominant traditions were the Yahwist, Elohist, Deuteronomist, and Priestly sources.

school, which became a hub for further critical studies, extending well into the twentieth century.[18]

British universities also witnessed a shift in their interpretive methodology, albeit a generation behind developments throughout Europe. As on the Continent, some of the earliest proponents of an alternative approach to the biblical text came from scholars outside the traditional disciplines of biblical studies. The poet and essayist Samuel Taylor Coleridge (1772–1834), who was described by the nineteenth-century historian and critic Julia Wedgwood as "the father of the broad church," was influenced by an extended stay in Germany from September 1798 through June 1799.[19] In January of 1799, Coleridge boasted in a letter that he was now able to "read German as English— that is, without any *mental* translation."[20] During his time at Göttingen, Coleridge attended the New Testament lectures of Johann Eichhorn. The time Coleridge spent in the German universities led him to a familiarity with higher criticism that was, according to Tod Jones, "years ahead" of his fellow English academics.[21] Following his death in 1834, Coleridge's writings continued to have a profound influence on British religious thought.[22]

Another seminal figure in British biblical studies was Benjamin Jowett (1817–1893), the Regius Professor of Greek at Balliol College, Oxford. Jowett's most influential publication on the topic was his essay titled "On the Interpretation of Scripture," which formed the final piece in the controversial *Essays and Reviews*.[23] Jowett's suggestion that readers should "read

---

[18]For a description of the school by a contemporary, see Ernst Troeltsch, "The Dogmatics of the 'Religionsgeschichtliche Schule,'" *The American Journal of Theology* 17, no. 1 (1913): 1-21; Larry Hurtado has offered a helpful synopsis of the movement in his "Fashions, Fallacies, and Future Prospects in New Testament Studies," *Journal for the Study of the New Testament* 36, no. 4 (2014): 303-5.

[19]Julia Wedgwood, "Samuel Taylor Coleridge," in *Nineteenth Century Teachers, and Other Essays by Julia Wedgwood* (London: Hodder & Stoughton, 1909), 21.

[20]Quoted in Tod E. Jones, *The Broad Church: A Biography of a Movement* (Lanham, MD: Lexington Books, 2003), 21.

[21]Jones, *Broad Church*, 37; also, Mark Knight and Emma Mason, *Nineteenth-Century Religion and Literature: An Introduction* (Oxford: Oxford University Press, 2006), 72.

[22]Spurgeon directly referenced Coleridge more than any of the other scholars listed in this section, amounting to nearly a dozen instances across his sermons. The majority of Spurgeon's quotations pertain to Coleridge's mastery of poetic imagery, with several direct acknowledgements to his 1798 poem *The Rime of the Ancient Mariner*.

[23]Benjamin Jowett, "On the Interpretation of Scripture," in *Essays and Reviews*, ed. John William Parker (London: John W. Parker and Son, 1860), 330-433.

Scripture like any book" commended the tools of higher criticism as beneficial to the academic study of the Bible.[24] The publication, in the words of
Stewart J. Brown, "aroused revulsion and outrage" among significant
sectors of the church in Britain.[25] While German methodology was evident
in Jowett's approach, his essay consisted primarily of theoretical exploration
rather than original research employing the methods that he espoused.

Not long after the publication of the *Essays*, John William Colenso, the
Anglican bishop of Natal, published the first volume of his multi-volume
commentary on the Pentateuch and the book of Joshua.[26] As we have seen,
Colenso's work added fuel to the fires of controversy surrounding critical
engagement with the Bible. Colenso's commentary was met with fierce opposition by many Christians upon its publication in Britain.[27] Another
influential figure in the Victorian British reception of biblical criticism was
Samuel Driver, an English Old Testament professor at New College, Oxford,
who was thoroughly influenced by the German school. In 1891, Driver published his *Introduction to the Literature of the Old Testament*, which was the
first major work of higher criticism written by an Englishman at an English
university.[28] Driver's landmark work introduced many scholars and cler-
gymen in Britain to an account of the Pentateuch and Isaiah that suggested
these books were written by multiple authors, and he ascribed far later

---

[24]Jowett, "On the Interpretation of Scripture," 338.

[25]Stewart J. Brown, *Providence and Empire: Religion, Politics, and Society in the United Kingdom,
1815–1914* (Harlow: Pearson Longman, 2008), 235. Contemporary critiques of Jowett's *Essays*
included Anonymous, *"Essays and Reviews" Anticipated: Extracts from a Work Published in the
Year 1825 and Attributed to the Lord Bishop of St. David's* (London, 1861). For further work on the
controversy, see Edward Meyrick Goulburn, *Replies to "Essays and Reviews"* (Oxford: J. Henry
and J. Parker, 1862); Ieuan Ellis, *Seven Against Christ: A Study of "Essays and Reviews,"* Studies in
the History of Christian Thought 23 (Leiden: Brill, 1980); Josef L. Altholz, *Anatomy of a Controversy: The Debate over Essays and Reviews, 1860–1864* (Aldershot, Hants, UK: Scolar Press, 1994).

[26]John William Colenso, *The Pentateuch and Book of Joshua Critically Examined* (London: Longman, Green, Longman, Roberts & Green, 1862).

[27]Spurgeon, for his part, rarely addressed Colenso directly. He did, however, proclaim the following
regarding Jewish and Christian responses to Colenso's mathematical approach to the text: "In the
debate brought on by Colenso, we were able, in comparing notes, to feel the same zeal for the
value of the Old Testament and for the glory of the ever-blessed God. Whether we were Christians or Jews, we were equally zealous to repel the infidel assaults of the famous master of arithmetic." C. H. Spurgeon, "The Vine of Israel," sermon no. 3243, given May 9, 1878, from Psalm
80:14, *The Metropolitan Tabernacle Pulpit*, vol. 57 (London: Passmore & Alabaster, 1911), 150-51.

[28]Samuel Rolles Driver, *An Introduction to the Literature of the Old Testament* (Edinburgh: T&T
Clark, 1891).

dates for the writing of several other Old Testament books. These datings would have been familiar to biblical scholars working on the Continent, but not necessarily in Britain. Driver's volume, as Mark Noll observes, in some ways represented the "triumph" of higher criticism within British academic circles.[29]

Many of the developments within British Old Testament studies occurred during Spurgeon's lifetime. Jowett's controversial essay was published in 1860, just as Spurgeon returned from a successful preaching tour throughout France. As Colenso was publishing his commentary on the Pentateuch, Spurgeon was in the final stages of the construction of the Metropolitan Tabernacle's new building at Elephant and Castle. Finally, Driver's Old Testament *Introduction* appeared just a few short months before Spurgeon traveled on what would be his final trip to the French Riviera before his death in 1892. While Spurgeon had not studied either the Bible or Christian theology in a formal university setting, his appetite for scholarship led him to consult a wide range of biblical commentaries and surveys. Though he valued biblical scholarship, as we will see in the next section, Spurgeon was deeply critical of volumes that could cause Christians to doubt the divine inspiration or authority of the Bible.

SPURGEON'S THEOLOGY OF THE BIBLE

A sustained investigation of Spurgeon's biblical interpretation will benefit from a brief summary of his beliefs regarding the nature of the Bible. As we have seen, both before and after his conversion, the young Spurgeon frequently consulted biblical commentaries. In his essay against Roman Catholicism, written as a precocious fifteen-year-old in the months before his conversion, he suggested that Catholicism was actively subjugating the Bible to church tradition, writing that "the Bible, that light divine was taken from man and then like the blind he groped his way through life assured by his blind guide that tradition and man's invention—mere sparks flying upwards from the bottomless pit—were the light upon the wicket gate

---

[29]Mark A. Noll, *Between Faith and Criticism: Evangelicals, Scholarship, and the Bible in America*, 2nd ed. (Vancouver: Regent College Publishing, 2004), 72.

which leads to eternal life."[30] Following his conversion, he studied the ancient Greek language and began to study ancient history in order to further
immerse himself in the biblical landscape.

In his first published volume of sermons, coinciding with his first year
of pastoral ministry in London at the New Park Street Chapel, Spurgeon
included a sermon simply titled "The Bible," which provides helpful context
for his theology of the Bible and divine revelation. In the sermon, he insisted that God was the author working behind and through the human
writers, maintaining that the Bible is

> the writing of the living God: each letter was penned with an Almighty
> finger; each word in it dropped from the everlasting lips, each sentence was
> dictated by the Holy Spirit. . . . It is God's voice, not man's; the words are
> God's words, the words of the Eternal, the Invisible, the Almighty, the
> Jehovah of this earth.[31]

Spurgeon's emphasis on the plenary inspiration of the Bible was consistent
throughout his ministry. Over thirty years later, Spurgeon made similar
comments, suggesting that his listeners "accept every syllable of God's Word
as infallible while we turn our unbelief towards man and his philosophies
and infidelities!"[32] While he claimed that appeals to "reason" potentially led
people away from a simple faith in the authority of the Bible, Spurgeon went
on to say, "Reason! Thy place is to stand and find out what this volume
means, not to tell what this book ought to say. Come thou, my reason, my
intellect, sit thou down and listen, for these words are the words of God."[33]
Formal articulation of the doctrine of biblical inerrancy was then in its in-
fancy and centered largely in conservative Protestant circles in the United
States, yet Spurgeon appears to have championed similar ideas in this
sermon, particularly when he proclaimed, "O Bible! It cannot be said of any

---

[30]C. H. Spurgeon, *Antichrist and Her Brood; or, Popery Unmasked*, 5. Located in Box A2.06 in the
   Heritage Room at Spurgeon's College, London. The "wicket gate" is a reference to John Bunyan's
   Pilgrim's Progress. In the allegorical novel, the gate is the entryway to the King's Highway.
[31]C. H. Spurgeon, "The Bible," sermon no. 15, given March 18, 1855, from Hosea 8:12, *The New Park
   Street Pulpit*, vol. 1 (London: Passmore & Alabaster, 1855), 110.
[32]C. H. Spurgeon, "Folly of Unbelief," sermon no. 1980, given August 28, 1887, from Luke 24:25,
   The Metropolitan Tabernacle Pulpit, vol. 33 (London: Passmore & Alabaster, 1887), 487.
[33]Spurgeon, "Bible," 111.

other book, that it is perfect and pure; but of thee we can declare all wisdom is gathered up in thee, without a particle of folly. This is the judge that ends the strife where wit and reason fail. This is the book untainted by any error; but is pure, unalloyed, perfect truth. Why? Because God wrote it."[34]

Spurgeon did not seem to sense any tension between divine and human authorship of the Bible, embracing an almost dictation model of verbal, plenary inspiration. He often looked to the Princeton theologian Charles Hodge (1797–1878) for guidance on theological matters, particularly when it came to his theological positions on the nature of the Bible.[35] In Spurgeon's words, "The more we use Hodge, the more we value him."[36] The mid-nineteenth century is noted as a significant time in the development and further articulation of the doctrine of biblical inerrancy. Hodge sought to refute trends in higher criticism by questioning whether human rationalism was able adequately to evaluate whether the Bible was divinely inspired, and hence, inerrant.[37] In his popular *Systematic Theology*, originally published in 1871, Hodge argued that from a Rationalist's perspective, "the Scriptures, therefore, abound with misapprehensions, with inconclusive arguments, and accommodations to Jewish errors, superstitions, and popular beliefs. It is the office of reason to sift these incongruous materials, and separate the wheat from the chaff."[38] Hodge viewed this approach as unacceptable, writing, "Rationalism assumes that the human intelligence is the measure of all truth. This is an insane presumption on the part of such a creature as man."[39]

---

[34]Spurgeon, "Bible," 111.

[35]Tom Nettles, *Living by Revealed Truth: The Life and Pastoral Theology of Charles Haddon Spurgeon* (Ross-shire, UK: Christian Focus, 2013), 194-95; Larsen, *People of One Book*, 249.

[36]C. H. Spurgeon, *Lectures to My Students*, vol. 4, *Commenting and Commentaries; Lectures Addressed to the Students of the Pastors' College, Metropolitan Tabernacle* (New York: Sheldon and Company, 1876), 247; Spurgeon corresponded with Hodge's son, Archibald Alexander Hodge (1823–1886), with regard to a manuscript of one of his father's addresses. Their correspondence was dated 1879, which was shortly after Hodge's father's death and not long after A. A. Hodge had been named the principal of Princeton Theological Seminary. See C. H. Spurgeon, *C. H. Spurgeon's Autobiography, Compiled from His Diary, Letters, and Records, by His Wife and His Private Secretary*, vol. 4, *1878–1892* (Chicago: Fleming H. Revell, 1900), 298.

[37]See George Michael Coon, "Recasting Inerrancy: The Doctrine of Scripture in Carl Henry and the Old Princeton School" (PhD thesis, University of St. Michael's College, 2009), 69-79.

[38]Charles Hodge, *Systematic Theology*, vol. 1 (New York: Charles Scribner, 1872), 40.

[39]Hodge, *Systematic Theology*, 1:41.

In addition to Hodge, Spurgeon drew support for his position on biblical inspiration from the Swiss theologian Louis Gaussen (1790–1863), republishing a translation of Gaussen's volume on the subject, titled *Theopneustia*, during the height of the Downgrade Controversy.[40] The book, originally published in Paris in 1840, defended a dictation model of inspiration, aimed in part at challenging the conclusions of several prominent scholars, including de Wette and Michaelis.[41] Spurgeon, preaching to his congregation in an 1885 sermon, suggested that he read widely throughout the fields of biblical and theological studies and proclaimed,

> If you can read a tainted book that denies the inspiration of the Scriptures, and attacks the truth of God, and if you derive any profit from it, you must be a very different being from myself. I have to read such books, I must read them sometimes to know what is being said by the enemies of the gospel, that I may defend the faith, and help the weaklings of the flock, but it is a sorry business.[42]

Though Spurgeon did not explicitly emphasize the doctrine of inerrancy in his sermons or other writings, his confidence in the Bible's reliability was fundamentally rooted in what he believed to be its divine origin, and his belief in the truth of the gospel message hinged upon the divine inspiration of the biblical text.

With regard to translation, Spurgeon preferred the Authorized, or King James, Version (AV) of the Bible; however, Peter Morden is correct in observing that he was well aware of the translation errors contained within it.[43] He advised students to "correct where correction must be for truth's

---

[40]Louis Gaussen, *Theopneustia: The Plenary Inspiration of the Holy Scriptures. With a Prefatory Note by C. H. Spurgeon*, ed. B. W. Carr, trans. David Dundas Scott (London: Passmore & Alabaster, 1888). See also Kenneth J. Stewart, "A Bombshell of a Book: Gaussen's *Theopneustia* and Its Influence on Subsequent Evangelical Theology," *The Evangelical Quarterly* 75, no. 3 (2003): 228-29; Keith A. Ives, *Voices of Nonconformity: William Robertson Nicoll and the British Weekly* (Cambridge: Lutterworth Press, 2011), 119-21.

[41]See Stewart, "Bombshell of a Book," 220-22.

[42]C. H. Spurgeon, "Deadness and Quickening," sermon no. 2521, given October 29, 1885, from Psalm 119:37, *The Metropolitan Tabernacle Pulpit*, vol. 43 (London: Passmore & Alabaster, 1897), 280.

[43]Peter J. Morden, *"Communion with Christ and His People": The Spirituality of C. H. Spurgeon* (Oxford: Regent's Park College, 2010), 108.

sake, but never for the vainglorious display of your critical ability."[44] He admitted that the AV "is faulty in many places" but insisted that it "still is a grand work, taking it for all in all, and it is unwise to be making every old lady distrust the only Bible she can get at, or what is more likely, mistrust you for falling out with her cherished treasure."[45] In the latter years of Spurgeon's ministry, a major new English translation of the Bible was prepared and published by a body of renowned scholars.[46] The Revised Version (RV) was commissioned as an updated edition of the King James Version, which had been the standard English biblical text. Elijah Hixson has helpfully suggested that Spurgeon "often supported the critical text underlying the RV" yet he "disliked the RV as an English translation."[47] Spurgeon studied both Hebrew and Greek, which he referred to as the "two sacred languages," and while he valued critical engagement, he continued using the AV, though he did occasionally amend its translation.[48]

Finally, Spurgeon emphasized that lay Christians, in reading the Bible, had an opportunity to engage directly with God. Cautioning his congregation against placing too much confidence in rote memorization, Spurgeon said that

> the mere words of Scripture are no better than any other words, only so far as they contain a higher and nobler sense. . . . Dear friend, you want to get the meaning—the inner sense. Nuts must be cracked, so must Scripture—you must get out the meaning or you have got nothing. . . . Pray, dear friends, as you read the Scriptures, that God may illuminate you; ask that you may not read in the dark as many do, who therefore stumble at the words in disobedience. The best interpreter of a book is generally the man who wrote it. The Holy Ghost wrote the Scriptures. Go to him to get their meaning, and you will not be misled.[49]

---

[44]Spurgeon, *Lectures to My Students*, 4:57.

[45]Spurgeon, *Lectures to My Students*, 4:57.

[46]The RV had a staggered release: the New Testament was published in 1881, and the Old Testament in 1885. The translation of the Apocrypha was not published until 1894.

[47]Elijah Hixson, "New Testament Textual Criticism in the Ministry of Charles Haddon Spurgeon," *Journal of the Evangelical Theological Society* 57, no. 3 (2014): 557.

[48]C. H. Spurgeon, *C. H. Spurgeon's Autobiography, Compiled from His Diary, Letters, and Records, by His Wife and His Private Secretary*, vol. 2, *1854–1860* (Chicago: Fleming H. Revell, 1899), 237.

[49]C. H. Spurgeon, "The Secret Food and the Public Name," sermon no. 1079, from Jeremiah 15:16, n.d., *The Metropolitan Tabernacle Pulpit*, vol. 18 (London: Passmore & Alabaster, 1872), 616.

For Spurgeon, the Holy Spirit was the guide for faithful readers, directing them to the truth contained within the Bible's pages. He did not, however, go so far as to intimate that the Holy Spirit's illumination would supersede human study. Spurgeon suggested that his congregation should read through individual biblical books in their entirety, "carefully and prayerfully," rather than "surface-skimming." He urged his listeners to read the Bible deliberately, for studying "verse by verse and word by word" would mean readers would be "far more likely to find what was the true meaning of the words which the Holy Spirit used."[50] Thus, in Spurgeon's estimation, readers of the Bible could not simply rely on the strength of their own research, nor could they simply skim the text and await the Holy Spirit's illumination; rather, the two must go hand in hand.

Spurgeon's advice, however, does not necessarily reflect his own practice nor the instruction that he gave to his students. Rather than systematically preaching through books of the Bible, throughout his ministry he delivered sermons drawn from either single verses or small groups of verses. When he discussed the topic of sermon text selection with his students, Spurgeon suggested that the best method was to "pause over our opened Bibles, and devoutly seek to be guided to that portion of Holy Writ which shall be most likely to be made useful."[51] He was critical of the clergy of the Established Church who followed a liturgical calendar, referring to this practice as a "slavish habit of following the course of the sun and the revolution of the months, instead of waiting upon the Holy Spirit."[52] Rather than following a calendar or working through a particular book of the Bible, Spurgeon believed that the Holy Spirit would guide him to the right text at the right time. While he was quick to assign the guidance of the Holy Spirit in his selection of a text, Spurgeon admitted that he held this alongside hours of "hard labour" that he spent "manipulating topics, ruminating upon points of doctrine, making skeletons out of verses and then

---

[50]Spurgeon, "Secret Food," 615.

[51]C. H. Spurgeon, *Lectures to My Students*, vol. 1, *A Selection from Addresses Delivered to the Students of the Pastors' College, Metropolitan Tabernacle* (London: Passmore & Alabaster, 1875), 84.

[52]Spurgeon, *Lectures to My Students*, 1:87.

burying every bone of them in the catacombs of oblivion."[53] His view of the role of the Holy Spirit in text selection was so strong that he recounted a story when, while singing the final hymn before he was meant to preach, a text on the opposite page of his Bible, in his words, "sprang upon me like a lion from a thicket, with vastly more power than I had felt when considering the text which I had chosen."[54] In rather striking language for a Particular Baptist, he recounted, "I was naturally desirous to run in the track which I had carefully planned, but the other text would take no refusal, and seemed to tug at my skirts, crying, 'No, no, you must preach from me. God would have you follow me.'"[55] Spurgeon was particularly emphatic on his text selection because he believed that the whole of the worship service should be carefully arranged to convert any unbelievers who might be in attendance, which was evident when he said, "When we remember that the salvation of a soul may hang, instrumentally, upon the choice of a hymn, we should not consider so small a matter as the selection of the psalms and hymns to be a trifle."[56] Thus text selection was viewed with conversionistic intent.

In addition to the role of the Holy Spirit in biblical interpretation, Spurgeon also closely linked Christ to the text. In a sermon titled "The Word a Sword," Spurgeon told his congregation, "As Christ reveals God, so this Book reveals Christ, and therefore it partakes, as the Word of God, in all the attributes of the Incarnate Word; and we may say many of the same things of the written Word as that of the embodied Word; in fact, they are now so linked together that it would be impossible to divide them."[57] Christocentrism was central to Spurgeon's engagement with the biblical text. As we will see in the sections that follow, this emphasis would lead him to include discussions of Christ in texts where Christ did not appear either explicitly or implicitly. We can also see Spurgeon's christocentrism at work in the preface to his first collection of sermons, particularly in a

---

[53]Spurgeon, *Lectures to My Students*, 1:88.
[54]Spurgeon, *Lectures to My Students*, 1:95.
[55]Spurgeon, *Lectures to My Students*, 1:95.
[56]Spurgeon, *Lectures to My Students*, 1:84.
[57]C. H. Spurgeon, "The Word a Sword," sermon no. 2010, given May 17, 1887, from Hebrews 4:12, *The Metropolitan Tabernacle Pulpit*, vol. 34 (London: Passmore & Alabaster, 1888), 110.

section where he outlined his fervent intentions for his published works. The paragraph, which is worth quoting at length, highlights both the christocentric and evangelistic essences of Spurgeon's preaching:

> Our hope is, that inferior matters in dispute will not so much be regarded as "the things which we have spoken touching the king." Jesus is the Truth. We believe in Him,—not merely in his words. He himself is Doctor and Doctrine, Revealer and Revelation, the Illuminator and the Light of Men. *He is exalted in every word of truth, because he is its sum and substance.* He sits above the gospel, like a prince on his own throne. Doctrine is most precious when we see it distilling from his lips and embodied in his person. Sermons are valuable in proportion as they speak of him and point to him. A Christless gospel is no gospel and a Christless discourse is the cause of merriment to devils.[58]

Additionally, Morden has helpfully observed that, along with many preachers of his day, Spurgeon's "dominant argument for the truth and power of the scriptures" was an experiential one.[59] This is evident in the aforementioned sermon, where he went on to argue that Christians accepted the Bible

> as the very word of the living God . . . not so much because there are external evidences which go to show its authenticity—a great many of us do not know anything about those evidences, and probably never shall— but because we discern an inward evidence in the words themselves. They have come to us with a power no other words ever had in them, and we cannot be argued out of our conviction of their superlative excellence and divine authority.[60]

Finally, while Spurgeon championed biblical infallibility throughout his ministry, there was a noted increase in his references to the nature of the Bible coinciding with the Downgrade Controversy of 1887 and 1888.[61] The

---

[58]C. H. Spurgeon, "Preface," *The New Park Street Pulpit*, vol. 1 (London: Passmore & Alabaster, 1855), vi. Emphasis mine.

[59]Morden, *"Communion with Christ,"* 112; See also Mark Hopkins, *Nonconformity's Romantic Generation: Evangelical and Liberal Theologies in Victorian England* (Milton Keynes, UK: Paternoster, 2004), 135-36.

[60]Spurgeon, "Secret Food," 618-19.

[61]The Downgrade Controversy will be discussed further in chapter five.

Downgrade Controversy was given its name by members of the Baptist Union who felt that several distinctive theological traits of the union were being "downgraded" by those who shared more liberal opinions.[62] The doctrine of substitutionary atonement, as well as the authority and inspiration of the Bible were among Spurgeon's deepest concerns. Spurgeon became a figure that conservative members of the Baptist Union could rally around. Morden notes that the 1887 volume of the *Metropolitan Tabernacle Pulpit* featured eight different sermons relating in some way to the topic of biblical infallibility, the following year's volume contained eleven references.[63] The controversy took its toll on Spurgeon, who went so far as to say in written correspondence that it was not his many health ailments but the Downgrade Controversy that was killing him.[64] For the purposes of the present study, it should be noted that the areas causing the greatest concern to Spurgeon, namely those that connected to the atonement and biblical authority, included theological elements that were essential to his crucicentric and conversionistic hermeneutical method.

SPURGEON AND OLD TESTAMENT COMMENTATORS

Before approaching Spurgeon's Old Testament sermons, it will be helpful to highlight a cross section of commentaries that he particularly favored. A key source for this task remains Spurgeon's *Commenting and Commentaries*, originally published in 1876 as a guide for students of the Pastors' College. His summaries of commentaries were not intended to serve as comprehensive reviews; rather, they generally provided two- to three-sentence overviews of what Spurgeon perceived to be the key strengths and weaknesses of the particular volumes. One contemporary review of *Commenting and Commentaries* suggested that the volume allowed

---

[62]The best historical survey of the Downgrade Controversy remains Hopkins, *Nonconformity's Romantic Generation*, 193-248. The controversy also receives a mention in Noll, *Between Faith and Criticism*, 75-79.

[63]Morden, "Communion with Christ," 115.

[64]Larsen, *People of One Book*, 247; Mark Hopkins, in a popular-level article, referred to the Downgrade Controversy as "the most disastrous episode in Spurgeon's career." Mark Hopkins, "The Down-Grade Controversy: What Caused Spurgeon to Start the Most Bitter Fight of His Life?," *Christian History* 10, no. 29 (1991).

Spurgeon to convey "his peculiar views with remarkable constancy."[65] The book also contained two lectures, which focused on the interplay between the academic nature of commentaries and general biblical interpretation and offered practical advice to pastors. From there, Spurgeon separated the books by type. Single-volume commentaries on the entirety of the Bible were evaluated, followed by single-volume Old and New Testament commentaries, respectively. Finally, Spurgeon evaluated commentaries on each of the sixty-six individual books of the biblical canon. In all, he surveyed 1,439 commentaries.

The two lectures that precede the commentary survey were titled "A Chat About Commentaries" and "On Commenting." In both lectures, Spurgeon spoke about commentaries in broad terms, addressing many authors from the Reformation era to the present day. Favorite commentators emerge in the course of his assessments; perhaps the foremost was the Nonconformist commentator Matthew Henry (1662–1714). Henry, who was born in Wales but spent the majority of his life in England, wrote a multi-volume commentary that spanned the entire Old Testament, as well as the Gospels and book of Acts.[66] In one of the lectures that preceded the commentary survey, Spurgeon said of Henry that he

> delights in apposition and alliteration. . . . He is not critical, but he quietly gives the result of an accurate critical knowledge of the original fully up to the best critics of his time. He is not versed in the manners and customs of the East, for the Holy Land was not so accessible as in our day; but he is deeply spiritual, heavenly, and profitable; finding good matter in every text, and from all deducing most practical and judicious lessons.[67]

Just behind Henry in Spurgeon's estimation was the Reformer John Calvin (1509–1564). In describing Calvin's work, Spurgeon praised his interpretive method, noting that

---

[65]"Commenting and Commentaries," *The Literary World; a Monthly Review of Current Literature* (August 1, 1876), 29.

[66]Matthew Henry, *A Commentary on the Whole Bible, Wherein Each Chapter Is Summed up in Its Contents; the Sacred Text Inserted at Large in Distinct Paragraphs; Each Paragraph Reduced to Its Proper Heads, the Sense Given, and Largely Illustrated*, 3 vols. (London: London Printing and Publishing, 1710).

[67]Spurgeon, *Lectures to My Students*, 4:110.

in his expositions his is not always what moderns would call Calvinistic; that is to say, where Scripture maintains the doctrine of predestination and grace he flinches in no degree, but inasmuch as some Scriptures bear the impress of human free action and responsibility, he does not shun to expound their meanings in all fairness and integrity. He was no trimmer and pruner of texts.[68]

Spurgeon also cautioned his readers concerning strong biases on the part of the authors. This is evident in his treatment of John Gill, the former pastor of the New Park Street Chapel. Spurgeon, aware that Gill leaned toward a high Calvinist theological position, qualified his recommendation accordingly. He identified Gill as an expert Hebraist and commented that "his great work on the Holy Scriptures is greatly prized at the present day by the best authorities."[69] In the following sentence, however, Spurgeon noted that even "amid the decadence of his own rigid system, and the disrepute of even more moderate Calvinism, Gill's laurels are still green."[70] He added in reference to Gill's high Calvinism that "when he falls upon a text which is not congenial with his creed," he "hacks and hews terribly to bring the word of God into a more systematic shape."[71]

Beyond the introductory lectures, Spurgeon's survey of biblical commentaries presented a diverse range of biblical scholarship spanning several centuries. His remarks on the volumes often included practical considerations, including whether he considered the book to be good value for its price. He encouraged students to purchase some commentaries regardless of their cost while suggesting that others were worth consulting if they were able to find them in a library. On this point, in the preface to the survey, Spurgeon wrote that

> students do not find it easy to choose which books to buy, and their slender stores are often wasted on books of a comparatively worthless kind. If I can save a poor man from spending his money for that which is not bread, or, by

---

[68]Spurgeon, *Lectures to My Students*, 4:16.
[69]Spurgeon, *Lectures to My Students*, 4:22.
[70]Spurgeon, *Lectures to My Students*, 4:22.
[71]Spurgeon, *Lectures to My Students*, 4:23.

directing a brother to a good book, may enable him to dig deeper into the
mines of truth, I shall be well repaid.[72]

Spurgeon offered his own assessments of both the pastoral practicality and
theological fidelity of many of the volumes. In his section on the Pentateuch, for instance, Spurgeon praised the work of E. W. Hengstenberg
(1802–1869), a scholar at the University of Berlin, recommended another
for weeknight instruction but not preaching, and referred to another,
written by an eighteenth-century Church of England clergyman, as "a pile
of paper, valuable to housemaids for lighting fires."[73] The levity present in
some reviews was intentional; Spurgeon indicated that he sought to use a
"degree of pleasantry" in his comments, "for a catalogue is a dry affair, and
as much for my own sake as for that of my readers, I have indulged the
mirthful vein here and there."[74]

Amid Spurgeon's combination of mirth and critique, the consistent
trend evident throughout the pages of *Commenting and Commentaries* is
his dedication to guide students toward what he believed to be the best
resources available, whether they were edited Puritan sermons or modern
critical commentaries. For Spurgeon the best material, more often than not,
consisted of books that either supported or could be used to support interpretations that were both crucicentric and evangelistic. His estimation of a
book could rise or fall based upon the manner in which the author handled
particular discussions of the work of Christ and the atonement. This is
evident, among other places, in his treatment of selected works on the book
of Isaiah. For instance, Spurgeon commended a commentator for keeping
"to the literal sense" and being "severe upon spiritualizers of whose vagaries
he gives specimens"; however, as he continued his review, he noted that "in
aiming at one excellence he misses others, and fails to see Christ where he
certainly is, thus rendering his remarks less valuable to the Christian
mind."[75] This is contrasted with his review of the Yorkshire Puritan Thomas

---

[72]Spurgeon, *Lectures to My Students*, 4:5.
[73]Spurgeon, *Lectures to My Students*, 4:75-79.
[74]Spurgeon, *Lectures to My Students*, 4:5.
[75]Spurgeon, *Lectures to My Students*, 4:177. Review of Samuel White, *Commentary on Isaiah,
Wherein the Literal Sense is Briefly Explained* (London: Printed by J. B. for Arthur Collins, 1709).

Calvert (1606–1679), whose *Mel Cœli, Medulla Evangelii: or The Prophet Isaiah's Crucifix*, originally published in 1657, met with Spurgeon's glowing endorsement.[76] Calvert's work was, according to Spurgeon, "precious and practical. Just what the title would lead us to expect—marrow and fatness; honey from the Rock, Christ Jesus."[77] Spurgeon appreciated both academic rigor and critical interpretation, but he relaxed his convictions on both if he thought that a volume would help to enable preachers to present Christ more vividly in their sermons. This is perhaps most evident in his discussion of the work of Robert Hawker (1753–1827), an evangelical Anglican clergyman who wrote a popular level work titled *Dr. Hawker's Poor Man's Commentary*.[78] Of Dr. Hawker, Spurgeon noted that he was

> the very least of commentators in the matter of criticism; he had no critical capacity, and no ability whatever as an interpreter of the letter; but *he sees Jesus,* and that is a sacred gift which is most precious whether the owner be a critic or no. It is to be confessed that he occasionally sees Jesus where Jesus is not legitimately to be seen. He allows his reason to be mastered by his affections, which, vice as it is, is not the worst fault in the world. There is always such a savor of the Lord Jesus Christ in Dr. Hawker that you cannot read him without profit.[79]

Spurgeon found Hawker's approach of viewing Christ as present in every Psalm particularly problematic but ultimately defended his work, suggesting to his readers that they should "not as a substantial dish, but as a condiment, place the Plymouth vicar's work on the table. His writing is all sugar, and you will know how to use it, not devouring it in lumps, but using it to flavor other things."[80]

Many of the critical works featured in *Commenting and Commentaries* appear to be presented only to be heavily criticized or simply dismissed.

---

[76]Thomas Calvert, *Mel Cœli, Medulla Evangelii: or The Prophet Isaiah's Crucifix. Being an Exposition of the Fifty Third Chapter of the Prophecie of Isaiah* [. . .] (London: Printed for Tho. Pierrepont, 1657). Spurgeon referred to an edition published in 1867 but did not include the publisher's information.

[77]Spurgeon, *Lectures to My Students*, 4:178.

[78]Robert Hawker, *Dr. Hawker's Poor Man's Commentary* (London: Printed for T. Williams by W. Nicholson, 1816).

[79]Spurgeon, *Lectures to My Students*, 4:29.

[80]Spurgeon, *Lectures to My Students*, 4:29.

Conversely, he placed a high value on volumes that emphasized a crucified Christ and could be used to forward an evangelistic impetus. This is evident throughout his commentary survey, but particularly in his review of a work by Henry Law (1797–1884), the Anglican dean of Gloucester, which he praised thoroughly, noting that it was "deservedly popular. Simple, instructive, full of Christ. Law abounds in gospel."[81]

SPURGEON'S INTERPRETATION
OF OLD TESTAMENT HISTORICAL BOOKS

As we have noted, the Old Testament historical books faced increased scrutiny in the nineteenth century, particularly in the light of contemporary advances in linguistic and archaeological work. For his part, Spurgeon frequently preached from the Old Testament historical books, but while he was interested in the archaeological explorations that had begun throughout the Near East, his sermons did not always reflect his reading. Spurgeon generally assumed that the historical texts in the Bible were factual and eschewed suggestions to the contrary. While Spurgeon was deeply unsatisfied with the conclusions of many historical-critical scholars, he occasionally consulted them and even recommended some to his students. As space does not permit a full investigation of Spurgeon's views of each Old Testament historical book or every controversial passage, the balance of the chapter will consider a series of representative sermons that provide further evidence of the degree to which crucicentrism and evangelistic intent drove Spurgeon's interpretation.

The book of Genesis contains significant theological themes that continue throughout the subsequent biblical canon. Among them is Genesis 3:15, which is called the *protoevangelium* by biblical and theological scholars. The existing collection of sermonic material from Spurgeon indicates that he preached on this text twice, once in 1876 and again in 1890.[82]

---

[81]Spurgeon, *Lectures to My Students*, 4:78. Review of Henry Law, *Christ Is All: The Gospel in the Pentateuch* (London: Religious Tract Society, 1867).

[82]See, respectively, C. H. Spurgeon, "Christ the Conqueror of Satan," sermon no. 1326, given November 26, 1876, from Genesis 3:15, *Metropolitan Tabernacle Pulpit*, vol. 22 (London: Passmore & Alabaster, 1876), 661; "The Serpent's Sentence," sermon no. 2165, given September 21, 1890, from Genesis 3:14-15, *The Metropolitan Tabernacle Pulpit*, vol. 36 (London: Passmore & Alabaster,

The verse in question, which takes place during the narrative of Adam and Eve's expulsion from the Garden of Eden, reads, "And I will put enmity between thee and the woman, and between thy seed and her seed; it shall bruise thy head, and thou shalt bruise his heel" (Gen 3:15). Preaching in 1876, Spurgeon began his sermon by referring to the verse as "the first gospel sermon that was ever delivered upon the surface of the earth."[83] Spurgeon's crucicentrism and conversionism were on display as he boldly proclaimed, "We preach Christ crucified, and every sermon shakes the gates of hell. We bring sinners to Jesus by the Spirit's power, and every convert is a stone torn down from the wall of Satan's mighty castle."[84] His conclusion further emphasized the conversionistic interpretation of the text, suggesting to his listeners that they might consider their "reception of Christ's righteousness as an instalment of the final overthrow of the devil."[85] Spurgeon's other sermons addressing the Adam and Eve narrative had moments of direct crucicentric application as well, with language like "escape for thy life . . . escape to mount Calvary"[86] or that those listeners who realized themselves to be in the same predicament as Adam and Eve could know that their sins "were put away by him when he bore our sins in his body on the tree."[87] While this narrative has been interpreted christologically from the early days of the Christian tradition, Spurgeon also connected it to evangelistic aims. Furthermore, he often wove a dichotomy between the garden and the cross into sermons that were drawn from texts

1890), 517. Additionally, Rev. Liam Garvie of Charlotte Chapel, Edinburgh, graciously invited me to see his copy of Spurgeon's handwritten sermon corrections from "The Serpent's Sentence."

[83]Spurgeon, "Christ the Conqueror of Satan," 661.

[84]Spurgeon, "Christ the Conqueror of Satan," 665.

[85]Spurgeon, "Christ the Conqueror of Satan," 671.

[86]C. H. Spurgeon, "God's First Words to the First Sinner," sermon no. 412, given October 6, 1861, from Genesis 3:9, *The Metropolitan Tabernacle Pulpit*, vol. 7 (London: Passmore & Alabaster, 1861), 520.

[87]C. H. Spurgeon, "A Look and Its Lessons," sermon no. 3194, given October 12, 1873, from Isaiah 51:1, *The Metropolitan Tabernacle Pulpit*, vol. 56 (London: Passmore & Alabaster, 1910), 201. Spurgeon connected this scene from the Garden of Eden to Christ's crucifixion in a number of other examples. See, for example: "Grace Abounding," sermon no. 3304, given April 15, 1866, from Romans 5:20, *The Metropolitan Tabernacle Pulpit*, vol. 58 (London: Passmore & Alabaster, 1912), 253-61; "The Water and the Blood," sermon no. 3311, from John 19:34, n.d., *The Metropolitan Tabernacle Pulpit*, vol. 58 (London: Passmore & Alabaster, 1912), 337-46; "How God Comes to Man," sermon no. 2900, given July 13, 1876, from Genesis 3:8-9, *The Metropolitan Tabernacle Pulpit*, vol. 50 (London: Passmore & Alabaster, 1904), 433-42.

that mentioned neither event.[88] This differs from several of his contemporaries. The evangelical Free Church of Scotland minister Robert Candlish
(1806–1873), for instance, observed,

> How far the phrase, "the seed of the woman" . . . should be limited to the
> Messiah personally is not very clear. . . . Undoubtedly it is Christ who is prin-
> cipally pointed out; though, at the same time, as the seed of the serpent may
> have a wider signification, denoting all of his party among men . . . so, also,
> the seed of the woman may'be held to mean all who take part with the Lord.[89]

John Henry Newman (1801–1890), when a young clergyman with evangelical sympathies in the Church of England, preached a sermon on the
same text in October 1825.[90] Newman stressed that Adam and Eve could
not have known the full christological magnitude of the promise set out in
Genesis 3:15; however, he did remind his congregation that they themselves
were able to grasp the theological significance of the text. This is evident
particularly in his concluding remarks, where he said that "while the good
men of old were left to collect, as they could, scattered intimations on the
subject, and gather up what gleanings of knowledge the fall had left, *for us*
the Son of man has reaped an harvest, and to us it is given to know Him by
whom life and immortality are brought to light."[91] While Candlish,
Newman, and Spurgeon took different approaches in their interpretation,
each of them identified a christological meaning in the Old Testament
passage. Of the three preachers, only Spurgeon interpreted the passage in
both crucicentric and conversionistic terms. Whereas Candlish and
Newman offered christological foreshadowing in their sermons, Spurgeon

---

[88]See, for instance, C. H. Spurgeon, "A Hearer in Disguise," sermon no. 584, given July 31, 1864,
from 1 Kings 14:6, *The Metropolitan Tabernacle Pulpit*, vol. 10 (London: Passmore & Alabaster,
1864), 449-60; "The Perpetuity of the Law of God," sermon no. 1660, given May 21, 1882, from
Matthew 5:18, *The Metropolitan Tabernacle Pulpit*, vol. 28 (London: Passmore & Alabaster,
1882), 277-88.

[89]Robert Candlish, *Contributions Towards the Exposition of the Book of Genesis*, vol. 1 (Edinburgh:
Johnstone and Hunter, 1853), 101-2.

[90]Newman's much-discussed conversion to Roman Catholicism would not occur for another
twenty years.

[91]John Henry Newman, *Sermons 1824–1843*, ed. Vincent Ferrer Blehl, SJ, vol. 2, *Sermons on Biblical
History, Sin and Justification, the Christian Way of Life, and Biblical Theology* (Oxford: Clarendon
Press, 1993), 358.

invoked directly crucicentric language and directly inquired of his listeners which "side" they were on and whether they were "born from above."[92]

Spurgeon was not always at odds with broader evangelical interpretation, as we will see with another historical text, namely the episode concerning Moses and the bronze serpent in Numbers 21.[93] In the passage, the Israelites, while wandering through the desert, had been plagued by the bites of poisonous snakes. As the narrative continues, God issued a command to Moses to craft a snake made from bronze, place it on a pole, and consequently any Israelite who had been bitten could look at the bronze snake and be healed. In his introduction, Spurgeon employed crucicentric language as he said, "My tongue longs to resound Christ alone, and give forth no other strain, but Christ on the cross; Christ uplifted, the salvation of a dying world; Christ crucified, the life of poor dead sinners."[94] He went on to draw a connection between the plight of the Israelites and that of his listeners, proclaiming that "the children of Israel in the wilderness were bitten with fiery serpents, whose venom soon tainted their blood, and after intolerable pain, at last brought on death. Thou art much in the same condition."[95] Spurgeon returned to this text and preached a second sermon on it at the Metropolitan Tabernacle in 1879.[96] This sermon was a significant one, as Spurgeon noted that it would be the fifteen-hundredth sermon published during his tenure in London.[97] Throughout

---

[92]Spurgeon, "Serpent's Sentence," 525.

[93]Spurgeon's *Commenting and Commentaries* contains uncharacteristically few commentaries on Numbers and Deuteronomy, listing just five and two, respectively. Spurgeon attributed this to a general lack of available material. Two noteworthy commentators who made the cut were the English Presbyterian minister John Cumming (1807–1881) and the Irish Plymouth Brethren writer Charles Henry Mackintosh (1820–1896). The latter required "filtering" according to Spurgeon, on the basis that "Darbyism" gave his commentaries "an unpleasant and unhealthy savour." Spurgeon, *Lectures to My Students*, 4:98.

[94]C. H. Spurgeon, "Man's Ruin and God's Remedy," sermon no. 284, given November 20, 1859, from Numbers 21:8, *The New Park Street Pulpit*, vol. 5 (London: Passmore & Alabaster, 1859), 482.

[95]Spurgeon, "Man's Ruin," 481.

[96]C. H. Spurgeon, "Number 1,500, or, Lifting Up the Brazen Serpent," sermon no. 1500, given October 19, 1879, from Numbers 21:9, *The Metropolitan Tabernacle Pulpit*, vol. 25 (London: Passmore & Alabaster, 1879), 589-600.

[97]He acknowledged this during his sermon's introduction, saying,

I do not know of any instance in modern times in which fifteen hundred sermons have thus followed each other from the press from one person, and have continued to command a large circle of readers. I desire to utter most hearty thanksgivings to God for divine help

the latter sermon, Spurgeon emphasized connections between Numbers 21 and John 3, which directly referenced the bronze serpent while discussing Christ's work in first-century Palestine. In his conclusion, Spurgeon suggested that his congregation's evangelistic efforts would be a contemporary equivalent of raising the healing bronze snake in the air. "You put the brazen serpent into a chest and hide it away," he observed. "Is that right? Bring it out, and set it on a pole. Publish Christ and his salvation. He was never meant to be treated as a curiosity in a museum; he is intended to be exhibited in the highways that those who are sin-bitten may look at him."[98] In this instance, Spurgeon was not alone in his crucicentric and conversionistic reading of this text. The Scottish-born Nonconformist Alexander Maclaren (1826–1910), a contemporary of Spurgeon who pastored in Southampton and Manchester, interpreted the text along similar lines.[99] He wrote that "the sole condition of receiving into ourselves that new life which is free from all taint of sin, and is mighty enough to arrest the venom that is diffused through every drop of blood, is faith in Jesus lifted on the Cross to slay the sin that is slaying mankind."[100] Spurgeon's crucicentric and conversionistic reading of this text was, in one sense, similar to that of his contemporaries. However, his hermeneutical priorities led him to frequently use the brazen serpent narrative as a metaphor for Christ's crucifixion in sermons drawn from a variety of texts.[101]

---

in thinking out and uttering these sermons—sermons which have not merely been printed, but have been *read* with eagerness, and have also been translated into foreign tongues; sermons which are publicly read on this very Sabbath day in hundreds of places where a minister cannot be found; sermons which God has blessed to the conversion of multitudes of souls.

This sermon was referenced throughout several subsequent volumes and included in multiple anthologies of Spurgeon's noteworthy sermons. Spurgeon, "Number 1,500," 589.

[98]Spurgeon, "Number 1,500," 599.

[99]In a survey of books written on sermon illustrations, Spurgeon reserved high praise for Maclaren, writing that "this beloved author needs no letters of commendation to our readers. He hath dust of gold. Even his leaf should not wither. Here we have a wealth of symbol and emblem which cannot be surpassed." C. H. Spurgeon, *Lectures to My Students*, vol. 3, *The Art of Illustration; Addresses Delivered to the Students of the Pastors' College, Metropolitan Tabernacle* (London: Passmore & Alabaster, 1905), 182.

[100]Alexander Maclaren, *The Books of Exodus, Leviticus, and Numbers* (London: Hodder & Stoughton, 1907), 367.

[101]See, for instance, C. H. Spurgeon, "The Pierced One Pierces the Heart," sermon no. 575, given June 19, 1864, from Zechariah 12:10, *The Metropolitan Tabernacle Pulpit*, vol. 10 (London:

Further along in the historical books, Spurgeon preached a number of sermons from the book of Joshua. Preaching from Joshua 1:11, which reads, "Pass through the host, and command the people," Spurgeon leapt from the context of the ancient Israelite army straight to the contemporary church. The first line of his sermon illustrates this as he said, "Believers are called to be good soldiers of Jesus Christ."[102] In the balance of the sermon, he contrasted the spiritual and moral discipline of the church to the Army Discipline and Regulation Bill, which had recently been brought before the House of Commons. As one who frequently highlighted militaristic illustrations in his sermons, Spurgeon linked the charges of desertion and abandonment of a soldier's post to Christians who forsook their personal evangelistic obligations.[103] After quoting a line from the military regulations that condemned any soldier who "shamefully casts away his arms, ammunition, or tools in the presence of the enemy," he exhorted his congregation to "speak up for the blessed truth, and stand to your gun; this will gall the enemy, and protect yourself. Rally to the colours, and wrap them around your heart when they seem to be in peril; I mean, the blood-red colours of the cross of Christ."[104] In the closing paragraph of the sermon, Spurgeon bade any potential deserters in his congregation to "come to Christ, he will receive you graciously, and love you freely, and his anger shall be turned away from you."[105] Spurgeon was not alone in interpreting the opening of Joshua in a christological context. Alexander Maclaren also directed his readers to a militaristic metaphor, though his sermon reflected neither crucicentric nor conversionistic language.[106] For Maclaren, the text

---

Passmore & Alabaster, 1864), 341-52; "A Sermon to Open Neglecters and Nominal Followers of Religion," sermon no. 742, given March 24, 1867, from Matthew 21:28-32, *The Metropolitan Tabernacle Pulpit*, vol. 13 (London: Passmore & Alabaster, 1867), 169-80; "The Sprinkling of the Blood of the Sacrifice," sermon no. 1780, given May 11, 1884, from Leviticus 4:6-7, *The Metropolitan Tabernacle Pulpit*, vol. 30 (London: Passmore & Alabaster, 1884), 265-76.

[102]C. H. Spurgeon, "Discipline in Christ's Army," sermon no. 3188, given July 13, 1879, from Joshua 1:11, *The Metropolitan Tabernacle Pulpit*, vol. 56 (London: Passmore & Alabaster, 1910), 121.

[103]This is perhaps most notable in C. H. Spurgeon, *The Greatest Fight in the World (Final Manifesto)* (New York: Funk & Wagnalls, 1891). Militaristic language was common throughout the Victorian Christian world, perhaps typified most by General Booth and the Salvation Army.

[104]Spurgeon, "Discipline in Christ's Army," 124.

[105]Spurgeon, "Discipline in Christ's Army," 132.

[106]Alexander Maclaren, *The Books of Deuteronomy, Joshua, Judges, Ruth, and First Book of Samuel* (London: Hodder & Stoughton, 1906), 92.

was fundamentally concerned with obedience to the law.[107] Spurgeon's evangelistic preaching from the book of Joshua was not limited to these sermons and texts. In an 1877 sermon to the London Missionary Society, he returned to the military themes in Joshua to rally support for the missionary endeavors of the Society as well as the broader domestic work of Christians in London. This is particularly evident when he observed that "if we ever neglect to render universal service as a church in the cause of Christ we shall depart from our trust and call, for the Lord has sent all his disciples to testify of him and contend against sin." "He has," he added, "sent us all to make known everywhere, according to our ability, the glad tidings of his salvation."[108] This sermon, in a similar manner to other addresses Spurgeon offered to Christian societies, shows a shift in his traditional style, in which Christian activism was moved to the foreground, and conversionism and crucicentrism became the basis for his exhortation rather than the substance of the exhortation itself.

These illustrations might indicate that Spurgeon routinely bypassed the context of the verses that he preached. But this is not necessarily the case. In numerous instances of sermons preached from Old Testament historical narratives, Spurgeon's delivery remained tightly focused on the passage and its context, though even in these sermons he often concluded with a turn toward a crucified Christ and an evangelistic invitation.[109] As we have seen, it was through an Old Testament sermon preached in the language of crucicentrism and conversionism that Spurgeon himself was converted, and his own sermons indicate that he felt it his duty always to preach Christ regardless of his text. George Landow observes that "Spurgeon, who

---

[107] Maclaren, *Books of Deuteronomy, Joshua*, 98.

[108] C. H. Spurgeon, "All the People at Work for Jesus," sermon no. 1358, given May 9, 1877, from Joshua 7:3; 8:1, *The Metropolitan Tabernacle Pulpit*, vol. 23 (London: Passmore & Alabaster, 1877), 328.

[109] See, for instance, C. H. Spurgeon, "The Snare of the Fowler," sermons no. 124-25, given March 29, 1857, from Psalm 91:3, *The New Park Street Pulpit*, vol. 3 (London: Passmore & Alabaster, 1857), 137-44; "Hezekiah and the Ambassadors, or Vainglory Rebuked," sermon no. 704, given August 5, 1866, from 2 Kings 20:12-13, *The Metropolitan Tabernacle Pulpit*, vol. 12 (London: Passmore & Alabaster, 1866), 433-44; "A Miniature Portrait of Joseph," sermon no. 1610, given July 24, 1881, from Genesis 39:2, *The Metropolitan Tabernacle Pulpit*, vol. 27 (London: Passmore & Alabaster, 1881), 413-24; "Who Found It Out?," sermon no. 1903, given June 6, 1886, from 2 Kings 7:3-7, *The Metropolitan Tabernacle Pulpit*, vol. 32 (London: Passmore & Alabaster, 1886), 301-12.

fervently believes that the Old Testament types can permit the prepared worshipper to experience the presence of Christ in both his own life and that of ancient believers, thus draws upon his own conversion as he moves from a merely explanatory to a dramatic, meditative mode."[110] Landow's emphasis on the autobiographical element in Spurgeon's preaching helps to set his evangelistic work in context, and this is evident in many of his Old Testament sermons. For instance, in a sermon drawn from 1 Samuel 7:12, Spurgeon devoted the majority of his text to explaining the historical and theological context of the place given the name Ebenezer.[111] The immediate context of the verse establishes a narrative whereby the Israelites, under Samuel's leadership, fought a battle against the Philistines at a place called Mizpah. The Israelites were victorious, according to the chapter, because they followed Samuel's instruction and confessed their sins, following which he sacrificed a lamb as a burnt offering to God. At this moment, the advancing Philistine army encountered thunder sent from God, and the Israelite army attacked them amid the confusion. Spurgeon's interpretation of this text was partly personal. Noting that this particular sermon represented a milestone in his ministry, he said, "In the spirit of these two observations then, looking at God's hand in our own life, and acknowledging that hand with some record of thankfulness, I, your minister, brought by divine grace to preach this morning the five hundredth of my printed sermons, consecutively published week by week, set up my stone of Ebenezer to God."[112] In the minutes that followed, Spurgeon reminded his congregation of the struggles that the Israelites endured as they wandered in the wilderness. He even drew an illustration from his own congregation's history, proclaiming that

> greater multitudes than ever flocked to listen to the word, and some here
> who otherwise might have never attended the preaching of the gospel,

---

[110]George P. Landow, *Victorian Types, Victorian Shadows: Biblical Typology in Victorian Literature, Art, and Thought* (Boston: Routledge & Kegan Paul, 1980), 70.

[111]C. H. Spurgeon, "Ebenezer," sermon no. 500, given March 15, 1863, from 1 Samuel 7:12, *The Metropolitan Tabernacle Pulpit*, vol. 9 (London: Passmore & Alabaster, 1863), 157. The sermon also includes several references to the line "Hitherto the Lord hath helped us" from the hymn "Come Thou Fount of Every Blessing," which references 1 Samuel 7 throughout its text.

[112]Spurgeon, "Ebenezer," 159.

remain as living monuments of God's power to save. Of all evil things out of which good has arisen, we can always point to the Surrey Hall catastrophe as one of the greatest goods which ever befel this neighbourhood, notwithstanding the sorrows which it brought.[113]

Spurgeon was also quick to read the lamb sacrificed in the narrative typologically as he said, "When we have pictured Christ slaughtered, have described the agonies which he endured upon the cross, when we have tried to preach fully though feebly the great doctrine of his substitutionary sacrifice, have set him forth as the propitiation for sins, then it is that the victories have begun."[114] The autobiographical sketch came full circle in Spurgeon's conclusion, where he echoes the fervent invitation that he heard on the morning of his conversion in Colchester.

Oh, if there should be a soul led to believe in Christ this morning, if some heart would give itself up to Christ to-day! Why not so? Why not? The Holy Ghost can melt flint and move mountains. Young man, how long are we to preach at you, how long to invite you, how long to pain you, how long to entreat you, to implore you? Shall this be the day that you will yield? Dost thou say, "I am nothing?" Then Christ is everything. Take him, trust him.[115]

Spurgeon's perspective on this passage may have influenced his fellow Baptist minister F. B. Meyer (1847–1929), who referenced the same hymn that Spurgeon emphasized and wrote that his readers "will never raise your stone of Eben-ezer until you have stood on the watch-tower of Mizpeh and put away all known sin, all complicity with what is grievous in the eyes of Christ. Only so will even his keeping power avail."[116] Meyer's reading of the

---

[113]Spurgeon, "Ebenezer," 161. Spurgeon is referring to a tragic event that occurred seven years earlier, on October 19, 1856, while the congregation was meeting in the Music Hall of the Royal Surrey Gardens. During the service, a small group of people yelled out "Fire!" and the room, crowded with thousands of listeners, quickly descended into a chaotic state. Despite Spurgeon's efforts to calm the crowd from the platform, seven people were killed in the ensuing stampede. The affair put Spurgeon into a state of deep depression. Nettles, *Living by Revealed Truth*, 90-93; Spurgeon, *Autobiography*, 2:195-221. A recent popular-level book investigates this issue at length. See Zach Eswine, *Spurgeon's Sorrows: Realistic Hope for Those Who Suffer from Depression* (Ross-shire, UK: Christian Focus, 2015).

[114]Spurgeon, "Ebenezer," 163.

[115]Spurgeon, "Ebenezer," 167.

[116]Frederick Brotherton Meyer, *Samuel the Prophet* (London: Morgan and Scott, n.d.), 58.

text is certainly christological, but rather than following Spurgeon down conversionistic and crucicentric interpretation, Meyer read the text as a call for moral living among Christians.[117]

In our assessment of Spurgeon's Old Testament interpretation thus far, we have observed several trends. First and foremost, Spurgeon saw no conflict in preaching christologically from the historical narrative accounts, even going so far as to import language of Christ's crucifixion into Old Testament texts, whether or not there was an apparent exegetical basis for doing so. Furthermore, his sermons maintained an evangelistic aim, regardless of the original meaning of the text or whether his contemporaries took different interpretations. Finally, he was not hesitant to interpret these narrative events alongside contemporary issues facing either Victorian Christianity or specifically his own congregation. In the next section, focusing on the wisdom literature in the Old Testament, we will see this trend continue.

SPURGEON'S INTERPRETATION
OF OLD TESTAMENT WISDOM LITERATURE

Wisdom literature is an ancient literary genre typified by didactic instruction, which may or may not be connected to actual historical events. Several books contained within the Old Testament canon are among the most circulated examples of the wisdom genre; they include Psalms, Proverbs, Ecclesiastes, Song of Songs, and Job.[118] The content of these books ranges from narrative parables and prayers to propositional maxims. The history of interpretation with regard to the wisdom books also contains a broad spectrum of opinions. Some psalms have been interpreted as thoroughly christological, while the book of Ecclesiastes represents the cautionary lament of a wise teacher. Spurgeon engaged the wisdom genre in a number of venues, ranging from *The Treasury of David*, his commentary

---

[117]Meyer and Spurgeon shared several friends, including American evangelist Dwight Lyman Moody (1837–1899), and Meyer took up a pastorate at the Regent's Park Chapel in London in 1888. Spurgeon praised Meyer's written work in *The Sword and the Trowel*, suggesting that he "still brings forth from the old mine many nuggets of new gold." *The Sword and the Trowel* 22 (1886): 139.

[118]The Apocrypha also includes Sirach (Ecclesiasticus) and the book of Wisdom (Wisdom of Solomon).

on the Psalms, to over five dozen sermons on the Song of Songs. In his engagement with wisdom literature, Spurgeon maintained his pattern of crucicentric and conversionistic preaching.

Within the wisdom genre, there are some texts that have traditionally been interpreted christologically for a variety of reasons. One such text would be Psalm 22, which begins with the line famously quoted by Christ during his crucifixion, "My God, my God, why hast thou forsaken me? why art thou so far from helping me, and from the words of my roaring?" (Ps 22:1).[119] Spurgeon preached a noteworthy sermon from this text on November 2, 1856.[120] It was his first sermon following the tragic loss of life in the stampede at the Surrey Gardens Hall the previous month.[121] The psalm, which is not attributed to any particular author, addresses the psalmist's sense of dread of present and future trials. Spurgeon, however, interpreted the text as referring exclusively to Christ's suffering on the cross, beginning his sermon by saying that "no other place so well shows the griefs of Christ as Calvary, and no other moment at Calvary is so full of agony as that in which this cry rends the air."[122] Spurgeon, still shaken from the tragedy the previous month, delivered a far shorter sermon than usual and spent the final third imploring any in his congregation who were not reconciled to Christ to reconcile themselves to him. He utilized particularly striking and personal language in this appeal, saying,

> O sinner, come! Come! Come! Jesus bids thee come; and as his ambassador to thee, I bid thee come, as one who would *die* to save your souls if necessary,—as one who knows how to groan over you, and to weep over you,—one who loves you even as he loves himself,—I, as his minister, say to you, in God's name and in Christ's stead, "Be ye reconciled to God."[123]

---

[119]Matthew 27:46 quotes Christ's exclamation in Aramaic as "Eli, Eli, lama sabachthani."

[120]C. H. Spurgeon, "Cries from the Cross," sermon no. 2562, given November 2, 1856, from Psalm 22:1, *The Metropolitan Tabernacle Pulpit*, vol. 44 (London: Passmore & Alabaster, 1898), 145-50.

[121]The published sermon indicates that Spurgeon acknowledged this fact as he began his address, saying, "The observations I have to make will be very brief, seeing that afterward we are to partake of the Lord's supper. I shall make no allusion to the recent catastrophe,—that theme of my daily thoughts and nightly dreams, ever since it has occurred." Spurgeon, "Cries from the Cross," 145.

[122]Spurgeon, "Cries from the Cross," 145.

[123]Spurgeon, "Cries from the Cross," 149.

While it could appear that Spurgeon turned to a more crucicentric interpretation in light of the tragic circumstances surrounding the sermon, further evidence suggests otherwise. For instance, in a sermon preached a decade later from the following verse, he makes a very similar application, saying,

> What sayest thou, sinner. . . . Canst now fall flat before his cross? Oh! The happy day when I learned that I was no longer to look to self, but found that the gospel was "Look unto me, and be ye saved, all ye ends of the earth." Many of you have looked, brethren and sisters! Look again to that sacred head once wounded, and filled with pain and grief, but which now is crowned with glory![124]

Spurgeon's commentary on the Psalms, *The Treasury of David*, contains a lengthy entry for Psalm 22.[125] In the format of his commentary, Spurgeon provided an exposition of the text, further explanatory notes, and then a section titled "helpful hints to preachers." In his expository section, Spurgeon addressed the first half of the first verse, which was quoted by Christ. But he also connected the second portion of the verse to Christ, though this did not occur in the New Testament account. He wrote, "*Why art thou so far from helping me, and from the words of my roaring?*' The Man of Sorrows had prayed until his speech failed him, and he could only utter moanings and groanings as men do in severe sicknesses, like the roarings of a wild animal."[126] Spurgeon's thoroughly crucicentric interpretation becomes clearer in the references in his "explanatory notes" section from the *Treasury*. He quoted Martin Luther as saying, "This is a kind of gem among the Psalms, and is peculiarly excellent and remarkable. It contains these deep, sublime, and heavy sufferings of Christ."[127] Similarly, he referenced the early church historian Eusebius of Caesarea, who identified the Psalm

---

[124]C. H. Spurgeon, "Unanswered Prayer," sermon no. 3344, given September 20, 1866, from Psalm 22:2, *The Metropolitan Tabernacle Pulpit*, vol. 59 (London: Passmore & Alabaster, 1913), 119. The reference in Spurgeon's sermon is to Isaiah 45:22, which was, as we have seen, the verse preached when he was converted in Colchester.

[125]C. H. Spurgeon, *The Treasury of David*, vol. 1, *Psalms 1-26* (London: Marshall Brothers, 1869), 324-52.

[126]Spurgeon, *Treasury of David*, 1:325.

[127]Spurgeon, *Treasury of David*, 1:335.

as "a prophecy of the passion of Christ."[128] In light of the New Testament reference as well as the history of interpretation that Spurgeon highlighted, we may conclude that he was justified in utilizing a crucicentric approach for this text.

Other wisdom texts offer less direct connections to the sort of crucicentric and evangelistic ends that Spurgeon preferred. The book of Job, for example, combines poetic dialogue and prose as it discusses the justice of God amid the suffering of a faithful man. Spurgeon preached a number of sermons from Job, including two on a passage that may represent a reference to Christ, namely Job 19:25, which reads, "For I know that my redeemer liveth, and that he shall stand at the latter day upon the earth." The first sermon, preached at the Metropolitan Tabernacle in April 1863, began with Spurgeon noting his frustration with commentators who did not view the passage as a direct reference to Christ. While he did not often criticize commentators from the pulpit, he made an exception that morning, saying,

> I am sorry to say that a few of those who have written upon this passage cannot see Christ or the resurrection in it at all. Albert Barnes, among the rest, expresses his intense sorrow that he cannot find the resurrection here, and for my part I am sorry for him. If it had been Job's desire to foretel [sic] the advent of Christ and his own sure resurrection, I can not see what better words he could have used.[129]

In the latter sermon, preached thirteen years later, the more mature Spurgeon began with a more skeptical tone, acknowledging that the text was "a very complicated piece of Hebrew, partly, I suppose, owing to its great antiquity, being found in what is, probably, one of the oldest Books of the Bible."[130] Continuing in that theme, he admitted, "It has occurred to me

---

[128]Spurgeon, *Treasury of David*, 1:335.

[129]C. H. Spurgeon, "I Know That My Redeemer Liveth," sermon no. 504, given April 12, 1863, on Job 19:25-27, *The Metropolitan Tabernacle Pulpit*, vol. 9 (London: Passmore & Alabaster, 1863), 206. Albert Barnes (1798–1870), whom Spurgeon references here, was an American Presbyterian minister known for his pastoral ministry in New Jersey, his strong abolitionist stance, and a series of Old and New Testament commentaries that were written with Sunday-school teachers in mind. Spurgeon, for his part, described Barnes as "a learned and able divine, but his productions are unequal in value." Spurgeon, *Lectures to My Students*, 4:30.

[130]C. H. Spurgeon, "Job's Sure Knowledge," sermon no. 2909, given September 10, 1876, from Job 19:25, *The Metropolitan Tabernacle Pulpit*, vol. 50 (London: Passmore & Alabaster, 1904), 541.

that, possibly, Job himself may not have known the full meaning of all that he said. . . . He may but dimly have perceived a future state, but his condition revealed to him the necessity for such a state. . . . Possibly, Job was seeing more than he had ever seen before of that mysterious One who pleads the cause of those who are oppressed."[131] Despite his somewhat hesitant introduction, by the sermon's conclusion Spurgeon had embraced fully crucicentric and conversionistic language, with reference to the "wondrous redemption which he wrought for you on the cross of Calvary."[132]

Spurgeon was not alone in seeing Christ in the unfolding prose of Job. Franz Delitzsch (1813–1890), a German theologian and Hebraist who taught at the Universities of Erlangen and Leipzig, came to similar conclusions. Delitzsch's commentary on Job, translated into English and published by T&T Clark in 1866, represented a more conservative voice of German scholarship, yet he did not make overt christological observations within the exegetical section of his commentary, instead merely suggesting that the "rescuer" of Job's "honour lives and will rise up as one who will speak the final decisive word."[133] While his comments on the specific passage did not indicate any specific christological interpretation, it should be noted that the introduction of the same commentary suggested that "the right expositor of the book of Job must before everything else bring it to a believing apprehension of the work of Christ, in order that he may be able to comprehend this book from its connection with the historical development of the plan of redemption, whose unity is the work of Christ."[134] Another interpreter, closer to Spurgeon geographically though not theologically, was Oxford professor of Hebrew E. B. Pusey (1800–1882).[135] Pusey was a leading figure in the Oxford Movement and represented a conservative, High-Church voice within the Church of England. His

---

[131]Spurgeon, "Job's Sure Knowledge," 541-42.

[132]Spurgeon, "Job's Sure Knowledge," 547.

[133]Franz Delitzsch, *Biblical Commentary on the Book of Job*, trans. Francis Bolton, vol. 1 (Edinburgh: T&T Clark, 1869), 353.

[134]Delitzsch, *Biblical Commentary on the Book of Job*, 1:43.

[135]Spurgeon criticized Pusey in some areas and generally condemned those who followed in his path, suggesting that he "pilots men to Rome," but he simultaneously commended him for doing "good service in the other part of his work, in which he exposes the points of Popery from which he and other Tractarians at present shrink." *The Sword and the Trowel* 1 (1865): 544.

published sermon on the text from Job bore similarities to Spurgeon's conclusions, particularly as he wrote of how the passage reflected

> the mystery of our Easter joy . . . not a mere continuance of our being, not only a life to come, but a life through the life of our Redeemer, a life through his victory over death, a life wherein this very flesh, now poor, corruptible, suffering, fainting, shrinking, easily affrighted, we shall, ourselves for ourselves, face to Face, behold our God.[136]

Although both Delitzsch and Pusey agreed that a christological interpretation was appropriate when considering this text, neither went to the length of drawing sustained appeals for conversion from this passage. Their hesitancy was not shared by Spurgeon, who asked his listeners,

> Can you, beloved friends, not merely rejoice in Christ as *the* Redeemer, but also as *your* Redeemer? Have you personally accepted him as your Redeemer? Have you personally trusted him with your soul, wholly and really; and do you already feel, in your own heart, a kinship to this great Kinsman, a trust in this great Vindicator, a reliance upon his great redemption?[137]

Some of Spurgeon's sermons drawn from wisdom texts featured more tenuous connections with crucicentrism and conversionism, yet as we have seen in these instances, he often increased language of Christian activism. In an 1859 sermon, he addressed Ecclesiastes 9:10, which reads, "Whatsoever thy hand findeth to do, do it with thy might; for there is no work nor device, nor knowledge, nor wisdom, in the grave, whither thou goest."[138] Spurgeon used the didactic language of the text to construct a message of Christian service. This service, according to Spurgeon, was rooted in the cross work of Christ himself. To this end, he suggested that

> if Christ Jesus should leave the upper world, and come into the midst of this hall this morning, what answer could you give, if after showing you his wounded hands and feet, and his rent side, he should put this question,

---

[136]Edward Bouverie Pusey, *Parochial and Cathedral Sermons* (Oxford and London: Parker, 1882), 408.

[137]Spurgeon, "Job's Sure Knowledge," 547. The reference here to a "kinsman" is drawn from the Hebrew word *go'el.*

[138]C. H. Spurgeon, "A Home Mission Sermon," sermon no. 259, given June 26, 1859, from Ecclesiastes 9:10, *The New Park Street Pulpit*, vol. 5 (London: Passmore & Alabaster, 1859), 273-80.

"I have done all this for thee, what hast thou done for me?" . . . He has done all this for you, he has bled away his precious life, has died in agonies most exquisite upon the cross. What have you done for him?[139]

The crucicentric and conversionistic language continued as the sermon's theme drew to a close, particularly when Spurgeon said, "If ye do not believe this Bible, I care not what ye are—earnest or dull. But if ye do believe it, act as ye believe; if ye think men are perishing, if the Lord's right hand is dashing in pieces his enemy, then I beseech you to be strengthened by the same right hand, to endeavour to bring those enemies to Christ that they may be reconciled by the blood of the cross."[140] Thus, in this example, Spurgeon emphasized each of the four tenets of evangelical theology in calling Christians to active evangelism that would produce conversions through a particularly crucicentric engagement with the Bible.

Several of Spurgeon's sermons from the Song of Songs represent similar forms of creative interpretation. The book, a collection of love poetry, has led preachers from virtually all eras of the church to employ some degree of allegorical interpretation. One verse that stands out as an example is Song of Songs 4:16, which reads, "Awake, O north wind; come, thou south; blow upon my garden, that the spices thereof may flow out. Let my beloved come into his garden, and eat his pleasant fruits." Octavius Winslow, a contemporary of Spurgeon, interpreted the passage as referring to Christian unity. For Winslow, "The *unity of Christ's Church* is strikingly illustrated by the similitude of a 'garden.' A garden is a spot single and complete in itself; in which there exists in all its essential landscape features, the most perfect harmony of character and design. Such is the great truth the similitude illustrates in reference to the Church of God. It is a Divine and sacred *unity*."[141] Spurgeon's interpretation saw each Christian as a "garden," and he told his congregation that "in a garden there are flowers and fruits, and in every Christian's heart you will find the same evidences of culture and care; not in all alike, for even gardens and fields vary in

---

[139]Spurgeon, "Home Mission Sermon," 278.

[140]Spurgeon, "Home Mission Sermon," 279.

[141]Octavius Winslow, *The Ministry of Home; or, Brief Expository Lectures on Divine Truth* (London: William Hunt, 1857), 302.

productiveness."[142] Spurgeon's christocentrism at work in this sermon appeared alongside an appeal for conversion, as he proclaimed, "Do you not feel, beloved, that *the one thing you want to stir your whole soul is that Christ should come into it?* Have you lost your company lately? Oh, do not try to do without it!"[143] A century earlier, John Gill, Spurgeon's predecessor at the New Park Street Chapel, read the passage not merely in a christological fashion but as a fully Trinitarian text.[144] Gill wrote that

> when Christ is here represented, saying to the Spirit, "come and blow upon my garden;" it must be understood of him as mediator, calling unto, and as it were demanding of the Spirit to do his work assigned him in the church . . . for all the three persons having jointly agreed in the everlasting council and covenant of peace, to take their several distinct parts in man's salvation.[145]

It is perhaps fitting that Gill's commentary should correspond most closely with Spurgeon's sermon, as Spurgeon regarded Gill's work on the Song of Songs as "the best thing Gill ever did."[146]

As we have seen, Spurgeon's engagement with the wisdom genre in many ways mirrored his engagement with historical narrative. He drew christological and crucicentric interpretations from passages whether or not his contemporaries saw the connection, and his sermons contained fervent evangelistic appeals. Further, particularly in the case of Spurgeon's sermon on Psalm 22, he turned to the wisdom genre amid significant personal turmoil.

SPURGEON'S INTERPRETATION
OF OLD TESTAMENT PROPHETIC BOOKS

For our final investigation of Spurgeon's Old Testament interpretation, we will turn to the prophetic books. The role of prophecy in the Old Testament

---

[142]C. H. Spurgeon, "My Garden—His Garden," sermon no. 2475, given July 20, 1882, from Song of Songs 4:16, *The Metropolitan Tabernacle Pulpit*, vol. 42 (London: Passmore & Alabaster, 1896), 349.

[143]Spurgeon, "My Garden—His Garden," 356.

[144]John Gill, *An Exposition of the Book of Solomon's Song, Commonly Called Canticles*, vol. 2 (Edinburgh: Thomas Turnbull, Canongate, 1805), 19-32.

[145]Gill, *Exposition of the Book of Solomon's Song*, 2:25.

[146]Spurgeon, *Lectures to My Students*, 4:165. In the same review, Spurgeon also said that those who disliked Gill's work on Song of Songs "have never read it, or are incapable of elevated spiritual feelings."

has intrigued and challenged interpreters from the earliest days of Christianity, and the nineteenth century represents a period of significant engagement with the prophetic books. In Germany, one scholar particularly noteworthy in the study of the prophets was Bernhard Duhm (1847–1928), who studied under Julius Wellhausen at Göttingen and spent the majority of his academic career at the University of Basel.[147] Building on Wellhausen's work, which separated the book of Isaiah into different sections with different authors, Duhm's commentary represented an attempt to "enter as deeply as possible into the personality of the [biblical] writer," and he regarded the biblical authors as "good writers who do not bungle and murder the language, but speak correctly and sensibly."[148] The prophetic genre contains several different thematic elements; significant among them were social criticisms directed at specific groups as well as predictive statements regarding the coming messiah. The social criticisms, which were often messages of warning to Israelites in both the northern kingdom of Israel and the southern kingdom of Judah, were purportedly written by such figures as Isaiah and Jeremiah. The prophetic warnings often contained exhortations and calls to repentance intended to guide and reform not only the religious culture but also external society at large. The didactic language employed by the prophets often proved useful to preachers centuries later who wished to critique the cultures around them, and there is an element of this sort of discourse in Spurgeon's sermons.[149] As well as social criticism, Spurgeon's engagement with Old Testament prophecy further expresses his crucicentric and conversionistic interpretive priorities.

One significant element of the prophetic books is *messianic* prophecy, that is, prophetic claims that served to foretell the coming of a savior, or Messiah. Within these passages, Christians have sought to identify references to aspects of the life of Christ, including his birthplace, his role as

---

[147]Smend, *From Astruc to Zimmerli*, 103-17.

[148]These quotes are from a letter written by Duhm to a colleague, translated by Smend. Smend, *From Astruc to Zimmerli*, 112.

[149]Donald Smith has made some helpful observations regarding social criticism in sermons; however, this study is limited to congregations in Scotland. Donald C. Smith, *Passive Obedience and Prophetic Protest: Social Criticism in the Scottish Church 1830–1945*, American University Studies, Series 9: History 15 (New York: Peter Lang, 1987).

teacher, his execution, and his resurrection. A noteworthy text containing elements of messianic prophecy regarding the birthplace of Christ is Micah 5:2, which reads, "But thou, Beth-lehem Ephrathah, though thou be little among the thousands of Judah, yet out of thee shall come forth unto me that is to be ruler in Israel; whose goings forth have been from of old, from everlasting." This was the verse Spurgeon chose in delivering a sermon at the New Park Street Chapel in December 1855. The twenty-one-year-old pastor, in preparing for his first Christmas with his new congregation, did not opt to preach from the narrative accounts of the nativity. Rather, he preached a sermon from the messianic prophecy in the book of Micah.[150] As he expounded on Christ's purpose in the Incarnation, the language in Spurgeon's Christmas sermon grew increasingly graphic, with the young pastor noting that Christ "signed the compact with his Father, that he would pay blood for blood, wound for wound, suffering for suffering, agony for agony, and death for death, in the behalf of his people."[151] His closing prayer emphasized conversionistic themes as he invited Christ to "subdue hard hearts—to break the iron gates of sinners' lusts, and cut the iron bars of their sins in pieces."[152]

Spurgeon occasionally used prophetic texts to address contemporary issues. This is illustrated in a sermon he gave during an outbreak of cholera in London in 1866.[153] The outbreak ravaged London's East End, killing nearly four thousand people.[154] Breaking from his usual habit, Spurgeon preached from several verses rather than just one. In the passage, the prophet Amos proclaims that the Lord raised up the people of Israel, and

---

[150]In a rare move for Spurgeon, he began his sermon by criticizing the Puritans, in this case criticizing the degree to which they eschewed traditional English celebrations of Christmas, suggesting that they "made a parade of work on Christmas-day, just to show that they protested against the observance of it. But we believe they entered that protest so completely, that we are willing, as their descendants, to take the good accidentally conferred by the day, and leave its superstitions to the superstitious." C. H. Spurgeon, "The Incarnation and Birth of Christ," sermon no. 57, given December 23, 1855, from Micah 5:2, *The New Park Street Pulpit*, vol. 2 (London: Passmore & Alabaster, 1856), 25.

[151]Spurgeon, "Incarnation and Birth of Christ," 30.

[152]Spurgeon, "Incarnation and Birth of Christ," 32.

[153]C. H. Spurgeon, "The Voice of the Cholera," sermon no. 705, given August 12, 1866, from Amos 3:3-6, *The Metropolitan Tabernacle Pulpit*, vol. 12 (London: Passmore & Alabaster, 1866), 445-56.

[154]W. Luckin, "The Final Catastrophe: Cholera in London, 1866," *Medical History* 21 (1977): 32-42.

when they committed sins as a nation, they placed themselves in a position whereby the Lord could bring righteous destruction upon them. Spurgeon began his sermon by acknowledging the tragic events occurring in the East End. From there, he praised the work of those in the scientific and medical professions who were working to contain the outbreak, saying, "I am thankful that there are many men of intelligence and scientific information who can speak well upon this point, and I hope that they will never cease to speak."[155] He noted that "the gospel has no quarrel with ventilation, and the doctrines of grace have no dispute with chloride of lime. We preach repentance and faith, but we do not denounce whitewash. . . . We would promote with all our hearts that which may honour God, but we cannot neglect that which may bless our neighbours whom we desire to love even as ourselves."[156] His tone shifted as he then offered theological reflections on the present situation. He began by reminding his congregation that he was not "among those, as you know, who believe that every affliction is a judgment upon the particular person to whom it occurs. We perceive that in this world the best of men often endure the most of suffering, and that the worst of men frequently escape."[157] While Spurgeon made clear his belief that *individuals* were not the target of specific judgment in such events as the cholera epidemic, he did claim that *nations* could be and often were judged by God. He identified several characteristics of England as being particularly offensive to God: these ranged from drunkenness and debauchery to breaking the Sabbath, as well as what he believed to be the "Romanism" now at work within the Established Church.[158] While Spurgeon emphasized England's culpability, he stopped short of directly connecting the present cholera outbreak to the sinful behavior of the nation, though he suggested that the sins committed on a daily basis throughout the country warranted national punishment. Additionally, this sermon typifies Spurgeon's pattern of referring to the cross of Christ as the

---

[155]Spurgeon, "Voice of the Cholera," 445.
[156]Spurgeon, "Voice of the Cholera," 446.
[157]Spurgeon, "Voice of the Cholera," 446.
[158]Uncharacteristically, in the same section he did admit that within the Church of England "a little band of good and faithful men still linger . . . and are like a handful of salt amid general putrefaction." Spurgeon, "Voice of the Cholera," 449.

basis for both reconciliation with God and protection from God's judgment. This is most clear as Spurgeon proclaimed, "Can you bear to be at disagreement with God . . . you ask his protection, but how can you expect it if you are not agreed with him? Now, if two men walk together, there must be a place where they meet each other. Do you know where that is? It is at the cross. Sinner, if thou trustest in Jesus, God will meet thee there."[159] In his conclusion, he suggested that the affliction of the people of London's East End should serve as an impetus for his congregation to share the gospel with others, noting that "men are always dying, time like a mighty rushing stream is always bearing them away, but now they are hurried down the torrent in increasing numbers. If you and I do not exert ourselves to teach them the gospel, upon our heads must be their blood."[160] Thus the content of the prophetic text, combined with the cholera epidemic in London, became grounds for Spurgeon to preach the cross and intensify his call on his congregation's evangelistic efforts.

Prophetic literature was also the basis for one of the most noteworthy sermons of Spurgeon's tenure in London. Following the Mutiny in India, Queen Victoria designated October 7, 1857, as a day for a "solemn fast, humiliation, and prayer before Almighty God: in order to obtain pardon for our sins, and for imploring His blessing and assistance on our arms for the restoration of tranquillity in India."[161] Spurgeon was invited to give a sermon to mark the fast day by the directors of the Crystal Palace, an immense glass and iron structure originally built for the Great Exhibition in London in 1851.[162] Their invitation may have come as a result of a sermon he had given the previous month, titled "India's Ills and England's Sorrows."[163] The Fast-Day sermon drew the largest recorded crowd

---

[159]Spurgeon, "Voice of the Cholera," 454.

[160]Spurgeon, "Voice of the Cholera," 455. Spurgeon's reference to time as a "mighty rushing stream" is a reference to Isaac Watts's 1719 hymn, "O God, Our Help in Ages Past."

[161]Spurgeon, *Autobiography*, 2:239. For further discussion of British responses to the mutiny, see Brian Stanley, "Christian Responses to the Indian Mutiny of 1857," in *The Church and War, Studies in Church History* 20 (Oxford: Blackwell, 1983), 277-89; Michael R. Watts, *The Dissenters*, vol. 3, *The Crisis and Conscience of Nonconformity* (Oxford: Oxford University Press, 2015), 323.

[162]Spurgeon, *Autobiography*, 2:239.

[163]Spurgeon, "India's Ills and England's Sorrows," sermon no. 150, given September 6, 1857, from Jeremiah 9:1, *The New Park Street Pulpit*, vol. 3 (London: Passmore & Alabaster, 1857), 341-48.

Spurgeon would ever address, with 23,654 people counted in attendance.[164] His text was from Micah 6:9, which read, "Hear ye the rod, and who hath appointed it."[165] Spurgeon's social criticism is visible from the onset of the sermon, as he told his congregation that he felt "persuaded that there are such things as national judgements, national chastisements for national sins—great blows from the rod of God, which every wise man must acknowledge to be, either a punishment of sin committed, or a monition to warn us to a sense of the consequences of sins, leading us by God's grace to humiliate ourselves, and repent of sin."[166] Spurgeon made no attempt to conceal his disdain for the mutinous sepoys or his belief that their rising should be met with swift and deadly military action. However, he also attempted to balance his strong critiques with a deeply Calvinistic view of divine providence as he noted, "I see God in this war. The wheels of providence may revolve in a mysterious manner, but I am certain that wisdom is the axle upon which they revolve, so that at last it shall be seen that God, who ordained the rod, only permitted it that greater good might follow, and that his name might be exalted throughout the earth."[167] Spurgeon lashed out with uncharacteristically graphic language, proclaiming that "if it be any man's religion to blow my brains out, I shall not tolerate it."[168]

Though he supported the suppression of the mutiny, Spurgeon also placed blame on the British governors and the East India Company, who did not adequately suppress the offenders. The judgment of God, according to Spurgeon, represented a double-edged sword, which is evident as he proclaimed, "The rod has smitten; the scourge has ploughed deep furrows upon India's back. . . . Now, it is an opinion published by

---

The Jeremiah text from this sermon is also representative of prophetic social criticism. The verse Spurgeon preached began with the lament, "Oh that my head were waters, and mine eyes a fountain of tears, that I might weep day and night for the slain of the daughter of my people!"

[164]Spurgeon, *Autobiography*, 2:239.

[165]C. H. Spurgeon, "Fast-Day Service," sermons no. 154-55, given October 7, 1857, from Micah 6:9, *The New Park Street Pulpit*, vol. 3 (London: Passmore & Alabaster, 1857), 373-88. Unlike the majority of Spurgeon's printed sermons, this text included his invocation, biblical exposition (Dan 9:1-19), and pastoral prayer.

[166]Spurgeon, "Fast-Day Service," 380.

[167]Spurgeon, "Fast-Day Service," 381.

[168]Spurgeon, "Fast-Day Service," 382.

authority . . . that one part of the reason for this dreadful visitation, is the sin of the people of England themselves . . . who am I, that I should dispute such a high authority as that?"[169] Thus, in Spurgeon's view, India's sins were not solely to blame for the tragedy. He directed the next section of his sermon to identify particular sins that, in his estimation, had plagued the English nation. Following critiques of alcohol abuse and theater attendance, Spurgeon proceeded to insist that Britain's "*class sins are the most grievous.*"[170] He portrayed oppressive mill owners who viewed the working class as "stepping stones to wealth," suggesting that factories became like cauldrons, with the wealthy owners treating the working class like logs in a fire, shouting, "*Put them in*; heap the fire, boil the cauldron; stir them up; never mind their cries."[171] It should be noted that while Spurgeon indeed directed harsh words toward the wealthy in London, they were not the only targets of his social criticism. He also suggested that the working class contributed to national sin as well, noting that "many are the sins of the poor" and calling on the working class to "humble yourselves with the rich; bow your heads and weep for your iniquities; for these things God doth visit us, and ye should hear the rod."[172] Spurgeon closed the sermon with a fervent appeal to any "despisers of Christ" who might have come to the sermon at the Crystal Palace, proclaiming that "'Jesus Christ of the seed of David' was nailed to a cross; he died that we might not die, and to every believer heaven's gate is open. . . . Sinner! Dost thou believe?"[173] Thus, amid Spurgeon's harsh critique of the behavior of both the mutinous Indians and the British nation, his conclusion reflected the same cross and gospel theme that we have noted throughout his engagement with the Old Testament.

In this section, we have seen how both crucicentrism and conversionism were woven throughout his prophetic sermons. Furthermore, in some instances we have seen Spurgeon attempting to step into a prophetic role,

---

[169]Spurgeon, "Fast-Day Service," 383.
[170]Spurgeon, "Fast-Day Service," 384.
[171]Spurgeon, "Fast-Day Service," 384.
[172]Spurgeon, "Fast-Day Service," 385.
[173]Spurgeon, "Fast-Day Service," 387.

reinterpreting the warnings of the Israelite prophets for the inhabitants of nineteenth-century London. In his sermons Spurgeon captured what Ellison summarized as a "call to action" for his congregation.[174] While some of his calls to action involved matters of Christian unity or social justice, the majority of his sermons featured a call on members of the congregation to repent and reconcile themselves to God. Though the prophetic texts contain a number of passages that have been understood to refer to Christ, throughout Spurgeon's sermons Christ was present throughout virtually all texts of the genre, and from this position he saw no difficulty or indiscretion in preaching crucicentric and conversionistic sermons drawn from a wide range of prophetic texts.

CONCLUSIONS

Throughout this chapter, we have identified key developments within the field of Old Testament interpretation and noted that the nineteenth century was a time of significant change with regard to the methods of biblical criticism. Higher criticism drew from Enlightenment scholarly approaches and found acceptance within universities on the Continent before British scholars began to interact with it in a serious manner. British engagement with higher criticism increased throughout the nineteenth century, concurrent with Spurgeon's pastorate in London. For Spurgeon, and indeed for all Christians, the Bible contained the words of God, and there was an increased emphasis upon the divine inspiration of the Bible in response to scholarship that called into question the Bible's accuracy as a historical record. This led Spurgeon to familiarize himself with contemporary works in biblical studies, though as we have seen Spurgeon was quick to discard volumes he believed were too critical in their assessments, and he particularly condemned books that disagreed with his position on Christology and the atonement.

We have noted throughout this chapter that Spurgeon held a particularly christocentric view of the Bible, viewing Christ as the Bible's "sum and substance," and in this view he saw no interpretive conflict in preaching

---

[174]Ellison, *Victorian Pulpit*, 19.

christological sermons from both the Old and New Testaments.[175] Spurgeon's focus on Christ, and more specifically Christ's crucifixion, alongside a conservative theology of the atonement and his desire to produce converts to Christianity through his sermons, led him to find references to Christ in his text whether or not there was any overt or apparent christological content. While the Old Testament contains numerous instances of prophecies that have commonly been understood to refer to Christ, in many of Spurgeon's sermons crucicentric and conversionistic language would be explicitly woven into virtually any Old Testament text, a practice that was not often followed by his contemporaries. This enabled him to say, in an 1861 sermon, that study into the content of the Old Testament was akin to the study of hieroglyphics, shapes that pointed to a "glorious one, a Son of David."[176] He continued on, noting how

> these wondrous hieroglyphs traced of old by Moses in the wilderness, must be left unexplained, till one comes forward and proclaims, "The cross of Christ and the Son of God incarnate," then the whole is clear, so that he that runs may read, and a child may understand . . . in thee we discover everything carried out in substance, which God has set forth us in the dim mist of sacrificial smoke.[177]

Thus Spurgeon's engagement with the Old Testament, both in pulpit and print, is indicative of the crucicentric and conversionistic interpretation we have seen throughout our study. In the next chapter we will continue our analysis of Spurgeon's biblical engagement, exploring his preaching and writing on the books of the New Testament.

---

[175]C. H. Spurgeon, "Preface," *The New Park Street Pulpit*, vol. 1 (London: Passmore & Alabaster, 1855), vi.

[176]C. H. Spurgeon, "It Is Finished!," sermon no. 421, given December 1, 1861, on John 19:30, *The Metropolitan Tabernacle Pulpit*, vol. 7 (London: Passmore & Alabaster, 1861), 587.

[177]Spurgeon, "It Is Finished," 587. Emphasis mine.

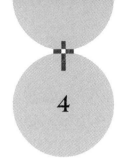

THE CROSS
AND CONVERSION
IN SPURGEON'S
NEW TESTAMENT
INTERPRETATION

If a man can preach one sermon without mentioning
Christ's name in it, it ought to be his last sermon.

C. H. SPURGEON

As we have seen in the previous chapter, Spurgeon's sermons indicated that he read the whole of the Old Testament in light of the atoning work of Christ on the cross, with an aim to produce conversions. In his engagement with the New Testament, Spurgeon's preaching moved in a similar direction, in that he unashamedly and boldly interpreted texts in light of crucicentrism and conversionism, irrespective of their immediate context. In Spurgeon's preaching, the Pastoral Epistles, Gospel narratives, and apocalyptic genres included material that pointed to the cross and, ultimately, to individual conversion. While the overall content of the New Testament books often bears significant christological and crucicentric emphases, there are few individual verses that feature

---

C. H. Spurgeon, "A Prayer for the Church Militant," sermon no. 768, from Psalm 28:9, n.d., *The Metropolitan Tabernacle Pulpit*, vol. 13 (London: Passmore & Alabaster, 1867), 489.

these topics as their specific focus. This is significant for the present study, as we have noted that Spurgeon's preference to preach from single verses led him to draw crucicentric emphases from a diverse range of texts, many of which did not contain overt christological content.

In this chapter we will investigate Spurgeon's focus on crucicentrism and conversionism as interpretive guides in preaching on various New Testament texts. In keeping with the structure of the previous chapter, we will begin our investigation with a discussion of the state of New Testament interpretation in the nineteenth century, highlighting key figures in the development of modern New Testament scholarship. From there, we will consider Spurgeon's engagement with biblical scholarship, noting his estimation of particular biblical interpreters and their methods. The remainder of the chapter will explore Spurgeon's New Testament sermons, divided by biblical genres of the New Testament, which include Gospel narratives, General and Pastoral Epistles, and apocalyptic literature. Additionally, an extended study of his interpretation of the Sermon on the Mount will provide further insight into Spurgeon's perspective on the language invoking the kingdom of God, and clues to how his church in London pursued a mission to shape a society reflecting the virtues that Christ proclaimed.[1]

DEVELOPMENTS IN MODERN
NEW TESTAMENT STUDIES

As we have seen in the previous chapter, the nineteenth century witnessed a significant turning point with regard to the methodologies employed in biblical studies. Alongside developments in Old Testament interpretation, New Testament studies also witnessed dramatic changes. There is a rich variety of historical literature on these developments.[2]

---

[1]Though Spurgeon is certainly not alone among evangelicals with regard to his social outlook, he does represent an example of an evangelical preacher with abundant resources in a city with abundant need. For broader context of late nineteenth-century Christian social movements, see Peter Jones, *The Christian Socialist Revival, 1877–1914: Religion, Class, and Social Conscience in Late-Victorian England* (Princeton, NJ: Princeton University Press, 1968).

[2]John Barton, *The Cambridge Companion to Biblical Interpretation* (Cambridge: Cambridge University Press, 2009); Hans W. Frei, *The Eclipse of Biblical Narrative: A Study in Eighteenth and*

This literature includes such valuable works as Stephen Neill's survey of New Testament interpretation (updated in recent years by N. T. Wright) as well as William Baird's expansive *History of New Testament Research* series.[3] Developments in New Testament interpretive methodology were associated with the Enlightenment, as developments in cosmology, physics, and philosophy began to call long-held interpretations of certain biblical texts into question. As Louis Dupré has observed, the language of the Bible "suddenly appeared utterly incongruous with the scientific worldview."[4]

As the early modern period unfolded, German universities were instrumental in the development of critical New Testament studies. Hans Frei notes that eighteenth-century German scholarship featured a significant number of scholars who were interested in "the Bible as a written document."[5] Eighteenth-century biblical scholars began to specialize in particular sections of the Bible, as evidenced by the work of Johann David Michaelis (1717–1791) and Johann Salomo Semler (1725–1791), both of whom studied at the University of Halle in the mid-eighteenth century and both of whom would become specialists in New Testament studies. Semler, who was raised in the Pietist tradition, attempted to find a theological path between Pietist subjectivity and Lutheran dogmatism. He championed the right of the individual to interpret the Bible outside the confines of a dogmatic framework, writing that "true Christians" could apply the "powers of their souls honestly and without reservation to these books which altogether are called *Holy Scripture*, in order ever better to know God and be useful to him. . . . Every rational man, if he is fortunate enough to apply his

---

Nineteenth Century Hermeneutics, rev. ed. (New Haven, CT: Yale University Press, 1980); Horton Harris, *The Tübingen School* (Oxford: Oxford University Press, 1975); Scott Mandelbrote and Michael Ledger-Lomas, eds., *Dissent and the Bible in Britain, c. 1650–1950* (Oxford: Oxford University Press, 2013); Henry Wansbrough, *The Use and Abuse of the Bible: A Brief History of Biblical Interpretation* (London: T&T Clark, 2010).

[3]Stephen Neill and N. T. Wright, *The Interpretation of the New Testament, 1861–1986*, 2nd ed. (Oxford: Oxford University Press, 1988); William Baird, *History of New Testament Research*, vol. 1, *From Deism to Tübingen* (Minneapolis: Fortress, 1992); William Baird, *History of New Testament Research*, vol. 2, *From Jonathan Edwards to Rudolf Bultmann* (Minneapolis: Fortress, 2002).

[4]Louis Dupré, *The Enlightenment and the Intellectual Foundations of Modern Culture* (New Haven, CT; London: Yale University Press, 2004), 230.

[5]Frei, *Eclipse of the Biblical Narrative*, 157.

soul's power seriously, is free, indeed obligated, to judge for himself on this matter without fear of man."[6]

Johann Michaelis, who also studied at the University of Halle, would become the first professor of the University of Göttingen's department of Oriental and Biblical Studies. Michaelis's historical introduction to the New Testament, published in 1788, balanced linguistic, text-critical, and historical surveys and represented a significant shift toward critical engagement with the New Testament.[7] As Neill and Wright observed, "The orthodoxy of the time took it for granted that, because the New Testament is divinely inspired in every part, it is *a priori* impossible that there should be any contradictions between the Gospels. . . . Michaelis was prepared to face the possibility that there might be contradictions."[8]

Michaelis was succeeded at the University of Göttingen by one of his students, Johann Gottfried Eichhorn (1752–1827). While we have previously noted Eichhorn's aptitude for Old Testament research, he was also a significant figure in New Testament interpretation, writing a five-volume *Introduction to the New Testament.*[9] Eichhorn's *Introduction* contained several controversial propositions, including the claim that the writers of the Gospel accounts consulted an *Urgospel,* a hypothetical lost source from which the Gospel writers drew.[10] Additionally, he questioned the traditional Pauline authorship of the Pastoral Epistles on the basis of linguistic content.[11]

The nineteenth century saw the development of biblical theology as a discipline distinct from both biblical studies and dogmatic theology. Biblical theology is often associated with Johann Philipp Gabler (1753–1826), whose inaugural address at the University of Altdorf in 1787, "Discourse on the Proper Distinction between Biblical and Dogmatic Theology, and the

---

[6]J. S. Semler, *Abhandlung von freier Untersuchung des Kanons* (Leipzig, 1771), quoted in Frei, *Eclipse of the Biblical Narrative,* 112.

[7]Johann David Michaelis, *Einleitung in die göttlichen Schriften des neuen Bundes* (Göttingen: Vandenhoeck & Ruprecht, 1788).

[8]Neill and Wright, *Interpretation of the New Testament,* 6.

[9]Originally published as Johann Gottfried Eichhorn, *Einleitung in das Neue Testament,* 5 vols. (Leipzig: Weidmann, 1820).

[10]Baird, *History of New Testament Research,* 1:150-53.

[11]The Pastoral Epistles include 1 and 2 Timothy, Titus, and Philemon.

Right Determination of the Aims of Each," argued for a middle way between the disciplines of biblical studies and dogmatic theology. Biblical theology, he argued, should be rooted in historic understandings of religion rather than dogmatic theology. Gabler's address was a pivotal moment in the development of biblical theology. He built his work on the framework established by Semler and others, which enabled him to employ myth as a category of biblical communication. Myth, as Gabler wrote in the introduction to Eichhorn's *Urgeschichte*, could best be understood as "legends of the ancient world expressed in the sensual way of thinking and speaking of that time."[12]

Perhaps the most noteworthy nineteenth-century German New Testament critic was F. C. Baur (1792–1860), whose career as a lecturer began at a seminary at Blaubeuren. Following this post, he was given a chair at his alma mater, the University of Tübingen, in 1826.[13] Baur was an expert in the fields of history, theology, and biblical studies, and a significant portion of his work involved the combination of those academic disciplines to construct a complex and nuanced Christology. Baur, as helpfully summarized by Baird, attempted "to bridge the chasm between the Christ of faith and the Jesus of history by asserting that God acts in Jesus and that faith is a response to the historical Jesus."[14] Baur's methodology led him to engage the books of the New Testament critically, and he was influential in what became known as the Tübingen school, which stood at the forefront of new trends in biblical scholarship. Dialectical thought, a central conception of Hegelian philosophy, played a formative role in the approach of the school. "According to the [Tübingen] school," Owen Chadwick observed, "the New Testament arose from the conflict between Peter and Paul, between Gentile and Jewish Christianity; a conflict which was slowly resolved into the synthesis of the second century which is Catholic Christianity."[15]

---

[12] Johann Philipp Gabler, introduction to *Urgeschichte* by Johann Gottfried Eichhorn (bey Monath und Kutzler, 1790), quoted in Baird, *History of New Testament Research*, 1:186.

[13] For a helpful introduction to Baur and his work, see Harris, *Tübingen School*, 11–54.

[14] Baird, *History of New Testament Research*, 1:260.

[15] Owen Chadwick, *The Victorian Church: Part Two (1860–1901)* (London: SCM Press, 1987), 68.

Baur attempted to construct a comprehensive "life" of Jesus Christ by evaluating and combining accounts from the Gospel narratives. Another who attempted this task was Friedrich D. E. Schleiermacher (1768–1834), who lectured on the life of Christ in 1819 at the newly established University of Berlin.[16] Key to Schleiermacher's work was the "God-consciousness" of Christ, which he used to refer to the unfolding degree to which Jesus understood his own divinity and mission.

Other lives of Christ followed, perhaps most notably David Strauss's *Leben Jesu*.[17] Strauss (1808–1874), who studied and later lectured for a time at the University of Tübingen, used the conception of myth as an analytic tool in New Testament studies. Strauss defined myth as "a narrative relating directly or indirectly to Jesus, which may be considered not as the expression of a fact, but as the product of an idea of his earliest followers."[18] In *Leben Jesu*, Strauss relegated the majority of supernatural accounts within the Gospel narratives to forms of myth rather than historical fact. In his conclusion, he wrote that "the results of the inquiry which we have now brought to a close, have apparently annihilated the greatest and most valuable part of that which the Christian has been wont to believe concerning his Saviour Jesus."[19] Jesus, he concluded, "can have been nothing more than a person, highly distinguished indeed, but subject to the limitations inevitable to all that is mortal."[20] The work cost him his post at the university. In Britain, Mary Ann Evans (1819–1880) translated *Leben Jesu* in 1846 under her pseudonym, George Eliot. Relatively few in Britain were fluent in the German language at that time, and Eliot's translation was among the earliest publications of German scholarship critical of the Gospel accounts to be published in Britain.[21] Strauss's conclusions received

---

[16]His work on the life of Christ was published posthumously, thirty years after his death. Friedrich Daniel Ernst Schleiermacher, *Das Leben Jesu. Vorlesungen an Der Universität Berlin im Jahr 1832*, ed. K. A. Rutenik (Berlin: G. Reimer, 1864).

[17]David Friedrich Strauss, *Das Leben Jesu kritisch bearbeitet* (Tübingen: C. F. Osiander, 1835).

[18]David Friedrich Strauss, *The Life of Jesus, Critically Examined*, ed. Peter C. Hodgson, trans. George Eliot (Philadelphia: Fortress, 1972), 86.

[19]Strauss, *Life of Jesus*, 757.

[20]Strauss, *Life of Jesus*, 780.

[21]For an overview of the controversy, see Timothy Larsen, "Biblical Criticism and the Crisis of Belief: D. F. Strauss's *Leben Jesu* in Britain," in *Contested Christianity: The Political and Social*

criticism from many Christians, including Spurgeon, who suggested that Strauss, Renan, and other "thinking men" were "very great at anything metaphysical, geological, anthopological [sic], or any other ology, except theology."[22] Spurgeon continued, suggesting that "among the working population, the real sinew, and the blood and bone of England, there is no further space for the superficial intellectualism which has vaunted itself."[23] For Spurgeon, the ideal minister would eschew "all flighty notions, specious novelties, mental eccentricities and philosophisings, he determines to know nothing among men save Jesus Christ and him crucified."[24]

Developments in approaches to New Testament studies were not restricted to the Continent. Debates concerning the New Testament occurred at several British universities in the nineteenth century, including Oxford and Cambridge.[25] A noteworthy figure in early nineteenth-century English New Testament studies was Samuel Taylor Coleridge (1772–1834), who had studied in Germany under Johann Eichhorn.[26] His *Confessions of an Inquiring Spirit*, originally published in 1825, consisted of seven letters written on the subject of the "literalism" at work in English biblical interpretation. These letters suggested that Christian biblical interpreters in England subscribed to a wooden, inflexible approach to the Bible. While Coleridge's work was embraced by liberal Anglicans, it was received coldly by high Anglicans, with the high Anglican *English Review* suggesting that Coleridge's writings were among "those of the most notorious amongst our modern infidels . . . wholly and absolutely subversive of the Christian religion."[27]

Context of Victorian Theology (Waco, TX: Baylor University Press, 2004), 43-58; Owen Chadwick, *The Victorian Church: Part One (1829–1859)* (London: A&C Black, 1971), 530-33.

[22] *The Sword and the Trowel* 7 (1871): 219.

[23] *The Sword and the Trowel* 7 (1871): 219.

[24] *The Sword and the Trowel* 7 (1871): 219.

[25] See Chadwick, *Victorian Church: Part Two (1860–1901)*, 60-74; David M. Thompson, *Cambridge Theology in the Nineteenth Century* (Aldershot: Ashgate, 2008), 95-121.

[26] Tod Jones notes that Coleridge favored Lessing's written works and hoped to write a biography of him. See Tod E. Jones, *The Broad Church: A Biography of a Movement* (Lanham, MD: Lexington Books, 2003), 21.

[27] Anonymous, "Review of Confessions of an Enquiring Spirit, and Some Miscellaneous Pieces," *English Review* 12 (1849): 267, quoted in Jeffrey W. Barbeau, "'Songs for My Joy . . . Pleadings for My Shame': Coleridge, Divine Revelation and Confessions of an Inquiring Spirit" (PhD diss., Marquette University, 2002), 20.

Another significant figure in New Testament scholarship was Fredrick Denison Maurice (1805–1872), who was raised in the Unitarian tradition but joined the Church of England in his twenties. A professor at King's College, London, he was dismissed from his chair for questioning the doctrine of eternal punishment in his 1853 publication *Theological Essays.*[28] Maurice built his case largely from the Gospel accounts of Matthew and John, arguing that the category of eternal punishment was not defensible from a careful reading of the Gospels. Significantly, changing attitudes within the church meant there was no major opposition when Cambridge University appointed him to the chair of moral philosophy in 1866.

While such scholars as Coleridge and F. D. Maurice had encountered significant opposition, critical interpretation of the New Testament became more accepted in colleges and universities during the latter half of the nineteenth century. While there was a distance between traditional views and modern critical approaches to the New Testament, several scholars worked to bridge the gap. Among them was Joseph Barber Lightfoot (1828–1889), professor at Cambridge and then bishop of Durham, who, in the words of biblical scholar Barnabas Lindars, "formed a middle ground of conservative and scrupulously honest scholarship, which exerted a moderating influence and helped to reconcile people to the inevitable march of historical criticism."[29] Most widely known for his commentaries on the Pauline Epistles, Lightfoot published his first commentary, a survey of Galatians, in 1865.[30] In it, he presented a nuanced view of potential drawbacks to the embrace or exclusion of German interpretation, writing,

> I feel very confident that the historical views of the Tübingen school are too extravagant to obtain any wide or lasting hold over the minds of men. But even in the extreme cases mere denunciation may be unjust and is certainly

---

[28]J. W. Rogerson, *The Bible and Criticism in Victorian Britain: Profiles of F. D. Maurice and William Robertson Smith*, Journal for the Study of the Old Testament Supplement Series 201 (Sheffield, UK: Sheffield Academic Press, 1995), 11.

[29]J. W. Rogerson, Christopher Rowland, and Barnabas Lindars, *The Study and Use of the Bible*, vol. 2, *The History of Christian Theology* (Basingstoke, Hants, UK: Marshall Pickering, 1988), 350. For broader discussion of Lightfoot's life and work, see Geoffrey R. Treloar, *Lightfoot the Historian* (Tübingen: Mohr Siebeck, 1998).

[30]J. B. Lightfoot, *St. Paul's Epistle to the Galatians: A Revised Text with Introduction, Notes, and Dissertations*, 2nd ed. (Andover, MA: Warren F. Draper, 1870).

unavailing . . . we should try and discover the element of truth which underlies even the greatest exaggerations of able men, and correct our impressions thereby.[31]

Many of the developments of New Testament interpretation outlined above occurred within Spurgeon's lifetime. George Eliot's 1846 translation of *Leben Jesu* occurred during Spurgeon's adolescent years; and F. D. Maurice published his *Theological Essays* while Spurgeon was preaching his first sermons to the congregation at Waterbeach. He was well-established as a pastor and president of the Pastors' College when Westcott and Hort published their Greek New Testament. As we have seen in the previous chapter, though Spurgeon did not receive a higher education, he maintained an interest in biblical and theological scholarship—both ancient and modern—and often engaged a wide variety of sources in his sermon preparation. Several of the higher critics' conclusions, such as Strauss's assertion that Christ was not divine or Maurice's arguments against the doctrine of eternal punishment, stood in opposition to Spurgeon's conservative Particular Baptist theology, as well as his interpretive emphasis on the cross and conversion. As we will see in the following section, Spurgeon's assessments of New Testament scholarship provide helpful context through which to approach his own biblical interpretation.

SPURGEON AND NEW TESTAMENT COMMENTATORS

In the latter years of his ministry, through his roles as President of the Pastors' College and general editor of *The Sword and the Trowel*, Spurgeon had broad access to the new biblical scholarship. Many books in Spurgeon's personal library included notes from their respective authors thanking him for his previous reviews of their work for *The Sword and the Trowel* and sometimes requesting him to review the present volume. Spurgeon's survey of biblical commentaries, published in 1876, is also a helpful guide to his perspectives on New Testament scholarship.[32]

---

[31]Lightfoot, *St. Paul's Epistle to the Galatians*, 5.

[32]C. H. Spurgeon, *Lectures to My Students*, vol. 4, *Commenting and Commentaries; Lectures Addressed to the Students of the Pastors' College, Metropolitan Tabernacle* (New York: Sheldon, 1876).

Spurgeon appears to have only encountered German works that were translated and published in English. Christian George's description of Spurgeon's "limited but attempted understanding of German" is likely correct.[33] In the introductory section of his *Commenting and Commentaries*, Spurgeon wrote that he was "not so enamored of the German writers as certain of my brethren appear to be, for they are generally cold and hard, and unspiritual."[34] Spurgeon's criticism of German scholarship took two forms. First, he sweepingly denounced what he called "German philosophy," a discipline he never expressly defined. His critical comments occasionally mentioned neology, an early modern movement embraced by some German academics that envisioned Christianity "as a practical religion consonant with modern knowledge and grounded in the self-reflection of the pious, reasonable individual."[35] Spurgeon's chief complaint against neology was that it obfuscated what he believed to be the clear message of the Bible, as he noted in an 1872 sermon,

> I have sometimes tried to muddle my way through chapters of German neology. Thank God I have felt this is not the way of life, or else certainly I should never find it, though I had a doctor of divinity on either side to assist me. . . . He that will not believe the simple revelation of God, will presently find himself committed to systematic misbeliefs, which distract reason, oppress the heart, and trammel the conscience.[36]

In a more concise sentiment, he suggested that "professed ministers of the gospel have taught the German mind to doubt everything, and now the basis of society is shaken, and law and order are undermined. What could they expect otherwise? He who does not fear God is not likely to honour the king."[37]

---

[33]For further discussion on Spurgeon's foreign language aptitude, see Christian T. George, "Jesus Christ, the 'Prince of Pilgrims': A Critical Analysis of the Ontological, Functional, and Exegetical Christologies in the Sermons, Writings, and Lectures of Charles Haddon Spurgeon (1834–1892)" (PhD thesis, University of St. Andrews, 2011), 37-38.

[34]Spurgeon, *Lectures to My Students*, 4:38.

[35]Eric Carlsson, "Eighteenth-Century Neology," in *The Oxford Handbook of Early Modern Theology, 1600–1800*, ed. Ulrich L. Lehner, Richard A. Muller, and A. G. Roeber (Oxford: Oxford University Press, 2016), 642.

[36]C. H. Spurgeon, "The Two Yokes," sermon no. 1032, given January 14, 1872, from Jeremiah 23:13, *The Metropolitan Tabernacle Pulpit*, vol. 18 (London: Passmore & Alabaster, 1872), 58.

[37]C. H. Spurgeon, "The Hold Fast," sermon no. 1418, given June 9, 1878, from Proverbs 4:13, *The Metropolitan Tabernacle Pulpit*, vol. 24 (London: Passmore & Alabaster, 1878), 332.

Spurgeon's second and more pressing concern was that modern German scholarship could lead Christians to distrust doctrines that he deemed central to the faith. Among these doctrines was the plenary inspiration of the Bible, which led Spurgeon to lament,

> Those fine books of the broad school which came from Germany years ago, but which we now produce at home, it is a pity to have seen the binding of them. Even doctors of divinity favour us with denials of plenary inspiration, and aid in that form of undermining work: they may have all their books so long as we can keep our Bibles, and God gives us firm faith in himself.[38]

Spurgeon regarded a conservative interpretation of penal substitutionary atonement as equally important to that of plenary inspiration. Substitution, a doctrine held closely by many evangelicals throughout the nineteenth century, would eventually become a rallying point for him, particularly in the latter years of his ministry. His comments regarding modern theology's varied expressions of atonement theology reflect both his frustration with the way in which the doctrine was articulated and, more important, his concern that it could hinder the evangelistic efforts of the church.

For Spurgeon and other conservative Christians, theological speculation on the nature of the atonement was perceived as dangerous on the basis that it cast doubt upon the means by which individuals were reconciled to God. As Bebbington observes, there was "normally a substantive difference between evangelicals and other Christians in the weight or the interpretation—or in both—that they put on the event of the crucifixion. Teaching about the cross was therefore the supreme means by which souls were turned to Christ."[39] Spurgeon not only distanced himself from works that contradicted the traditional Reformed position on substitutionary atonement, but he also criticized those who in his estimation had abandoned it. This is evident as he made statements noting that

---

[38]C. H. Spurgeon, "God Glorified by Children's Mouths," sermon no. 1545, given June 27, 1880, from Psalm 8:2, *The Metropolitan Tabernacle Pulpit*, vol. 26 (London: Passmore & Alabaster, 1880), 382.

[39]David W. Bebbington, *The Dominance of Evangelicalism: The Age of Spurgeon and Moody* (Downers Grove, IL: InterVarsity Press, 2005), 26.

the gentlemen of the modern-thought school, who have been to Germany for their theology, do not like that glorious doctrine of substitution. They think that the atonement is a something or other, that in some way or other, somehow or other, has something or other to do with the salvation of men; but I tell them that their cloudy gospel might have surrounded me till my hair grew grey, but I should never have been any the better for it.[40]

Though he was critical of some aspects of German scholarship, Spurgeon's negative comments were usually focused on what he termed the "German philosophers" or the "modern school of theology." As we will note, he held several German scholars in high regard. Furthermore, he recognized that there were evangelical ministers at work in Germany and routinely praised their efforts. He maintained a friendship with the German Baptist preacher Johann Gerhard Oncken (1800–1884) and used Oncken's successes in Germany as sermon illustrations on multiple occasions.[41]

Spurgeon's concern over theological liberalism and higher criticism was not limited to the German universities. Although he appreciated some perspectives from British scholars, he was particularly critical of others. For instance, Spurgeon strongly criticized Benjamin Jowett, the Regius Professor of Greek at the University of Oxford, writing that "Jowett's most unseemly attack on Paul, as an apostle, as a thinker, as a writer, and as a man, only proves his own incapacity for forming a just judgment either of the apostle or of himself."[42] Spurgeon cautiously endorsed a set of lectures on the book of Romans by Thomas Chalmers (1780–1847), a leader in the Church of Scotland and later the Free Church of Scotland.[43] Although his "preferences as to expositions lie in another direction," Spurgeon observed that "we cannot be insensible to the grandeur and childlike simplicity

[40]C. H. Spurgeon, "Christ's Past and Present Witnesses," sermon no. 2709, given March 7, 1880, from John 15:27, *The Metropolitan Tabernacle Pulpit*, vol. 47 (London: Passmore & Alabaster, 1901), 18.

[41]See, for instance, C. H. Spurgeon, "Fire! Fire! Fire!," sermon no. 397, given June 23, 1861, from Isaiah 43:2, *The Metropolitan Tabernacle Pulpit*, vol. 7 (London: Passmore & Alabaster, 1861), 398; Spurgeon, "The Gospel in Power," sermon no. 3551, given April 28, 1872, from 1 Thessalonians 1:5-10, *The Metropolitan Tabernacle Pulpit*, vol. 63 (London: Passmore & Alabaster, 1917), 82.

[42]Spurgeon, *Lectures to My Students*, 4:239; Benjamin Jowett, *Epistles to the Thessalonians, Galatians, and Romans. With Critical Notes and Dissertations*, 2nd ed., 2 vols. (London: John Murray, 1859).

[43]Thomas Chalmers, *Lectures on Romans*, 4 vols. (Edinburgh: Edmonston & Company, 1854).

which were combined in Chalmers."[44] Spurgeon's comments on Chalmers's writing indicate a broader tendency, namely that he often commended biblical study material for different interpretive ends. He noted where readers might find some commentaries valuable for personal study or family devotion, whereas more technical volumes were highlighted as beneficial to those who desired a closer study of the text, particularly with regard to the original languages. Though Spurgeon did not often actively promote critical German scholarship, he did commend a commentary on the Epistles to the Corinthians by Gustav Billroth (1808–1836), a lecturer at the University of Halle. Spurgeon's note on the commentary reveals a sense of his perspective on critical scholarship. He wrote that Billroth's work should

> be prized for its criticism. The author tries to bring forth from each passage the sense which the Apostle intended it to convey. Observations and reflections there are none; but we are not among those who throw away "the dry bones of criticism"—bones are as needful as meat, though not so nourishing.[45]

While Spurgeon interacted with German criticism, he rarely mentioned it in his sermons. His suggestion to his students that he preferred "Puritanic gold to the German silver which is now in fashion" adequately summarizes his viewpoint.[46] He made a similar reference in an 1885 sermon, proclaiming, "We want nowadays a sterling Christianity. We cannot do with German silver now: we must have the real metal. I was about to say I would sooner you had no religion, and made no pretence to having any, than to have the imitation of it."[47] His comparison of German scholarship with German silver, a compound commonly used in nineteenth century dining utensils that resembled silver but was actually

---

[44]Spurgeon, *Lectures to My Students*, 4:241.

[45]Spurgeon, *Lectures to My Students*, 4:246; Johann Gustav Fredrick Billroth, *A Commentary on the Epistles of Paul to the Corinthians*, trans. W. Lindsay Alexander, 2 vols. (Edinburgh: Thomas Clark, 1837).

[46]Spurgeon, *Lectures to My Students*, 4:256.

[47]C. H. Spurgeon, "The Foundation and Its Seal: A Sermon for the Times," sermon no. 1854, given August 9, 1885, from 2 Timothy 2:19, *The Metropolitan Tabernacle Pulpit*, vol. 31 (London: Passmore & Alabaster, 1885), 444.

comprised of copper, nickel, and zinc, indicates the extent to which he viewed their efforts as imitations of biblical engagement rather than helpful guides for the church.

Taken as a whole, Spurgeon's comments suggest that he attempted to engage with German scholarship and offered varied assessments throughout his ministry. Although Spurgeon did not possess a comprehensive understanding of eighteenth and nineteenth-century German philosophy and theology, he feared that some positions promoted by modern German scholars could raise doubts about both plenary inspiration of the Bible and substitutionary atonement. Spurgeon's own approach to biblical interpretation was predicated upon conservative evangelical positions on both biblical inspiration and the atonement, which worked in tandem with his broader crucicentric and conversionistic methodology.

In *Commenting and Commentaries*, Spurgeon recognized the value of engagement with the Greek text, although he knew that some ministers had not had the opportunity to master the ancient language. In keeping with this, he recommended that pastors consult *The Critical English Testament*, which sought "to enable a reader, unacquainted with Greek, to ascertain the exact English force and meaning of the New Testament, and to appreciate the latest result of modern criticism."[48] Additionally, he suggested that students purchase the *How to Study the New Testament* series, written by the Anglican textual critic Henry Alford (1810–1871), who Spurgeon praised for his "mature scholarship, the harvesting of a judgment, generally highly impartial, always worthy of respect, which has gleaned from the most important fields of Biblical research, both modern and ancient, at home and abroad."[49] Spurgeon suggested that Alford was "indispensible to the students of the original. With some faults, he has surpassing excellencies."[50] The faults Spurgeon alluded to may have been related to Alford's presentation, as he further wrote that his readers "will not look here for spirituality of thought or tenderness

---

[48]W. L. Blackley and James Hawes, eds., *The Critical English Testament*, 3rd ed. (London: Daldy, Isbister, 1876), vi.

[49]Spurgeon, *Lectures to My Students*, 4:36.

[50]Spurgeon, *Lectures to My Students*, 4:201.

of feeling" but noted that "the learned Dean does not forget to do full justice to his own views, and is quite able to express himself against his opponents."[51]

On the Gospel accounts, Spurgeon surveyed a variety of sources. Among them was *Catena Aurea*, a collection of comments on the Gospels from the church fathers, assembled by Thomas Aquinas (1225–1274), of which Spurgeon wrote, "This collection of extracts we always look into with curiosity, and sometimes we find a pearl."[52] While he consulted selected ancient and medieval commentaries, Spurgeon focused most of his attention on more recent volumes, particularly editions of Puritan authors and nineteenth-century commentaries. He particularly recommended Westcott's *Introduction to the Study of the Gospels*, observing that "the author knows the German writers, but is not defiled by their scepticism. He is a man of deep thought, but displays no pride of intellect."[53] Additionally, Spurgeon categorized other books under headings such as the "harmonies" of the Gospels; lives of Christ; and studies of the miracles and parables connected to Christ.[54]

Spurgeon followed his section on the Gospel accounts with a brief collection of sources on the book of Acts, the final narrative account in the New Testament canon. This section of the survey is significant in that it contained references to a number of commentaries written by German authors. While Spurgeon remained opposed to the more radical forms of higher criticism, the evidence suggests that he evaluated each work on its merits and did not reject books simply because they were published in Germany. For instance, he praised the work of the German Romantic August Neander (1789–1850), a student of Schleiermacher and convert from Judaism who lectured on theology and church history at the University of Berlin. Neander's survey of Acts, according to Spurgeon, was "bold, devout, learned, and, on the whole, sound. The result of wide

---

[51]Spurgeon, *Lectures to My Students*, 4:36.
[52]Spurgeon, *Lectures to My Students*, 4:209; Thomas Aquinas, *Catena Aurea: Commentary on the Four Gospels, Collected out of the Works of the Fathers*, ed. John Henry Newman, 6 vols. (London: James Parker, 1870).
[53]Spurgeon, *Lectures to My Students*, 4:214.
[54]Spurgeon, *Lectures to My Students*, 4:215-21.

research, and deep learning."[55] The work of Rudolf Stier (1800–1862), a German pastor and professor, received slightly more measured comments. While Spurgeon esteemed Stier's work to be "devout, scholarly, and full of thought" he suggested that it was best used "discreetly."[56] Finally, in a separate section titled "Lives of the Apostles," he critiqued F. C. Baur's survey of the apostle Paul, writing that it was "of the very Broad Church school. Not at all to our mind."[57]

The Pastoral Epistles, which consisted of the letters attributed to the apostle Paul and addressed to Timothy, Titus, and Philemon, were the subject of significant debate in the nineteenth century. The debate, instigated in part by Schleiermacher, centered on whether Paul could have written the letters; this doubt about the Pauline authorship was based largely upon the assumption that the authors of the Pastoral Epistles appeared to combat a form of Gnostic thought that was not believed to have been prevalent in the mid-first century. Spurgeon, who held tightly to traditional views regarding biblical authorship, deplored commentators who questioned this view and also commended scholars who upheld his position. This was evident when he praised a commentary written by the Free Church of Scotland theologian Patrick Fairbairn (1805–1874): "What with a good translation, full defence of the Apostolic authorship of the Epistles, fruitful comments, and profitable dissertations, this volume is about as complete a guide to the smaller epistles as one could desire."[58]

Finally, Spurgeon surveyed commentaries on apocalyptic literature, most notably contained in the Revelation to St. John. Debates regarding the nature, timing, and order of the return of Christ have characterized much of Christian scholarship, and these debates had been renewed in Britain in

---

[55]Spurgeon, *Lectures to My Students*, 4:234; August Neander, *History of the Planting and Training of the Christian Church by the Apostles*, trans. J. E. Ryland, 2 vols. (London: Bell & Sons, 1851).

[56]Spurgeon, *Lectures to My Students*, 4:234; Rudolf Ewald Stier, *The Words of the Apostles*, trans. G. H. Venables (Edinburgh: T&T Clark, 1869).

[57]Spurgeon, *Lectures to My Students*, 4:235; Ferdinand Christian Baur, *Paul, the Apostle of Jesus Christ, His Life and Work, His Epistles and His Doctrine: A Contribution to a Critical History of Primitive Christianity*, trans. Eduard Zeller, 2 vols. (London: Williams and Norgate, 1876).

[58]Spurgeon, *Lectures to My Students*, 4:261; Patrick Fairbairn, *The Pastoral Epistles: The Greek Text and Translation, with Introduction, Expository Notes, and Dissertations* (Edinburgh: T&T Clark, 1874).

part through the influence of John Nelson Darby (1800–1882), a Church of Ireland curate who left the Established Church to form the Christian movement that came to be referred to as the Plymouth Brethren. Darby hypothesized that the events described in the book of Revelation were occurring in the nineteenth-century world around him. He was known for developing and systematizing dispensationalism, a theological framework predicated on the belief that God's administration over and involvement in human affairs changed over measurable historical periods, or "dispensations." This included the notion of the rapture, by which some believed that Christ would return to take believers to heaven before the final judgment described in the latter chapters of Revelation. While Spurgeon's own positions on eschatology are difficult to discern, he consistently opposed dispensationalism.[59] Spurgeon introduced commentaries written on the Revelation to St. John with a lengthy section in which he warned readers of the competing perspectives to be found in apocalyptic study. He wrote, "As for the lucubrations upon parts of the book, they lie at the booksellers' 'thick as leaves in Vallambrosa.' Numbers of these prophecyings have been disproved by the lapse of time, and others will in due season share their fate."[60] His critique of the German Lutheran clergyman Johann Albrecht Bengel's (1687–1752) commentary may serve as an example. As he wrote of Bengel, "This great author was rather too precise in his dates. The end of the forty-two months was settled for the 21st of May, 1810, and the destruction of the beast for June 18th, 1836. When so princely an expositor maunders in this fashion it should act as a caution to less able men."[61] Spurgeon preferred the work of E. B. Elliott (1793–1875), an Anglican

---

[59]Spurgeon's engagement with the various Brethren groups is mixed. While he often critiqued J. N. Darby, he praised the work of George Müller at his orphanage in Bristol, as well as Hudson Taylor's (1832–1905) missionary work in China. Regarding the present topic, Spurgeon's reviews are indicative of what Randall refers to as his "lack of interest in premillennial interpretative minutiae." For further discussion of Spurgeon and the Brethren, see Ian M. Randall, "'Ye Men of Plymouth': C. H. Spurgeon and the Brethren," in *Witness in Many Lands*, ed. Tim Grass (Troon, UK: Brethren Archivists & Historians Network, 2013), 81.

[60]Spurgeon, *Lectures to My Students*, 4:278.

[61]Spurgeon, *Lectures to My Students*, 4:279; Johann Albrecht Bengel, *Bengel's Introduction to His Exposition of the Apocalypse, with His Preface to That Work and the Greatest Part of the Conclusion of It; and Also His Marginal Notes on the Text, Which Are Summary of the Whole Exposition*, trans. John Robertson (London: J. Ryall and R. Withy, 1757).

minister whose four-volume *Horæ Apocalypticæ* was regarded as "the standard work on the subject."[62] Further, Spurgeon's remarks on John Chappel Woodhouse's (1749–1833) translation of Revelation, the final volume listed in Spurgeon's commentary survey, may well describe his general perspective regarding surveys of apocalyptic literature. His commentary survey concluded with his brief statement on Woodhouse: "We give no opinion, for we are too much puzzled with these Apocalyptic books, and are glad to write Finis."[63] He might as easily have referred readers to a comment he made in a review in *The Sword and the Trowel* a few years earlier, in which he mused that "only fools and madmen are positive in their interpretations of the Apocalypse."[64]

Thus the trends noted in Spurgeon's engagement with Old Testament commentaries can also be discerned in his survey of New Testament commentaries. He presented readers with works written at various periods in Christian history, though his focus remained primarily upon the Puritan era and contemporary scholarship. While his most frequent criticisms were directed against what he perceived as departures from conservative, Protestant expressions of Christian doctrine, he was equally ready to grant or withhold recommendations on the grounds of clarity, accessibility, and even the publisher's pricing of the text. With regard to Spurgeon's overall position on higher critical texts, Peter Morden's suggestion that Spurgeon was "anti-critical" is largely correct but requires further qualification.[65] In his pulpit rhetoric, Spurgeon did occasionally speak against "the gentlemen of the higher criticism" and "scientific discoverers . . . and all the other braggers" who were "up in arms against the believers of Jesus," but this was not a frequent occurrence.[66] Furthermore, in his *Commenting and Commentaries*, written for pastors and students, Spurgeon noted, "Modern criticism has furnished many valuable additions to our materials for New

---

[62]Spurgeon, *Lectures to My Students*, 4:280. Spurgeon misidentifies the author as "C. B. Elliott."
[63]Spurgeon, *Lectures to My Students*, 4:281.
[64]*The Sword and the Trowel* 3 (1867): 115.
[65]Peter J. Morden, *"Communion with Christ and His People": The Spirituality of C. H. Spurgeon* (Oxford: Regent's Park College, 2010), 115.
[66]C. H. Spurgeon, "Faith's Sure Foundation," sermon no. 1429, given August 18, 1878, from 1 Peter 2:6, *The Metropolitan Tabernacle Pulpit*, vol. 24 (London: Passmore & Alabaster, 1878), 465.

Testament exegesis."[67] Spurgeon's commentary survey, intended for "thoughtful, discerning men," contained works from a variety of scholars and traditions. This was intentional on his part. Though he avoided including volumes "whose main drift is sceptical," he admitted material "by writers of doubtful doctrine, because of their superior scholarship, and the correctness of their criticism."[68] For Spurgeon, the final litmus test for a book remained whether it could be used to support conversionistic and crucicentric aims. In the sections that follow, we will highlight Spurgeon's own interpretation of New Testament literature according to genre, noting trends in his interpretation and contrasting his conclusions against those of several of his contemporaries.

SPURGEON'S NEW TESTAMENT SERMONS

In December 1874, Spurgeon delivered a sermon that specifically addressed methods of biblical interpretation. The sermon was drawn from 2 Timothy 2:15, a text in which the apostle Paul exhorts Timothy to "study to shew thyself approved unto God, a workman that needeth not to be ashamed, rightly dividing the word of truth."[69] Spurgeon began by outlining the importance of accurate biblical interpretation, suggesting that "rightly handling" the Bible was something that "every Christian minister must do if he would make full proof of his ministry, and if he would be clear of the blood of his hearers on that last great day. Of the whole twenty years of my printed sermons, I can honestly say that this has been my aim."[70] In the subsequent paragraph, Spurgeon equated the preaching of the Bible in general with the preaching of the gospel message within it, particularly as he said of the text, "It is like a sword, and *it was not meant to be played with*. This is not rightly to handle the gospel. It must be used in earnest and pushed home. . . . *The word of God is not committed to God's ministers to amuse men with its glitter, nor to charm them with the jewels in*

---

[67]Spurgeon, *Lectures to My Students*, 4:33.

[68]Spurgeon, *Lectures to My Students*, 4:62.

[69]C. H. Spurgeon, "Rightly Dividing the Word of Truth," sermon no. 1217, given December 27, 1874, from 2 Timothy 2:15, *The Metropolitan Tabernacle Pulpit*, vol. 21 (London: Passmore & Alabaster, 1875), 85-96.

[70]Spurgeon, "Rightly Dividing," 85.

its hilt, but to conquer their souls for Jesus."[71] His argument became more forceful in the following section, where he proclaimed that he desired "to handle the word of God so that no man may ever find an excuse in my ministry for his living without Christ."[72] Later in the sermon, he acknowledged that his method of preaching was not necessarily the norm in pulpits across Britain:

> There are preachers who are always dealing with the deep things, the very deep things. For them the coral caves of mystery, and the far descending shafts of metaphysics have a mighty charm. I have no quarrel with their tastes, but I do not think the word of God was given us to be a riddle-book. *To me the plain gospel is the part which I cut out, and rightly cut out of the word of God. . . . My business is to bring forth that which will save souls, build up saints, and set Christians to work for Christ.* I leave the mysteries, not because I despise them; but because the times demand we first, and above all other things, seek the souls of men.[73]

Having established the centrality of evangelism in his sermons, Spurgeon indicated that this goal was best accomplished through preaching that focused on Christ and his crucifixion. This is illustrated as he quoted the apostle Paul while also subtly including a reference to the text in Isaiah that prompted his own conversion: "'We preach Christ,' said the apostle, 'Christ and him crucified,' and I believe that if the preacher is rightly to divide the word, he will say to the sinner, 'Sinner, Christ died, Christ rose again, Christ intercedes; look to him. As for the difficult questions, leave them for awhile. . . . Now just believing in the Lord Jesus Christ is the main matter.'"[74] Following the format of the previous chapter, we will analyze Spurgeon's sermons from a variety of New Testament literary genres and from a broad chronological range. To provide broader homiletical context, Spurgeon's interpretation will occasionally be set alongside

---

[71]Spurgeon, "Rightly Dividing," 85-86. Emphasis mine.
[72]Spurgeon, "Rightly Dividing," 85-86.
[73]Spurgeon, "Rightly Dividing," 91-92. Emphasis mine.
[74]Spurgeon, "Rightly Dividing," 92. Spurgeon's reference to the apostle Paul is drawn from 1 Corinthians 2:2, which reads, "For I determined not to know any thing among you, save Jesus Christ, and him crucified."

his contemporaries, particularly in cases where his crucicentric and conversionistic focus leads him to eschew more straightforward interpretations of the biblical text.

SPURGEON'S INTERPRETATION
OF THE GOSPEL ACCOUNTS

The New Testament opens with four separate accounts of the life and ministry of Jesus Christ.[75] While each book crafts its own account in a unique way, all four contain descriptions of Christ's teaching and miracles, as well as his death and resurrection.[76] In this section we will consider Spurgeon's treatment of the Gospel accounts, concluding with a survey of Spurgeon's engagement with the Sermon on the Mount, which has a rich history of interpretation in its own right. Throughout we will continue to see Spurgeon's propensity to interpret his texts with a particular focus on the cross and conversion.

Spurgeon often preached from the Gospels, frequently addressing a single verse or even a portion of a verse.[77] One of his earliest sermons at the New Park Street Chapel in 1855 concerned Christ's revelation of himself, and it provided a particularly early example of his crucicentric and conversionistic interpretation.[78] This was evident in his introduction, in which he proclaimed, "When I pass a day without preaching my Master's name I feel that I have not done what I ought to have done, and I do not rest satisfied till I am within the four boards of the pulpit again."[79] As he concluded, he

---

[75]For a helpful overview highlighting the development of the interpretation of the Gospel genre in the nineteenth and twentieth centuries, see Richard A. Burridge, *What Are the Gospels? A Comparison with Graeco-Roman Biography*, 2nd ed. (Grand Rapids, MI: Eerdmans, 2004), 3-24.

[76]Substantive differences in style exist between the first three (the Synoptic Gospels) and John's account, particularly as John's Gospel is recognized by most scholars as having been written later than the others.

[77]He constructed an entire 1889 sermon on the shortest verse in the Bible, John 11:35, which simply reads, "Jesus wept." See C. H. Spurgeon, "Jesus Wept," sermon no. 2091, given June 23, 1889, from John 11:35, *The Metropolitan Tabernacle Pulpit*, vol. 35 (London: Passmore & Alabaster, 1889), 337-48. In a separate portion of the worship service, Spurgeon did provide expositions of chapters, often in the form of running commentaries. Unfortunately, for the majority of his ministry at the Metropolitan Tabernacle these expositions were not recorded by the stenographers.

[78]C. H. Spurgeon, "Christ Manifesting Himself to His People," sermon no. 29, given June 10, 1855, from John 14:22, *The New Park Street Pulpit*, vol. 1 (London: Passmore & Alabaster, 1855), 221-28.

[79]Spurgeon, "Christ Manifesting Himself," 223.

told the congregation that they could learn about the living Christ only through the lens of the dying Christ. He said, "Let thy feet be shod with light once more; trip lightly across the plain of trouble; get to the side of Calvary; ascend to the very summit; and from Calvary I tell thee; thou canst see across the plain as far as heaven itself."[80] The language of conversion came in as the conclusion intensified, and Spurgeon warned that his listeners should

> take heed, lest the first revelation you have of Christ be, when he shall be revealed in flaming fire, taking vengeance on his enemies; for if he is not revealed in mercy, he will be in justice. God give you grace to see him on Calvary before you see him on Sinai; to behold him as the Saviour of sinners, before you see him as the judge of the quick and the dead.[81]

One of Spurgeon's most noteworthy sermons came from Luke's Gospel. In it, Spurgeon broke from his usual behavior and preached from five verses rather than one isolated verse.[82] The sermon was preached following a tragic train collision in August 1861 at the Clayton Tunnel, near Brighton. The collision and subsequent fire in the tunnel killed twenty-three passengers and severely injured 176 more. In the sermon, Spurgeon sought to reassure his congregation and subsequent readers that such tragedies were not necessarily divine punishments.[83] He observed that

> the wicked man sometimes falls dead in the street; but has not the minister fallen dead in the pulpit? . . . The path of righteousness has often conducted men to the rack, to prison, to the gibbet, to the stake; while the

---

[80]Spurgeon, "Christ Manifesting Himself," 228.
[81]Spurgeon, "Christ Manifesting Himself," 228.
[82]The text read:

> There were present at that season some that told him of the Galileans, whose blood Pilate had mingled with their sacrifices. And Jesus answering said unto them, Suppose ye that these Galileans were sinners above all the Galileans, because they suffered such things? I tell you, Nay: but, except ye repent, ye shall all likewise perish. Or those eighteen, upon whom the tower in Siloam fell and slew them, think ye that they were sinners above all men that dwelt in Jerusalem! I tell you, Nay: but, except ye repent, ye shall all likewise perish. (Luke 13:1-5)

[83]C. H. Spurgeon, "Accidents, Not Punishments," sermon no. 408, given September 8, 1861, from Luke 13:1-5, *The Metropolitan Tabernacle Pulpit*, vol. 7 (London: Passmore & Alabaster, 1861), 481-88.

road of sin has often led a man to empire, to dominion, to high esteem among his fellows.[84]

In his second point, Spurgeon directed his listeners to Christ, telling them that while events on earth were not necessarily acts of divine judgment, final judgment did await all men and women. Speaking of the necessity of an individual's reconciliation to God through Christ, he encouraged his listeners to ask themselves, "Do I hate sin? Have I learned to abhor it? . . . Am I washed in his blood? Do I bear his likeness?"[85] He concluded with heightened conversionistic language, proclaiming that every person will face death "not with the crash of broken timbers, perhaps, not with the darkness of the tunnel, not with the smoke and with the steam, not with the shrieks of women and the groans of dying men, but yet with terrors."[86] "If we be not in Christ," he added, "and if the shepherd's rod and staff do not comfort us, to die must be an awful and tremendous thing."[87] The sermon, preached two weeks after the event, was widely circulated in print.[88]

A later sermon, preached in 1885, illustrated a creative interpretation on Spurgeon's part.[89] The title, "He Ran, and He Ran," referred both to the demon-possessed man in Mark's Gospel running to Christ, and to the father of the prodigal son, from the parable in Luke's Gospel, running to greet his lost son. Spurgeon merged the texts together, admonishing his congregation that he "must briefly remind you of the secret hope for sinners,—that while you are yet a great way off, the Father himself will see you, and will run to you. While you are running to his Son, the Father will run to you, and you and he shall meet in Christ,—the only safe

---

[84]Spurgeon, "Accidents," 483.

[85]Spurgeon, "Accidents," 486.

[86]Spurgeon, "Accidents," 488.

[87]Spurgeon, "Accidents," 488.

[88]Spurgeon noted in his *Autobiography* that David Livingstone (1813–1873), the celebrated Scottish physician and missionary, owned a copy of the sermon. Following his death in Zambia, the managers of Livingstone's estate sent his copy of the sermon back to Spurgeon, who noted that the words "Very good.–D.L." had been inscribed at the top. C. H. Spurgeon, *C. H. Spurgeon's Autobiography, Compiled from His Diary, Letters, and Records, by His Wife and His Private Secretary*, vol. 2, *1854–1860* (Chicago: Fleming H. Revell, 1899), 214.

[89]C. H. Spurgeon, "He Ran, and He Ran," sermon no. 2507, given July 2, 1885, from Mark 5:6; Luke 15:20, *The Metropolitan Tabernacle Pulpit*, vol. 43 (London: Passmore & Alabaster, 1897), 109-17.

meeting-place for God and man."[90] Spurgeon's interpretation of the text bypassed extended discussion of the nature of the man's demon possession.[91] In a bold interpretive maneuver, Spurgeon equated exorcism with conversion, particularly as he proclaimed,

> It may be that it is so with you also, dear friends, who are so far away from Christ in the misapprehensions of your want of hope; yet it may be that this very hour is the time when you are to be set free from the power of the devil, and brought to sit at Jesu's feet, clothed, and in your right mind.[92]

His conclusion directed his listeners to the cross, particularly in his last lines, as he said, "In the name of the bleeding Christ, seek his mercy even now; by his bloody sweat and crown of thorns, seek him now. I know no better argument except it be by his death-cry, 'It is finished.' Come ye to Christ; look to him and live, even now."[93]

Spurgeon's crucicentric interpretation of the account in Mark 5 was not shared by several of his contemporaries. J. C. Ryle (1816–1900), the evangelical Anglican Bishop of Liverpool, commented that while this narrative focused upon a particular triumph of Christ over Satan, Christians awaited the time when "He will finally triumph over Satan completely, when He shall come forth at the second advent, and bind him in the bottomless pit."[94] The Baptist minister Alexander Maclaren (1826–1910) portrayed the man's "deliverance" from the power of Satan, and explained that he was "sent to proclaim it among friends who had known his dreadful state, and old associations which would help him to knit his new life to his old, and to treat his misery as a parenthesis."[95] Neither the bishop nor the Baptist minister went so far as to consider the episode to be a narrative about

---

[90]Spurgeon, "He Ran," 115.

[91]Spurgeon, "He Ran," 110.

[92]Spurgeon, "He Ran," 111. The American biographer Russell Conwell (1843–1925) highlighted several apparently supernatural elements of Spurgeon's life in ministry, including scenes of Spurgeon's prayers for the sick and injured resulting in miraculous healing, as well as a potential exorcism. See Russell H. Conwell, *Life of Charles Haddon Spurgeon, the World's Great Preacher* (Philadelphia: Edgewood, 1892), 172-94.

[93]Conwell, *Life of Charles Haddon Spurgeon*, 117.

[94]J. C. Ryle, *Expository Thoughts on the Gospels for Family and Private Use: St. Mark* (London: Wertheim, Macintosh, & Hunt, 1859), 92.

[95]Alexander Maclaren, *The Gospel of St. Mark* (London: Hodder & Stoughton, 1893), 87-88.

conversion. In contrast to the interpretation of his contemporaries, Spurgeon's emphasis on crucicentric and conversionistic preaching meant that he could preach on virtually any episode from the Gospel narratives with reference to the Christ's atoning death.

SPURGEON'S INTERPRETATION
OF THE SERMON ON THE MOUNT

Encompassing three chapters in Matthew's Gospel, the Sermon on the Mount contains the longest recorded discourse attributed to Jesus Christ.[96] Luke Timothy Johnson, a historian of early Christianity, helpfully observes, "In the history of Christian thought—indeed in the history of those observing Christianity—the Sermon on the Mount has been considered an epitome of the teaching of Jesus and therefore, for many, the essence of Christianity."[97] Spurgeon recognized the significance of the Sermon and preached at least twenty-five sermons from it. Additionally, in the months prior to his death, Spurgeon completed the manuscript for his second and final biblical commentary, a survey of Matthew's Gospel titled *The Gospel of the Kingdom*.[98] While the Sermon on the Mount was often used in the nineteenth century as a text for social criticism, Spurgeon's preaching and writing from the Sermon continued to feature the crucicentric and conversionistic interpretation that we have seen more broadly within the Gospel genre as a whole. This is evident across the range of Spurgeon's sermons on the Sermon. His first message from this discourse, in 1858, was drawn from the first line of the Lord's Prayer, and Spurgeon focused on the concept of adoption as a theological metaphor.[99] His conclusion offered both

---

[96]The Sermon is found in Matthew 5–7. For a brief history of interpretation of the Sermon, see Graham N. Stanton, *A Gospel for New People: Studies in Matthew* (Edinburgh: T&T Clark, 1992), 285-325. The Sermon has also been the subject of several historical theology projects. See, for instance, Jaroslav Pelikan, *Divine Rhetoric: The Sermon on the Mount as Message and as Model in Augustine, Chrysostom, and Luther* (Crestwood, NY: St. Vladimir's Seminary Press, 2001).

[97]Luke Timothy Johnson, "The Sermon on the Mount," in *The Oxford Companion to Christian Thought*, ed. Adrian Hastings (Oxford: Oxford University Press, 2000), 654.

[98]Spurgeon's widow, Susannah, published the book a year after his death. C. H. Spurgeon, *The Gospel of the Kingdom: A Commentary on the Book of Matthew* (London: Passmore & Alabaster, 1893).

[99]C. H. Spurgeon, "The Fatherhood of God," sermon no. 213, given September 12, 1858, from Matthew 6:9, *The New Park Street Pulpit*, vol. 4 (London: Passmore & Alabaster, 1858), 385-92.

encouragement for the converted and caution for the unconverted, particularly as he pressed on, "Thank God you have got a father that can be angry, but that loves you as much when he is angry as when he smiles upon you. Go away with that upon your mind, and rejoice. But if you love not God and fear him not, go home, I beseech you, to confess your sins, and to seek mercy through the blood of Christ."[100]

Another sermon, delivered in December 1861, gave Spurgeon more latitude to discuss contemporary topics in light of the Sermon on the Mount.[101] Preaching on the blessing for the peacemakers, who would be "called the children of God," Spurgeon began by admonishing his listeners to work as peacemakers in their own contexts, saying, "The peacemaker is *a citizen*, and though he be a Christian, he remembers that Christianity does not require him to forego his citizenship, but to use and to improve it for Christ's glory. The peacemaker, then as a citizen, loveth peace."[102] Spurgeon portrayed Christ as the believer's best example of a peacemaker and echoed words used at the crucifixion to emphasize it. He said, "If ye have any strifes among you, or any divisions, I pray you, even as God, for Christ's sake, forgave you, so also do ye. By the bloody sweat of him who prayed for you, and by the agonies of him who died for you, and in dying said, 'Father, forgive them, for they know not what they do,' forgive your enemies."[103]

He concluded with a fervent evangelistic plea, addressing the unconverted directly as he said, "Are you willing to take Christ on his own terms, and they are no terms at all—they are simply that you should make no terms in the matter, but give yourself up, body, soul, and spirit, to be saved of him?"[104]

---

[100]Spurgeon, "Fatherhood of God," 392.

[101]C. H. Spurgeon, "The Peacemaker: A Sermon for the Times," sermon no. 422, given December 8, 1861, from Matthew 5:9, *The Metropolitan Tabernacle Pulpit*, vol. 7 (London: Passmore & Alabaster, 1861), 593-600. It is not immediately clear whether Spurgeon had a particular event in mind as he addressed his congregation. As several illustrations in the sermon referred to preachers who had worked in America such as John Wesley and Cotton Mather, it is possible that the "times" his sermon was meant to address referred to the American Civil War.

[102]Spurgeon, "Peacemaker," 593.

[103]Spurgeon, "Peacemaker," 597. Spurgeon's reference is to the account of the crucifixion in Luke 23:34.

[104]Spurgeon, "Peacemaker," 600.

In this rather fervent appeal for conversion, Spurgeon stands at a considerable distance from several of his contemporaries. The Scottish poet and Congregationalist minister George MacDonald (1824–1905), an admirer of F. D. Maurice, saw the text as a warning against unnecessary schism and division in the church, particularly as those who in his mind "care for canon and dogma more than for truth, and for the Church more than for Christ; who take uniformity for unity; who strain at a gnat and swallow a camel, not knowing what spirit they are of."[105] The Anglican J. C. Ryle viewed the peacemakers in the Sermon as "those who strive to make all men love one another, by teaching that Gospel which says, 'love is the fulfilling of the law.'"[106] Thus, while all three preachers saw the text as a basis for social criticism, Spurgeon was alone in his crucicentric and conversionistic reading of the text.

Spurgeon addressed matters of Christian life and practice as he navigated through the Sermon on the Mount. In a sermon appropriately titled "A Call to Holy Living," he suggested that there "are legitimate reasons why the world, the church, and our Lord Jesus Christ himself, may expect more from Christians than from the rest of mankind. And, the first is, because *they profess more.*"[107] Spurgeon constructed his ideal of the Christian life using the language of conversion and transformation. This is evident as he admonished his congregation that "a Christian professes himself to be a renewed man; he has learned the evil of sin, repented of it, and fled from it to Christ Jesus. . . . Now, Christian, if you profess this, your life must prove it, or else, if your life gives the lie to your religious pretensions, you stand convicted of a flagrant falsehood, a fraud on men and a felony against God."[108] Spurgeon's appeal included crucicentric language scattered throughout his sermon. For instance, commenting on sexual purity, he implored, "Be ye chaste as the driven snow, let not an immodest glance

---

[105]George MacDonald, *The Hope of the Gospel* (New York: D. Appleton, 1892), 136.

[106]J. C. Ryle, *Expository Thoughts on the Gospels for Family and Private Use: St. Matthew* (New York: Robert Carter and Brothers, 1857), 34.

[107]C. H. Spurgeon, "A Call to Holy Living," sermon no. 1029, given January 14, 1872, from Matthew 5:47, *The Metropolitan Tabernacle Pulpit*, vol. 18 (London: Passmore & Alabaster, 1872), 14. Spurgeon preached from a portion of the verse, which read, "What do ye more than others?"

[108]Spurgeon, "Call to Holy Living," 15.

defile you. We do not like to say much about these things, they are so delicate, and we tremble lest we should suggest what we would prevent; but, oh, by the tears of Jesus, by the wounds of Jesus, by the death of Jesus, hate even the garment spotted by the flesh."[109] Finally, as he concluded, Spurgeon used the image of the dying Christ to illustrate the extent to which his listeners should seek to serve others. His conclusion, worth quoting at length, indicates the extent to which social action, crucicentrism, and conversion blended together in Spurgeon's interpretation of the sermon:

> Our Lord Jesus Christ's heart was expansive and unselfish. *He gave himself for his enemies, and died breathing a prayer over them*; he never lived for himself. . . . He saved others, but himself he would not save. His followers must in this follow him closely. Selfishness is as foreign to Christianity as darkness to light. The true Christian lives to do good, he looks abroad to see whom he may serve, and with this eye he looks upon the wicked, upon the fallen and the offcasts, seeking to reclaim them. Yes, in the same way he looks upon his personal enemies, and aims at winning them by repeated kindnesses. No nationality must confine his goodwill, no sect or clan monopolise his benevolence. No depravity of character or poverty of condition must sicken his loving-kindness, for Jesus received sinners and ate with them. Our love must embrace those who lie hard by the gates of hell, and *we must endeavour with words of truth and deeds of love to bring them to Christ, who can uplift them to heaven.*[110]

Spurgeon's sermons on this significant biblical passage show points of continuity and discontinuity with his contemporaries. As with Old Testament prophetic literature, the Sermon on the Mount was a text that was often used to promote Christian social action, and to an extent Spurgeon fits within that tradition. Spurgeon's interpretation of the Sermon, however, focused more upon transformation rooted in the Sermon's divine author, and as such his sermons from this noteworthy text continue the trend of crucicentric and conversionistic interpretation. Thus Timothy Larsen is correct to note that "Spurgeon's deepest desire

---

[109]Spurgeon, "Call to Holy Living," 22.
[110]Spurgeon, "Call to Holy Living," 22-23.

was that his preaching on the Sermon on the Mount would occasion spiritual conversion and moral formation. Moreover, he was convinced that the original speaker of this greatest of all sermons was aiming at the same effect."[111]

THE EPISTLES

A significant portion of the New Testament is made up of the Epistles, with authorship attributed to the early Christian writers Peter, Paul, John, James, and Jude.[112] Some of the Epistles were written to churches across Europe and Asia Minor, in cities such as Corinth, Ephesus, and Rome; others were written directly to church leaders, such as Paul's letters to Timothy. In the following section, we will note that although Spurgeon used the Epistles to address pastoral concerns within his own church, the overriding framework by which he interpreted the letters was crucicentric and conversionistic.

Spurgeon's sermons from the Epistles began in his earliest time in London. During his second week at the New Park Street Chapel, he turned to a text in the first epistle to the Corinthians, which read, "This do in remembrance of me."[113] The sermon addressed several noteworthy scenes in the life of Christ, contrasting most of them with his execution.[114] He preached, "What a mighty tragedy was the death of Christ! And his life too? Ushered in with a song, it closed with a shriek. 'It is finished.'"[115] He moved his illustrations from Christ's prayer at the Garden of Gethsemane to his trial before Pontius Pilate, before stopping at Christ's crucifixion at Calvary.

---

[111]Timothy Larsen, "Charles Haddon Spurgeon," in *The Sermon on the Mount Through the Centuries*, ed. Jeffrey Greenman, Timothy Larsen, and Stephen R. Spencer (Grand Rapids, MI: Brazos Press, 2007), 205.

[112]The author of the epistle to the Hebrews is not identified.

[113]C. H. Spurgeon, "The Remembrance of Christ," sermon no. 2, given January 7, 1855, from 1 Corinthians 11:24, *The New Park Street Pulpit*, vol. 1 (London: Passmore & Alabaster, 1855), 9-16.

[114]The text spanning 1 Corinthians 11:23-26, which retells the Last Supper narrative, setting precedent for the sacrament of the Eucharist, accounts for more sermons from Spurgeon than any other New Testament passage. He published eleven sermons from the broader text, six on 1 Corinthians 11:26 alone. He preached four sermons on another text relevant to the Eucharist, John 6:55. For further discussion on Spurgeon's theology of the sacraments see Morden, *"Communion with Christ,"* 165-89; Tim Grass and Ian Randall, "C. H. Spurgeon on the Sacraments," in *Baptist Sacramentalism*, ed. Anthony R. Cross and Philip E. Thompson (Milton Keynes, UK: Paternoster, 2003), 55-75.

[115]Spurgeon, "Remembrance of Christ," 11.

Amid Spurgeon's call to remember the suffering Christ, he noted that this might not be possible for some listeners, for "you cannot spiritually remember anything about Christ, because you never had him manifested to you, and what we have never known, we cannot remember."[116]

The phrase "this do in remembrance of me" also appears in Luke 22:19. Spurgeon preached a sermon drawn from this identical passage over thirty years later.[117] In the latter sermon, Spurgeon reversed his structure, beginning by asking his congregation, "Do we know the Lord?"[118] He argued that "until you have believed in Jesus, and so know him, and know his power within you, and have come to personal dealings with him, instead of getting a blessing from the ordinance, you would eat and drink condemnation to yourselves . . . you are not capable of discerning that body if you have no faith."[119] The sermon also illustrated some of Spurgeon's more excessive christocentric language, particularly as he said, "I would have the image of my Lord printed on the palms of my hands, that I might *do* nothing without him; and I would have it painted on my eye-balls, that I might *see* nothing except through him. It were better still to have it stamped upon the heart, that my very life might not beat except to the music of his name."[120] As he concluded his sermon, Spurgeon offered one last evangelistic invitation, proclaiming that "If you desire Christ, Christ desires you. If you have a spark of love to him, he has a furnace full of love to you; and if you want to come to him and trust him to save you, come and welcome."[121]

Another illustration of Spurgeon's crucicentric emphasis can be found in a sermon titled "Contentment," drawn from Philippians 4:11, which reads, "For I have learned, in whatsoever state I am, therewith to be content."[122] The first half of Spurgeon's sermon took the form of social

---

[116]Spurgeon, "Remembrance of Christ," 12.

[117]C. H. Spurgeon, "The Lord's Supper: A Remembrance of Jesus," sermon no. 2038, given August 19, 1888, from Luke 22:19, *The Metropolitan Tabernacle Pulpit*, vol. 34 (London: Passmore & Alabaster, 1888), 445-56.

[118]Spurgeon, "Lord's Supper," 446.

[119]Spurgeon, "Lord's Supper," 447.

[120]Spurgeon, "Lord's Supper," 449.

[121]Spurgeon, "Lord's Supper," 456.

[122]C. H. Spurgeon, "Contentment," sermon no. 320, given March 25, 1860, from Philippians 4:11, *The New Park Street Pulpit*, vol. 6 (London: Passmore & Alabaster, 1860), 269-76.

criticism. He reminded his largely upper working-class and lower middle-class congregation that the wealth of the rich often did not bring about contentment.[123] Spurgeon then addressed the Christian poor, suggesting that in the midst of their plight, they were in a superior state to those outside the faith. He suggested that they should "seek, if you can, by superior skill, steady perseverance, and temperate thriftiness, to raise your position," and reminded them that "a Christian is a believer who hath fellowship with Christ; but a poor Christian hath in his poverty a special vein of fellowship with Christ opened up to him. *Your* Master wore a peasant's garb, and spoke a peasant's brogue."[124] Spurgeon then turned to the matter of finding contentment amid suffering. He instructed his congregation and readers to consider that "all these sufferings are less than his (Christ's) sufferings. 'Canst thou not watch with thy Lord one hour?' He hangs upon a tree with the world's miseries in his bowels; cannot you bear these lesser miseries that fall on you?"[125] Finally, having taken his listeners to the cross, Spurgeon appealed to the unconverted, saying, "You that love not Christ, recollect that you are the most miserable people in the world. Though you may think yourselves happy, there is no one of us that would change places with the best of you. . . . Saints have no hell but what they suffer here on earth; sinners will have no heaven but what they have here in this poor troublous world."[126] Spurgeon's nearly seamless transition from discussion of the apostle Paul's discourse on contentment to his invitation to the unconverted occurred through his employment of the language of atonement. This element of the crucifixion narrative served as a bridge between the text at hand and the evangelistic invitation.

Amid examples of Spurgeon preaching crucicentric sermons from varied and sometimes unexpected texts, it should be noted that his sermons based on explicitly crucicentric texts often indicate reflective, nuanced interpretation. For instance, Spurgeon preached a number of sermons from the

---

[123]Spurgeon, "Contentment," 272.

[124]Spurgeon, "Contentment," 273-74.

[125]Spurgeon, "Contentment," 276. Spurgeon's reference in this section is Christ's question to the disciples as he prayed in a moment of distress in the Garden of Gethsemane, in the moments immediately preceding his arrest and trial. See Matthew 26:40 and Mark 14:37, respectively.

[126]Spurgeon, "Contentment," 276.

Epistle to the Hebrews.[127] One of them, titled "The Shameful Sufferer," was featured in a list of noteworthy sermons in Spurgeon's *Autobiography* as "the means of a great blessing to very many."[128] The sermon, preached while the congregation met in the Music Hall of the Royal Surrey Gardens, focused on a particularly christological text from Hebrews that read, "Who for the joy that set before him endured the cross, despising the shame, and is now set down at the right hand of the throne of God."[129] Spurgeon took the occasion of a verse centered on the crucifixion scene to investigate both the historical and theological significance of the cross. Beginning his address, he acknowledged to his listeners that "all I can say concerning the sufferings of Jesus, this morning, will be but as a drop of the bucket."[130] To begin to appreciate the significance of the cross, according to Spurgeon, one must "understand [Christ's] previous glory in its height of majesty, and his incarnation upon the earth in all its depths of shame. . . . We must first understand infinite height, and then, infinite depth; we must measure, in fact, the whole infinity that is between heaven and hell, before we can understand the love of Jesus Christ."[131]

Spurgeon devoted a significant portion of the sermon to highlighting the nature and degree of the shame inflicted upon Christ. In particular he observed that the mocking of the Roman soldiers recorded in the crucifixion narrative served to undermine the offices attributed to Christ, namely those of prophet, priest, and king. Spurgeon used impassioned language to describe "the King of kings and Lord of lords, having for his adoration the

---

[127]The epistle to the Hebrews is unique in that, unlike the other books in the New Testament canon, its author does not list his or her name. While the authorship of the letter has been a question for scholars throughout the centuries, Spurgeon simply assumed that Hebrews was the work of the apostle Paul. He held this position throughout his ministry. For an early example, see C. H. Spurgeon, "Final Perseverance," sermon no. 76, given April 20, 1856, from Hebrews 6:4-6, *The New Park Street Pulpit*, vol. 2 (London: Passmore & Alabaster, 1856), 172. Over thirty years later, he still referred to Paul as the author. See Spurgeon, "Christ's One Sacrifice for Sin," sermon no. 2283, given June 19, 1890, from Hebrews 9:26, *The Metropolitan Tabernacle Pulpit*, vol. 38 (London: Passmore & Alabaster, 1892), 554.

[128]Spurgeon, *Autobiography*, 2:226. Hebrews 12:2.

[129]C. H. Spurgeon, "The Shameful Sufferer," sermon no. 236, given January 30, 1859, from Hebrews 12:2, *The New Park Street Pulpit*, vol. 5 (London: Passmore & Alabaster, 1859), 89-96. The end of the verse immediately preceding Spurgeon's text included the phrase "looking unto Jesus," which referenced the text in Isaiah that was preached on the morning of his conversion in 1850.

[130]Spurgeon, "Shameful Sufferer," 89.

[131]Spurgeon, "Shameful Sufferer," 89.

spittle of guilty mouths, for damage the smitings of filthy hands, for tribute the jests of brutal tongues."[132] With regard to Christ's prophetic office, Spurgeon proclaimed, "They blindfolded him; shut out the light of heaven from his eyes, and then they smote him, and did buffet him with their hands, and they said, 'Prophesy unto us who it is that smote thee.' The prophet must make a prophecy to those who taunted him to tell them who it was that smote him."[133] Finally, with regard to Christ's priesthood, Spurgeon observed that "Jesus Christ had come into the world to be a priest to offer sacrifice, and his priesthood must be mocked too. All salvation lay in the hands of the priests, and did not they say unto him, 'If thou be the Christ save thyself and us,' Ah! He saved others, himself he could not save."[134]

Spurgeon then turned to highlight Christ's suffering with an evangelistic appeal: "By the grace of God, let every Christian lift his hands to the Most High God, to the maker of heaven and earth, and let him say within himself, 'Now for the love I bear his name, what was my gain I count my loss. I pour contempt on all my shame, and nail my glory to his cross.'"[135] Spurgeon's focus on the cross event in this sermon stands in contrast to several of his contemporaries. Alexander Maclaren, for instance, did not highlight the suffering of Christ in his comments on the passage, which focused primarily on Christ's second coming.[136] John Henry Newman, while still within the Church of England, used the text as a basis to critique what he determined to be "dogmatic" definitions of the gospel, particularly within the evangelical traditions.[137] In contrast with Spurgeon, neither interpreter noted any connection between the mocking of Christ and his offices, nor did they utilize conversion language.

Spurgeon's sermons drawn from the apostle Paul's letters to Timothy are a helpful case study within this genre. He preached often from both letters,

[132]Spurgeon, "Shameful Sufferer," 92.

[133]Spurgeon, "Shameful Sufferer," 92-93.

[134]Spurgeon, "Shameful Sufferer," 93.

[135]Spurgeon, "Shameful Sufferer," 93. The verse quoted by Spurgeon is drawn from the hymn "No More, My God, I Boast No More," by the popular eighteenth-century English hymnwriter Isaac Watts (1674–1748).

[136]Alexander Maclaren, *The Epistle to the Hebrews (Chapters VII to XIII) and the General Epistle of James* (New York: A. C. Armstrong and Son, 1910), 199-208.

[137]John Henry Newman, *Parochial and Plain Sermons*, vol. 2 (London: Rivingtons, 1868), 163-74.

and among his sermons he particularly favored one verse, 1 Timothy 1:15, which he addressed in six different sermons throughout his ministry.[138] The text of the verse, which read, "This is a faithful saying, and worthy of all acceptation, that Christ Jesus came into the world to save sinners; of which I am chief," connected particularly well with Spurgeon's established crucicentric and conversionistic preaching. In his earliest sermon on the text, Spurgeon's evangelistic plea to his listeners began to emerge within his first paragraph, in which he proclaimed that "our message is no heavy one. No threatenings and no thunders compose the theme of the gospel minister. All is mercy; love is the sum and substance of our gospel—love undeserved. . . . May many of you gathered together, who have never as yet fled to Jesus for refuge, by the simple preaching of the word, now be persuaded to come in."[139] He continued, suggesting that the unconverted remained in their state in part because they had never truly seen Christ as he said, "A true view of Christ, a right-looking at him, will most assuredly beget faith in the soul."[140] The proper view of Christ, according to Spurgeon, was one that presented a crucified and resurrected Christ. He lamented, "Could I bring him before you, could I now bring him here to show you his hands and his side, if ye could now, like Thomas, put your fingers in the holes of the nails, and thrust your hand into his side, methinks you would not be faithless, but believing."[141]

In 1878, Spurgeon addressed this text from the pulpit at the Metropolitan Tabernacle for the third time.[142] This sermon's structure varied considerably

---

[138]See C. H. Spurgeon, "The Glorious Gospel," sermon no. 184, given March 21, 1858, from 1 Timothy 1:15, *The New Park Street Pulpit*, vol. 4 (London: Passmore & Alabaster, 1858), 153-60; "The Chief of Sinners," sermon no. 530, from 1 Timothy 1:15, n.d., *The Metropolitan Tabernacle Pulpit*, vol. 9 (London: Passmore & Alabaster, 1863), 517-28; "The Faithful Saying," sermon no. 1416, given May 26, 1878, from 1 Timothy 1:15, *The Metropolitan Tabernacle Pulpit*, vol. 24 (London: Passmore & Alabaster, 1878), 301-12; "A Great Gospel for Great Sinners," sermon no. 1837, given June 2, 1884, from 1 Timothy 1:15-17, *The Metropolitan Tabernacle Pulpit*, vol. 31 (London: Passmore & Alabaster, 1885), 229-40; "The Whole Gospel in a Single Verse," sermon no. 2300, given February 28, 1889, from 1 Timothy 1:15, *The Metropolitan Tabernacle Pulpit*, vol. 39 (London: Passmore & Alabaster, 1893), 133-44; "A Sermon on a Grand Old Text," sermon no. 3089, from 1 Timothy 1:15, n.d., *The Metropolitan Tabernacle Pulpit*, vol. 54 (London: Passmore & Alabaster, 1908), 193-202.

[139]Spurgeon, "Glorious Gospel," 153.

[140]Spurgeon, "Glorious Gospel," 155.

[141]Spurgeon, "Glorious Gospel," 155.

[142]Spurgeon, "Faithful Saying," 301-12.

from his previous explorations of the text. He began with a discussion of the nature of sin, reminding his congregation that *"the thrice holy God hates sin* with a hatred scarcely to be conceived by any of us, since we have lost the sensitiveness of perfect purity."[143] The thematic turning point of the sermon came next, with the cross central to his argument:

> Note also that even Christ Jesus could not save men had he stayed in heaven, he *came into the world* to save sinners. The Fall was so grievous that he must come right down into the place of our ruin; he must come to the dunghill that he might lift us out of it . . . he must needs come into the world to do so; down into this polluted creation the eternal Creator must himself descend.[144]

His use of imagery intensified and focused even more tightly on language of atonement for sin, particularly as he exclaimed, "I will only ask you to consider the crowning act of his work, when he hung upon the cross. What mean those bruisings of the scourge? What mean those deep furrows on his blessed back? What mean those pierced hands and feet? They mean this, that he is suffering on account of human sin."[145] Throughout the sermon, Spurgeon followed the highly personal language of the apostle Paul and was careful to include himself within his group of sinners, evident in comments such as, "I speak the language of every child of God when I say the top and bottom, the beginning and the ending of all my hope lies in this, that Jesus Christ came into the world to save sinners. I just trust myself as a sinner with him."[146] The sermon concluded with a fervent invitation, with Spurgeon exhorting his listeners, "Will you and I have Christ? I will, whether you will or not. Come along. Do not draw back. Take what God freely presents to you, and from this day trust Jesus to be your Saviour, and we will meet in heaven."[147]

A later sermon on the same passage offers a similar message, though his emphasis shifted from previous sermons on the text. The 1 Timothy text,

---

[143]Spurgeon, "Faithful Saying," 303.
[144]Spurgeon, "Faithful Saying," 304. Spurgeon is likely referencing John 4:4 here, which in the Authorized Version read, "He must needs go through Samaria."
[145]Spurgeon, "Faithful Saying," 306.
[146]Spurgeon, "Faithful Saying," 311.
[147]Spurgeon, "Faithful Saying," 312.

according to Spurgeon, "contains the gospel in brief, yet I may say that *it contains the gospel in full*. If you get condensed notes of a sermon or a speech, you often miss the very soul and marrow of it; but here you get all the condensation possible, as if the great truths of the gospel were pressed together by a hydraulic ram, and yet there is not a particle of it left out."[148] Spurgeon provided a comprehensive overview of the nature of sin, as he had in previous sermons; however, in this instance he criticized not only sins committed by individuals but also sins committed by society as a whole. Commenting on Victorian London, Spurgeon remarked,

> What a wonderful thing "society" is, itself rotten to the core very often; and yet if there happens to be a poor woman who has gone astray, "society" cries, "Put her out! Drive the wretched creature away from us." I have known one such turned out of hotel after hotel. They could not bear their righteous selves to come anywhere near to one who had in the least degree broken the laws of society.[149]

In his interpretation of this text, Spurgeon was quick to critique a public piety that left no room for the care of individuals whose indiscretions bristled against cultural stigmas. According to Spurgeon, his congregation and indeed all Christians should imitate Christ in their dealings with sinners. Elaborating further, he reminded the congregation that

> notwithstanding all his sense of horror of sin . . . [Christ] came into the world to save sinners, and with sinners he mixed, even with publicans and harlots. With sinners he sat at meat; with sinners he lived; with sinners he died; he made his grave with the wicked; he entered paradise with a thief; and to-day, those who sing the new song in heaven confess that they were sinners.[150]

His next section elaborated on the life of Christ, throughout which Spurgeon reiterated that Christ's life, teaching, and ministry all pointed to the cross, where Jesus "stretched out his hands and feet, and yielded up himself to die for sinners."[151] His sermon ended with the plea, "May the

---

[148]Spurgeon, "Whole Gospel," 133. Emphasis mine.
[149]Spurgeon, "Whole Gospel," 135.
[150]Spurgeon, "Whole Gospel," 135.
[151]Spurgeon, "Whole Gospel," 139.

Lord help thee to believe in Jesus immediately! Ere thou leavest this place, trust him! Trust him wholly. He came to save sinners. Let him save you. It is his business; it is not yours. Leave yourself in his hands, and he will save you, to the praise of his glory and grace."[152]

As we have seen throughout the chapter, Spurgeon's focus on the cross and conversion exceeded that of his contemporaries. Edwin Charles Dargan (1852–1930), an American Southern Baptist minister who wrote a two-volume history of preaching, addressed the broader theology of the gospel message in the text but focused his attention on the text as Pauline autobiography, with virtually none of the crucicentrism that characterized Spurgeon's interpretation.[153] In a similar vein, Marcus Dods (1834–1909), a Scottish New Testament scholar and Free Church minister, also highlighted Paul's self-identity in a sermon on this text, though his sermon focused primarily on the relationship between the Savior and those he saved, in contrast with Spurgeon's more direct appeal for conversion.[154]

Thus, while the epistles represent a variety of texts written by a variety of authors, Spurgeon's engagement with this genre followed the general pattern that we have observed. Whether he preached from Paul's text on the nature of the communion meal or from his instruction on Christian contentment, Spurgeon focused his sermons on the cross of Christ. Furthermore, as Spurgeon engaged texts that included crucicentric imagery, he intensified that imagery to further color his sermons, often to significant effect.

SPURGEON'S INTERPRETATION OF THE REVELATION OF JOHN AND APOCALYPTIC LITERATURE

The final genre in this survey of Spurgeon's New Testament interpretation is apocalyptic literature. The biblical scholar John Collins has defined apocalyptic literature as "a genre of revelatory literature with a narrative

---

[152]Spurgeon, "Whole Gospel," 142.
[153]Edwin Charles Dargan, *The Changeless Christ and Other Sermons* (Chicago: Fleming H. Revell, 1918), 121-36. Dargan was also the president of the Southern Baptist Convention from 1911–1913. Regarding his history of preaching, which included a section on Spurgeon, see Edwin Charles Dargan, *A History of Preaching*, vol. 2, *From the Close of the Reformation Period to the End of the Nineteenth Century, 1572–1900* (London: Hodder & Stoughton, 1912).
[154]Marcus Dods, *Christ and Man: Sermons* (London: Hodder & Stoughton, 1909), 176-87.

framework, in which a revelation is mediated by an otherworldly being to a human recipient, disclosing a transcendent reality which is both temporal, insofar as it envisages eschatological salvation, and spatial insofar as it involves another supernatural world."[155] Bearing some similarity to the prophetic genre in the Old Testament, we might further define New Testament apocalyptic literature as characterized by texts that presupposed Christ's incarnation and reflected upon his eventual return. New Testament apocalyptic texts include the Revelation of John, the longest apocalyptic text in the New Testament, as well as sections of the Gospels and portions of the apostle Paul's letters to the Thessalonians and the apostle Peter's epistles. In this last section, we will note that the interpretive priorities we have seen throughout Spurgeon's New Testament preaching remain consistent in his sermons from the apocalyptic genre.

Interestingly, while Spurgeon drew the gospel out of passages where it was not explicit, he guarded against drawing conclusions, aside from gospel messages, out of the obscure apocalyptic writings. On the one hand, Spurgeon was happy to read the gospel into a variety of biblical passages; on the other hand, he cautioned against reading anything into the Revelation of John apart from the cross and the gospel. As we have seen, the interpretation of apocalyptic literature was polarizing in the nineteenth century, and Spurgeon was wary of the influence of Darbyism and dispensational theology.[156] He did include a commentary from Darby in his *Commenting and Commentaries*, though the book was, in Spurgeon's estimation, "too mystical for ordinary minds. If the author would write in plain English his readers would probably discover that there is nothing very valuable in his remarks."[157] Literalistic interpretations of apocalyptic texts have been produced throughout Christian history, and the nineteenth century was no exception. Spurgeon, addressing the matter in an 1875 sermon, commented that "some hearers are crazy after the mysteries of the

---

[155]John J. Collins, "What Is Apocalyptic Literature?," in *The Oxford Handbook of Apocalyptic Literature*, ed. John J. Collins (Oxford: Oxford University Press, 2014), 2.

[156]See, for instance, an 1869 article that was critical of both the Plymouth Brethren and Darby himself that was included in *The Sword and the Trowel*. The author was James Grant (1802–1879), a Scottish editor of Christian periodicals. See *The Sword and the Trowel* 5 (1869): 65-75.

[157]Spurgeon, *Lectures to My Students*, 4:127.

future. Well, there are two or three brethren in London who are always trumpeting and vialing. Go and hear them if you want it, I have something else to do."[158] Criticizing the biblical interpretation of the Plymouth Brethren, Spurgeon suggested they "delight to fish up some hitherto undiscovered tadpole of interpretation, and cry it around the town as a rare dainty."[159] Spurgeon's estimation of his own task as a preacher follows the pattern we have seen throughout his biblical interpretation and broader ministry, particularly as he said, "I confess I am not sent to decipher the Apocalyptic symbols, my errand is humbler but equally useful, I am sent to bring souls to Jesus Christ."[160]

Preaching from an apocalyptic section of 2 Peter, Spurgeon cautioned his listeners against being too precise in their interpretations of biblical prophecy, suggesting that "we are but children, and our little plans of house-building, like children with their toy bricks, are very simple and elementary indeed; but God's architecture is of a high class, and we cannot, therefore, conjecture where this event will come in, or where that marvel will find its place."[161] Helpfully clarifying his objective, he continued, "instead of puzzling our brains over projects of interpretation, we may be quite satisfied to take each of the facts separately as we find them, believingly expect them, and, above all, deduce from them their legitimate practical conclusions."[162] Spurgeon addressed the text from 2 Peter straightforwardly, comparing the destructive power of the fire described in the passage to that of Vesuvius, and the lack of preparedness on part of the population to the bystanders who perished in the Great Flood. To the converted among his listeners, Spurgeon advocated a watchful outlook and a reminder that they should live as "pilgrims and strangers." The unconverted were directed fervently toward the cross: "If all you love is here below, it will all go! Your gold and silver will all go! Will you not have Christ? Will you not have a Saviour? For if you will not, there remains for

---

[158]Spurgeon, "Rightly Dividing," 91.
[159]Spurgeon, *Lectures to My Students*, 4:57.
[160]Spurgeon, *Lectures to My Students*, 4:57.
[161]C. H. Spurgeon, "The World on Fire," sermon no. 1125, given August 3, 1873, from 2 Peter 3:10-11, *The Metropolitan Tabernacle Pulpit*, vol. 19 (London: Passmore & Alabaster, 1873), 434.
[162]Spurgeon, "World on Fire," 434.

you only a fearful looking for of judgment and of fiery indignation. Tempt not the anger of God. Yield to his mercy now. Believe in his dear Son."[163]

The theme of watchfulness in prophetic literature is also seen in Spurgeon's sermons on an apocalyptic section of Paul's letter to the Thessalonians. Paul's admonition to the Thessalonian church to "watch and be sober" formed the basis for three separate Spurgeon sermons.[164] The first, preached at the New Park Street Chapel in 1856, was titled "The Enchanted Ground," a title drawn from John Bunyan's allegory, *Pilgrim's Progress*.[165] In this sermon, Spurgeon breaks from his usual practice by referring to Bunyan's allegory far more than to Paul's letter. Spurgeon suggested that the "Enchanted Ground" represented a place of comfort, a place where Christians could grow complacent. Cautioning his listeners, he observed that "there is no temptation half so bad as not being tempted. . . . There is no season in which we are so likely to fall asleep as that of high enjoyment. The disciples went to sleep after they had seen Christ transfigured on the mountain top. Take heed, joyous Christian, good frames are very dangerous; they often lull you into a sound sleep."[166] Spurgeon's antidote for complacency in Christian living was meditation upon the cross of Christ. He proclaimed, "There are some things, it is said, which will not let men shut their eyes if they are held before them. Jesus Christ crucified on Calvary is one of these. I never knew a Christian go to sleep at the foot of the cross."[167] Finally, in his last paragraph, Spurgeon turned his attention to the unconverted: "There are some here who do not sleep at all, because they are positively dead; and if it takes a stronger voice than mine to wake the sleeper, how much more mighty must be that voice which wakes the

---

[163]Spurgeon, "World on Fire," 443.

[164]C. H. Spurgeon, "The Enchanted Ground," sermon no. 64, given February 3, 1856, from 1 Thessalonians 5:6, *The New Park Street Pulpit*, vol. 2 (London: Passmore & Alabaster, 1856), 81-88; Spurgeon, "Awake! Awake!," sermon no. 163, given November 15, 1857, from 1 Thessalonians 5:6, *The New Park Street Pulpit*, vol. 3 (London: Passmore & Alabaster, 1857), 445-52; "Sleep Not," sermon no. 1022, from 1 Thessalonians 5:6, n.d., *The Metropolitan Tabernacle Pulpit*, vol. 17 (London: Passmore & Alabaster, 1871), 649-60.

[165]In Bunyan's allegory, the Enchanted Ground was a region where travelers would grow tired, fall asleep, and sleep so deeply that they would not awaken. Christian, the protagonist of Bunyan's novel, quotes 1 Thessalonians 5:6 in the narrative.

[166]Spurgeon, "Enchanted Ground," 86.

[167]Spurgeon, "Enchanted Ground," 86.

dead. Yet even to the dead I speak; for God can wake them, though I cannot!"[168]

While this sermon drew heavily from Bunyan, Spurgeon's other sermons on the passage from Thessalonians did not mention *Pilgrim's Progress*. They did, however, contain equally fervent crucicentric and conversionistic language. In a sermon on the same text given a year later, Spurgeon suggested that his congregation should consider itself involved in spiritual warfare, and he used graphic imagery from the Indian Rebellion of 1857, including references to atrocities by the "abominable Sepoys," to illustrate the significance with which he viewed the present spiritual conditions.[169] He exhorted his listeners that evangelistic work was not reserved for those in pastoral work, but that a congregation that was "watchful and sober" would recognize that "the world's imminent danger demands that we should be active, and not be slumbering."[170] In his final sermon from the text, Spurgeon took a different approach, presenting cautionary tales about noteworthy biblical figures who encountered unfortunate ends as a result of sleeping. Samson, Jonah, and the sluggard from the book of Proverbs all served as warnings. The caution against spiritual slumber, according to Spurgeon, was secondary to what he considered the ultimate danger: unbelief. "May we never," he proclaimed, "sleep under the word as do others, lest we die in our sins. . . . To die on a dunghill, or in a ditch, or on the rack, or on the gallows is nothing compared with this—*to die in your sins!*"[171]

Spurgeon also preached a number of sermons from the book of Revelation. Spurgeon's interpretation of the apocalyptic portrait of the last days accords with much of what we have seen in his interpretation of the rest of Scripture. In a sermon from the last chapter of Revelation, he focused on the image of the Tree of Life, drawn from Genesis, which is featured in the reconstructed New Earth. In his introduction, Spurgeon emphasized that the tree mentioned by John was not literally the Tree of Life from the Genesis account but a reference to Christ himself. He said, "We believe our

---

[168]Spurgeon, "Enchanted Ground," 88.
[169]Spurgeon, "Awake! Awake!," 450.
[170]Spurgeon, "Awake! Awake!," 451.
[171]Spurgeon, "Sleep Not," 658.

Lord Jesus Christ to be none other than the tree of life, whose leaves are for the healing of the nations. We can scarcely conceive of any other interpretation, as this seems to us to be so full of meaning, and to afford us such unspeakable satisfaction."[172] Spurgeon told his listeners that he intended to base his message on that interpretation, proclaiming "We are right enough, then, in saying that Jesus Christ is a tree of life, and we shall so speak of him in the hope that some may come and pluck of the fruit, and eat and live for ever. Our desire shall be so to use the sacred allegory that some poor dying soul may be encouraged to lay hold on eternal life by laying hold on Jesus Christ."[173] In statements such as these, Spurgeon suggested that his listeners' conversion justified his somewhat strained interpretation. This becomes evident as the sermon continued, with Spurgeon employing particularly crucicentric language. He continued,

> My dear friends, you will never see the tree of life aright unless you first look
> at the cross. It was there that this tree gathered strength to bring forth its
> after-fruit. It was there, we say, that Jesus Christ, by his glorious merits and
> his wondrous work achieved upon the cross, obtained power to become the
> Redeemer of our souls, the Captain of our salvation.[174]

In his conclusion, he suggested that the unconverted as well as troubled Christians should "shake the tree" with prayer, "until the mercy drops in your lap."[175]

Spurgeon's christological interpretation is at odds with several fellow Baptists. Andrew Fuller (1754–1815), a Baptist minister and founding member of the Baptist Missionary Society, saw the presence of the tree of life as a reference to healing trees in a prophecy from Ezekiel and assigned no christological significance to it.[176] Spurgeon's position was closer to the interpretation of Scottish minister Horatius Bonar (1808–1889), though Bonar was careful to qualify his position, observing that "we might in this

---

[172]C. H. Spurgeon, "Christ the Tree of Life," sermon no. 3251, from Revelation 22:2, n.d., *The Metropolitan Tabernacle Pulpit*, vol. 57 (London: Passmore & Alabaster, 1911), 241.

[173]Spurgeon, "Christ the Tree of Life," 242.

[174]Spurgeon, "Christ the Tree of Life," 242.

[175]Spurgeon, "Christ the Tree of Life," 247.

[176]See Andrew Fuller, *The Complete Works of the Rev. Andrew Fuller*, ed. Joseph Belcher, vol. 3 (Philadelphia: American Baptist Publication Society, 1845), 298-99.

aspect say, He is the river, He is the tree, He is the fruit, He is the healing leaf. But perhaps it is more correct to say, He is the fountain-head of all blessing in heaven and earth, in this world and that which is to come, and these material things are the channels through which He pours out His fulness."[177]

Spurgeon's apocalyptic sermons, then, follow his general pattern of crucicentric and conversionistic interpretation. Matters related to the second coming of Christ were filtered through the cross, which Spurgeon viewed as the culmination of his incarnation. Furthermore, matters of Christian instruction to churches throughout Asia Minor were often interpreted as an impetus for evangelism, and in keeping with his convictions Spurgeon extended the free offer of the gospel in a high number of his sermons from these texts.

CONCLUSIONS

As Spurgeon's interpretation of the Old Testament looked forward, beyond the immediate context to the cross of Christ, his New Testament sermons display a similar focus. In this chapter we have noted that the nineteenth century was a turning point in New Testament interpretation, with many universities and colleges both on the Continent and in Britain embracing the methodologies of higher criticism. The developments in biblical studies that we noted earlier in the chapter raised alarm among many Christians in Britain. Theologically conservative academics, clergy, and congregations resisted the new biblical scholarship, and Spurgeon in many ways reflected this position. While university and college professors debated the authorship and dating of the New Testament accounts, Spurgeon largely restricted himself to directing his listeners and readers to the cross in order to produce conversions. This is not to say that he did not read widely; on the contrary, Spurgeon engaged with a variety of works of biblical criticism and provided his own candid and critical comments about them. Although he had not had the opportunity for a university education, he respected

---

[177]Horatius Bonar, *Light and Truth: Or, Bible Thoughts and Themes. The Revelation* (New York: Robert Carter and Brothers, 1872), 390.

biblical and theological scholarship and saw it as necessary for the church. Though he read widely, he also resolved not to be deflected by biblical scholarship but rather to read the Bible always through the lens of a dominant cross-centered and conversionistic hermeneutic.

Spurgeon's interpretative method was not without its drawbacks. His almost singular focus upon the cross of Christ and the offer of the gospel occasionally led him to downplay or sidestep more straightforward interpretations of the biblical text in his insistence upon crucicentric and conversionistic readings. An 1879 sermon provides a helpful window into Spurgeon's approach.[178] In it, he suggested that his congregation should approach the Bible "like a little child." He emphasized this approach further, suggesting, "Here is this blessed Book, and I can honestly declare that, as a rule, *I see only one meaning to it*, yet, as I read it, I find that there are some difficult passages which I cannot understand."[179]

With a degree of optimism, he proceeded, noting that he was "even glad that there are some difficult passages, because they are a trial to my faith; yet all that is essential for me to know, it seems to me, is as plain as possible when I just read it as I would another book."[180] Spurgeon's advice to read the Bible like any other book is almost identical to the advice given by Benjamin Jowett in his celebrated essay "On the Interpretation of Scripture" in the controversial *Essays and Reviews*, a book that was vilified by most evangelicals.[181] Jowett, furthermore, suggested that "he who in the present state of knowledge will confine himself to the plain meaning of words and the study of their context may know more of the original spirit and intention of the New Testament than all the controversial writers of former ages put together."[182] Despite the significant rhetoric that was exchanged in the controversy surrounding the publication of *Essays and Reviews*, there is some overlap between the interpretive approaches

---

[178]C. H. Spurgeon, "Rest as a Test," sermon no. 2748, given May 4, 1879, from Jeremiah 6:16, *The Metropolitan Tabernacle Pulpit*, vol. 47 (London: Passmore & Alabaster, 1901), 481-92.

[179]Spurgeon, "Rest as a Test," 485. Emphasis mine.

[180]Spurgeon, "Rest as a Test," 485.

[181]Benjamin Jowett, "On the Interpretation of Scripture," in *Essays and Reviews*, ed. John William Parker (London: John W. Parker and Son, 1860), 338.

[182]Jowett, "On the Interpretation of Scripture," 340-41.

advocated by Jowett, a leading classicist, and Spurgeon, the nation's most famous preacher.[183]

A further drawback of Spurgeon's advocated method was that he called for plain and straightforward readings of the Bible, while not necessarily following his own instruction. Concluding the sermon, he suggested,

> I believe that you do not get any peace for your soul out of God's Word either by trying to clip it down to fit in with some system of your own making, or by spiriting it away in some metaphysical incomprehensibility; but if you take the Bible in its plain sense, and say, "That seems to me to be what my Heavenly Father means by this passage; it looks very simple and clear to me; I, an unsophisticated person, reading it after the Holy Spirit's instruction and guidance, think it is so; and I believe it, and I act upon it," you will find peace and rest of heart in that way of studying the Scriptures.[184]

These remarks exemplify Spurgeon's desired goal for his listeners; however, they were given in a sermon drawn from a prophetic text that reads, "Ask for the old paths, where is the good way, and walk therein, and ye shall find rest for your souls." From this single verse Spurgeon almost immediately referred to Jesus Christ as the "perfect quiet for your soul."[185] Spurgeon claimed to favor "plain" interpretations of biblical texts, and he conveyed his interpretation in straightforward, colorful, and winsome language. From his sermons, however, it appears that he saw no contradiction between calling for simple readings of texts and also including particularly crucicentric and conversionistic readings.

We have seen this interpretive method on display throughout Spurgeon's New Testament sermons. Our investigation began with a sermon titled "Rightly Dividing the Word of Truth," which featured Spurgeon offering a glimpse into his own perspective on the proper use of the Bible from the pulpit. To "rightly divide" the Bible, according to Spurgeon, was to "use it to push truth home upon men for their present conversion, to

---

[183]For more on this controversy, see Josef L. Altholz, *Anatomy of a Controversy: The Debate over Essays and Reviews, 1860–1864* (Aldershot, Hants, UK: Scolar Press, 1994); Peter Bingham Hinchliff, *Benjamin Jowett and the Christian Religion* (Oxford: Oxford University Press, 1987).

[184]Spurgeon, "Rest as a Test," 486.

[185]Spurgeon, "Rest as a Test," 482.

use it for the striking down of their sins, to use it to draw men to Christ, to use it to arouse sinners, and to use it to produce, not mere profession but a real work of grace in the hearts of men."[186] This focus was exemplified in his handling of the various genres of the New Testament books. In the Gospel accounts, which detailed the life, work, and death of Christ in four narratives, Spurgeon found ample opportunities to direct his listeners to Christ's sacrificial death and resurrection, with a high number of his sermons including fervent language of evangelistic invitation. We saw this same method at work in Spurgeon's preaching on the Sermon on the Mount. While he followed the pattern of many of his contemporaries in addressing broader social concerns, the conclusions of his sermons directed his listeners to the cross. The Sermon on the Mount was a text that captivated Spurgeon, and he spent the final months of his life editing a commentary that featured significant discussion on the passage. His widow Susannah noted that "within a few days of the termination of his lovely and gracious life, he was incessantly occupied in expounding this portion of God's Word."[187]

In addition to his crucicentric and conversionistic reading of the Gospels, Spurgeon's engagement with the Epistles revealed similar trends. Whether or not he was preaching from texts directly related to theological discussion of the atonement, Spurgeon often took his listeners to the cross, intending to bring them to a point of conversion. His occasionally creative interpretations were often at odds with those of his contemporaries, even contemporaries with whom he shared theological convictions. Finally, while some Christians were concerned with debates over the timing and nature of the end times, Spurgeon's sermons on apocalyptic texts focused primarily on the restoration of God's creation and God's redemption, which provided him with an opportunity to preach about Christ's life and death, and extend further evangelistic invitations.

Thus Spurgeon's engagement with the New Testament, in both his sermons and written material, affirms the broader crucicentric and

---

[186]Spurgeon, "Rightly Dividing," 87.
[187]Spurgeon, *Gospel of the Kingdom*, ii.

conversionistic approach that we have seen across the previous chapters. As higher critical scholars gained influence within the academy and some sectors of the church, Spurgeon maintained his emphasis on the cross and the gospel. In the next chapter we will continue our analysis of Spurgeon's biblical interpretation outside the pulpit, focusing particularly on the latter years of his ministry.

THE BIBLE BEYOND
THE PULPIT

Spurgeon's Later Years in Ministry

> *There is something definite in the Bible. It is not quite*
> *a lump of wax to be shaped at our will, or a roll of cloth*
> *to be cut according to the prevailing fashion.*

C. H. SPURGEON, 1874

AS WE NOTED IN THE PREVIOUS CHAPTERS, the latter half of the nineteenth century represented a significant shift in biblical engagement in both British universities and pulpits. The biblical scholar and historian John Rogerson notes that "it is no exaggeration to say that in the period 1815 to 1914 the study of the Bible experienced the biggest changes that had ever occurred in its history. This is particularly striking in the case of Britain."[1] In this chapter we will focus on the later years of Spurgeon's ministry, picking up where the second chapter ended, in the mid-1870s, and proceeding to the time of his death in 1892. We will engage with matters of biblical interpretation in this period, focusing primarily on sources connected to Spurgeon's broader ministries outside the pulpit of the Metropolitan Tabernacle.

From an address to students titled "The Need of Decision for the Truth," *The Sword and the Trowel* 10 (1874): 102.

[1]John Rogerson, "History and the Bible," in *World Christianities, c. 1815–c. 1914*, ed. Brian Stanley and Sheridan Gilley, The Cambridge History of Christianity 8 (Cambridge: Cambridge University Press, 2001), 195.

In this period, we find Spurgeon at his most productive phase of life. He was midway through the publication of his commentary on the Psalms, *The Treasury of David*, which eventually spanned nearly three thousand pages. The Pastors' College, which will be discussed in greater detail in the following chapter, had already begun to place graduates in churches in greater London and also around the world. Spurgeon had become a highly popular figure not only in Britain but around the world. By this time the Metropolitan Tabernacle had become a significant tourist site in central London. Tourists who could not gain access to the Metropolitan Tabernacle could still have an audience with Spurgeon in the form of a wax sculpture at Madame Tussauds famous gallery in London.[2] In short, Spurgeon had achieved celebrity status by this phase of his ministry.

In the chapter that follows, we will consider several themes. First, Spurgeon faced poor health during most of the latter years of his adult life. Peter Morden notes that Spurgeon was "frequently incapacitated" by "debilitating physical suffering" from 1879 until his death in 1892.[3] This was a frequent subject of his correspondence with friends and family, as an undated letter to his brother reveals, "Better, but broken-backed, and broken-kneed. No dealer would buy me except for cats' meat, and I'm not worth so much for that as I was, for I am many pounds lighter."[4] As Spurgeon's ministries grew, so did his workload. As early as 1870, the thirty-six-year-old Spurgeon noted the stress that these responsibilities placed on him, writing that

> the pastorate of a church of four thousand members, the direction of all its agencies, the care of many churches, arising from our college work: the selection, education, and guidance in their settlements of the students, the oversight of the Orphanage, the editing of a magazine, the production of

---

[2]Anonymous, *Madame Tussaud and Sons: Biographical Catalogue of Distinguished Characters* (London: F. W. Potter, 1888), 30. The catalogue indicates that the wax Spurgeon resided in Hall Number Four, which consisted of a somewhat curiously ecumenical group of figures, including the earl of Shaftesbury, Cardinal John Henry Newman, Cardinal Henry Edward Manning (1808–1892), and Pope Leo XIII (1810–1903).

[3]Peter J. Morden, *"Communion with Christ and His People": The Spirituality of C. H. Spurgeon* (Oxford: Regent's Park College, 2010), 259.

[4]Spurgeon to James Archer Spurgeon, undated, in *The Letters of Charles Haddon Spurgeon*, ed. Charles Spurgeon (London: Marshall Brothers, 1923), 67.

numerous volumes, the publication of a weekly sermon, an immense correspondence, a fair share in public and denominational action, and many other labours, besides the incessant preaching of the word, give us a right to ask our friends that we be not allowed to have one anxious thought about the funds needful for our enterprises.[5]

These commitments took a significant toll on Spurgeon's physical health. His physicians advised that he escape London's climate in the winter months, so he began to spend weeks, and later months, in Mentone, a seaside town on the French Riviera.[6] By 1879, his symptoms were so severe that "contrary to our innermost intention we must take the full three months of rest, hoping that the fine weather, which has we trust commenced, will have a beneficial effect of a lasting kind."[7] Other entries took on a more somber tone, with Spurgeon noting that he had been "laid aside by illness. . . . For the most part we have been a prisoner, under bonds to cease from work."[8]

Spurgeon's magazine, *The Sword and the Trowel*, circulated widely during this period of his ministry. He utilized the magazine as a venue to publish addresses, articles, and book reviews; the latter often focused on books written in the fields of biblical studies and theology. These reviews are often revealing with regard to Spurgeon's perspective on a variety of topics, and along with the wit he used in evaluating the various books, he often provided rather blunt conclusions.

Discussions of the latter years of Spurgeon's ministry inevitably refer to the Downgrade Controversy, a theological conflict that took place within the Baptist Union in 1887 and 1888. As several lengthy treatments of the controversy have already been published, this chapter will not discuss it at length.[9] Rather we will note instances where Spurgeon points to the

---

[5] *The Sword and the Trowel* 6 (1870): 143.
[6] See Ian M. Randall, "C. H. Spurgeon (1834–1892): A Lover of France," *European Journal of Theology* 24, no. 1 (2015): 57-65.
[7] *The Sword and the Trowel* 15 (1879): 146.
[8] *The Sword and the Trowel* 15 (1879): 86.
[9] Mark Hopkins, *Nonconformity's Romantic Generation: Evangelical and Liberal Theologies in Victorian England* (Milton Keynes, UK: Paternoster, 2004), 193-248; Ian M. Randall, "Charles Haddon Spurgeon, the Pastor's College and the Downgrade Controversy," in *Discipline and Diversity*, ed. Kate Cooper and Jeremy Gregory, Studies in Church History 43 (Suffolk: The Boydell Press, 2007),

implications of the controversy for matters of biblical interpretation and evangelism. The plenary inspiration of the Bible was among the central matters of disagreement within the Baptist Union. Plenary inspiration, the belief that God directly and fully inspired the biblical text, was the position that Spurgeon and many conservative evangelicals preferred, and we will see that while Spurgeon was in the minority on this position within the Baptist Union, he would receive support from other bodies.

Finally, we will discuss several of Spurgeon's later publications, noting particularly how Spurgeon used them to weigh in on matters pertaining to the Bible and biblical interpretation. Spurgeon was no stranger to controversy, and whether controversies followed him or were instigated by him is largely the matter for another study. What is evident is that Spurgeon began to cast his work in terms of military action, and this increased in the latter years of his work. The apostle Paul had described the Bible as "the sword of the Spirit" (Eph 6:17), and Spurgeon was likely to adopt such imagery when challenged, whether he was responding to higher critics or his fellow Baptists. Throughout, we will note that for Spurgeon, crucicentrism and conversionism functioned as boundaries not only for biblical interpretation but for Christian fellowship as well. As we will see, throughout the expansion of his peripheral ministries, the cross and the conversion of sinners remained central to Spurgeon's approach to the Bible.

THE BIBLE IN *THE SWORD AND THE TROWEL*

In his latter years, as poor health kept him from the pulpit, Spurgeon often maintained his writing output. Written works appeared in a number of forms, including his magazine, *The Sword and the Trowel,* as well as a range of devotional writings and biblical commentaries. In addition to these volumes, which we have discussed in previous chapters, Spurgeon also

---

366-76; Tom Nettles, *Living by Revealed Truth: The Life and Pastoral Theology of Charles Haddon Spurgeon* (Ross-shire, UK: Christian Focus, 2013), 541-78. Popular level works on the Downgrade Controversy include these: Mark Hopkins, "The Down-Grade Controversy: What Caused Spurgeon to Start the Most Bitter Fight of His Life?," *Christian History* 10, no. 29 (1991); Iain H. Murray, *The Forgotten Spurgeon* (London: Banner of Truth Trust, 1966), 145-91; R. J. Sheehan, *C. H. Spurgeon and the Modern Church: Lessons for Today from the "Downgrade" Controversy* (London: Grace Publications Trust, 1985).

published over a dozen practical Christian books, whose subjects ranged from topical investigations of theology to advice for parents.

As we have noted, Spurgeon began his magazine, *The Sword and the Trowel*, in 1865. One of his intentions for the magazine was to "report the efforts of those Churches and Associations, which are more or less intimately connected with the Lord's work at the Metropolitan Tabernacle, and to advocate those views of doctrine and Church order which are most certainly received among us."[10] Spurgeon set out to accomplish this through a variety of means, and as such the magazine often featured printed sermons, book reviews, articles, and reports of news. In the magazine's earliest years, Spurgeon often included sermons by other preachers, such as the Church of Scotland minister Robert Murray M'Cheyne (1813–1843), though by the mid-1870s there were fewer sermons published apart from those by Spurgeon and his regular contributors.[11] As Spurgeon's broader ministries expanded, *The Sword and the Trowel* began to include regular updates on his Pastors' College and orphanages, as well as reports of other similar Christian work throughout Britain.[12] As space became limited, Spurgeon eventually printed fewer of his own sermons in the magazine, offering additional space for articles by his friends such as Vernon J. Charlesworth and G. Holden Pike.[13]

In addition to the articles, book reviews remained a central part of *The Sword and the Trowel* from its inception. These reviews, featured in every issue, provide insights into Spurgeon's hermeneutic, as he reflected on the changing theological landscape surrounding him. The magazine reviewed a wide variety of books, though most were written by Christian authors,

---

[10]*The Sword and the Trowel* 1 (1865): 5.

[11]For instance, in 1866 alone, Spurgeon published eight M'Cheyne sermons in *The Sword and the Trowel*.

[12]Spurgeon also devoted regular space to inform readers with regard to Christian missionary endeavors, including frequent columns by his cousin, Robert Spurgeon, who worked as a missionary in India, and translated a number of his cousin's sermons.

[13]Charlesworth was the headmaster of Spurgeon's orphanage. Geoffrey Holden Pike (1836–1910) was an evangelical biographer who wrote an extensive biography of Spurgeon, as well as of Archibald Brown, and was a key assistant to Spurgeon in his latter years. Pike also served as one of editors of *The Sword and the Trowel*. G. Holden Pike, *The Life and Work of Charles Haddon Spurgeon*, 6 vols. (London: Cassell, 1892); G. Holden Pike, *The Life and Work of Archibald G. Brown, Preacher and Philanthropist* (London: Passmore & Alabaster, 1892).

with Christian readership in mind. For instance, Spurgeon and his editors often featured books related to foreign mission as well as a significant number of children's books.[14]

Patricia Kruppa has argued that the contents of Spurgeon's library provided "a fairly accurate measure of the range of his reading" and that this range was "extremely narrow."[15] Her argument is not convincing, as we cannot say that he only read the works in his own personal library. Further, his contemporaries did not observe a narrowness in his reading. For instance, C. Maurice Davies (1828–1910), in his *Unorthodox London*, was struck by the wide theological range of Spurgeon's references from the pulpit.[16] Reflecting on his visit to the Metropolitan Tabernacle, he wrote,

> Remembering what Mr Spurgeon was when he came to London seventeen years ago, a boy of nineteen, one cannot but congratulate him on the change; while the vast building, with all its varied works . . . bears witness to the sterling stuff there is in the man below all his eccentricity. What particularly struck me was his constant and copious reference to such authorities as Augustine, Chrysostom, and Gregory of Nazianzen.[17]

In *The Sword and the Trowel*, Spurgeon reviewed a range of books focused on theology and biblical commentary, as well as nonacademic books that sought to comment on contemporary Christian culture.[18] With regard

---

[14]The children's books were not immune to Spurgeon's critical pen; for instance, he suggested that one was "a *quiet* sort of book, unambitious, uneventful, we might almost say uninteresting." *The Sword and the Trowel* 13 (1877): 537. Review of Violet Fletcher, *Violet Fletcher's Home Work* (London: Religious Tract Society, 1870).

[15]Patricia S. Kruppa, *Charles Haddon Spurgeon: A Preacher's Progress*, Routledge Library Editions: 19th Century Religion (London: Taylor and Francis, 2017), 454.

[16]Davies, a deacon in the Church of England, kept a column in the *Daily Telegraph* in which he reflected on his visits to various religious institutions in London. He identified with the Broad Church and spent several years working under Bishop John William Colenso in Natal, South Africa.

[17]C. Maurice Davies, *Unorthodox London, or, Phases of Religious Life in the Metropolis* (London: Tinsley Bros., 1876), 41.

[18]This is perhaps the most noteworthy distinction between reviews appearing in *The Sword and the Trowel* and Spurgeon's *Commenting and Commentaries*, the fourth and final volume of his *Lectures to My Students*, which we referenced in the previous chapter. In addition to providing reviews on a wider range of subjects, the magazine's reviews were generally longer. The authorship of the book reviews in *The Sword and the Trowel* is admittedly varied, though Spurgeon appears to have established a practice of introducing guest reviewers, and some other reviews are followed by their author's initials, which potentially indicates that the majority of the reviews were

to the latter category, given the rise of Darbyism and other premillennial theological movements, the second half of the nineteenth century witnessed a significant increase in written material on apocalyptic subjects. Spurgeon reviewed several of these books in his magazine negatively, as he was critical of works that sought to harmonize current political events with the prophetic and apocalyptic literature of the Bible, and he was generally critical of Darby's work and theology.[19] For instance, Spurgeon began a review of a volume titled *The Keys of the Apocalypse* by stating, "No, good friend, your keys please your own fancy, and may do for winding up your own watch; but they do not admit us into the secret chambers of the Apocalypse."[20] Another book, written by Nathaniel Starkey, whom Spurgeon identified as the minister of Union Chapel in South Hackney, received similar criticism, particularly as he sought to connect Napoleon to the figure of the antichrist in the book of Revelation. Spurgeon suggested that in Starkey's work "there is some pure gospel, but it is overshadowed with paltry gossip; and a few good poetical extracts, yet they are mixed up with stilted talk about political economy, commercial short-comings, music parties, field sports, and other matters of doubtful relevance to the coming of the Lord."[21] Spurgeon's critique of these types of publication, as well as his own reluctance to engage with apocalyptic texts may stem from the position of one of his own expository heroes, John Calvin. Addressing a group of students, Spurgeon proclaimed, "Did you ever notice in Calvin's *Commentaries* that there is no exposition of the Book of Revelation? Why not? He said, 'I have not expounded that book because I do not understand

---

written by Spurgeon himself. Furthermore, Spurgeon retained editorial control of the magazine, and as such it is reasonable to conclude that he was in full agreement with the content and conclusions of the magazine's book reviews.

[19]For further information on the growth of dispensationalism, see Harriet A. Harris, *Fundamentalism and Evangelicals* (Oxford: Oxford University Press, 1998), 22-25; Crawford Gribben and Timothy C. F. Stunt, eds., *Prisoners of Hope? Aspects of Evangelical Millennialism in Britain and Ireland, 1800–1880* (Milton Keynes, UK: Paternoster, 2004); Ernest Robert Sandeen, *The Roots of Fundamentalism: British and American Millenarianism, 1800–1930* (Chicago: University of Chicago Press, 1970), 81-102.

[20]*The Sword and the Trowel* 13 (1877): 483. Review of Francis Henry Morgan, *The Keys of the Apocalypse* (London: Elliot Stock, 1877).

[21]*The Sword and the Trowel* 16 (1880): 35. Review of Nathaniel Starkey, *Things Which Must Shortly Come to Pass; for the Time Is at Hand* (London: Elliot Stock, 1879).

it.' . . . I have been amused by observing the manner in which speculators have been taken in when they have left the old ship of the gospel to become prophets."[22] In light of comments such as these, it appears as if Spurgeon assigned a higher priority to biblical interpretation that could fuel evangelism. Conversely, he often derided biblical engagement that, in his estimation, obfuscated a clear understanding of substitutionary atonement.

The Sword and the Trowel also featured reviews of a number of books written to inform and educate readers about potentially controversial theological topics, such as the age of the earth and the historical reliability of the Bible. Spurgeon, who maintained an interest in science from his youth, was nonetheless skeptical of attempts to harmonize the biblical text with scientific theory. That said, Spurgeon did not categorically deny the findings of scientific research; rather, he often sought to find a middle road, one that allowed for fidelity to the biblical text as well as engagement with scientific discovery. For instance, he endorsed a book titled *Conversations on the Creation*, published by the Sunday School Union, suggesting that "every Sunday-school teacher should read this volume."[23] Spurgeon insisted, "We have no fear for the result of the conflict between science and religion: the God of Nature is the God of the Bible, and when we read both aright we shall not see conflict, but deep unity and harmony."[24] In another review, Spurgeon wrote that "creation is revealed in the Scriptures so far as the race of man is concerned, and in harmony with its one great design. . . . Scripture does not profess to use the language of science, but that which is common to man."[25] Or again, he suggested, "It is enough for us to know that creation and revelation are from the same Being, so remove all fear of any other than an apparent disagreement between them."[26] However, Spurgeon did have limits with regard to interpretation of the biblical

---

[22]C. H. Spurgeon, "Inaugural Address at the Sixteenth Annual Conference of the Pastors' College Association," *The Sword and the Trowel* 15 (1880): 257.

[23]*The Sword and the Trowel* 18 (1882): 88.

[24]*The Sword and the Trowel* 18 (1882): 88.

[25]*The Sword and the Trowel* 12 (1876): 43-44. Review of George W. Victor, *The Twin Records of Creation, or Geology and Genesis* (Le Vaux: Lockwood, 1867).

[26]*The Sword and the Trowel* 11 (1875): 401. Review of John Radford Young, *Science Not Antagonistic to Scripture* (London: Lockwood, 1863).

creation narrative. He had little regard for the "mediocrity" he saw within a book of poems titled *The Wonders of Creation* and recommended that authors of such Christian poetry should "write carefully, correct seventy-two times, keep the manuscript ninety-nine years, and give orders for it to be buried in their coffins with them."[27] He cautioned readers about another volume, written by the Free Church minister James Brodie, noting that he had "less sympathy with certain speculative ideas respecting the creation and the flood."[28] While critiquing some of Brodie's argument, Spurgeon insisted, "We have been glad to find here more of Scripture than of science, and more of that part of Scripture which speaks of him whom to know is life eternal, than of any other part."[29] This concern about finding eternal life through knowing God suggests that for Spurgeon the evangelistic message of a book was central to its value. This is evident in the final sentences of his review, where he wrote that "the peculiarities to which we have referred are harmless, and stand by themselves, while that which is in unison with known truth, and which is far more abundant, is evangelically animating and pure."[30]

With regard to the historical reliability of the Bible, as well as biblical commentaries, Spurgeon followed a similar format to what we have seen previously in his *Commenting and Commentaries*, though the reviews in *The Sword and the Trowel* were often longer and allowed for a more thorough engagement with the texts.[31] As higher criticism gained a place within British universities, a number of books were published by conservative Christians with the aim of combating critical approaches to the Bible and of instilling confidence in the historical reliability of the biblical text. These works varied considerably in quality. Some were written by established scholars who sought to offer an academically rigorous alternative to

---

[27] *The Sword and the Trowel* 12 (1876): 233. Review of Matthew Josephs, *The Wonders of Creation, and Other Poems* (London: F. E. Longley, 1876).

[28] *The Sword and the Trowel* 11 (1875): 342. Review of James Brodie, *Science and Scripture* (Edinburgh: Johnstone, Hunter, 1875).

[29] *The Sword and the Trowel* 11 (1875): 342.

[30] *The Sword and the Trowel* 11 (1875): 342.

[31] For instance, Spurgeon occasionally commends a specific publication of a book for reasons such as affordability or durability.

the critical approaches that had been accepted by many of their colleagues. Spurgeon, for his part, offered mixed reactions to such efforts. In 1875, reviewing a book titled *The Miracles of our Lord in Relation to Modern Criticism*, Spurgeon suggested that "to those who care to see how the infidel observations of Strauss and others of that school can be met by a man of equal thought and learning, this work will be full of value."[32] Spurgeon spent the balance of the review denouncing what he deemed to be skeptical biblical scholarship, suggesting, "For our own part this work is not one which would ever fascinate us, *we have a keen appetite for the marrow of the gospel*, but in the snarling of dogs over the bones, or even in the whips of those who lash the dogs away, we take no interest."[33]

In the latter years of the nineteenth century, publishing houses produced a large number of books responding to higher criticism as well as to theological liberalism more generally. Spurgeon's engagement with these volumes, which were often written by nonacademics, was also mixed. While he recognized the need for a response, he was largely dismissive of the enterprise if and when it distracted from the "marrow" of the gospel. For instance, he praised a book written in response to the French Semitic linguist J. E. Renan's (1823–1892) *Life of Jesus*. Spurgeon recommended the work to "the various doubters upon the verity of gospel facts and the validity of the gospel truths" and suggested that it was "an able and masterly reply to nearly all the attacks of modern sceptics upon the credibility of the Scriptures."[34] The review's conclusion indicated Spurgeon's priorities, as he praised the book because it was not "a contention for truth merely, but for truth as it is in Jesus, and it is evidently the result of great research and a genuine zeal for the defence of the New Testament as alone able, in what is styled its evangelical interpretation, *to make men wise unto salvation*."[35] The desire for "evangelical interpretation" is evident in a great deal of Spurgeon's interaction with biblical and theological scholarship.

---

[32] *The Sword and the Trowel* 11 (1875): 236. Review of F. L. Steinmeyer, *The Miracles of Our Lord in Relation to Modern Criticism* (Edinburgh: T&T Clark, 1875).

[33] *The Sword and the Trowel* 11 (1875): 236. Emphasis mine.

[34] *The Sword and the Trowel* 13 (1877): 86. Review of E. Stephens, *Modern Infidelity Disarmed* (London: Bemrose & Sons, 1876).

[35] *The Sword and the Trowel* 13 (1877): 86. Emphasis mine.

In the following year, Spurgeon reviewed a pamphlet that engaged with critical scholarship on the Pentateuch, observing that the work was "called forth by the rationalistic treatment of the Old Testament records by such critics as De Wethe [sic], Davidson, and Ewald."[36] His frustration with higher critical scholarship became evident as the review continued: "While there is so much theory-spinning by theological professors, we suppose there will be the necessity for these criticisms of the critics; but after all, it is a sorry business, and the game is scarcely worth the candle."[37] Spurgeon was more emphatic in another review, questioning, "Why need 'Essays and Reviews' and Dr. Colenso be put up, just to show how elegantly they can be knocked down? Orthodox divines too often do the advertising for heretics, and turn bill stickers to the devil. Why should they? We are getting tired of ghost-hunting."[38] Finally, Spurgeon speculated that evangelical books responding to higher critical scholarship might have the unintended consequence of introducing readers to concepts of which they might have been otherwise unaware. This is particularly evident in his review of a conservative evangelical book titled *The Wave of Scepticism and the Rock of Truth*, where he suggested that "our readers who know nothing of the sceptical work Mr. Habershon has answered, need not take the poison for the sake of appreciating the antidote."[39]

As noted in the previous chapter, though Spurgeon could be dismissive of German scholarship, there were exceptions. Among them was Franz Delitzsch, the German Lutheran professor of Semitic studies. Reviewing Delitzsch's volume on the Song of Songs and Ecclesiastes, Spurgeon particularly favored his position that the Song was evocative of the love of Christ and the church, eschewing interpretations that suggested erotic imagery present within the text.[40] He wrote that the "commentary is mainly

---

[36] *The Sword and the Trowel* 14 (1878): 482. Review of C. T. Rust, *The Higher Criticism: Some Account of Its Labours upon the Primitive History* (London: W. Hunt, 1878).

[37] *The Sword and the Trowel* 14 (1878): 482.

[38] *The Sword and the Trowel* 16 (1880): 532. Review of Selina Ditcher, *Life, Lost or Saved* (London: James Nisbet, 1868).

[39] *The Sword and the Trowel* 11 (1875): 236. Review of Matthew Henry Habershon, *The Wave of Scepticism and the Rock of Truth: A Reply to "Supernatural Religion; an Inquiry into the Reality of Divine Revelation"* (London: Hodder & Stoughton, 1875).

[40] *The Sword and the Trowel* 13 (1877): 392. Review of Franz Delitszch, *Commentary on the Song of Songs and Ecclesiastes* (Edinburgh: T&T Clark, 1877).

critical, and though dry, as nearly all German works are, it is sound, and likely to be of great assistance in discovering the literal sense. It is pleasing to know that evangelical teaching is now the ascendant in the German universities."[41] In the same year, Spurgeon set aside several pages of the magazine to publish a section of Delitzsch's introduction to the Song of Songs. Delitzsch's prose, which readily referred to academic German and French works, stood in stark contrast to the usual content of *The Sword and the Trowel*. However, the section that Spurgeon selected advanced a christological interpretation that would allow himself and other like-minded interpreters to focus on "the love subsisting between Christ and his church."[42]

Spurgeon's favoring of a christological interpretation of the Song of Songs provided a way for him to avoid an interpretation that allowed for erotic imagery within the Bible. In this case, Spurgeon preferred the same typological interpretation taken by many commentators in the patristic and medieval periods, though it is unclear whether his interpretation was driven by fidelity to historical interpretations or by Victorian unease with explicit sexual content.[43] His 1880 review of a New Testament commentary may shed more light on his practice. The commentary offered a new, more literal translation of Galatians 5:12, in which the apostle Paul brazenly suggests that members of a rival sect who required circumcision upon conversion to Christianity should go the full measure and "make themselves eunuchs."[44] Spurgeon, who preferred the Authorized Version's rendering of the verse, "I would they were even cut off that trouble you," went so far as to suggest that "the writers are evidently disbelievers in plenary inspiration."[45] His basis for this was that in translating the verse in such a manner as to suggest language of castration, "the commentator ascribes to these words a meaning so filthy that we are

---

[41] *The Sword and the Trowel* 13 (1877): 392.

[42] *The Sword and the Trowel* 13 (1877): 362.

[43] For a comprehensive overview of Victorian typology, see George P. Landow, *Victorian Types, Victorian Shadows: Biblical Typology in Victorian Literature, Art, and Thought* (Boston: Routledge & Kegan Paul, 1980), 15-63.

[44] Charles John Ellicott, ed., *A New Testament Commentary for English Readers* (London: Cassell, Petter, & Galpin, 1878), 457.

[45] *The Sword and the Trowel* 16 (1880): 132. Review of Ellicott, *A New Testament Commentary for English Readers*.

certain that it never occurred to Paul's mind, and were he among us he would reject the abominable imputation with disgust."[46] In this instance, Spurgeon's reaction to this particular interpretation may have been influenced by Victorian sensibilities on sexuality, particularly as subsequent English biblical translations have consistently corrected the Authorized Version's translation.[47] Though he generally favored straightforward renderings of the grammar present in the original languages, in this instance Spurgeon's squeamish reaction to the explicit language within the biblical passage led him to prefer a less accurate translation. Thus, while Spurgeon's engagement with the Bible was largely guided by his crucicentrism and conversionism, he was also occasionally influenced by social conventions.

Finally, Spurgeon also highlighted books that evaluated and critiqued contemporary culture in light of Christian theology. These reviews enabled him to call attention to social and political issues. As we saw in chapter three, in the case of the Indian Mutiny of 1857, Spurgeon was not afraid to criticize the British government when he felt that it was drifting from its Christian moorings.[48] This was particularly clear in his criticism of Britain's role in the opium trade throughout Asia, which had been made the subject of several books designed to inform and mobilize Christian readers.[49] While reviewing one of these volumes, Spurgeon bemoaned that Britain could "make a monopoly of the growth of opium, and then claim a right to sell it to China, a right enforced by cannon and gun-boats; practically a right to poison the Chinese. We sent out missionaries to the heathen Chinese, while acting more heathenly than he does. Was ever inconsistency

---

[46]*The Sword and the Trowel* 16 (1880): 132.

[47]For further elaboration on Spurgeon's perspective on biblical translation, see Elijah Hixson, "New Testament Textual Criticism in the Ministry of Charles Haddon Spurgeon," *Journal of the Evangelical Theological Society* 57, no. 3 (2014): 555-70.

[48]See chapter three of this book, as well as Michael R. Watts, *The Dissenters*, vol. 3, *The Crisis and Conscience of Nonconformity* (Oxford: Oxford University Press, 2015), 323-24; Brian Stanley, "Christian Responses to the Indian Mutiny of 1857," in *The Church and War*, ed. M. J. Shells, Studies in Church History 20 (Oxford: Blackwell, 1983), 277-89.

[49]For broader investigation of this subject, see Immanuel C. Y. Hsü, *The Rise of Modern China*, 6th ed. (Oxford: Oxford University Press, 2000); James Hevia, *The Imperial Security State: British Colonial Knowledge and Empire-Building in Asia* (Cambridge: Cambridge University Press, 2012).

more glaring?"[50] As the review continued, Spurgeon continued to rail against British politicians, and called on them to renounce the opium trade, though he was skeptical that any immediate relief would come, recognizing that the Indian government would be reluctant to forsake the revenue associated with the opium trade. Speaking of that potential loss of revenue, he observed, "It may be that one of these days Christianity will enable those in high places to make the sacrifice, but we fear it will not be just yet, for religion and financing do not often go together. 'Gold and the gospel seldom do agree.'"[51]

Spurgeon's engagement with scholarship in *The Sword and the Trowel* indicates several conclusions. First and foremost, he read widely within the world of biblical and theological studies.[52] In these reviews Spurgeon revealed his perspectives, often with minimal gloss, not only on selected works but also on trends within broader scholarship. He was skeptical of the benefits of higher criticism, but he occasionally praised the efforts of those from the more conservative wing of the discipline. He was equally critical of his evangelical contemporaries when he felt that their work was of poor quality or misguided. Spurgeon's estimation apparently rested on a single criterion, namely whether he thought the book's contents helped or hindered efforts toward conversion. Given Spurgeon's theological convictions, it is not surprising to see this sort of position on volumes that dealt directly with matters of Christology, or theology of the atonement, but it remained constant throughout his reviews of books on a variety of topics. We can see this clearly in two final book reviews, one negative example and one positive. The former was a review of a theological volume titled *The Fatherhood of God*. This review captures both Spurgeon's evangelistic priorities and wit, as he describes the book as "one of the most poetic, beautiful, pseudo-philosophic but altogether erroneous books on the Fatherhood of God which we have ever read. *As insidious and attractive as it can be, but altogether subversive of the very fundamental truths of the*

---

[50] *The Sword and the Trowel* 11 (1876): 433.
[51] *The Sword and the Trowel* 11 (1876): 433.
[52] Additionally, his personal library included numerous volumes of history, science, and popular novels, including authors such as Charles Dickens and Louisa May Alcott.

gospel concerning man's ruin, regeneration, and redemption."[53] Spurgeon's further recommendation was this: "Our advice concerning it would be the same as given with respect to the proper way of preparing cucumber. Carefully peel and slice it, flavour with pepper, salt, and vinegar, and then— eat it?—oh no! *Throw it on the dung hill!*"[54] Conversely, we can see a positive example in a review of a book titled *Teaching the Scriptures*, which Spurgeon emphatically endorsed, on the basis that

> the one design of the whole Scriptures is kept throughout. Every part is shown to have its seed within itself, yielding fruit for spiritual life and nourishment to the soul of man. *The Bible is not given to teach man history, or science, or literature, or mere morality, but to restore him to God.* To those who approach it with that design it is a light that shineth more and more unto that perfect day. To all others it is a light that shineth in darkness, and the darkness comprehendith it not.[55]

THE BIBLE AND THE NEWSPAPER

The Bible and the Newspaper is something of an oddity in Spurgeon's collected writings.[56] In it, he collected newspaper headlines from the 1870s and listed them alongside biblical passages, using the two together as a basis for theological reflection.[57] In explaining his approach, he observed that "the worlds of nature and of providence are full of parallels to things moral and spiritual, and serve as pictures to make the written book of inspiration more clear to the children of God. The Bible itself abounds in metaphors, type, and symbols; it is a great picture book."[58] Spurgeon added, with reference to his readers, that he compiled the book "not merely for their entertainment, but that we may encourage them in the habit of

---

[53] *The Sword and the Trowel* 15 (1880): 187. Review of Robert Mitchell, *The Fatherhood of God* (London: Hamilton, Adams, 1879). Emphasis mine.

[54] *The Sword and the Trowel* 15 (1880): 187.

[55] *The Sword and the Trowel* 14 (1878): 463. Review of Dr. Anderson, *Teaching the Scriptures* (London: Morgan and Scott, n.d.).

[56] This volume, part of Spurgeon's "Shilling Series," is not frequently referenced in more recent secondary literature. A noteworthy exception is Timothy Larsen, *A People of One Book: The Bible and the Victorians* (Oxford: Oxford University Press, 2011), 266-68.

[57] Some of the headlines reflected major national news events, whereas others appear to have been drawn from miscellanea that Spurgeon had collected.

[58] C. H. Spurgeon, *The Bible and the Newspaper* (London: Passmore & Alabaster, 1878), iii.

looking for emblems and analogies. It is a mental exercise as profitable as it is pleasant."[59] The volume granted Spurgeon freedom to explore social and theological issues with his trademark wit.

For instance, in the entry "Chaotic Theology," Spurgeon highlighted an article from the United States, namely a West Virginia newspaper that bemoaned difficulties related to the transfer of the state legislature between Wheeling and Charleston, the former and current capital cities of the state.[60] Spurgeon suggested that the ever-shifting state capital, which the article suggested could be located "on a steamboat somewhere between Wheeling and Charleston," bore a similar resemblance to "the minds of many who claim to be preachers of the gospel of 'the advanced school.'"[61] He believed that liberal scholarship could lead Christians away from historic, confessional Christianity into a state of "human jelly-fish, or something more gelatinous still."[62] Moving further, he wrote that "even the main and fundamental points of the atonement of Christ, and his divine person, are unsettled with some of the Broad School. Their capital is on a steamboat somewhere between Unitarianism and Pantheism."[63]

It is difficult to assess precisely how Spurgeon defined theological liberalism, as he often assigned terms such as *liberal* and *modern thought* indiscriminately to a broad range of authors with whom he disagreed on various points. Spurgeon's criticism of liberal theology, as we have seen, was primarily rooted in his concern that any uncertainty cast upon historic Christian doctrine was potentially detrimental to the faith of ordinary churchgoers. This is particularly evident as he wrote, "Their manifest indecision for truth is a clear gain to the side of unbelief. These rolling stones in the road cause many to stumble who else would have held on their way. With their cloudy speculations they throw an air of uncertainty over the most settled truths. They cause faith to dwindle into mere opinion and throw thousands into a condition of miserable suspense."[64] While this entry

---

[59]Spurgeon, *Bible and the Newspaper*, v.
[60]Spurgeon, *Bible and the Newspaper*, 179-81.
[61]Spurgeon, *Bible and the Newspaper*, 179.
[62]Spurgeon, *Bible and the Newspaper*, 180.
[63]Spurgeon, *Bible and the Newspaper*, 180.
[64]Spurgeon, *Bible and the Newspaper*, 180.

features Spurgeon speaking out against liberal theology in broad terms, several entries in *The Bible and the Newspaper* cover topics related to biblical interpretation. These entries in particular provide a particularly helpful vantage point for further assessment of Spurgeon's interpretive preferences.

In "Blasting Prohibited," for instance, Spurgeon highlighted an article reporting a debate in the House of Commons over the prevalence of and dangers associated with the use of dynamite in Britain's coal mines, particularly in instances where open flames were required for illumination.[65] He suggested that careless preaching, in which the preacher presented his theological musings, was akin to an open flame near dynamite, writing that "we have heard of ministers whose speculations in theology are no better than so many firings of shots in dangerous mines; their blasts are ruinous to multitudes of young men. . . . If these divines were heard to swear a profane oath, or known to pick a pocket, they would be scouted from society, but they are doing worse, and yet retain their position."[66] He concluded the entry with a stern warning, suggesting that congregations should take steps to safeguard themselves, suggesting, "If a man will play with powder and shot he must be kept out of the way, for we cannot afford to risk hundreds of lives for the amusement of a so-called 'thoughtful man.' Let him play off his gunpowder 'thinkings' and his dynamite 'culture' in some other sphere, *but not among subjects which concern eternity, immortality, glory, and perdition*."[67] His conclusion indicates his concern that liberal biblical interpretation might muddle the efforts of evangelistic preachers like himself. This is evident in another article, titled "Spurious Imitations."[68] Referencing an advertisement featured in several newspapers that simply read, "Beware of Spurious Imitations," Spurgeon suggested that the that imitations of the gospel were the most spurious ones of all. He noted that the imitations could take a number of forms, such as the sacramental theology of the Church of England, which he dismissed as "done up in tasteful mediaeval

---

[65]Spurgeon, *Bible and the Newspaper*, 187-90.
[66]Spurgeon, *Bible and the Newspaper*, 189-90.
[67]Spurgeon, *Bible and the Newspaper*, 190. Emphasis mine.
[68]Spurgeon, *Bible and the Newspaper*, 201-8.

wrappers."[69] Spurgeon was also critical of speculative thinking within higher education: "We are ready to accept all that science teaches us when it has made up its mind what it is. We never despise knowledge, but on the contrary seek after it as for hidden treasure; but we do not want to be duped by conjectures and fooled by speculations."[70]

One entry in particular gives what may be the clearest and most extended example of Spurgeon's perspective on German higher criticism, illustrated by a well-known shipwreck involving German frigates near the coast of Dover. Titled "Sinking of the Ironclad," Spurgeon began by summarizing the naval incident, noting that

> three ironclad ships, the *Grosser Kurfurst, Koenig Wilhelm*, and *Preussen* . . . were reported off Dover at 8:00 A.M. on Friday morning, May 31st [1878]. The weather was calm and a slight wind blowing, when about five miles due south of Sandgate Castle, the *Koenig Wilhelm* ran into the *Grosser Kurfurst* and sank her. The ship went down in a few seconds with the larger part of her crew.[71]

Following his description of the events, Spurgeon wrote that "we mourn over this sudden wreck and the dreadful loss of life, and then we take breath and moralize . . . men who seemed capable of great deeds perished before our eyes by the hand of one of their own comrades, and *that not by wicked intent but by an unwise movement never meant to involve such ruin*."[72] This acknowledgment that higher criticism did not begin with the intent of undermining the church could not be missed. However, as he proceeded, it became clear that Spurgeon did not intend to engender sympathy for the higher critics. As we have seen, Spurgeon opposed critical scholarship that called into question traditional Christian doctrines, including biblical inspiration. In this particular case he was highly critical of those who promoted what he deemed a dangerous interpretive approach. He compared the German higher critics to the unfortunate ironclads, observing that the

---

[69]Spurgeon, *Bible and the Newspaper*, 202.

[70]Spurgeon, *Bible and the Newspaper*, 203.

[71]Spurgeon, *Bible and the Newspaper*, 144. The verses paired with this reading were 2 Samuel 1:27 and Job 6:21.

[72]Spurgeon, *Bible and the Newspaper*, 144-45. Emphasis mine.

"'German Squadron of Evolution,' fit name, and fit country to remind us of the school of modern-thought who proudly float upon our seas at this time and threaten the peace of our churches. These philosophers are all iron-clads, and cannot be touched by the heaviest guns of those poor simple souls who believe in the Bible and its plenary inspiration."[73]

As we have seen, Spurgeon did not believe that ordinary Christians should concern themselves with the affairs of academic biblical studies. For example, he wrote of the higher critics that "we need not fear them, for happily they destroy one another, and that very readily, as if they were created on purpose for this and nothing else. A little change in the steering and they ram each other to the bottom. . . . One school of unbelief effectually sweeps away another. So let it be."[74] Perhaps most telling in Spurgeon's assessment of liberal biblical scholarship is his recommendation to his readers. Returning to the nautical disaster, he observed,

> The fishing boats in the neighbourhood of the huge monitors did admirable service by rescuing many of the drowning sailors, and so may true-hearted men hover around the huge infidelities of the period, and snatch here and there a sinking doubter from destruction. It would be idle for smacks and luggers to attack an ironclad; they can far better distinguish themselves by coming to the rescue in the hour of distress; and in the same way simple-minded believers, who know nothing of controversy, can do a vast amount of service by bringing salvation to those who are ready to perish. Let us not argue, but let us love. We will not confront the sceptical with reasoning, but by God's Spirit, we will save them by the gospel and by believing prayer.[75]

The conclusion indicates two noteworthy observations on Spurgeon's part. First, he suggested that men and women who were untrained in the methods of biblical interpretation could prove themselves to be more useful interpreters of the text than university professors whose methods clouded the text and whose conclusions called the text's reliability, as God's

---

[73]Spurgeon, *Bible and the Newspaper*, 146. The phrase "German Squadron of Evolution" referred to the new class of ships in the German navy, a group that included the ships mentioned in this article.

[74]Spurgeon, *Bible and the Newspaper*, 146-47.

[75]Spurgeon, *Bible and the Newspaper*, 147.

Word, into question. Thus, in Spurgeon's estimation, a lay Christian offering an interpretation featuring the cross and conversion offered more useful biblical engagement than some biblical scholars. Second, and perhaps more significant, he emphasized that plain communication of the gospel, coupled with prayer, would prove far more successful than attempts to address or combat the critical scholarship in a more academic manner. Spurgeon could be viewed as speaking autobiographically here, particularly as his recommendation to readers to put forth simple, straightforward evangelistic efforts mirrored his own approach from the pulpit.

In another entry called "Battered Scripture," he addressed an article in the *Deal Telegram* from June 29, which noted that several Beefeater guards at the Tower of London were guilty of damaging inscriptions in the side of the building as they pointed at them with their bayonets.[76] Following his own skeptical estimation of the charge leveled at the soldiers, Spurgeon wrote that in a similar manner, "texts of Scripture are rapped and tapped, poked and smitten by preachers who are endeavouring to call attention to them and are at the same time misrepresenting them. . . . Scripture probably suffers more often from the hands of its friends than its foes."[77] In his criticisms, Spurgeon suggested that texts were often "explained away, or expounded into confusion, or spiritualized into nonsense. . . . Great bruises remain upon some passages of Scripture, and these will never be effaced, for the shameful maltreatment has not only fixed itself upon the memory, but affected the judgment of the hearer."[78] As his critique continued, Spurgeon offered an extended paragraph, worth quoting at length, in which his criticism of some preacher's alleged mishandling of the Bible helpfully indicates some aspects of his preferred interpretive method. He wrote,

> True reverence for the inspired word should lead a man to *guard carefully the most delicate shades of meaning*; the mind of the Spirit should be carefully

---

[76]Spurgeon, *Bible and the Newspaper*, 213-16. Each chapter contained a verse or two upon which Spurgeon based his reflection. In this chapter he referenced Jeremiah 23:28, "He that hath my word, let him speak my word faithfully," and Deuteronomy 4:2, "Ye shall not add unto the word which I command you, neither shall ye diminish ought from it."

[77]Spurgeon, *Bible and the Newspaper*, 214.

[78]Spurgeon, *Bible and the Newspaper*, 214.

ascertained, and then as carefully declared to the people. *There should be no forcing of meanings, no twisting of words, no concealment of evident teachings.* The word was written by God and not by man, and therefore it deserves to be protected even at the cost of life if need be; never under any circumstances should it be made the martyr of prejudice, or the victim of learned wrestlings, or the slave of ignorant misrepresentation. When atheists and infidels batter the word of God we can very well understand their object, but it is grievous when a man of God in order to call attention to a passage darkens its meaning, and in order to show his esteem for every letter smites it with an exaggerated emphasis which utterly mars it.[79]

Spurgeon's discussion of "careful" interpretation in this section is particularly telling. As we have seen, his sermons frequently cast his text in the light of crucicentric, conversionistic interpretation, often whether or not the immediate context warranted such interpretation. Spurgeon's warnings against sermons that were "spiritualized into nonsense" and comments in favor of the pursuit of "the most delicate shades of meaning" are somewhat metered by the reality that many of his sermons could potentially fall under his own rebuke. Amid the dangers of overly spiritualized interpretation, Spurgeon evidently offered a great deal of leniency when these interpretations featured the cross and the free offer of the gospel, both in his own work and his assessments of others. Perhaps sensing that some readers might make this very objection, Spurgeon closed the section with an illustration from his visit to Nero's Golden House in Rome, where tour guides would raise candles on a long rod to illuminate the gilded frescoes on the ceilings. This practice, according to Spurgeon, led to significant accumulation of soot on the ceiling, further obscuring the object the guides sought to illuminate. He wrote, "It will be a sad thing for us if, while we are endeavouring to exhibit divine truth, we at the same time destroy or becloud its loveliest tints with our ignorance or prejudice. Our candles had better be put out rather than they should do permanent damage to the glorious doctrines of grace, which are the masterpiece of Infinite Wisdom."[80]

---

[79]Spurgeon, *Bible and the Newspaper*, 214-15.
[80]Spurgeon, *Bible and the Newspaper*, 216.

In conclusion, in *The Bible and the Newspaper* Spurgeon attempted a literary experiment with nontraditional methods of biblical interpretation and application. He set out to show his readers that it was possible to connect everyday affairs with biblical matters. As the book was clearly intended toward a Christian readership, while traces of crucicentric and conversionistic language were woven through the book, there was also significant attention paid toward activism, particularly in areas where Spurgeon exhorted his readers to take an active role in evangelism. Furthermore, the book contained several sustained sections where Spurgeon revealed his misgivings with contemporary preaching and biblical interpretation, offering a window into his own preferences in the process. Along with this effort, however, Spurgeon cautioned readers against overly spiritualized interpretations, though he himself could occasionally be guilty of the same charge.

THE BIBLE AND THE BAPTIST UNION: THE DOWNGRADE CONTROVERSY

The Downgrade Controversy, which took place in 1887 and 1888, has been referred to as the "biggest conservative rearguard action against the growth of liberal theology in Victorian England."[81] Several valuable accounts of this controversy have appeared, especially that of Mark Hopkins, who dedicated the final chapter of his *Nonconformity's Romantic Generation* to an exploration of the principal events and figures.[82] The controversy is largely agreed to have begun with the publication of two articles in *The Sword and the Trowel* in the spring of 1887. Spurgeon himself was not the author of the articles; they were written by Robert Shindler, a frequent contributor to the magazine.[83] As we have seen, Spurgeon had long been critical of liberal biblical scholarship, and he frequently denounced what he considered to be

---

[81]Hopkins, *Nonconformity's Romantic Generation*, 193.

[82]Hopkins, *Nonconformity's Romantic Generation*, 193-248.

[83]This is over and against several earlier volumes that assumed Spurgeon himself wrote the articles, including H. F. Colquitt in his doctoral thesis of 1951. See Hopkins, *Nonconformity's Romantic Generation*, 193; Henry Franklin Colquitt, "The Soteriology of Charles Haddon Spurgeon Revealed in His Sermons and Controversial Writings" (PhD thesis, University of Edinburgh, 1951), 114-15. For further discussion, see Hopkins, *Nonconformity's Romantic Generation*, 193.

"broad" theology. Further, Spurgeon had previously suspected liberal leanings within the Baptist Union. In 1883, the Baptist Union elected Richard Glover (1837–1919) of Bristol to their presidency. Some delegates at the annual meeting in Leicester felt that Glover's inaugural address as president contained traces of universal restitution, implicitly denying a future punishment for the unrepentant.[84] Spurgeon did not attend the Baptist Union meeting and learned of its proceedings second-hand from his former student, Archibald Brown (1844–1922).[85] In a letter to Spurgeon, Brown expressed a fear that "'the spirit of the age' seems to have found a welcome in our midst, but in my humble judgment—it is a spirit of anti-Christ—there is nothing left for those loyal to Christ except to protest against it and refrain from all fellowship with it."[86] Spurgeon's suspicions of the Baptist Union increased during the 1880s, and he became progressively more vocal in expressing frustration with ministers in his denomination who he believed were embracing liberal theology. Having resolved to "have no fellowship with modern doubt," and relying largely on printed sermons and reports relayed from friends still within the union, Spurgeon began to speak out against his fellow Baptists more forcefully. Spurgeon made his case clear in November 1887, when he cast doubt upon the future viability of a Baptist Union where "believers in Christ's atonement are now in declared religious union with those who make light of it; believers in holy Scripture are in confederacy with those who deny plenary inspiration; those who hold evangelical doctrine are in open alliance with those who call the fall a fable."[87]

As this study explores Spurgeon's biblical interpretation, we will focus only on those aspects of the controversy that have bearing on our topic. Willis Glover has argued that higher criticism was not a key issue leading

---

[84]The most comprehensive account of this event is found in Kruppa, *Charles Haddon Spurgeon: A Preacher's Progress*, 515-23.

[85]Brown was a conservative evangelical Baptist, cut from a similar cloth as his mentor. In 1872 he opened the East End Tabernacle in London, which had a seating capacity for 2,500 and ultimately became the second-largest congregation in Britain. For further background on Brown, see Pike, *Life and Work of Archibald G. Brown*; Iain H. Murray, *Archibald Brown: Spurgeon's Successor* (Edinburgh: Banner of Truth Trust, 2011).

[86]Brown to C. H. Spurgeon, October 11, 1883, located in the Heritage Room at Spurgeon's College, quoted in Kruppa, *Charles Haddon Spurgeon: A Preacher's Progress*, 515.

[87]*The Sword and the Trowel* 23 (1887): 558.

Spurgeon to charge into the Downgrade conflict. Rather, he suggests, Spurgeon's concern was tied to the plenary inspiration of the Bible.[88] Spurgeon accepted plenary inspiration as dogma and had little patience for interpreters who rejected the doctrine. This is particularly evident as he wrote, "We must part company altogether with the errorist, who overrides prophets and apostles, and practically regards his own inspiration as superior to theirs. We fear that such a man will before long *prove himself to be an enemy of the cross of Christ*, all the more dangerous because he will profess loyalty to the Lord whom he dishonours."[89] We have previously seen that Spurgeon was intensely critical of movements that cast doubt on biblical infallibility, particularly if he thought they would undermine evangelistic work. He held a similar position on the atonement, proclaiming, "If, sirs, you take away the atoning sacrifice, you make that blessed Book to be a mere husk from which the kernel has been withdrawn. If you take away expiation by the precious blood of Jesus, you tear away the sinner's only ground of hope."[90] His tone and rhetoric throughout the Downgrade Controversy was no different, particularly in his use of *The Sword and the Trowel* as a sounding board for his theological reflections. He suggested that his audience

> read those newspapers that represent the Broad School of Dissent, and ask yourself, how much farther could they go? What doctrine remains to be abandoned? What other truth to be the object of contempt? A new religion has been initiated, which is no more Christianity than chalk is cheese; and this religion, being destitute of moral honesty, *palms itself off as the old faith with slight improvements, and on this plea usurps pulpits which were erected for gospel preaching.*[91]

Spurgeon's indictment against liberalism within the Dissenting community caused a significant stir and drew increased attention to the developing

---

[88]Willis Borders Glover, *Evangelical Nonconformists and Higher Criticism in the Nineteenth Century* (London: Independent Press, 1954), 166.

[89]*The Sword and the Trowel* 24 (1888): 207. Emphasis mine.

[90]C. H. Spurgeon, "Prisoners Delivered," sermon no. 2883, given April 2, 1876, from Zechariah 9:11-12, *The Metropolitan Tabernacle Pulpit*, vol. 50 (London: Passmore & Alabaster, 1904), 234.

[91]*The Sword and the Trowel* 23 (1887): 397. Emphasis mine.

controversy. A contributing factor to the difficulty of handling the controversy was that there were no formal disciplinary procedures within the Baptist Union, which had, in Spurgeon's words, "no doctrinal basis whatever."[92] Because of this, he wrote that "there is no use in blaming the Union for harbouring errors of the extremest kind, for, so far as we can see, it is powerless to help itself, if it even wished to do so. Those who originally founded it made it 'without form and void,' and so it must remain."[93] Tensions continued to rise, both within the Baptist Union as well as subsequent coverage within newspapers and periodicals. Spurgeon could not find a point of agreement with the leaders of the Baptist Union, and he had begun to lose support among some of his former students at the Pastors' College.[94] He conclusion regarding the union was that "no one thought my appeals worthy of notice," leading him to resign in October 1887.[95]

As he resigned from the Baptist Union, language of unity in the gospel was present throughout his comments, particularly as he wrote, "In the isolation of independency, tempered by the love of the Spirit which binds us to all the faithful in Christ Jesus, *we think the lovers of the gospel will for the present find their immediate safety.* Oh, that the day would come when, in a larger communion than any sect can offer, all those who are one in Christ may be able to blend in manifest unity!"[96] Hopkins's analysis of Spurgeon's motivation is particularly helpful; he argues that any attempt to paint his resignation from the union as a tactical decision overlooks the more straightforward explanation, namely that Spurgeon's "main interest in resigning was escape—from fellowship with people who in his view denied the gospel, from the responsibilities involved in membership of the Baptist Union, and even from the effort and pain involved in theological conflict."[97] Spurgeon's departure from the Baptist Union did not provide the escape he wanted, however. In the months that followed, the

---

[92] *The Sword and the Trowel* 23 (1887): 560.

[93] *The Sword and the Trowel* 23 (1887): 560.

[94] Hopkins, *Nonconformity's Romantic Generation*, 203; Randall, "Charles Haddon Spurgeon, the Pastor's College and the Downgrade Controversy."

[95] *The Baptist*, December 23, 1887. Quoted in Hopkins, *Nonconformity's Romantic Generation*, 203.

[96] *The Sword and the Trowel* 23 (1887): 560.

[97] Hopkins, *Nonconformity's Romantic Generation*, 207.

dispute intensified, particularly when the union issued a censure against him while he was away in France. This reignited tensions on both sides and led to Spurgeon's return to the conflict in full force. As the particular doctrines of contention vacillated between plenary inspiration and the eternality of hell, Spurgeon held fast to his position. Notably, in this instance, Spurgeon's Calvinistic theology put him at odds with many Baptists represented in the union. Spurgeon, moreover, saw the doctrine of penal substitutionary atonement as fundamental to Christianity as a whole. For him, any attempts toward compromise would lead to the collapse of the church.

Though the Downgrade Controversy put Spurgeon at odds with many of his fellow Baptists, it did not, as Michael R. Watts has argued, leave him isolated.[98] Amid the trials of the controversy, Spurgeon's frustration with the Baptist Union helped him to foster closer relationships with evangelicals in other denominations. Though Watts did portray the older Spurgeon as an isolated, "autocratic egotist," there is evidence to suggest that in his later years Spurgeon enjoyed a broad fellowship.[99] For instance, in his early years in London Spurgeon lashed out against the Church of England over the doctrine of baptismal regeneration, criticizing evangelicals who refused to leave the Established Church as hypocrites.[100] By the 1880s, however, Kruppa notes that Spurgeon "drew closer to the Evangelicals in the Church of England, for he recognized that in the larger fight they were better allies than many members of his own Baptist community. His staunchest supporters during the Downgrade Controversy were the Church of England Evangelicals, the very group he had once charged with hypocrisy."[101] His relationships within the Established Church went further than his evangelical contemporaries. Canon Basil Wilberforce's (1841–1916) correspondence with him indicated a "union of spirit" in their friendship. Wilberforce suggested that "when we knelt together there is nothing which

---

[98]Watts, *Dissenters*, 3:59-64.

[99]Watts, *Dissenters*, 3:129.

[100]For an extensive treatment of Spurgeon and the Baptismal Regeneration controversy, see Kruppa, *Charles Haddon Spurgeon: A Preacher's Progress*, 316-40.

[101]Kruppa, *Charles Haddon Spurgeon: A Preacher's Progress*, 511.

separates those who love the Lord."[102] Larsen expands on this theme, noting that Spurgeon's inner circle was denominationally diverse.[103] In addition to Anglicans, he maintained close connections with Congregationalists, the denomination of his youth, particularly in his friendships with the American evangelist D. L. Moody as well as Vernon J. Charlesworth, who oversaw all of Spurgeon's orphanages and frequently contributed to *The Sword and the Trowel*.[104] He was on even better terms with the Presbyterians. Charles Hodge, the American theologian at Princeton, was among Spurgeon's most trusted authors. Spurgeon enjoyed a warm reception from Presbyterian congregations in Scotland, would often worship in Presbyterian churches when he was on holiday, and became a friend of the leading Highland Free Church Evangelical, John Kennedy of Dingwall (1819–1884).[105] Perhaps most interesting of all was his close relationship with the American Presbyterian Arthur Tappan Pierson (1837–1911). Pierson, who had embarked on a preaching tour of Britain in 1890, met Spurgeon during his trip and was invited to preach at the Metropolitan Tabernacle. Spurgeon held Pierson in particularly high esteem, to the extent that he invited him to preach full-time at the Tabernacle while he convalesced in France.[106] In the year before his death, Spurgeon began a gathering of like-minded conservative evangelicals in London. The "Fraternal Union," as he called it, was structurally based on the Baptist Union but included members from Baptist, Congregational, and Presbyterian churches.

---

[102]Wilberforce to C. H. Spurgeon, November 19, 1881, located in the Heritage Room at Spurgeon's College, quoted in Kruppa, *Charles Haddon Spurgeon: A Preacher's Progress*, 362.

[103]Larsen, *People of One Book*, 248-51.

[104]The best treatment of Spurgeon's relationship with Moody remains Gregg William Quiggle, "An Analysis of Dwight Moody's Urban Social Vision" (PhD thesis, The Open University, 2009), 141-53; For further information on Moody's revival work in Britain, see John Coffey, "Democracy and Popular Religion: Moody and Sankey's Mission to Britain, 1873–1875," in *Citizenship and Community: Liberals, Radicals, and Collective Identities in the British Isles, 1865–1931*, ed. Eugenio F. Biagini (Cambridge: Cambridge University Press, 1996), 93-119.

[105]Spurgeon enjoyed a close friendship with Kennedy, though their relationship was tested when Kennedy published a pamphlet critical of D. L. Moody's evangelistic campaign. Spurgeon, attempting to make peace, suggested in *The Sword and the Trowel* that Kennedy misunderstood Moody's approach. See *The Sword and the Trowel* 11 (1875): 142.

[106]The congregation at the Metropolitan Tabernacle, equally favorable to the American, asked Pierson to stay on following Spurgeon's death, and he remained with the congregation for two more years.

The years of the Downgrade Controversy qualify as perhaps the most turbulent period in Spurgeon' ministry. These years reveal the extent to which Spurgeon was willing to sacrifice friendships and relationships with former pupils in what he viewed as a fight to uphold the authority of the Bible, substitutionary atonement, and the doctrine of eternal punishment. While his uncompromising position put him at odds with many in the Baptist Union, it won him admirers from other Christian traditions and provided an opportunity for him to gather support from a wider community.

THE GREATEST FIGHT IN THE WORLD: SPURGEON'S "FINAL MANIFESTO"

As Spurgeon's health worsened, he was increasingly unable to preach at the Metropolitan Tabernacle. Since illness kept him from his pulpit, he focused his attention on several writing projects, including his autobiography and a commentary on the Matthew's Gospel titled *The Gospel of the Kingdom*.[107] Another noteworthy publication from this time period was a volume titled *The Greatest Fight in the World*, which was based on Spurgeon's final presidential address at the Pastors' College Evangelical Association in 1891. The editors of the final volume of Spurgeon's *Autobiography* noted that it was "a fitting climax to the long series of Inaugural Addresses, which were always reckoned, by those who were privileged to hear them, as the most solemn and forceful of all Mr. Spurgeon's utterances."[108] The book was published shortly before Spurgeon's death and was translated into French and German later in the year. Following Spurgeon's death, the book was described as Spurgeon's "Final Manifesto," and the *Autobiography* noted that a "generous gentleman" donated enough funds to secure the distribution of the book to "every clergyman and minister of every denomination in England."[109]

---

[107]As we have seen, the commentary was nearly finished when Spurgeon died and was published posthumously in the subsequent months.

[108]C. H. Spurgeon, *C. H. Spurgeon's Autobiography, Compiled from His Diary, Letters, and Records, by His Wife and His Private Secretary*, vol. 4, *1878–1892* (Chicago: Fleming H. Revell, 1900), 314.

[109]Spurgeon, *Autobiography*, 4:315.

In Spurgeon's mind, the "greatest fight" that lay ahead of Christians was that for evangelism, and his discussion of the fight was more forceful than solemn. In addition to furthering Spurgeon's increased usage of military imagery, the book includes some of Spurgeon's most candid comments with regard to the nature and appropriate use of the Bible. In this address, Spurgeon is part crusading evangelist and part mystic.[110] Despite failing health, the rebuttal of the Baptist Union, and dwindling support from some fellow ministers, Spurgeon's determination to guide and encourage those who remained within his sphere of influence was on display in these lectures on evangelism.

This convergence of evangelist and mystic is evident even in his introduction, where, noting his poor health, Spurgeon said, "I would be willing to speak with stammering tongue if God's purpose could be answered more fully; and I would even gladly lose all power of speech if, by being famished as to human words, you might feed the better on the spiritual meat which is to be found alone in Him, who is the incarnate Word of God."[111] As he continued, Spurgeon kept the cross of Christ and the necessity of evangelism central, noting, "*My topics have to do with our life-work, with the crusade against error and sin in which we are engaged.* I hope every man here wears the red cross on his heart, and is pledged to do and dare for Christ and for his cross, and never to be satisfied till Christ's foes are routed and Christ himself is satisfied."[112]

The Bible, according to Spurgeon, was the ultimate "armoury" for Christian ministers. He suggested,

> If we want weapons we must come here for them, and here only. Whether
> we seek the sword of offence or the shield of defence, we must find it within
> the volume of inspiration. If others have any other storehouse, I confess at

---

[110]Spurgeon's mystical side is not prevalent in many of the more conservative published works; however, it does appear in several more recent scholarly volumes, including Morden, *"Communion with Christ"*; Christian T. George, "Jesus Christ, the 'Prince of Pilgrims': A Critical Analysis of the Ontological, Functional, and Exegetical Christologies in the Sermons, Writings, and Lectures of Charles Haddon Spurgeon (1834–1892)" (PhD thesis, University of St. Andrews, 2011).

[111]C. H. Spurgeon, *The Greatest Fight in the World (Final Manifesto)* (New York: Funk & Wagnalls, 1891), 5.

[112]Spurgeon, *Greatest Fight*, 8.

once that I have none. I have nothing else to preach when I have got through with this book. Indeed, I can have no wish to preach at all if I may not continue to expound the subjects which I find in these pages. What else is worth preaching? Brethren, the truth of God is the only treasure for which we seek, and the Scripture is the only field in which we dig for it.[113]

As we have seen in previous chapters, Spurgeon's own excavations in the text very often led him to conclusions that focused upon evangelistic pleas for his listener's conversion, which were often rooted in the cross of Christ. Spurgeon's crucicentric and conversionistic focus ensured that theories of the atonement that could not coincide with the framework of penal substitution were roundly rejected, as we will see below.

The Bible, according to Spurgeon, was the only appropriate starting point in matters of Christian conversion. He rhetorically asked his listeners, "Have any of you known or heard of such a thing as conversion wrought by any other doctrine than that which is in the Word? I should like to have a catalogue of conversions wrought by modern theology. I would subscribe for a copy of such a work."[114] Modern theology, according to Spurgeon, would produce "conversions to the love of God, and to faith in his Christ, by hearing that the death of the Saviour was only the consummation of a grand example, but not a substitutionary sacrifice! Conversions by a gospel out of which all the gospel has been drained!"[115] Concluding his section on the Bible and conversion, he stated, "In a word, in our warfare *we shall keep to that old weapon of the sword of the Spirit, until we can find a better.*"[116]

As he developed his argument, Spurgeon spent a considerable amount of his lecture addressing the nature and inspiration of the Bible. Having previously spoken primarily through the language of doctrine, Spurgeon now took on a more experiential tone. He invited his listeners to consider their own experiences in light of his address. In a lengthy but telling paragraph, he urged his listeners to remember that

---

[113]Spurgeon, *Greatest Fight*, 9.
[114]Spurgeon, *Greatest Fight*, 14.
[115]Spurgeon, *Greatest Fight*, 14.
[116]Spurgeon, *Greatest Fight*, 15.

it was not so long ago that you will have forgotten how, like a hammer, the Word of God broke your flinty heart, and brought down your stubborn will. *By the Word of the Lord you were brought to the cross, and comforted by the atonement.* That Word breathed a new life into you; and when, for the first time, you knew yourself to be a child of God, you felt the ennobling power of the gospel received by faith. *The Holy Spirit wrought your salvation through the Holy Scriptures. . . .* Whoever may have been the man who spoke it, or whatever may have been the book in which you read it, *it was not man's Word, nor man's thought upon God's word, but the Word itself, which made you know salvation in the Lord Jesus.* It was neither human reason, nor the force of eloquence, nor the power of moral suasion, but the omnipotence of the Spirit, applying the Word itself, that gave you rest and peace and joy through believing. We are ourselves trophies of the power of the sword of the Spirit.[117]

In this quotation there are faint echoes of the comments Spurgeon made with regard to his own conversion, namely that he did not particularly remember the finer details of the service, to the extent that he was never able to identify the minister who preached the morning's sermon. In Spurgeon's estimation the sermon, and indeed the preacher, were ultimately less influential than the supernatural power of the Holy Spirit working through the biblical text. Spurgeon's perspective on Bible reading implies that he regarded the Bible in almost sacramental language, particularly when he suggested that "the prayerful study of the Word is not only a means of instruction, but an act of devotion wherein the transforming power of grace is often exercised, changing us into the image of him of whom the word is a mirror."[118] Spurgeon's suggestion of the best way to internalize the Bible is again indicative of a mystical view of Scripture. His language is particularly striking as he finished his point, saying, "Let the great transactions of the gospel story be to you as really and practically facts, as any fact which meets you in the domestic circle, or in the outside world: let them be as vividly true to you as your own ever present body, with its aches and pains, its appetites and joys."[119]

---

[117]Spurgeon, *Greatest Fight*, 18. Emphasis mine.
[118]Spurgeon, *Greatest Fight*, 19.
[119]Spurgeon, *Greatest Fight*, 24.

Later in the lecture, Spurgeon addressed the topic of biblical inspiration directly. The topic that had created significant tension during the controversy in the Baptist Union in previous years had not waned in Spurgeon's mind. His comments, among the last he made on the subject, are telling. For example, he insisted that "we care little for any theory of inspiration: in fact, we have none. To us the plenary verbal inspiration of Holy Scripture is fact and not hypothesis. It is a pity to theologize about a subject which is deeply mysterious, and makes a demand upon faith rather than fancy."[120] Further elaborating on his theology of the Bible, Spurgeon made a case for biblical infallibility. His chief concern was with the continued outworking of biblical higher criticism within the universities, whose graduates, in his mind, thought they could decide for themselves which particular texts were authentic. Spurgeon naturally rejected this approach and described the new batch of higher critics as "a horde of little popelings fresh from college."[121] Under the system, "German silver" was being substituted for gold, and "doctrines which produced the godliest generation that ever lived on the face of the earth are scouted as sheer folly."[122]

At the heart of Spurgeon's argument was his aversion to the "pretension" surrounding the proponents of biblical criticism. He believed, against such elitism, that men and women who had not attained advanced theological degrees were nonetheless able to interpret the Bible. Spurgeon sought to bolster his listeners' confidence in the Bible so that they might engage with it confidently in both their devotional reading and evangelism. It should be noted that he was by no means alone in this position. Joseph Parker (1830–1902), a Congregationalist minister, offered similar views, writing that "even Baur or Colenso may, contrary to his own wishes, be almost unconsciously elevated into a literary deity under whose approving nod alone we can read the Bible without any edification. Have we to await a communication from Tübingen, or a telegram from Oxford, before we can read the Bible?"[123] Spurgeon, who shared this view, noted that

---

[120]Spurgeon, *Greatest Fight*, 27.

[121]Spurgeon, *Greatest Fight*, 27.

[122]Spurgeon, *Greatest Fight*, 27-28. The "godliest generation" to which Spurgeon refers were the Puritans.

[123]Quoted in Glover, *Evangelical Nonconformists and Higher Criticism in the Nineteenth Century*, 230.

we shall gradually be so bedoubted and becriticized, that only a few of the most profound will know what is Bible, and what is not, and they will dictate to all the rest of us. I have no more faith in their mercy than in their accuracy: they will rob us of all we hold most dear, and glory in their cruel deed. The same reign of terror we shall not endure, for we still believe that God revealeth himself rather to babes than to the wise and prudent and we are fully assured that *our own old English version of the Scriptures is sufficient for plain men for all purposes of life, salvation, and godliness.* We do not despise learning, but we will never say of culture or criticism, "These be thy gods, O Israel."[124]

He launched equal criticism against Christians who attempted to construct elaborate arguments in an attempt to harmonize biblical accounts with modern scientific theories. As we have seen in the previous discussion on *The Sword and the Trowel,* Spurgeon maintained a personal interest in science, though he took a significant section of his speech to target Christians who were especially fixated on matters of scientific discovery. This is noteworthy particularly as he addressed the subject of the age of the earth, saying,

I do not know, and I do not care, much about the question; but I want to say that, if you smash up an explanation you must not imagine that you have damaged the Scriptural truth which seemed to require the explanation: you have only burned the wooden palisades with which well-meaning men thought to protect an impregnable fort which needed no such defence.[125]

As he continued his address, Spurgeon noted that it was incumbent on ministers who prioritized the gospel message in their sermons to in turn bid their congregations to engage in evangelism themselves. Most men and women had the capacity to be evangelists, Spurgeon argued, but they lacked motivation from their ministers, who ought to be models. "The man who is all aglow with love to Jesus," according to Spurgeon, "finds little need for amusement. He has no time for trifling. He is dead earnest to save

[124]Spurgeon, *Greatest Fight*, 28-29. Emphasis mine.
[125]Spurgeon, *Greatest Fight*, 32.

souls, and establish the truth, and enlarge the kingdom of his Lord."[126] He suggested that this was accomplished more fully in previous generations because of their heightened biblical literacy, noting that "old-fashioned believers could give you chapter and verse for what they believed; but how few of such remain . . . to try and shake them was by no means a hopeful task: you might as well have hoped to shake the pillars of the universe; for they were steadfast."[127] A church of this nature, according to Spurgeon, would become a "church of a missionary character." He continued, with passion, noting that "a church is a soul-saving company, or it is nothing. If the salt exercises no preservative influence on that which surrounds it, what is the use of it?"[128]

For all the attention that Spurgeon called to the work of the Holy Spirit in the efficacy of preaching, near the end of his addresses he suggested that the "Holy Ghost will not come in to rescue us from the consequences of willful neglect of the Word of God and study."[129] His remedy was to "prepare the sermon as if all depended upon us, and then we are to trust the Spirit of God knowing that all depends upon Him."[130] He concluded by imploring his listeners to preach Christ above all else:

> If we do not make the Lord Jesus glorious; if we do not lift him high in the esteem of men, if we do not labour to make him the King of kings, and Lord of lords; we shall not have the Holy Spirit with us. Vain will be rhetoric, music, architecture, energy, and social status: If our one design is not to magnify the Lord Jesus, we shall work alone and in vain.[131]

The Greatest Fight in the World is particularly helpful as a window into Spurgeon's view on how pastors, and indeed all Christians, should engage the biblical text. His chief concern was to promote an outward-looking, evangelistic focus. In these lectures, Spurgeon frequently appealed to his own personal experience, as well as the presumed shared Christian

---

[126]Spurgeon, *Greatest Fight*, 44.
[127]Spurgeon, *Greatest Fight*, 45-46.
[128]Spurgeon, *Greatest Fight*, 46.
[129]Spurgeon, *Greatest Fight*, 61.
[130]Spurgeon, *Greatest Fight*, 61.
[131]Spurgeon, *Greatest Fight*, 63.

experience of his listeners as he pleaded with them to preach in the same manner that he had during the four previous decades. His "final manifesto" was in one sense a rallying cry to his students, an encouragement for the coming academic year. In perhaps a fuller sense, we might see the themes Spurgeon addressed as a sort of culmination of the core elements of his ministry, a final reminder of the significance with which he viewed the preaching of the Bible in such a manner as to emphasize a crucified Christ and to seek the conversion of one's listeners.

CONCLUSIONS

As we have seen, Spurgeon's latter years were spent supporting and maintaining the ministries that he had established earlier in life. These demands took a significant toll upon his health; Bright's Disease, rheumatism, and chronic gout routinely constrained his schedule and restricted his physical mobility. While Spurgeon will always be most famous for his preaching, we have noted that his other written and spoken work are equally relevant in assessing his biblical interpretation.

As the staff at British universities and ministers of British churches and theological colleges increasingly explored different approaches to the Bible and theology, Spurgeon held fast to Puritan Nonconformity. His desire was to make *The Sword and the Trowel* live up to its namesake, as both an offensive weapon and a constructive tool. Spurgeon, however, was not entirely consistent in his views. He criticized Christian writers who sought to engage the higher critics, especially when they mentioned particular critics by name, yet Spurgeon occasionally gave himself license to do the same, both in his pulpit and magazine. In his book reviews, Spurgeon surveyed a wide range of material, both academic and devotional, though his reviews were relatively short. While his reviews often provided lively conclusions, they did not always convey a sense of careful critical engagement that would have been found in longer, more comprehensive reviews. This could leave a sense that he was prepared to condemn a book that he had not fully weighed and considered, which would, of course, have been unfair to the author. Spurgeon's book reviews were rarely impartial, but his rhetoric offers a window into his own biblical interpretation and coincides with the broader argument that Spurgeon preferred volumes that either forwarded or did not oppose interpretation that was crucicentric and conversionistic in nature.

In *The Bible and the Newspaper*, Spurgeon set out to evaluate the culture around him and draw material to further illustrate the biblical text. Ironically, while Spurgeon's musings were certainly within the bounds of conservative, evangelical theology, the verses that he associated with the given articles were often only mentioned in footnotes and rarely discussed in the body text of the entries themselves. Thus Spurgeon's exercise in proving the practicality of connecting the Bible to everyday life may have in reality simply proven the relative ease with which a verse or pair of verses could be moralized into a didactic lesson. *The Bible and the Newspaper* does, however, contain some of Spurgeon's clearest commentary on the contemporary state of biblical interpretation, and as such it is a helpful resource for the study of Spurgeon's hermeneutics.

The Downgrade Controversy, often regarded as the most trying time of Spurgeon's ministry, resulted in him taking a rather public stand against the Baptist Union. Throughout the controversy, however, perhaps the single most common thread in Spurgeon's discourse was his concern that the gospel would be undermined by his opponents' actions. While his judgment in handling the affair can certainly be called into question, he showed no vacillation with regard to his own priorities and positions throughout the conflict. The plenary inspiration of the Bible, the reality of hell, and the doctrine of penal substitutionary atonement represented core tenets of Spurgeon's theology, and for them he was willing to step away from the Baptist Union.

Finally, Spurgeon's last inaugural address to the students and academic staff of the Pastors' College could be described in some sense as definitive of the broader theology that had governed his life and ministry up to that point. The lecture's content does not represent any shift on Spurgeon's part but perhaps a finer articulation of his doctrine and practice. Given what we have observed about Spurgeon's interpretive method thus far, it is not surprising that he should identify crucicentric, evangelistic use of the Bible as the "greatest fight in the world." His address, which aimed to animate the students of the Pastors' College, would eventually become one of his most circulated lectures. In his fervor to promote evangelistic preaching, Spurgeon provided one of the clearest illustrations of his doctrinal positions regarding the nature of the Bible and how one should interpret and preach from it.

Spurgeon's engagement with the Bible in the latter years of his life mirrors what we have seen earlier. Reaching an elevated position of influence, financial security, and perhaps the greatest printed circulation of any preacher up to that time, he used his resources and influence to emphasize the cross of Christ and to encourage others to use the Bible for evangelistic ends. As he proclaimed to his listeners, "I wish that our ministry—that mine especially—might be tied and tethered to the cross. . . . You may wander from Dan to Beersheba, and you may not sin, for it is all holy ground between the two places; but he is wisest who does not ramble even there, but keeps to Calvary, and is content to speak only of Jesus crucified."[132] In the following chapter, we will evaluate Spurgeon in his role as an educator, analyzing the extent to which his crucicentric and conversionistic approach was used as a paradigm in his educational endeavors.

---

[132]C. H. Spurgeon, "The Best Bread," sermon no. 1940, given October 28, 1886, from John 6:48, *The Metropolitan Tabernacle Pulpit*, vol. 33 (London: Passmore & Alabaster, 1887), 25.

THE CROSS
IN THE COLLEGE

Biblical Engagement in Spurgeon's Training Institutions

> *Whatever forms of expression you may use as you advance in knowledge,*
> *ever keep the cross of Jesus Christ in the forefront, and let all*
> *the blessed truths which gather around it be heartily maintained.*

C. H. SPURGEON

IN A LETTER ADDRESSED TO HIS FATHER in May 1851, a teenaged Charles Haddon Spurgeon wrote that "a cap and gown are poor things to sell one's principles for."[1] The young Spurgeon's defiant tone here is likely a reference to the University of Cambridge's policy that excluded Dissenting students, a policy that was largely ended in 1856, before all remaining disabilities for undergraduate students were abolished in 1871.[2] Among the many social endeavors in which nineteenth century British evangelicals were involved, education was especially important, both at home and abroad.[3] These movements largely coincided with

---

C. H. Spurgeon, *An All-Round Ministry: Addresses to Ministers and Students* (Pasadena, TX: Pilgrim Press, 1983), 182.

[1] Spurgeon to John Spurgeon, May 15, 1851, in *C. H. Spurgeon's Autobiography, Compiled from His Diary, Letters, and Records, by His Wife and His Private Secretary*, vol. 1, *1834–1854* (Cincinnati: Curts & Jennings, 1898), 209.

[2] Michael Twaddle, "The Oxford and Cambridge Admissions Controversy of 1834," *British Journal of Educational Studies* 14, no. 3 (November 1966): 57; J. E. B. Munson, "The Education of Baptist Ministers, 1870–1900," *Baptist Quarterly* 26, no. 7 (1976): 321.

[3] See, for instance, Khim Harris, *Evangelicals and Education: Evangelical Anglicans and Middle-Class Education in Nineteenth-Century England* (Milton Keynes, UK: Paternoster, 2004); Paul Serda,

the general expansion of public education in Britain across the latter half of the nineteenth century.[4] Their influence was also felt in churches, where some congregants, particularly in the middle class, began to expect a higher standard of discourse from their ministers.[5] These efforts produced tremendous results: Whereas in 1841, literacy among adult males in England and Wales was 67.3 percent, by 1900 the figure had risen to 97.2 percent. The increase was even higher among women, whose literacy rates grew from 51.1 percent to 96.8 percent in the same time span.[6]

Although he never formally studied the Bible or Christian theology in an academic setting, Spurgeon respected theological study, and he eventually used his influence to promote a multifaceted campaign to provide accessible theological instruction at several levels. Spurgeon's engagement with education took several forms throughout his ministry. His desire to work as an educator, according to his *Autobiography*, was present even in his teenage years in Cambridge, where he advertised in a local newspaper that he intended to take on "six or seven young gentlemen as day pupils" and that he would "endeavour to the utmost to impart a good commercial Education."[7] Throughout his life, Spurgeon saw value in providing both general and theological education for a wide audience. His education schemes included vocational evening courses in London, a well-attended women's study, and his arguably most well-known foray into education,

---

From Mission to Modernity: Evangelicals, Reformers, and Education in Nineteenth Century Egypt (New York: I. B. Tauris, 2011); Michael R. Watts, *The Dissenters*, vol. 3, *The Crisis and Conscience of Nonconformity* (Oxford: Oxford University Press, 2015), 191-206.

[4]There was a strong tradition of Dissenting academies throughout Britain, beginning in the late seventeenth century; however, the nineteenth century witnessed an expansion of new training facilities. See Herbert McLachlan, *English Education Under the Test Acts: Being the History of the Nonconformist Academics 1662–1820* (Manchester: Manchester University Press, 1931); Irene Parker, *Dissenting Academies in England: Their Rise and Progress and Their Place Among the Educational Systems of the Country* (Cambridge: Cambridge University Press, 1914).

[5]See Munson, "Education of Baptist Ministers," 321.

[6]T. W. Heyck, *The Transformation of Intellectual Life in Victorian England*, Croom Helm Studies in Society and History (London & Canberra: Croom Helm, 1982), 199.

[7]Spurgeon, *Autobiography*, 1:341. The balance of the entry suggests a degree of youthful optimism, as he suggested that his students would be able to study "Arithmetic, Algebra, Geometry, and Mensuration; Grammar and Composition; Ancient and Modern History; Geography, Natural History, Astronomy, Scripture, and Drawing. Latin and the elements of Greek and French, if required," all for the fee of £5 per year.

the Pastors' College.[8] In each of these educational endeavors, the study of the Bible was central to the curriculum, and both Spurgeon and his fellow educators encouraged their students to deepen their knowledge of the Bible through further study. The nineteenth century was a time of increased biblical literacy in Britain, even among nonbelievers. As Larsen has observed, the Bible was "the common cultural currency of the Victorians."[9] Spurgeon, who was the most popular preacher of his day, also recognized the benefit of a training ministry. While his printed sermons reached most corners of the world, he saw a particular value in training Bible teachers. The training he offered, in some ways, stood in contrast to divinity instruction elsewhere in Britain. Though he emphasized biblical and theological study, Spurgeon's ultimate goal for his students was that they would replicate the style of preaching and ministry in the Metropolitan Tabernacle. Remarking on the work of the Pastors' College, he simply said, "By it, I multiply myself."[10] In a culture saturated with biblical references and imagery, Spurgeon's mission to further biblical and theological education across several venues was indicative of his desire to see men and women from all backgrounds using the Bible to proclaim Christ crucified and to see individuals converted.

To accomplish his educational aims, Spurgeon gathered a select group of men and women. These included Vernon J. Charlesworth, who oversaw the education of the boys and girls living at Spurgeon's orphanage. Additionally, Spurgeon recruited George Rogers (1799–1892), who like Charlesworth came from an Independent background, and both were hired despite their convictions regarding baptism.[11] In addition to the staff at his orphanage and college, Spurgeon looked to a woman in his congregation, Lavinia Bartlett (1806–1875), to head what would become an extensive

---

[8]The institution was initially called the Pastor's College, though in the mid-1870s the title changed to the Pastors' College. Following its founder's death, it was finally renamed Spurgeon's College. For consistency in this book, I have used "Pastors' College" throughout.

[9]Timothy Larsen, *A People of One Book: The Bible and the Victorians* (Oxford: Oxford University Press, 2011), 2.

[10]J. C. Carlile, *C. H. Spurgeon: An Interpretive Biography* (London: Religious Tract Society and the Kingsgate Press, 1934), 169.

[11]Charlesworth had a noteworthy change in his position regarding baptism, and prior to his second baptism he gave a lengthy testimony to his new position.

evangelistic teaching ministry to women in London.[12] Spurgeon's team of educators, a team that included paedobaptists and women, is indicative of the degree to which he was prepared to appoint a diverse group of instructors to key positions, so long as they were in agreement with his overall aim, which was to train and deploy individuals who would teach the Bible with evangelistic intent.

As scholarly interest in Spurgeon has increased in the past three decades, there have also been several works written about his Pastors' College. These accounts are largely associated with three historians. Michael Nicholls, a former lecturer and vice principal at Spurgeon's College, has written two articles surveying Spurgeon's work as an educator as well as a popular-level history of the college.[13] David Bebbington has written a concise survey of the college and its goals in a chapter contributed to a volume on theological education in the evangelical tradition.[14] Finally, Ian M. Randall, who is also a former lecturer and current Senior Research Fellow at Spurgeon's College, has written several recent studies of the Pastors' College, works which include discussion of the college's engagement with global mission, the involvement of current and former students in the broader context of the Downgrade Controversy, and a general history of the college.[15]

---

[12]The most extensive, though uncritical, account of Bartlett's life and work is the following, written by her son. Edward H. Bartlett, *Mrs. Bartlett and Her Class at the Metropolitan Tabernacle: Being a Brief Account of the Life and Labours of Mrs. Lavinia Strickland Bartlett* (London: Passmore & Alabaster, 1877).

[13]Mike Nicholls, "Charles Haddon Spurgeon, Educationalist: Part 1—General Education Concerns," *Baptist Quarterly* 31, no. 8 (October 1986): 364-401; Mike Nicholls, "Charles Haddon Spurgeon, Educationalist: Part 2—The Principles and Practice of the Pastors' College," *Baptist Quarterly* 32, no. 2 (April 1987): 73-94; Mike Nicholls, *C. H. Spurgeon: The Pastor Evangelist* (Didcot, UK: Baptist Historical Society, 1992), 69-96; Mike Nicholls, *Lights to the World: A History of Spurgeon's College 1856–1992* (Harpenden, UK: Nuprint, 1994).

[14]David W. Bebbington, "Spurgeon and British Evangelical Theological Education," in *Theological Education in the Evangelical Tradition*, ed. D. G. Hart and R. Albert Mohler (Grand Rapids, MI: Baker, 1996), 217-34.

[15]Ian M. Randall, "The World Is Our Parish: Spurgeon's College and World Mission, 1856–1892," in *Baptists and Mission: Papers from the Fourth International Conference on Baptist Studies*, ed. Ian M. Randall and Anthony R. Cross, Studies in Baptist History and Thought 29 (Milton Keynes, UK: Paternoster, 2007), 64-77; Ian M. Randall, "Charles Haddon Spurgeon, the Pastor's College and the Downgrade Controversy," in *Discipline and Diversity*, ed. Kate Cooper and Jeremy Gregory, Studies in Church History 43 (Suffolk, UK: The Boydell Press, 2007), 366-76; Ian M. Randall, *A School of the Prophets: 150 Years of Spurgeon's College* (London: Spurgeon's College, 2005).

In this final chapter, we will survey Spurgeon's involvement with several educational ministries, analyzing both these ministries and their curricula with particular regard to biblical interpretation and evangelistic preaching. We will note that it is perhaps in the arena of education that Spurgeon's desire to raise up "soul winners" is most visible. The chapter will illustrate the degree to which Spurgeon and his fellow educators encouraged students to read and teach the Bible through the lens of crucicentrism and conversionism, with the goal of training and sending as many gospel-centered preachers as possible.

EVENING CLASSES

With the growth of commercial society, there was a growing need for men and women—particularly those living in urban centers like London—to possess basic education in English grammar and arithmetic. Christians from diverse denominational and confessional traditions recognized this need and took steps to provide education particularly for those who did not have the opportunity to attend formal schools and colleges. For instance, F. D. Maurice (1805–1872) and a group of influential Christian Socialists in London founded the Working Men's College, which opened in 1854, offering day and evening courses for working men.[16] Spurgeon, who had ample classroom space in his church buildings and a team of instructors already on staff at his Pastors' College, began offering his own evening classes in 1862.[17] By 1867, the available course list included Bible and Writing classes on Monday evenings, Elementary English classes on Tuesdays, and Advanced English, Elementary Greek & Latin, Advanced Greek & Latin, French language, and Science classes on Wednesday evenings.[18] The course offerings varied, and on occasion the evening classes

---

[16]For further information on the Working Men's College, see Frederick Denison Maurice, *The Workman and the Franchise: Chapters from English History on the Representation and Education of the People* (London: A. Strahan, 1866); J. F. C. Harrison, *A History of the Working Men's College, 1854–1954* (Boston: Routledge & Kegan Paul, 1954); Kristin Mahoney, "Work, Lack, and Longing: Rossetti's 'The Blessed Damozel' and the Working Men's College," *Victorian Studies* 52, no. 2 (January 2010): 219-48.

[17]For further information on the Evening Classes, see Nicholls, "Charles Haddon Spurgeon, Educationalist: Part 1," 388-90; Nicholls, *Lights to the World*, 78-81; Bebbington, "Spurgeon and British Evangelical Theological Education," 227-28.

[18]Referenced in Nicholls, "Charles Haddon Spurgeon, Educationalist: Part 1," 388.

offered courses tailored to specific trades. For instance, in late 1878, *The Sword and the Trowel* advertised that the Evening School intended to offer a course in shorthand writing.[19] Rather than follow a fixed curriculum, the tutors were given freedom to adapt the coursework to suit the particular needs of individual students. Nicholls has noted that the evening classes "purposed both to help the inadequate beginner in his education and to make available the benefits of the College's classes to a wider clientele."[20] The students were not required to be members of the Metropolitan Tabernacle, and as such the classes were open to people from a variety of denominational backgrounds. The evening classes also gave Spurgeon an ideal place to both identify and train men with the intention of eventually admitting them to the Pastors' College. John Jackson, a minister in Sevenoaks, Kent, trained at both the evening classes and the college. Writing of his experience in the evening classes, he noted that

> for two years I was thus helped in my business and at the same time in my Christian life and work. On entering College I found nothing new. I was acquainted with the tutor and the students and to some extent with all the subjects for study. The Evening Classes afforded the best preparation for the College and for the ministry. Poverty is no disqualification. Here is the way for all who have the will.[21]

While the evening classes were ultimately geared toward vocational training, Spurgeon and his lecturers viewed the courses as an opportunity to introduce biblical and theological topics to their students. For instance, Nicholls has noted that there was significant interest in a class that studied A. A. Hodge's *Outlines of Theology*, and the main text for the Greek-language class was the *Gospel of John*.[22] The evening classes continued, though by the end of the nineteenth century a number of additional vocational and polytechnic schools had been established throughout London, which caused attendance at the evening classes to decline accordingly.

---

[19]*The Sword and the Trowel* 14 (1878): 601. Spurgeon himself depended on team of stenographers who recorded his sermons.

[20]Nicholls, "Charles Haddon Spurgeon, Educationalist: Part 1," 388.

[21]Nicholls, "Charles Haddon Spurgeon, Educationalist: Part 1," 389.

[22]Nicholls, "Charles Haddon Spurgeon, Educationalist: Part 1," 389.

SUNDAY AND MIDWEEK WOMEN'S CLASSES

In addition to the evening classes, one of the key ministries of the Metropolitan Tabernacle was a class run specifically for women, which met on Sunday afternoons. The primary figure associated with these courses was Lavinia Bartlett, who joined the church in 1856.[23] Though Spurgeon, like most Baptists of his era, opposed women preaching sermons to mixed groups, he was quite happy for women to preach to women and girls, and he accordingly supported the efforts of women's ministry within the Tabernacle. The church had an existing ministry to women, though by 1859 attendance at the women's Bible study had dwindled to three women. Thomas Olney, one of the Tabernacle's elders, invited Mrs. Bartlett to take over the weekly study. Within two years, the group had grown to include fifty women.[24] By 1866, an article in *The Sword and the Trowel* noted that the attendance in Mrs. Bartlett's class had grown to seven hundred women.[25] As the ministry grew, the Tabernacle began female prayer meetings on Tuesday evenings, and Mrs. Bartlett also invited women to pray at her home on Friday evenings. These classes were not only popular among women in London; they were also featured in Christian periodicals in the United States, where the *New York Evangelist* wrote, "May there be many more such devoted women as Mrs. Bartlett raised up to begin and carry on this good work!"[26] In contemporary discussions of the women's study, three noteworthy traits were commonly referenced. First and foremost, Mrs. Bartlett was renowned for her capacity as a Bible teacher. Edward Leach, one of the part-time lecturers at the Pastors' College, visited the women's meeting and described Mrs. Bartlett's address as "painting bright pictures of coming joys and communions to be realised by faith in the far-stretched future. Better still—it was savoury, full of Jesus."[27] Second, the women's ministry mirrored

---

[23] The most recent, though brief, investigation of Mrs. Bartlett's work is Tom Nettles, *Living by Revealed Truth: The Life and Pastoral Theology of Charles Haddon Spurgeon* (Ross-shire, UK: Christian Focus, 2013), 274-75.

[24] *The Sword and the Trowel* 15 (1879): 127.

[25] *The Sword and the Trowel* 2 (1866): 114.

[26] "An Afternoon with Mrs. Bartlett's Class," *New York Evangelist* (December 8, 1870): 3.

[27] *The Sword and the Trowel* 2 (1866): 115. Leach stressed that Mrs. Bartlett preferred the term *addresses* rather than sermons, as she was "anxious that the public should not be possessed with the idea that she preaches."

the larger focus of the Tabernacle with regard to ministry to the poor in London. Leach noted that "some members of the class are in respectable stations in life; others are of the Lord's poor. But these latter are carefully looked after by their sisters, and their wants are as far as may be supplied according to their varied necessities."[28] For the purposes of this study, what is most noteworthy about the women's ministry was that they reflected the evangelistic priorities of the Tabernacle and its pastor. Describing Mrs. Bartlett's instruction, Leach recorded that "peculiarly tender and eloquent was her appeal to the unconverted. Convince a sinner of your real anxiety for his eternal welfare, and you have opened a channel in his heart for further communications. Few could resist admiring the exuberant and passionate utterances of this Bible-teacher."[29] Leach commended the work of the women's ministry and its leader, suggesting that her teaching in some ways equaled Spurgeon's own as he wrote, "Who can estimate the influence of one converted woman upon the world? Where does not her power extend? . . . The sacred labour of Mrs. Bartlett's is not excelled even by a minister's most earnest work."[30] Another account suggested that "it should be a matter of praise to the Lord that He has so blessed this Bible class at the Tabernacle, many hundreds since its commencement professed their repentance toward God and their faith in our Lord Jesus Christ."[31] Perhaps the most telling remark is a passing comment by Leach in which he suggests that his male colleagues in ministry would benefit from attending Mrs. Bartlett's ministry. Commenting on her teaching, he wrote that "it was a simple, tender, earnest, powerful, and prevailing address to a real present Father. If [a] woman can thus approach the Lord in supplication, how much do we not lose, my male friends, by not occasionally hearing her voice?"[32]

Spurgeon himself frequently praised Mrs. Bartlett's efforts, particularly with regard to her commitment to evangelistic teaching. In the preface to her biography, written by her son, Spurgeon wrote,

---

[28] *The Sword and the Trowel* 2 (1866): 114-15.
[29] *The Sword and the Trowel* 2 (1866): 115.
[30] *The Sword and the Trowel* 2 (1866): 118.
[31] "Afternoon with Mrs. Bartlett's Class," 3.
[32] "Afternoon with Mrs. Bartlett's Class," 115.

Her addresses were always practical, never speculative or merely enter-
taining. *She aimed at soul-winning every time she met the class, and that in*
the most direct and personal manner. . . . She was troubled if at any time the
brethren whom she invited to address her young women wandered from
the one great subject, or treated it in a flowery or cold-hearted style.
Nothing suited her but the gospel preached in a gospel spirit, with the Holy
Ghost sent down from heaven. . . . She had asked the Lord to give her the
young women's souls, she expected Him to do so; and she went up in the
name of the Lord to win them, and she did win them, as our Church-
meetings continually proved.[33]

Additional accounts suggest that Mrs. Bartlett's teaching converted some
who had previously remained unconverted under Spurgeon's preaching.
The volume *Mrs. Bartlett and Her Class* notes that

an elderly person, who had listened to Mr. Spurgeon's voice for two years
without being led to the Saviour, was entering the room when Mrs. Bartlett
looked round and said, without intending the words for the late comer in
question, "Flee from the wrath to come, my sisters." . . . These words, so appropriately spoken, were the means of her conversion.[34]

Although the evening classes and Mrs. Bartlett's weekly meetings have not
received much attention in recent scholarship, they were influential in
their day. Furthermore, the support they enjoyed from Spurgeon suggests
that he placed a high priority on biblical study for laypeople as well as
future pastors. The similarities between the content of their preaching is
particularly telling as Spurgeon himself wrote of Mrs. Bartlett, "Her talk
was of the 'old, old story,' and never of the new-fangled doctrines, or
imaginary attainments. She kept to the cross, extolled her Saviour, pleaded
with sinners to believe, and stirred up saints to holy living."[35] Thus both
the evening classes and Mrs. Bartlett's meetings complemented Spurgeon's broader biblical ministry, with their particular emphasis on the
cross and conversion.

---

[33]Bartlett, *Mrs. Bartlett and Her Class*, xii-xiii. Emphasis mine.
[34]"Afternoon with Mrs. Bartlett's Class," 164.
[35]Bartlett, *Mrs. Bartlett and Her Class*, x.

THE PASTORS' COLLEGE

Perhaps to the chagrin of his twin sons, Spurgeon often referred to the Pastors' College as his "firstborn and best beloved."[36] The college, the most noteworthy of his educational endeavors, began in 1856. In the college's earliest days, the instruction was more akin to an apprenticeship than classroom education, though as interest increased Spurgeon quickly assembled a small group of lecturers and tutors to instruct the growing number of students. From its small beginnings, the Pastors' College would expand to become a key training facility for Baptists in Britain, and its students would learn to read the Bible in the same manner as Spurgeon himself, through a lens of crucicentrism and conversionism.

As we have noted, until the mid-1850s Baptists could not earn a degree at England's ancient universities, and many chose to prepare for ministry at Baptist colleges.[37] In the early nineteenth century, the most noteworthy Baptist training facility in London was the Stepney Academy. This changed when in 1856 its principal, Joseph Angus, oversaw the college's move to Regent's Park, where it became known as Regent's Park College.[38] As Michael Ledger-Lomas has observed, Regent's Park maintained a traditional academic structure, which some believed did not provide enough practical training in the ministry. Ledger-Lomas noted the frustrations of Baptist pastors such as John Howard Shakespeare (1857–1928) who complained that Regent's Park graduated "'theologians, essayists, Hebraists, Dryasdusts, and men with brilliant degrees' rather than preachers."[39]

Spurgeon's educational model was not antagonistic toward the liberal arts and sciences. As we will see, his curriculum was decidedly Bible-focused. However, students were also required to complete coursework in a variety of subjects, including English grammar, arithmetic, and classical literature.

---

[36]C. H. Spurgeon, *C. H. Spurgeon's Autobiography, Compiled from His Diary, Letters, and Records, by His Wife and Private Secretary*, vol. 3, *1856–1878* (Cincinnati: Curts & Jennings, 1899), 137.

[37]Scottish universities had fewer restrictions, leading many English Baptists to pursue training at institutions such as the Universities of Edinburgh, Glasgow, and St. Andrews.

[38]Regent's Park College would move a third time, in 1927, taking up its current residence in Oxford. It became a permanent, private hall of the University of Oxford in 1957.

[39]Michael Ledger-Lomas, "Ministers and Ministerial Training," in *The Oxford History of Protestant Dissenting Traditions*, vol. 3, *The Nineteenth Century*, ed. Timothy Larsen and Michael Ledger-Lomas (Oxford: Oxford University Press, 2017), 484.

Though Spurgeon retained ambitious goals for the breadth of education, biblical, theological, and preaching courses formed the core of the Pastors' College curriculum. Spurgeon was not anti-intellectual, but his vision for the college allowed no room for abstract thinking that clouded the plain teachings of the Bible. In a letter assessing the pastoral needs of Britain, he observed that "it seems to me that many of our churches need a class of ministers who will not aim at lofty scholarship, but at the winning of souls;—men of the people, feeling, sympathizing, fraternizing with the masses of working-men;—men who can speak the common language, the plain blunt Saxon of the crowd;—men ready to visit the sick and the poor."[40] His final sentence, however, captured the essence of not only the college's aim but Spurgeon's broader philosophy of pastoral ministry. He wrote, "Whether the student be rich or poor, *the object is the same,—not scholarship, but preaching the gospel,*—not the production of fine gentlemen, but of hardworking men."[41] In his college, Spurgeon could ensure that the students in his care read and preached the Bible through a lens of crucicentrism and conversionism.

The curricula at many British universities saw significant change at this time.[42] This included the ancient universities and also new establishments such as the London University, later known as University College, London, which embodied the philosopher Jeremy Bentham's vision for secularized university education. British universities were expanding their course offerings to include increased professional training, a change spurred on in great part by developments in science. Many university theology departments also saw significant changes in their curriculum. British academics such as Benjamin Jowett and Samuel Driver were influenced by the German university model, including higher criticism of the Bible. Spurgeon grew increasingly suspicious of the manner in which some divinity schools taught biblical interpretation, writing that the Bible

> is not quite a lump of wax to be shaped at our own will, or a roll of cloth to be cut according to the prevailing fashion. Your great thinkers evidently look

---

[40]Spurgeon, *Autobiography*, 3:129.
[41]Spurgeon, *Autobiography*, 3:129. Emphasis mine.
[42]Heyck, *Transformation of Intellectual Life in Victorian England*.

upon the Scriptures as a box of letters for them to play with, and make what they like of, or a wizard's bottle, out of which they may pour anything they choose from atheism up to spiritualism.[43]

In a lengthy passage, Spurgeon drew several distinctions between his vision for a college and what he viewed as the educational approaches of other universities:

> They are not to be warped into philosophers, polished into debaters, carved into metaphysicians, fashioned into literati, or even sharpened into critics, they are to be "thoroughly furnished unto every good work." *The Scriptures must be their chief class-book, theology their main science, the art of teaching their practical study, and the proclamation and exposition of the gospel their first business. With all knowledge they may intermeddle; but upon the knowledge of Christ crucified they must dwell.* Books and parchments should be prized, but prayer and meditation should be supreme. The head should be stored, but the heart also should be fed with heavenly food. The tutors should be men of equal learning and grace, sound scholars, but much more sound divines, men of culture, but even more decidedly men of God.[44]

Goals of the Pastors' College. Recalling the earliest days of the college, Spurgeon noted,

> Some five or six years ago one of the young men of the Church gave promise of being a successful minister if he could but have a good education. With the assistance of a friend in the Church, I undertook to take him under my charge, put him under a suitable tutor, and train him for the ministry. So successful was that work, that I was induced to take another, and another, and another.[45]

The young man to whom Spurgeon referred was T. W. Medhurst (1834–1917), who was actually only four months younger than Spurgeon himself.[46]

---

[43] *The Sword and the Trowel* 10 (1874): 102.

[44] *The Sword and the Trowel* 11 (1875): 252. Emphasis mine.

[45] C. H. Spurgeon, "The Church—Conservative and Aggressive," sermon no. 393, given May 19, 1861, from 1 Timothy 3:15, *The Metropolitan Tabernacle Pulpit*, vol. 7 (London: Passmore & Alabaster, 1861), 361.

[46] Nettles has provided a helpful summary of Medhurst's ministry. See Nettles, *Living by Revealed Truth*, 358-60.

Medhurst had a limited educational background and had recently finished an apprenticeship as a rope-maker. The tutor was George Rogers, then an Independent minister in Camberwell, Southwark. Medhurst received instruction from both Spurgeon and Rogers for several years before he was commissioned to pastor his own church.[47] Spurgeon's tutoring of Medhurst became the basis for the Pastors' College, which had over eighty full-time students in attendance by 1865.[48] This coincided with a general improvement in the education of Dissenting ministers. The Pastors' College was part of a broader trend in England. As J. E. B. Munson has noted, "Whereas in 1870 half of the active ministry in England were without any formal education, by 1901 the number had dropped to 18 per cent."[49] By 1874, Spurgeon had raised enough money to construct a purpose-built building for the students, which relieved constraints on space at the Metropolitan Tabernacle. The Pastors' College left a significant imprint upon Baptist ministry through Britain. David Bebbington has observed that "by the end of Spurgeon's life, a total of 863 men had been trained at the college, and they constituted over 50 percent of the Baptist ministers in England and Wales."[50]

Training dozens of pastors year after year, particularly those from less prosperous backgrounds, was costly, and the college had to run on a tight budget. To help raise money, Spurgeon printed fundraising information on the last page of each issue of *The Sword and the Trowel*, and he dedicated the income of his sermon sales in America toward the college's expenses.[51] While he was fundraising, Spurgeon often mentioned the importance of the training work in public lectures. For example, in 1881 he gave an address titled "On the Worth of Colleges," in which he proclaimed,

---

[47]Medhurst would eventually serve in pastorates in London, Northern Ireland, and Scotland. He and Spurgeon engaged in consistent correspondence throughout their ministries, and Medhurst occasionally contributed articles to *The Sword and the Trowel* and provided lectures at the Pastors' College when invited. His most well-known written work was a pamphlet titled *Is Romanism Christianity*, which was eventually reproduced in the third volume of the noteworthy American publication, *The Fundamentals*. Medhurst's son, Charles Spurgeon Medhurst (1860–1927), worked as a missionary in China.

[48]*The Sword and the Trowel* 1 (1865): 36.

[49]Munson, "Education of Baptist Ministers," 321.

[50]Bebbington, "Spurgeon and British Evangelical Theological Education," 221.

[51]For further discussion on Spurgeon's fundraising tactics, see Bebbington, "Spurgeon and British Evangelical Theological Education," 224-26.

We have laboured with our heart, and soul, and strength to make the Pastors'
College a seed-garden for the church and for the world. . . . *Our word to all
our brethren is—Encourage and help the colleges more and more, but see to it
that those you aid are seminaries for the growth of unmistakable
gospel preachers.*[52]

Admission to the college was restricted to students who held to Baptistic
theology. Spurgeon regarded it as "unwarrantable" to interfere with the
training of pastors who belonged to different denominations, writing that
"we confine our College to Baptists; and, in order not to be harassed with
endless controversies, we invite those only who hold those views of divine
truth which are popularly known as *Calvinistic*,—not that we care for
names and phrases; but, as we wish to be understood, we use a term which
conveys our meaning as nearly as any descriptive word can do."[53] The
faculty and students appeared largely supportive of this aim. James Archer
Spurgeon (1837–1899), Charles's younger brother and the college's eventual
vice president, proudly proclaimed in an 1882 college report that "happily
we see no signs of any abatement in the love of our young brethren to the
old doctrines and principles of our denomination. We desire to train up no
band of bigots; but we urge a definite creed and a rigid discipline in our
churches, and first of all in our church-leaders."[54]

The staff of the Pastors' College. While Spurgeon only admitted credo-
baptist students, he was open to a degree of theological latitude in the college's teaching staff. The Independent minister George Rogers exemplified
this sort of latitude. Writing about Rogers, Spurgeon noted, "He has been a
Puritan from his childhood, and is a Puritan still. He has a well-defined
creed, and is not ashamed to own it. In all points, except upon the matter of
baptism, we are heartily agreed, and in spirit and temper he is a man with
whom our communion is perfect."[55] Rogers, who was described as "grim,
gaunt, and grey" by one of his students, was nonetheless a popular

---

[52] *The Sword and the Trowel* 17 (1881): 175. Emphasis mine.
[53] C. H. Spurgeon, *Lectures to My Students*, vol. 2, *Addresses Delivered to the Students of the Pastors'
College, Metropolitan Tabernacle* (New York: Robert Carter and Brothers, 1889), xiii.
[54] *The Sword and the Trowel* 18 (1882): 269.
[55] *The Sword and the Trowel* 10 (1874): 151-52.

instructor.[56] He ran the college's operation from his home for its first five years, and was the first principal, serving from 1856 to 1881.[57] Rogers's successor as principal, David Gracey (1841–1893), fit squarely into the Baptist context. Originally from County Down and converted during a revival in 1859, Gracey began studying theology at Glasgow University. In 1861, after hearing Spurgeon preach in Glasgow, Gracey left the University to study at the Pastors' College, where he was soon appointed to lecture in Classics.[58] In addition to Rogers and Gracey, there were two other noteworthy tutors at the college. Archibald Fergusson (1821–1900), originally from Scotland, lectured in English grammar. Finally, James Archer Spurgeon worked as both a tutor and the vice president of the college.[59] The younger Spurgeon graduated from the Stepney Academy prior to its move and had a stronger academic background than his brother.[60] The Pastors' College additionally employed several part-time lecturers. Among them was William Robbins Selway (1822–1893), a local surveyor who held a position on the Metropolitan Board of Works and taught science courses. In 1879, Spurgeon recruited Frederick Marchant (1839–1899), a former Baptist pastor in Birmingham, to teach part-time in classics and mathematics. An entry in the 1883 edition of *The Sword and the Trowel* provided a succinct if not idealized list of traits Spurgeon desired for tutors at the college, namely they should "thunder in preaching, and lighten in conversation, they should be flaming in prayer, shining in life, and burning in spirit. . . . The spirit of the gospel must be in him as well as its doctrine."[61] The college's tutors served for long terms: Fergusson worked for thirty years, and Gracey completed thirty-one years, ending his tenure in 1893. Rogers, who was fifty-seven years old

---

[56]Nicholls, "Charles Haddon Spurgeon, Educationalist: Part 2," 74.

[57]For more information on Rogers, see Nicholls, "Charles Haddon Spurgeon, Educationalist: Part 2," 73-76.

[58]For further biographical material on Gracey, see Archibald McCaig's preface in David Gracey, *Sin and the Unfolding of Salvation, Being the Three Years' Course of Theological Lectures Delivered at the Pastors' College, London* (London: Passmore & Alabaster, 1894), v-viii; Nicholls, "Charles Haddon Spurgeon, Educationalist: Part 2," 75.

[59]James Archer Spurgeon was also installed as the co-pastor of the Metropolitan Tabernacle and would often preach there when his brother's health declined.

[60]He would eventually receive two honorary doctor of divinity degrees, honors his brother routinely rejected.

[61]*The Sword and the Trowel* 19 (1883): 262-63.

when he began work at the college, worked there for an additional twenty-five years. Each of the primary lecturers often preached in London churches.

Students at the Pastors' College. Spurgeon was committed to admitting students to the college from a variety of socioeconomic backgrounds. For Spurgeon one of the most important criteria for admission was whether or not the applicant was already involved in preaching. He made abundantly clear that the

> institution receives no man in order to make him a preacher, but it is established to help in the further education of brethren who have been preaching with some measure of success for two years in the least. Many men of earnest spirit and established Christian character are hindered in their efforts to do good by the slenderness of their knowledge. Conscious of their own defects, they endeavour to improve themselves, but the absence of a guide, their need of books, and their scanty time, all prevent their making progress. These are the men whom the Pastors' College welcomes.[62]

While the majority of the Pastors' College students were British, Spurgeon's increasingly global reputation eventually attracted students from other parts of the world. Among these applicants was Thomas L. Johnson (1836–1921), who was born into slavery on a plantation in Virginia.[63] Following the end of the American Civil War in 1865, Johnson moved to New York, where he first began to preach. When he later applied to American mission boards to work as a missionary in Africa, his applications were denied, and he was encouraged to receive formal theological training. Upon traveling to England, Johnson met the Baptist minister Alexander Maclaren, who forwarded his name to the council of the Baptist Missionary Society in London.[64] When Spurgeon was made aware of Johnson's desire to pursue training in preparation for mission work in Africa, he sent a brief telegraph that simply read, "Yes, let the dear man come."[65]

---

[62]C. H. Spurgeon, *Lectures to My Students*, vol. 1, *A Selection from Addresses Delivered to the Students of the Pastors' College, Metropolitan Tabernacle* (London: Passmore & Alabaster, 1875), vii.

[63]Thomas L. Johnson, *Twenty-Eight Years a Slave, or the Story of My Life in Three Continents*, 7th ed. (Bournemouth, UK: W. Mate & Sons, 1909), 1.

[64]Johnson, *Twenty-Eight Years a Slave*, 85.

[65]Johnson, *Twenty-Eight Years a Slave*, 86.

Johnson's memoirs contain first-hand descriptions of the college's preaching course, which was run at the time by George Rogers. The students prepared sermons, which were delivered to the entire class, who were then invited to comment. While living in the United States, Johnson had been given a copy of the sermons of Andrew Fuller, from which he borrowed liberally in his first sermon at the college, despite the stern warnings he'd received regarding plagiarism. Johnson noted that he "thought the book, being old, no-one would detect it; the students would be sure to be taken up with the new books. But the students went for me when I finished my sermon."[66] Rogers recognized Johnson's embarrassment and defended the student and his sermon, saying, "I see in him an 'Andrew Fuller,'" though Johnson later wrote, "I felt like I had been detected by the ever vigilant Professor Rogers, and I sat looking into the fire in the grate and studied 'fireology' for the remainder of the sermon class. My sin found me out. This was indeed a great help to me."[67] Johnson's anxiety over the preaching course was shared by several of his peers at the college. For instance, J. C. Carlile, a friend and eventual biographer of Spurgeon, described the Pastors' College's building containing "on the ground floor a large hall, a students' common room, the arena in which student gladiators fought, mixing metaphors and chopping logic," while the first floor contained "small classrooms and the famous room at the end of the corridor where trial sermons were preached and many tears shed."[68]

Johnson continued on in his studies, befriending several of the lecturers; perhaps most noteworthy was his relationship with Archibald Fergusson, the grammar lecturer at the college, who frequently entertained Johnson and his wife at his home.[69] Regarding his time at the college, Johnson noted that it was

> the turning point in an important passage of my life's history, for which I feel continually grateful. . . . *My prayer is that God will continue to prosper the*

---

[66]Johnson, *Twenty-Eight Years a Slave*, 94.

[67]Johnson, *Twenty-Eight Years a Slave*, 94.

[68]Quoted in Nicholls, *Lights to the World*, 82.

[69]Johnson reprinted several lengthy obituaries for Fergusson in his memoir. See Johnson, *Twenty-Eight Years a Slave*, 94-100.

College which has been privileged to educate and send out a thousand men to
preach the Gospel . . . and I pray that many of them will turn towards Africa,
to labour among a long-oppressed and neglected race.[70]

Spurgeon, who took particular interest in Johnson and his ministry, wrote
a letter of recommendation for him, which read in part "he has the advantage of being like the spouse in the Song [of Songs] 'black, but comely,'
and perhaps he will therefore be more at home among his coloured
friends—but be his complexion shal [sic] it may, he is a beloved brother in
the Lord and should be received as such."[71]

Johnson's experience at the college in many ways captured the essence
of Spurgeon's goals for the institution, which set out to train "preachers
rather than scholars."[72] This was not to say that academic study was regarded as secondary to training in oratorical delivery, rather the college
promoted scholarship that would inform sermons, particularly crucicentric and evangelistic sermons. A glimpse of Spurgeon's broader social
vision is on display here. Randall is correct in writing that Spurgeon "was
determined to draw into the orbit of theological training many who felt
shut out."[73] Once those students were in Spurgeon's orbit, he trained them
to preach sermons that emphasized the cross and the gospel. In an early
edition of *The Sword and the Trowel*, George Rogers suggested that their
education scheme provided a different class of men with the basic skills
needed for the pastorate. He wrote that "collegiate training had hitherto
been limited to a particular class of candidates, and to a particular kind
and amount of education; and the tendency has recently been to restrict
the preliminary qualifications within still narrower bounds, and to bring
our Dissenting colleges into nearer approximation with the ancient Universities of our land."[74] Overstating his case, Rogers continued, suggesting

---

[70]Johnson, *Twenty-Eight Years a Slave*, 93. Emphasis mine.
[71]Spurgeon's letter, dated May 26, 1880, was reproduced in Johnson, *Twenty-Eight Years a Slave*,
   96-97. Spurgeon's language of beloved brother, a reference to Philemon 1:16, evokes the case of
   another former enslaved man who was regarded with family language.
[72]Spurgeon, *Lectures to My Students*, 1:vii.
[73]Randall, *School of the Prophets*, 89. Also, see David W. Bebbington, "Spurgeon and the Common
   Man," *Baptist Review of Theology* 5, no. 1 (1995): 63-75.
[74]*The Sword and the Trowel* 2 (1866): 42.

that "the men who are the most effective preachers of our day, as a rule, are not men of high scholastic attainments; but look among them for the rationalistic perverters of the simplicity that is in Christ, and you will not be in vain."[75] At the Pastors' College, the content and clear delivery of the students' preaching was of primary importance, irrespective of their previous training or social background. Spurgeon wrote that the college's ultimate aim was

> to develop the faculty of ready speech, to help them understand the word of God, and to foster the spirit of consecration, courage, and confidence in God, are objects so important that we put all other matters into a secondary position. *If a student should learn a thousand things, and yet fail to preach the gospel acceptably, his College course will have missed its true design.* Should the pursuit of literary prizes and the ambition for classical honours so occupy his mind as to divert his attention from his life work, they are perilous rather than beneficial. *To be wise to win souls is the wisdom that ministers should possess.*[76]

The college's tight focus on producing graduates capable of delivering thoroughly evangelistic sermons in many ways mirrored the drive of its founder and president.

Though he aspired to make an education at the Pastors' College available to a broad variety of potential students, Spurgeon turned away students in whom he did not see the qualifications for pastoral ministry. He suggested that one of his aims in overseeing the admissions of the college was "to keep out of the sacred office those who are not called to it. We are continually declining candidates because we question their fitness. Some of these have education and money and are supported by earnest requests from parents and friends, but all this avails them nothing!"[77] The student's application form contained no less than twenty-five questions, beginning with the applicants' age and inquiring about their present "secular calling," with a request of the name and address of their current

---

[75] *The Sword and the Trowel* 2 (1866): 43.
[76] Spurgeon, *Lectures to My Students*, 1:vii. Emphasis mine.
[77] *The Sword and the Trowel* 23 (1887): 206.

employer.[78] The form asked questions regarding the applicants' conversion, asking how long they had "known the Grace of God in Truth" as well as whether they had "made a profession of faith" through immersion. Though the application contained several questions that invited long responses, it did not ask the students to produce a conversion narrative.[79] The form also asked the applicant to list his position regarding "Gospel invitations," a question likely to disqualify students who tended toward a high Calvinist practice.[80]

Students at the college were not subject to external public examinations or encouraged to sit degree examinations at a university empowered to grant degrees. James Archer Spurgeon, in 1887, commented that he did not wish to bind the students to "the arbitrary regulations of some secular authority, with its demands for studies adapted to meet the requirements of its examiners, rather than the duties of a pastor's life."[81] Though this position in some ways undermined the academic credibility of the college, students who completed their courses typically found employment.

Curricula at the Pastors' College. Both the college's president and lecturers believed that courses in grammar, science, and theology would help train effective evangelistic preachers. In an 1885 edition of *The Sword and the Trowel*, Spurgeon outlined the ideal balanced curriculum that he desired, namely,

1. A knowledge of the Scriptures, studying whole books and making the best use of commentaries, expositions and introductions.

2. The study of doctrine.

---

[78]"Pastors' College Application Questions," located in folder marked "Black folder with various cuttings 1892–1900," Heritage Room, Spurgeon's College. Further questions on the form include "Are you a teetotaler?" and "What experience have you had in preaching?" With regard to theological matters, the form requested further information as to the student's positions on baptism by immersion, communion, and future punishment.

[79]"Pastors' College Application Questions." For instance, the form asked questions such as "What is your motive for wishing to become a Preacher of the Gospel?" and "What reason have you to conclude that you have abilities suited to such an undertaking?"

[80]"Pastors' College Application Questions."

[81]J. A. Spurgeon, *Annual Paper Concerning the Lord's Work in Connection with the Pastors' College, Newington, London, 1886–87*, located in the Heritage Room at Spurgeon's College, quoted in Bebbington, "Spurgeon and British Evangelical Theological Education," 228.

3. The history of the church and the history of the nation.

4. The rudiments of Astronomy, Chemistry, Zoology, Geology, and Botany.

5. Mental and Moral Science, Metaphysics and Casuistry.

6. Mathematics.

7. Latin, Greek and Hebrew.

8. Composition and Style.

9. Poetry.

10. Practical Oratory.

11. The conduct of Church work.[82]

Spurgeon's desire for a comprehensive education was, however, held in tension with his opposition to theological liberalism and his general distrust of the theology departments within most British universities. Spurgeon discouraged scholarship without evangelistic zeal, questioning,

> How many of our ministers are labouring to be grand orators or intellectual thinkers? That is not the thing. Our young ministers have been dazzled by that, and have gone off to bray like wild asses under the notion that they would have been reputed to have come from Jerusalem or to have been reared in Germany. . . . There is nothing now I believe that genuine Christians despise more than the foolish affectation of intellectualism.[83]

Conversely, Spurgeon believed that he and his fellow lecturers at the college could build upon a student's existing desire to evangelize with further instruction. This coincides with Bebbington's broader observation that nineteenth-century Nonconformist congregations had rising expectations with regard to the academic training for their ministers.[84] From this standpoint, Spurgeon was willing to defend his educational endeavors when criticized. For instance, in 1868, he wrote that "the whimsies of certain good people with regard to seminaries for ministers are founded in a misapprehension: it is both a good and necessary work to educate

---

[82]*The Sword and the Trowel* 21 (1885): 205-10.
[83]*The Sword and the Trowel* 10 (1874): 112.
[84]Bebbington, "Spurgeon and British Evangelical Theological Education," 218.

those whom the Lord has called."[85] In a later address, he boldly suggested, "There is little need to enlist the sympathy of our readers for our object, for all are now agreed that preachers of the gospel are all the better for being men of education."[86]

Because the curriculum of the Pastors' College was intentionally flexible so as to adapt to student abilities, it is difficult to ascertain the college's precise course offerings. An 1882 report contained summaries of the course material from several lecturers. In his report, David Gracey noted,

> I have continued my course of Lectures on Theology, and kept up the study of Hodge's "Outlines," "Homiletics," and "Church History." The Seniors have been engaged in the exegetical and grammatical study of the Greek text of the Acts, the Epistle to the Ephesians, and the Epistle to the Hebrews; and have read in connection herewith Trench's "Synonyms of the Greek Testament." In Hebrew the Seniors have been reading the Psalms and in the Book of Genesis, the latter of which the Juniors are beginning. In the Senior Classics the subjects have been Lucian's "Dialogue" and the "Oedipus Rex" of Sophocles; the 6th book of Virgil's "Aeneid," and "Cicero De Senectute."[87]

The works referred to here reflect Gracey's background in classics, as well as the diversity of the courses' reading assignments in the curriculum. Archibald Alexander Hodge (1823–1886), the son of Princeton Theological Seminary principal Charles Hodge, was a noteworthy theologian in his own right.[88] His *Outlines of Theology* text referenced by Gracey was a standard work in Presbyterian systematic theology and included significant discussion on paedobaptism.[89] Richard Chenevix Trench (1807–1886), the Anglican archbishop of Dublin, was a poet and academic who contributed to the translation of the Revised Version of the Bible. His volume on the *Synonyms of the Greek Testament* was republished several times and reflected critical, though conservative, Christian engagement

---

[85] *The Sword and the Trowel* 4 (1868): 99.
[86] *The Sword and the Trowel* 18 (1882): 258.
[87] *The Sword and the Trowel* 18 (1882): 270.
[88] He was named after Archibald Alexander (1772–1851), the first principal of Princeton Seminary and a close associate of his father.
[89] Archibald Alexander Hodge, *Outlines of Theology* (New York: Robert Carter, 1863).

with the text.[90] In the volume, Trench surveyed common terms throughout the New Testament that were represented by a range of words in the original Greek and discussed whether they could be appropriately understood to be synonymous with one another. He set out to accomplish his task via comparative studies across the New Testament as well as broader Greek literature. His approach, in one sense, seems to mirror the sort of higher-critical approach that Spurgeon often criticized; however, Trench's high Christology and his language of the cross as the place of reconciliation between humanity and God—over and against the intent of those who displayed "a foregone determination to get rid of the reality of God's anger against the sinner"—likely led Spurgeon's instructor to regard it as an orthodox and helpful resource.[91]

A separate summary of the curriculum of the biblical studies department from the lecturer Archibald Fergusson indicates that his students were required to read "Blaikie's 'Bible Geography' and Angus's 'Bible Handbook.'"[92] William Garden Blaikie (1820–1899) taught theology at New College, Edinburgh, from 1868 and also served as the moderator of the Free Church of Scotland. His *Outlines of Bible Geography, Physical and Political* contained high-quality maps of the ancient Near East and detailed introductions to the political, cultural, and religious dimensions of each territory.[93] Joseph Angus (1816–1902), who studied at the University of Edinburgh, was among Spurgeon's predecessors as pastor of the New Park Street Chapel, serving there from 1837 to 1839. As we have seen, he became the president of Stepney Academy and oversaw its move to Regent's Park. His *Bible Handbook* contained not only commentary-like surveys of the respective genres of Scripture but also long chapters on biblical interpretation.[94] Fergusson praised Angus's work in particular because it introduced

---

[90]Richard Chenevix Trench, *Synonyms of the New Testament: Being the Substance of a Course of Lectures Addressed to the Theological Students, King's College, London*, 9th ed. (London: Macmillan, 1880).

[91]Trench, *Synonyms of the New Testament*, 292.

[92]*The Sword and the Trowel* 18 (1882): 270.

[93]William Garden Blaikie, *Outlines of Bible Geography, Physical and Political* (Edinburgh: T. Nelson and Sons, 1877).

[94]Joseph Angus and Samuel G. Green, *The Bible Hand-Book: An Introduction to the Study of Sacred Scripture* (Chicago: Fleming H. Revell, 1900).

students "through a style at once crisp, rigid, and graphic, to the great themes of their life-work, exposition and biblical criticism."[95] In his description of these volumes, Fergusson wrote, "Should our men carry into their ministry the same hunger for Bible knowledge, the same energy in turning it to account, and still keep unspoiled the same sensitiveness of soul in appreciating the fine touches of the Spirit in His delineation of truth, they must and they will excel in the great business of soul-winning."[96]

The college's use of these texts written by contemporary authors representing a range of theological traditions suggests that Spurgeon's academic staff were willing to consult and engage with sources from outside the Baptist or Puritan traditions.[97] While the academic staff at the college clearly preferred conservative theological textbooks, the students were reading and interacting with contemporary writings from academics who held positions at significant universities in Britain and the United States. This coincides with the pattern we have noted in previous investigations of Spurgeon's reviews in *The Sword and the Trowel* and *Commenting and Commentaries*, namely that differing Christian traditions and dense academic prose would not necessarily disqualify a book from endorsement, so long as the book maintained a high Christology, upheld a conservative position on biblical history, and could be utilized by readers to aid in the preparation of crucicentric and conversionistic sermons.

The legacy of the Pastors' College. Attendance at the Pastors' College held steady during Spurgeon's lifetime, even throughout the 1880s when positions for new Baptist ministers grew scarce, particularly in rural areas. Spurgeon adjusted for this in two primary ways: he extended the duration of study at the college from two to three years, and he increased his involvement in establishing new churches for his former students to lead. These churches were established as independent congregations. They had no formal ties under either the Metropolitan Tabernacle or Pastors' College;

---

[95] *The Sword and the Trowel* 18 (1882): 270.

[96] *The Sword and the Trowel* 18 (1882): 270-71.

[97] This is contrary to claims by Patricia Kruppa that Spurgeon was intellectually tethered to antiquated English theologians, "a lonely Victorian Elijah, stand fast against the modern priests of Baal." Patricia S. Kruppa, *Charles Haddon Spurgeon: A Preacher's Progress*, Routledge Library Editions: 19th Century Religion (London: Taylor and Francis, 2017), 451.

however, they shared the core ethos of both institutions: cross-centered, evangelistic preaching. On this topic, Spurgeon suggested,

> The oftener brethren can create their own spheres the more glad shall I be. It is not needful to repeat the details of former reports, but many churches have been founded through the College, and there are more to follow. I announced at the beginning of this enterprise that it was not alone for the education of ministers, *but for the general spread of the gospel*, and this has been adhered to, a part of the income being always expended in that direction.[98]

Largely through the intervention of the Spurgeon brothers, the college helped to establish dozens of congregations throughout England and also sent pastors to work overseas.[99]

Additionally, Spurgeon sought to facilitate camaraderie and lasting relationships among the students, connections that would continue beyond their time in the classroom. He accomplished this through a series of conferences, which were attended by both current students and alumni. At a conference in 1880, Spurgeon highlighted the college's goal of encouraging lifelong learning. He noted, "Many among you entered the College with no education whatsoever; but when you left it you had learned enough to have formed the resolution to study with all your might."[100] Spurgeon then used the students' principal as an illustration, admonishing that "no man should ever dream that his education is complete. I know that my friend, Mr. Rogers, though he has passed his eightieth year, is still a student, and perhaps has more of the true student spirit about him now than ever: will any of the younger sort sit down in self-content?"[101] At the conferences, distinguished former students such as Medhurst were often invited to address the assembled body. The conferences, irrespective of the speakers, often emphasized evangelistic themes, which will be explored in greater detail in the following section. For instance, Spurgeon admonished his listeners to "rally to the old standard. Fight to the death for the old gospel, for it is your life. Whatever forms of expression you may use as you advance in

---

[98] *The Sword and the Trowel* 17 (1881): 308. Emphasis mine.
[99] Spurgeon's son, Thomas, spent several years in pastoral ministry in Australia.
[100] *The Sword and the Trowel* 17 (1881): 261.
[101] *The Sword and the Trowel* 17 (1881): 261.

knowledge, ever keep the cross of Jesus Christ in the forefront, and let all the blessed truths which gather around it to be heartily maintained."[102]

The Pastors' College was in many ways a bold experiment, driven largely by Spurgeon's desire to recruit, train, and establish preachers whose primary focus was the cross and the gospel. The college additionally placed a high value on devotional life. All students attended a daily prayer meeting at the college, as well as evening prayer meetings at the Metropolitan Tabernacle. Bebbington is likely correct in his assessment that the training, which included modules in mathematics and science, was "remarkably diverse" but that most disciplines were not studied in much depth.[103] The college's core strength was biblical studies and preaching.

Though Spurgeon attracted a significant number of students, the college was not without its detractors. As early as 1866, a London magazine suggested that "more and more Spurgeon is separating himself from the general organisation of the religious world, and even of the Baptist denomination, and concentrating his work upon his immense Church, his College, and the Churches throughout the kingdom that have taken his pupils for pastors."[104] In his own magazine, Spurgeon responded to this charge, writing, "He who searches all hearts knows that our aim and object is not to gather a band around self, but to unite a company around the Saviour."[105] In a follow-up article, he concluded, "Whether we are officially in the Baptist body or out of it, *is small care to us so long as we can advance the gospel of our Lord Jesus.*"[106] The centrality on evangelism that Spurgeon emphasizes here is emblematic of not only his own pastoral ministry but also of his work as an educator.

LECTURES TO MY STUDENTS AND OTHER PUBLICATIONS

While there are a small number of published lectures from the academic staff at the Pastors' College, the most substantial collection of addresses

---

[102]*The Sword and the Trowel* 17 (1881): 317.
[103]Bebbington, "Spurgeon and British Evangelical Theological Education," 229.
[104]"Spurgeonism."
[105]*The Sword and the Trowel* 2 (1866): 138.
[106]*The Sword and the Trowel* 2 (1866): 284. Emphasis mine.

to students were those given by Spurgeon himself.[107] Spurgeon's *Lectures to My Students* was a volume of selections from his weekly addresses, some of which had previously appeared in *The Sword and the Trowel*.[108] Additionally, popular Spurgeon books such as *The Soul Winner* and *An All-Round Ministry* were based on student lectures.[109] These lectures covered a broad range of texts and topics; however, Spurgeon's emphasis on crucicentric and conversionistic preaching was frequently woven through a number of the addresses. In this final section, we will analyze the content of Spurgeon's lectures, noting the degree to which crucicentrism and conversionism informed both his own approach and subsequent instruction.

Spurgeon's lectures, often given on Fridays, were seen by many students as the highlight of their academic week. In his college lectures, Spurgeon took on a more informal and conversational tone than he typically used in public speaking, and as Bebbington helpfully observes, Spurgeon's "devastating capacity for wit, sarcasm, and mimicry, usually kept within bounds in the pulpit, was allowed full play in the college."[110] In the introduction to his first published series of addresses, Spurgeon gave some indication of the tenor of his student lectures: "I am as much at home with my young brethren as in the bosom of my family, and therefore speak without restraint. Generous minds will take this into account in reading these lectures, and I shall hope that all who favour me with their criticisms will be of that noble order."[111]

One of Spurgeon's lectures regarding biblical interpretation was titled "On Spiritualizing."[112] In the lecture, Spurgeon disagreed with homiletical writers who recommended that biblical interpretation should be restricted

---

[107]See Gracey, *Sin and the Unfolding of Salvation*; Arthur T. Pierson, *The Divine Art of Preaching* (New York: Baker and Taylor, 1892).

[108]In the preface to the first volume, Spurgeon suggested that he was hesitant to publish them, as they "were not originally prepared for the public eye, and are scarcely presentable for criticism." Spurgeon, *Lectures to My Students*, 1:v.

[109]C. H. Spurgeon, *The Soul Winner: How to Lead Sinners to the Saviour* (Chicago: Fleming H. Revell, 1895); Spurgeon, *All-Round Ministry*.

[110]Bebbington, "Spurgeon and British Evangelical Theological Education," 226.

[111]Spurgeon, *Lectures to My Students*, 1:v.

[112]Spurgeon, *Lectures to My Students*, 1:102-16.

to a "plain, literal sense."[113] As we have seen, Spurgeon's crucicentric and conversionistic emphases in his preaching and writing often led him to creative interpretations of texts that were not directly or indirectly related to the atonement. He encouraged his students to "employ spiritualizing within certain limits and boundaries," though he also cautioned them that "an allowable thing carried to excess is a vice, even as fire is a good servant in the grate, but a bad master when raging in a burning house."[114] He established the church father Origen of Alexandria (185–254) as a negative example, criticizing his "wild, daring interpretations," suggesting that his students avoid "the follies into which even his marvellous mind was drawn by allowing a wild fancy to usurp absolute authority over his judgment."[115] For Spurgeon, there was a "legitimate range for spiritualizing," suggesting that his students expound upon biblical types and metaphors in order to provide richer sermons for their listeners.[116] Throughout the balance of the lecture, Spurgeon drew illustrations of various texts and themes that could become an ideal basis for a spiritualized interpretation, referencing several preachers including Benjamin Keach, John Gill, and John Bunyan. Spurgeon, who had a particular affinity for Bunyan, suggested that his students should be cautious in imitating his approach, noting that Bunyan "is the chief, and head, and lord of all the allegorists, and is not to be followed by us into the deep places of typical and symbolical utterance. He was a swimmer, we are but mere waders, and must not go beyond our depth."[117] Amid Spurgeon's discussion of spiritualized interpretation, the trends toward crucicentrism and conversionism that we have noted throughout our study are apparent. His introduction noted that the freedom to spiritualize in biblical interpretation equipped "many great soul-winners . . . to give a fillip to their ministry, and to arrest their people's attention."[118] This address has been noted in several recent secondary works. Peter Morden has observed that Spurgeon believed "that typologising should only take

---

[113]Spurgeon, *Lectures to My Students*, 1:102.
[114]Spurgeon, *Lectures to My Students*, 1:103.
[115]Spurgeon, *Lectures to My Students*, 1:107.
[116]Spurgeon, *Lectures to My Students*, 1:108.
[117]Spurgeon, *Lectures to My Students*, 1:114.
[118]Spurgeon, *Lectures to My Students*, 1:103.

place within certain limits," though he also noted, "Spurgeon was not especially clear as to what the limits to such typologising were."[119] Christian
George discusses the lecture at length, suggesting that "Spurgeon's exegesis
displayed Alexandrian and medieval characteristics."[120] Morden is largely
correct in concluding that Spurgeon "overstepped the bounds he set for his
own students," ultimately concluding that in Spurgeon's preaching "the
gospel of Christ was to be shared with Christ's people, and those who did
not yet know Christ were encouraged to look to him."[121] Though Morden
and George place a high emphasis on this lecture, Spurgeon gave several
other addresses to his students that provide a broader context for his
biblical interpretation.

While the previous single lecture indicates that Spurgeon saw little issue
with spiritualizing biblical texts, several additional student lectures focus
not on spiritualizing and allegory but on language of the cross and
conversion. For instance, in a lecture titled "Sermons—Their Matter,"
Spurgeon placed a high emphasis on crucicentrism and conversionism. He
began by cautioning his students that "all the rhetoric in the world is but as
chaff to the wheat in contrast to the gospel of our salvation."[122] He additionally warned against amplifying points of "minor doctrine" such as "pre
or post millenarian schemes," noting that whether or not his students
might find them interesting they would be "of very little concern" to a
hypothetical "godly widow woman, with seven children to support by her
needle, who wants far more to hear of the loving-kindness of the God of
providence than of these mysteries profound."[123] Spurgeon's instruction to
his students closely reflects the themes we have noted in his own preaching,
particularly as he proclaimed, "Our great master theme is the good news
from heaven; the tidings of mercy through the atoning death of Jesus,

---

[119]Peter J. Morden, *"Communion with Christ and His People": The Spirituality of C. H. Spurgeon* (Oxford: Regent's Park College, 2010), 123.

[120]Christian T. George, "Jesus Christ, the 'Prince of Pilgrims': A Critical Analysis of the Ontologi-cal, Functional, and Exegetical Christologies in the Sermons, Writings, and Lectures of Charles Haddon Spurgeon (1834–1892)" (PhD thesis, University of St. Andrews, 2011), 110.

[121]Morden, *"Communion with Christ,"* 123, 136; George makes a similar point in George, "'Prince of Pilgrims,'" 111.

[122]Spurgeon, *Lectures to My Students,* 1:72.

[123]Spurgeon, *Lectures to My Students,* 1:78.

mercy to the chief of sinners upon their believing in Jesus."[124] A further
section, worth quoting at length, summarizes his perspective:

> We must throw all our strength of judgment, memory, imagination, and elo-
> quence into the delivery of the gospel; and not give to the preaching of the
> cross our random thoughts while wayside topics engross our deeper medita-
> tions. . . . Brethren, first and above all things, keep to plain evangelical doc-
> trines; whatever else you do or do not preach, be sure incessantly to bring
> forth the soul-saving truth of Christ and him crucified.[125]

Additionally, Spurgeon saw danger in preachers addressing matters of
higher criticism from the pulpit. He strongly critiqued "those who waste
time in insinuating doubts concerning the authenticity of texts, or the correctness of Biblical statements concerning natural phenomena."[126] In his
conclusion, Spurgeon spoke in very crucicentric and conversionistic language. He suggested that "the world needs still to be told of its Saviour and
of the way to reach him. . . . We are not called to proclaim philosophy and
metaphysics, but the simple gospel."[127] Furthering his claim, he continued,
"More and more am I jealous lest any views upon prophecy, church government, politics, or even systematic theology, should withdraw one of us
from glorying in the cross of Christ."[128]

Spurgeon's christocentrism and crucicentrism were also on display in an
1881 Pastors' College address titled "Preach Christ in a Christly Manner."[129]
In his introduction, he admonished his listeners that

> Thomas Aquinas and others wrote commentaries upon the works of Peter
> the Lombard, who was surnamed *Magister Sententiarum*, or the Master of
> the Sentences. I will for a while join these schoolmen, and discourse upon a
> sentence. I know not whence it came, but it is floating in my brain; here it is:
> "PREACH CHRIST IN A CHRISTLY MANNER." It comes to me in associ-
> ation with another, "*Preach the cross in a crucified style*," an equally weighty

---

[124]Spurgeon, *Lectures to My Students*, 1:78.
[125]Spurgeon, *Lectures to My Students*, 1:78.
[126]Spurgeon, *Lectures to My Students*, 1:79.
[127]Spurgeon, *Lectures to My Students*, 1:82.
[128]Spurgeon, *Lectures to My Students*, 1:83.
[129]*The Sword and the Trowel* 17 (1881): 105-11.

word, which we may handle at another time. Ministers of the gospel, let Christ be your *subject*, and let Christ be your *model*: find in him not only the truth you utter, but the way and life of your utterance.[130]

His address was topical. Rather than expounding a particular verse, Spurgeon referenced a string of biblical texts throughout the sermon. This was fitting, as he recommended that the students "preach all that you know about Christ—all that you have learned from the Scriptures, all that you have experienced at his hands, all that his Spirit has enabled you to perceive and enjoy. . . . Preach all that Christ set forth in his life; and all that he commanded, all that he did, all that he suffered, and all that he was."[131] He continued on, proclaiming that

> the central sun of your whole system must be his glorious sacrifice for sin. As
> the starry cross holds the chief place among the southern constellations, so let
> it be the main glory of your ministry. Set before the people not only Christ,
> but Christ crucified, and when you are engaged upon the work, not only
> preach him in a dull, didactic manner, but, by a lively, spiritual, earnest,
> hearty, mode of address, set him forth "before their eyes evidently crucified
> among them."[132]

Highlighting the degree to which he held this position, he noted that "nothing else will keep a congregation in a gracious condition. Nothing else will win souls."[133]

While Spurgeon advocated for lively discourse, he was equally concerned that his students would produce sermons that were instructive in the way they expounded upon the text:

> Seek not to produce a wondering but an instructed audience. Obscurity
> more befits the Delphic shrine than the oracles of God. *Be as plain as a pike-*
> *staff in your doctrine and clear as the sun in the heavens in your gospel.* Let
> there be nothing difficult about what you preach, except that which naturally
> and inevitably surrounds truths of surpassing sublimity and spirituality.[134]

---

[130] *The Sword and the Trowel* 17 (1881): 105.
[131] *The Sword and the Trowel* 17 (1881): 105-6.
[132] *The Sword and the Trowel* 17 (1881): 106. Emphasis mine.
[133] *The Sword and the Trowel* 17 (1881): 106.
[134] *The Sword and the Trowel* 17 (1881): 109. Emphasis mine.

Finally, Spurgeon suggested the ultimate test for sermons preached in a "Christly" manner was the degree to which they reflected the preacher looking to Christ as not only the interpretive lens of the text but also as a model of effective preaching. As he closed his address, he proclaimed, "I hold up to you Jesus Christ as the model preacher. I hold up no man beside, and I earnestly advise you never to become slavish copyists of any living preachers. . . . You may find faults in all other preachers, for the best of men are men at the best; but there are no flaws, eccentricities, or infirmities in him, for he is perfection."[135]

One of Spurgeon's best-known books, *The Soul Winner*, was drawn in part from a series of lectures at a conference at the Pastors' College.[136] It was published in 1895, three years after his death.[137] In the collected lectures, Spurgeon set out a particularly clear mandate that drew strong connections between weekly preaching and evangelistic ministry:

> The weapon with which the Lord conquers men is the truth as it is in Jesus. *The gospel will be found equal to every emergency: an arrow which can pierce the hardest heart, a balm which will heal the deadliest wound. Preach it, and preach nothing else.* Rely implicitly upon the old, old gospel. You need no other nets when you fish for men; those your Master has given you are strong enough for the great fishes, and have meshes fine enough to hold the little ones. Spread those nets and no others, and you need not fear the fulfillment of his word, "I will make you fishers of men."[138]

Though Spurgeon put significant emphasis on the doctrinal content of the sermon, he was equally concerned that his listeners might overcorrect and produce dull sermons. He compared doctrine and emotion in

---

[135]*The Sword and the Trowel* 17 (1881): 111.

[136]The preface notes that "the first six chapters contain the College Lectures; then follow four Addresses delivered to Sunday-school teachers, open-air preachers, and friends gathered at Monday evening prayer-meetings at the Tabernacle; while the rest of the volume consists of Sermons in which the work of winning souls is earnestly commended to the attention of every believer in the Lord Jesus Christ." Spurgeon, *Soul Winner*, 5.

[137]In the preface, it was noted that Spurgeon "had already prepared for the press the greater part of the material here published" and "it was his intention to deliver to the students of the Pastors' College a short course of Lectures upon what he termed 'that most royal employment.'" Spurgeon, *Soul Winner*, 5.

[138]Spurgeon, *Soul Winner*, 18. Emphasis mine.

sermon delivery to the preacher's legs, suggesting that a lack of one at the expense of the other would always generate an imbalance. Elaborating further, he said,

> To win a soul it is necessary, not only to instruct our hearer and make him know the truth, but *to impress him so that he may feel it*. A purely didactic ministry, which should always appeal to the understanding and should leave the emotions untouched, would certainly be a limping ministry. It is a horrible thing for a man to be so doctrinal that he can speak coolly of the doom of the wicked, so that he does not actually praise God for it, it costs him no anguish of heart to think of the ruin of millions of our race. This is horrible![139]

The Soul Winner contained over a dozen addresses, though perhaps its most pointed section was the entry titled "Soul-saving Our One Business," which offers an ideal final study. In it, Spurgeon began by voicing his concern that the contemporary church could be too concerned with educating their congregations. He said, "The object of Christianity is not to educate men for their secular callings, or even to train them in the politer arts, or the more elegant professions, or to enable them to enjoy the beauties of nature or the charms of poetry."[140] His intensity increased as he proclaimed that

> Jesus Christ came not into the world for any of these things, but He came to seek and save that which was lost; and on the same errand he has sent His Church, and she is a traitor to the Master who sent her if she is beguiled by the beauties of taste and art to forget that to preach Christ and Him crucified is the only object for which she exists among the sons of men. The business of the church is salvation.[141]

This approach was in keeping with Spurgeon's stated pastoral aim, particularly as he claimed that he "never sought anything but the conversion of souls, and I call heaven and earth to witness, and your consciences, too, that I have never laboured for anything except this, the bringing of you to Christ. . . . I have not sought to gratify depraved appetites either by novelty of doctrine

---

[139]Spurgeon, *Soul Winner*, 18.
[140]Spurgeon, *Soul Winner*, 251.
[141]Spurgeon, *Soul Winner*, 251-52.

or ceremonial, but I have kept up the simplicity of the gospel."[142] Spurgeon's tone throughout the address captures much of what we've seen throughout this chapter, namely his view that crucicentric and conversionistic preaching was the primary means of seeing the church grow and flourish, and its absence would ultimately leave church buildings empty. This is evident as he continued, saying, "I have noticed that, as a general rule, wherever the new 'thinking' drives out the old gospel, there are more spiders than people, but where there is the simple preaching of Jesus Christ, the place is crowded to the doors. Nothing else will crowd a meeting-house, after all, for any length of time, but the preaching of Christ crucified."[143] While Spurgeon's observations are likely not reflective of particularly accurate knowledge of all the sermons and congregations of churches throughout Britain, the quote reveals the extent to which he prioritized the necessity of crucicentric and conversionistic preaching, and his comments are consistent both with his own practice and his desired goal for the graduates of his college.

CONCLUSIONS

Spurgeon's foray into education was, as we have seen, both multifaceted and yet ultimately singular in purpose. That purpose was to support and train individuals for a variety of roles, from Sunday School work through ordained ministry, all of which were focused on engagement with the Bible that focused on the cross of Christ and the message of salvation. Spurgeon's sermons reached a spread of audiences that were unprecedented for any preacher in his day, yet he devoted significant time and energy to the Pastors' College, even in years when failing health made travel and even movement difficult. He recognized the need for educated preachers, and in the course of meeting that need, he also provided accessible instruction for students for whom the traditional venues of education were out of reach.

Spurgeon's approach was not without drawbacks. Students at the Pastors' College were offered a wide breadth of topics to study; however, standards lagged in many of the peripheral subjects, and the lack of external

---

[142]Spurgeon, *Soul Winner*, 256.
[143]Spurgeon, *Soul Winner*, 265.

examination made the overall assessment of the students' education difficult to discern. These shortcomings aside, Spurgeon and his team of lecturers trained nearly one thousand students in the latter half of the nineteenth century, a significant number of whom went on to pastor churches throughout Britain. Arguably the key strength of the college was Spurgeon himself. Though he detested the term *Spurgeonite*, the classification apparently did not harm job prospects for his students, particularly in churches sympathetic to his theology. By the end of Spurgeon's life, over fifty percent of Baptist ministers working in England and Wales had trained at the Pastors' College.[144] The influence of the college also extended into denominational leadership, as Bebbington has noted, "Of the twenty-nine ministers who became president of the Baptist Union between 1897 and 1933, ten had studied there."[145]

Spurgeon's convictions with regard to the necessity of crucicentric, evangelistic sermons led him and his fellow educators to construct their biblical studies curriculum as a wheel, the hub of which was the cross and gospel. For Spurgeon, there was no more important focus, and this enabled him to boldly proclaim from his pulpit that "the motto of all true servants of God must be, 'We preach Christ, and him crucified.' A sermon without Christ in it is like a loaf of bread without any flour in it. No Christ in your sermon, sir? Then go home, and never preach again until you have something worth preaching."[146] Through his work as an educator, Spurgeon ensured that congregants in Britain would continue to hear sermons centered around the cross of Christ and the message of conversion long after his death. This is perhaps best exemplified in the college motto, which remains to the present day: "We labour to hold forth the cross of Christ with a bold hand among the sons of men, because that cross holds us fast by its attractive power. Our desire is, that every man may hold the truth, and be held by it; especially the truth of Christ crucified."[147]

---

[144]Bebbington, "Spurgeon and British Evangelical Theological Education," 221.

[145]Bebbington, "Spurgeon and British Evangelical Theological Education," 231.

[146]C. H. Spurgeon, "Exposition of Acts 13:13-49," sermon no. 2899, given July 9, 1876, from Acts 13:13-49, *The Metropolitan Tabernacle Pulpit*, vol. 50 (London: Passmore & Alabaster, 1904), 431.

[147]C. H. Spurgeon, *C. H. Spurgeon's Autobiography, Compiled from His Diary, Letters, and Records, by His Wife and His Private Secretary*, vol. 2, *1854–1860* (Chicago: Fleming H. Revell, 1899), 150.

CONCLUSION

ON MARCH 25, 1861, Spurgeon gave his first sermon at the newly constructed Metropolitan Tabernacle.[1] His text was Acts 5:42, which read, "And daily in the temple, and in every house, they ceased not to teach and preach Jesus Christ." For the occasion, Spurgeon emphasized the nature of the sermons that would be preached from the new pulpit:

> We ought to preach the law, we ought to thunder out the threatenings of God, but they must never be the main topic. Christ, Christ, Christ, if we would have men converted. Do you want to convince yonder careless one? Tell him the story of the cross. . . . Whatever I have not preached, *I have preached Christ*, and into whatever mistakes I have fallen, I have sought to point to his cross, and say, "Behold the way to God."[2]

Spurgeon went on to preach over three thousand sermons to his congregation, most of which directly followed his aim to "point to the cross." When his health permitted, he preached most of the sermons at the Tabernacle, though his sermon on June 7, 1891, would be his final address to his congregation.[3] A combination of chronic rheumatism, gout, and Bright's Disease led Spurgeon to convalesce in Mentone, France, a destination that he frequented during periods of ill health. While in Mentone, on December 31, 1891, Spurgeon gave a brief address to a small group of visiting friends, an address that was later published as one of his final sermons. In it, he offered a summary of his ministry, noting,

[1]C. H. Spurgeon, "The First Sermon in the Tabernacle," sermon no. 369, given March 25, 1861, from Acts 5:42, *The Metropolitan Tabernacle Pulpit*, vol. 7 (London: Passmore & Alabaster, 1861), 169-76.

[2]Spurgeon, "First Sermon in the Tabernacle," 176.

[3]C. H. Spurgeon, "The Statute of David for the Sharing of the Spoil," sermon no. 2208, given June 7, 1891, from 1 Samuel 30:21-25, *The Metropolitan Tabernacle Pulpit*, vol. 37 (London: Passmore & Alabaster, 1891), 313-24.

"This is a faithful saying, and worthy of all acceptation, that Christ Jesus came into the world to save sinners." On that blessed fact I rest my soul. Though I have preached Christ crucified for more than forty years, and have led many to my Master's feet, I have at this moment no ray of hope but that which comes from what my Lord Jesus has done for guilty men.[4]

A month later, he fell into a coma at the Hotel Beau-Rivage and died late in the evening on January 31, 1892, at the age of fifty-seven.

Although he lacked a university education and was largely self-taught, Spurgeon attracted thousands of sermon listeners, and his sermons, in their published form, reached a truly global audience. Spurgeon engaged in a number of publishing endeavors from his earliest days in London, and through the efforts of translators his printed sermons reached a global readership in dozens of languages. Additionally, his magazine, biblical commentaries, and other books sold in significant volume throughout his life.

What may account for his unparalleled success? Spurgeon's ministry was distinct for a number of reasons. First, he was able to communicate effectively to men and women in the working and lower middle classes. His lack of formal education, though a weakness in some areas, also enabled him to communicate to a wide range of people in a compelling and engaging style. Second, Spurgeon read widely and engaged works of higher criticism, though he admittedly dismissed much of it as scholarly pretension. He emphasized that the Bible was not a book that could only be fully understood by academics who were able to read it in the original languages. Rather, for Spurgeon, the Bible held enduring power because God inspired its words and continued to speak through it as preachers proclaimed sermons each week. Thus he actively encouraged his congregation and readers to engage with the biblical text in their homes and created several guides to help them in that pursuit. This brings us to the central element of Spurgeon's success.

---

[4]Anonymous, *From the Pulpit to the Palm-Branch: A Memorial of C. H. Spurgeon. Sequel to the Sketch of His Life, Entitled "From the Usher's Desk to the Tabernacle Pulpit." Including the Official Report of the Services in Connection with His Funeral* (New York: A. C. Armstrong and Son, 1892), 23. Spurgeon is referencing 1 Timothy 1:15. For more information on the funeral proceedings, see Peter Shepherd, "Spurgeon's Funeral," *Baptist Quarterly* 41, no. 2 (April 2005): 72-79.

Throughout this book, it has been argued that the evangelical tenets of crucicentrism and conversionism were the guiding principles of Spurgeon's biblical interpretation. This is not to say that David Bebbington's tenets of biblicism and activism did not also appear in his biblical engagement; rather, Spurgeon's discussion of these themes often grew out of his theological priorities. He emphasized the cross, seeking conversions through his preaching, writing, and instruction. He also personally sought to foster the same priorities in the lives of every Christian, whether or not they were involved in vocational ministry. Moreover, this biblical engagement contributed greatly to Spurgeon's success in ministry. Through his magazine, commentaries, lectures, and especially his sermons, Spurgeon addressed complex theological themes and presented them in an engaging and accessible format. While liberal Christians in his day viewed the Bible as a history of the Hebrew people and the teachings of early Christianity, Spurgeon maintained a different view. His ministry was characterized by the conviction that the primary task of biblical interpretation was not to instruct men and women in biblical history or morality but to "restore them to God."[5] For him, this was a theological imperative and an interpretive guide. Thus each verse of Scripture could be used in some way to emphasize Christ's sacrifice for the sins of the world and the necessity of personal salvation. For his largely working-class and lower middle-class congregation, it became a message of great personal hope.

As Spurgeon's contemporaries gathered to honor him in his death, they clearly discerned the same emphases that contributed to his effectiveness. Spurgeon's crucicentric and conversionistic interpretation of the Bible was highlighted in the eulogies offered by a number of his friends and colleagues at the multiple memorial services held in his honor. Sir Arthur Blackwood (1832–1893), a veteran of the Crimean War and the chairman of the Mildmay Conference, attempted to identify the source of Spurgeon's success as a preacher, asking,

> What was it that gave Charles Haddon Spurgeon his power? What may we
> learn from the testimony of his life? Is it not this above all things, that the

---

[5] *The Sword and the Trowel* 14 (1878): 463.

glorious gospel of the blessed God which so permeated his whole being . . .
it was the firm grasp that he had of the gospel of Christ, the unflinching earnestness and faithfulness with which he preached it, the valour with which
he stood in the gap when men fled on all sides, his adherence to the doctrines of grace, *and his determination to know nothing among men save Jesus
Christ and him crucified.*[6]

Thomas Bowman Stephenson (1839–1912), a noted Wesleyan Methodist
minister who shared Spurgeon's concern for the better care of London's
orphaned children, offered a similar reflection. With regard to Spurgeon's
handling of the Bible, Stephenson remarked that "his quick eye recognized
the essential truth wherever it was found, and he called every man brother
who was true to the Master, Christ, and who desired that *all his work should
find its centre at the cross of Calvary."*[7] Colonel J. T. Griffin, the president
of the Baptist Union, was invited to give a eulogy despite the significant
friction that had built up between Spurgeon and the union during the
Downgrade Controversy. Commenting specifically on Spurgeon's biblical
interpretation, Griffin said,

> *It was his delight to preach Christ Jesus and him crucified. He had but one text,
> but what a marvellous text it was,* from which over 3,000 separate sermons
> could be preached, which have been scattered far and wide throughout the
> length and breadth of the world. . . . *Christ and his cross was his song here on
> earth. . . .* In that Book he found first the promise of a Saviour to redeem;
> then the prophecy regarding that Christ; then the realization of the proph-
> ecies by Christ on earth; his grand mission, his glorious work; his sufferings
> and his death. This was where Mr. Spurgeon found his power.[8]

Some who approached Spurgeon later adjudged him similarly. Owen
Chadwick, the eminent historian of Victorian Christianity, noted that
Spurgeon "knew his Bible, was widely read outside his Bible, never
preached without preaching a cross, and perfectly understood how to array
his gospel."[9] The twentieth-century German theologian Helmut Thielicke,

---

[6]Anonymous, *From the Pulpit to the Palm-Branch,* 158-59. Emphasis mine.
[7]Anonymous, *From the Pulpit to the Palm-Branch,* 140. Emphasis mine.
[8]Anonymous, *From the Pulpit to the Palm-Branch,* 170. Emphasis mine.
[9]Owen Chadwick, *The Victorian Church: Part One (1829-1859)* (London: A&C Black, 1971), 421.

who translated a portion of Spurgeon's *Lectures to My Students* into German, stressed the practical application of Spurgeon's methods to his mid-twentieth century Lutheran seminary students, noting that

> Spurgeon's aim . . . is the saving of souls. . . . And there it is, so simple and so naïve—and suddenly all the worldliness, all the modernity of speech is wiped away. . . . We stand in need of the simple way in which Spurgeon dares to say what really and ultimately counts is to save sinners.[10]

One important catalyst in the formation of Spurgeon's hermeneutic discussed earlier was his own conversion experience. Alongside his hermeneutic, his own conversion was linked to the content of his preaching. The connection between Spurgeon's conversion and the content of his preaching was drawn by both his closest friends and also his critics. A character sketch of Spurgeon by the celebrated Congregationalist journalist, W. T. Stead, in his *Review of Reviews,* referenced the Colchester sermon and the unnamed man who preached it, noting that "the echo of that man's text has been audible in every discourse that Mr. Spurgeon has ever preached. He has always cried, 'Look, look, look to Christ.' That trust, which has been the central essence of the whole Christian faith in all its forms, constituted . . . one of the greatest sources of his power."[11] There was also a reference to the sermon that converted Spurgeon in his funeral procession, which attracted tens of thousands of mourners as it wound its way over five miles from the Metropolitan Tabernacle to the West Norwood Cemetery. Resting atop the coffin, in place of a sword, was Spurgeon's pulpit Bible, which was opened to Isaiah 45, with the passage "Look unto me, and be ye saved, all the ends of the earth" marked, providing one last reference to the verse and the sermon that led to his conversion over forty years earlier.[12]

This is not to say that there were not other influences present in Spurgeon's ministry. Throughout this study, we have noted that Spurgeon

---

[10]Helmut Thielicke, *Encounter with Spurgeon*, trans. John W. Doberstein (Philadelphia: Fortress, 1963), 41, 44.

[11]W. T. Stead, "Character Sketch: March. Charles Haddon Spurgeon," *The Review of Reviews* 5, no. 27 (March 1892): 247.

[12]Anonymous, *From the Pulpit to the Palm-Branch*, 205.

drew from past expressions of Christianity as he addressed contemporary London. It was in the context of village Nonconformity that Spurgeon first encountered both the Bible and the Puritans, and he would continue to hold the two hand in hand throughout the balance of his ministry. His conversion, however, did not take place through the Congregational ministries of his father or grandfather but rather through a sermon delivered in a Primitive Methodist chapel. The sermon, which was drawn from an Old Testament text, was preached with a conversionistic and crucicentric emphasis that was not immediately present in the biblical text. Spurgeon's own biblical interpretation eventually took on both of these elements.

Like his sermons, Spurgeon's written works provide a different vantage point through which his interpretive prioritization of crucicentrism and conversionism becomes all the more apparent. This is evident particularly in his evaluation of contemporary books, in which he displayed both a wide range of reading and a narrowly focused concern with regard to the theological implications of the respective volumes. Furthermore, the many articles, addresses, and books authored by Spurgeon frequently focused on the cross and conversion.

Even the controversies of Spurgeon's ministry highlight the centrality of his crucicentric and evangelistic commitments. Significantly, several of the controversies in which he was embroiled focused upon his theology of the atonement. In his youth, high Calvinists bristled against the free offer of the gospel that characterized his sermons, and in his later years the Downgrade Controversy put him at odds with some of his Baptist colleagues over the doctrine of the atonement, among other issues. These confrontations, which bookended Spurgeon's ministry in London, and both were interlocked with his crucicentric and evangelistic commitments.

Amid Spurgeon's strengths there were also weaknesses. His almost singular focus on preaching the cross and conversion from a wide variety of biblical texts meant that he often provided rather strained interpretations. While he engaged with current biblical scholarship, his reviews indicate that he did not always give books a fair or objective reading, particularly if he was already disinclined to agree with their subject. Furthermore, his straightforward and bold preaching manner, which won him favor in the working and lower middle classes, did not always have the same effect among more educated demographics.

Finally, Spurgeon's work as an educator provides an additional dimension by which to view his biblical interpretation. The nearly one thousand students who attended the Pastors' College during Spurgeon's lifetime were taught from a curriculum that emphasized both the preaching of the cross and appeals for the conversion of their listeners. Spurgeon endeavored to provide affordable and accessible education for individuals he deemed gifted and competent for ministry yet who lacked the opportunity to pursue training elsewhere. Throughout his tenure as president of the Pastors' College, Spurgeon and his faculty members sought to train students to lead their own pastorates in a manner that was "tied and tethered to the cross . . . keeps to Calvary, and is content to speak only of Jesus crucified."[13] In the Pastors' College, which Spurgeon called his "first-born, and best beloved," he created a culture that sought to train pastors whose sermons would reflect the principles and priorities of its founder.[14] The Pastors' College, now called Spurgeon's College, continues to perpetuate his legacy into the twenty-first century.

This book has sought to contribute to the history of Victorian Christianity by offering the first sustained analysis of the biblical interpretation of one of its most well-known preachers. It is, in one sense, located within the broader category of historical investigations of C. H. Spurgeon. Though there have been a number of studies on Spurgeon's life and work by scholars such as Patricia Kruppa, Peter Morden, and Christian George, there has not yet been a comprehensive analysis of Spurgeon's biblical interpretation. As such, I've sought to identify and clarify Spurgeon's approach to hermeneutics from different vantage points, including his sermons, written work, and instruction.

---

[13]C. H. Spurgeon, "The Best Bread," sermon no. 1940, given October 28, 1886, from John 6:48, *The Metropolitan Tabernacle Pulpit*, vol. 33 (London: Passmore & Alabaster, 1887), 25.

[14]C. H. Spurgeon, *C. H. Spurgeon's Autobiography, Compiled from His Diary, Letters, and Records, by His Wife and Private Secretary*, vol. 3, *1856–1878* (Cincinnati: Curts & Jennings, 1899), 137.

This book has also addressed approaches to the history of biblical interpretation and the history of preaching. It has provided a study of a preacher's hermeneutical method, attempting to bridge a gap between two existing fields. On the one hand, some recent scholars, typically those connected to the history of theology and philosophy, have produced a number of useful surveys of the history of hermeneutical methodology.[15] A weakness of these projects has been their heavy focus on the hermeneutics of influential philosophers and theologians. As such, they do not frequently engage with the interpretive methods employed within the sermons of influential preachers who were not professional philosophers or theologians. On the other hand, there are also a number of scholarly investigations of the history of preaching by historians and literary scholars; however, many of these focus on sermon content, delivery, and reception rather than identifying methods of biblical interpretation.[16]

Thus this present book has attempted to carve out a space between these two types of study to attempt a third category, namely a study of the hermeneutics of popular preachers, who would have in many cases held far more popular influence in their respective times than academic writers. Though it is appropriate and indeed necessary to consult theologians and philosophers when painting a portrait of the history of biblical interpretation, that portrait receives further clarity and color through detailed analysis of the biblical interpretation of preachers who were not also academics.

For Spurgeon, the Bible was a book that demanded a crucicentric interpretation, and his sermons, written work, and instruction convey the extent to which the cross and the free offer of the gospel were central to his ministry. While Spurgeon was certainly not the only preacher in Victorian

---

[15]Stephen E. Fowl, ed., *The Theological Interpretation of Scripture: Classic and Contemporary Readings*, Blackwell Readings in Modern Theology (Cambridge, MA: Blackwell, 1997); Jens Zimmermann, *Recovering Theological Hermeneutics: An Incarnational-Trinitarian Theory of Interpretation* (Grand Rapids, MI: Baker Academic, 2004).

[16]See, for instance, Keith A. Francis and William Gibson, *The Oxford Handbook of the British Sermon, 1689–1901* (Oxford: Oxford University Press, 2012); Robert H. Ellison, *The Victorian Pulpit: Spoken and Written Sermons in Nineteenth-Century Britain* (Selinsgrove, PA: Susquehanna University Press, 1998); Paul T. Phillips, ed., *The View from the Pulpit: Victorian Ministers and Society* (Toronto: Macmillan, 1978).

Britain to utilize this hermeneutical approach, he nonetheless harnessed it to an effect that was unrivaled in his day. Spurgeon's congregation, the largest in Britain, would have been well acquainted with their pastor's near singular emphasis on conversion, and indeed on most Sundays, they would indeed hear sermons that were tied and tethered to the cross.

BIBLIOGRAPHY

PRIMARY SOURCES

Anonymous. "An Afternoon with Mrs. Bartlett's Class." *New York Evangelist*, December 8, 1870.

———."Commenting and Commentaries." *The Literary World; a Monthly Review of Current Literature*, August 1, 1876.

———."Character Sketch: March. Charles Haddon Spurgeon." *The Review of Reviews.* London, March 1892, 5.27 edition.

———. *Ecce Homo: A Survey of the Life and Work of Jesus Christ.* London: Macmillan, 1866.

———. *"Essays and Reviews" Anticipated: Extracts from a Work Published in the Year 1825 and Attributed to the Lord Bishop of St. David's.* London, 1861.

———. *From the Pulpit to the Palm-Branch: A Memorial of C. H. Spurgeon. Sequel to the Sketch of His Life, Entitled "From the Usher's Desk to the Tabernacle Pulpit." Including the Official Report of the Services in Connection with His Funeral.* New York: A. C. Armstrong and Son, 1892.

———."The Rev. Charles H. Spurgeon." *Illustrated Times.* October 11, 1856.

———."Spurgeonism." *Baltimore Daily Commercial.* Baltimore, March 8, 1866.

———."Spurgeonism in Belfast." *Morning Chronicle.* London, August 20, 1858.

Aquinas, Thomas. *Catena Aurea: Commentary on the Four Gospels, Collected out of the Works of the Fathers.* Edited by John Henry Newman. 6 vols. London: James Parker, 1870.

Astruc, Jean. *Conjectures sur les mémoires originaux dont il paroit que Moyse s'est servi pour composer le Livre de la Genese: Avec des Remarques, qui appuient ou qui éclaircissent ces Conjectures.* Bruxelles: Chez Fricx, 1753.

Baur, Ferdinand Christian. *Paul, the Apostle of Jesus Christ, His Life and Work, His Epistles and His Doctrine: A Contribution to a Critical History of Primitive Christianity.* Translated by Eduard Zeller. 2 vols. London: Williams and Norgate, 1876.

Bengel, Johann Albrecht. *Bengel's Introduction to His Exposition of the Apocalypse, With His Preface to That Work and the Greatest Part of the Conclusion of It; And Also His Marginal Notes on the Text, Which Are Summary of the Whole Exposition.* Translated by John Robertson. London: J. Ryall and R. Withy, 1757.

Billroth, Johann Gustav Fredrick. *A Commentary on the Epistles of Paul to the Corinthians.* Translated by W. Lindsay Alexander. 2 vols. Edinburgh: Thomas Clark, 1837.

Blackley, W. L., and James Hawes, eds. *The Critical English Testament*. 3rd ed. 3 vols. London: Daldy, Isbister & Co., 1876.

Blaikie, William Garden. *Outlines of Bible Geography, Physical and Political*. Edinburgh: T. Nelson and Sons, 1877.

Bonar, Andrew A. *Memoir and Remains of the Rev. Robert Murray M'Cheyne*. Edinburgh: William Oliphant, 1878.

Bonar, Horatius. *Light and Truth: Or, Bible Thoughts and Themes. The Revelation*. New York: Robert Carter and Brothers, 1872.

Bunyan, John. *Grace Abounding to the Chief of Sinners*. Edited by Roger Sharrock. Oxford: Oxford University Press, 1962.

Candlish, Robert. *Contributions Towards the Exposition of the Book of Genesis*. Vol. 1. Edinburgh: Johnstone and Hunter, 1853.

Chalmers, Thomas. *Lectures on Romans*. 4 vols. Edinburgh: Edmonston, 1854.

Dargan, Edwin Charles. *The Changeless Christ and Other Sermons*. New York: Fleming H. Revell, 1918.

Davies, C. Maurice. *Unorthodox London, or, Phases of Religious Life in the Metropolis*. London: Tinsley Bros., 1876.

Delitzsch, Franz. *Biblical Commentary on the Book of Job*. Translated by Francis Bolton. Vol. 1. 2 vols. Edinburgh: T&T Clark, 1869.

Dods, Marcus. *Christ and Man: Sermons*. London: Hodder & Stoughton, 1909.

Driver, Samuel Rolles. *An Introduction to the Literature of the Old Testament*. Edinburgh: T&T Clark, 1891.

Eichhorn, Johann Gottfried. *Einleitung in Das Neue Testament*. 5 vols. Leipzig: Weidmann, 1820.

Ellicott, Charles John, ed. *A New Testament Commentary for English Readers*. London: Cassell, Petter, & Galpin, 1878.

Fairbairn, Patrick. *The Pastoral Epistles: The Greek Text and Translation, with Introduction, Expository Notes, and Dissertations*. Edinburgh: T&T Clark, 1874.

Fuller, Andrew. *The Complete Works of the Rev. Andrew Fuller*. Edited by Joseph Belcher. Vol. 3. 3 vols. Philadelphia: American Baptist Publication Society, n.d.

Gaussen, Louis. *Theopneustia: The Plenary Inspiration of the Holy Scriptures. With a Prefatory Note by C. H. Spurgeon*. Edited by B. W. Carr. Translated by David Dundas Scott. London: Passmore & Alabaster, 1888.

Gill, John. *An Exposition of the Book of Solomon's Song, Commonly Called Canticles*. Vol. 2. Edinburgh: Thomas Turnbull, Canongate, 1805.

Goulburn, Edward Meyrick. *Replies to "Essays and Reviews."* Oxford: J. Henry and J. Parker, 1862.

Gracey, David. *Sin and the Unfolding of Salvation, Being the Three Years' Course of Theological Lectures Delivered at the Pastors' College, London*. London: Passmore and Alabaster, 1894.

Henry, Matthew. *A Commentary on the Whole Bible, Wherein Each Chapter Is Summed up in Its Contents; the Sacred Text Inserted at Large in Distinct Paragraphs; Each Paragraph Reduced to Its Proper Heads, the Sense Given, and Largely Illustrated.* 3 vols. London: London Printing and Publishing Company, 1710.

Higgs, William Miller. *The Spurgeon Family: Being an Account of the Descent and Family of Charles Haddon Spurgeon, with Notes on the Family in General, Particularly the Essex Branch, from 1465 (5 Edward IV) to 1905 (4 Edward VII).* London: Elliot Stock, 1906.

Hodge, Archibald Alexander. *Outlines of Theology.* New York: Robert Carter, 1863.

Hodge, Charles. *Systematic Theology.* Vol. 1. 3 vols. New York: Charles Scribner, 1872.

Johnson, Thomas L. *Twenty-Eight Years a Slave, or the Story of My Life in Three Continents.* Seventh Edition. Bournemouth: W. Mate & Sons, 1909.

Jowett, Benjamin. *Epistles to the Thessalonians, Galatians, and Romans. With Critical Notes and Dissertations.* 2nd ed. 2 vols. London: John Murray, 1859.

———. "On the Interpretation of Scripture." In *Essays and Reviews*, edited by John William Parker, 330–433. London: John W. Parker and Son, 1860.

Lightfoot, J. B. *St. Paul's Epistle to the Galatians: A Revised Text with Introduction, Notes, and Dissertations.* 2nd ed. Andover, MA: Warren F. Draper, 1870.

MacDonald, George. *The Hope of the Gospel.* New York: D. Appleton, 1892.

Maclaren, Alexander. *The Books of Deuteronomy, Joshua, Judges, Ruth, and First Book of Samuel.* London: Hodder & Stoughton, 1906.

———. *The Books of Exodus, Leviticus and Numbers.* London: Hodder & Stoughton, 1907.

———. *The Epistle to the Hebrews (Chapters VII to XIII) and the General Epistle of James.* New York: A. C. Armstrong and Son, 1910.

———. *The Gospel of St. Mark.* London: Hodder & Stoughton, 1893.

Maurice, Frederick Denison. *The Workman and the Franchise: Chapters from English History on the Representation and Education of the People.* London: A. Strahan, 1866.

Meyer, Frederick Brotherton. *Samuel the Prophet.* London: Morgan and Scott, n.d.

Michaelis, Johann David. *Einleitung in Die Göttlichen Schriften Des Neuen Bundes.* Göttingen: Vandenhoeck & Ruprecht, 1788.

Neander, August. *History of the Planting and Training of the Christian Church by the Apostles.* Translated by J. E. Ryland. 2 vols. London: Bell & Sons, 1851.

Newman, John Henry. *The Idea of a University.* London: Basil Montagu Pickering, 1873.

———. *Parochial and Plain Sermons.* Vol. 2. 8 vols. London: Rivingtons, 1868.

———. *Sermons 1824-1843.* Vol. 2, *Sermons on Biblical History, Sin and Justification, the Christian Way of Life, and Biblical Theology.* Edited by Vincent Ferrer Blehl, SJ. Oxford: Clarendon Press, 1993.

Owen, John. *The Reason of Faith or, An Answer unto That Enquiry, Wherefore We Believe the Scripture to Be the Word of God?* Glasgow: W. Falconer, 1801.

Pierson, Arthur T. *The Divine Art of Preaching.* New York: The Baker and Taylor Co., 1892.

Pusey, Edward Bouverie. *Parochial and Cathedral Sermons.* Oxford and London: Parker, 1882.

Randolf, John. *Remarks on "Michaelis's Introduction to the New Testament, Vols. III, IV, Translated by the Rev. Herbert Marsh, and Augmented with Notes," by Way of Caution to Students in Divinity, Second Edition, with Preface and Notes, in Reply to Mr. Marsh.* London: T. Bensley, 1802.

Ryle, J. C. *Expository Thoughts on the Gospels for Family and Private Use: St. Mark.* London: Wertheim, Macintosh, & Hunt, 1859.

———. *Expository Thoughts on the Gospels for Family and Private Use: St. Matthew.* New York: Robert Carter and Brothers, 1857.

Schleiermacher, Friedrich Daniel Ernst. *Das Leben Jesu.* Vorlesungen an Der Universität Berlin Im Jahr 1832. Edited by K. A. Rutenik. Berlin: G. Reimer, 1864.

Smith, Ebenezer. *Two Centuries of Grace: Being a Brief History of the Baptist Church, Waterbeach. An Address at the Centenary Meeting.* Cambridge: University Press, 1903.

Spurgeon, C. H. *An All-Round Ministry: Addresses to Ministers and Students.* Pasadena, TX: Pilgrim Press, 1983.

———. *Antichrist and Her Brood, or, Popery Unmasked.* Spurgeon's College Heritage Room: Box A2.06, 1849.

———. *Autobiography: Compiled from His Diary, Letters, and Records by His Wife and His Private Secretary.* 4 vols. London: Passmore and Alabaster, 1897.

———. *The Bible and the Newspaper.* London: Passmore and Alabaster, 1878.

———. "The Bible (Part Second)." In *Speeches at Home and Abroad,* edited by G. Holden Pike. London: Passmore & Alabaster, 1878.

———. *The Chequebook of the Bank of Faith: Being Precious Promises Arranged for Daily Use with Brief Comments.* New York: American Tract Society, 1893.

———. *"Come, Ye Children": A Book for Parents and Teachers on the Christian Training of Children.* London: Passmore & Alabaster, 1897.

———. *Evening by Evening.* New York: Sheldon, 1869.

———. *The Gospel of the Kingdom: A Commentary on the Book of Matthew.* London: Passmore and Alabaster, 1893.

———. *The Greatest Fight in the World (Final Manifesto).* Toronto; New York; London: Funk & Wagnalls, 1891.

———. "Home Missions." In *Speeches at Home and Abroad,* edited by G. Holden Pike. London: Passmore & Alabaster, 1878.

———. *How Spurgeon Found Christ.* London: James E. Hawkins, n.d.

———. *The Interpreter, or, Scripture for Family Worship.* London: Passmore & Alabaster, 1888.

———. *John Ploughman's Pictures; or, More of His Plain Talk for Plain People.* Philadelphia: H. Altemus, 1896.

———. *John Ploughman's Talk; or, Plain Advice for Plain People.* Philadelphia: H. Altemus, 1896.

———. *Lectures to My Students: A Selection from Addresses Delivered to the Students of the Pastor's College, Metropolitan Tabernacle.* 4 vols. London: Passmore and Alabaster, 1875.

———. *The Letters of Charles Haddon Spurgeon.* London; Edinburgh; New York: Marshall Brothers, Limited, 1923.

———. *The Metropolitan Tabernacle Pulpit.* 56 vols. London: Passmore and Alabaster, 1861.

———. *Morning by Morning.* New York: Robert Carter and Brothers, 1865.

———. *My Sermon Notes: A Selection from Outlines of Discourses Delivered at the Metropolitan Tabernacle.* Vol. 1. New York: Funk & Wagnalls, 1891.

———. *The New Park Street Pulpit.* 6 vols. London: Passmore and Alabaster, 1855.

———. *The Saint and His Savior: The Progress of the Soul in the Knowledge of Jesus.* New York: Sheldon, Blakeman, 1858.

———. *The Soul Winner: How to Lead Sinners to the Saviour.* New York; Chicago; Toronto: Fleming H. Revell, 1895.

———. *Speeches at Home and Abroad.* London: Passmore and Alabaster, 1878.

———, ed. *The Sword and the Trowel.* 28 vols. London: Passmore and Alabaster, 1865–1892.

———. *The Treasury of David.* 7 vols. London; Edinburgh; New York: Marshall Brothers, 1869-1885.

Spurgeon, C. H., and Benjamin Beddow. *Memories of Stambourne: With Personal Remarks, Recollections, and Reflections.* London: Passmore & Alabaster, 1892.

Stevenson, John. *Christ on the Cross: An Exposition of the Twenty-Second Psalm.* London: J. H. Jackson, Islington Green, 1845.

Stier, Rudolf Ewald. *The Words of the Apostles.* Translated by G. H. Venables. Edinburgh: T&T Clark, 1869.

Strauss, David Friedrich. *Das Leben Jesu Kritisch Bearbeitet.* Tübingen: C. F. Osiander, 1835.

———. *The Life of Jesus, Critically Examined.* Edited by Peter C. Hodgson. Translated by George Eliot. Philadelphia: Fortress Press, 1972.

Trench, Richard Chenevix. *Synonyms of the New Testament: Being the Substance of a Course of Lectures Addressed to the Theological Students, King's College, London.* 9th ed. London: Macmillan, 1880.

Troeltsch, Ernst. "The Dogmatics of the 'Religionsgeschichtliche Schule.'" *The American Journal of Theology* 17, no. 1 (1913): 1-21.

Wellhausen, Julius. *Geschichte Israels.* Berlin: G. Reimer, 1878.

———. *Prolegomena to the History of Israel: With a Reprint of the Article Israel from the Encyclopedia Britannica.* Translated by J. Sutherland Black and Allan Menzies. Edinburgh: A&C Black, 1885.

Winslow, Octavius. *The Ministry of Home; or, Brief Expository Lectures on Divine Truth.* London: William Hunt, 1857.

SECONDARY SOURCES

Allen, James T. *The Essex Lad Who Became the Prince of Preachers.* London; Glasgow: Pickering & Inglis, 1893.

Altholz, Josef L. *Anatomy of a Controversy: The Debate over Essays and Reviews, 1860–1864.* Aldershot, Hants, England; Brookfield, VT: Scolar Press, 1994.

Angus, Joseph, and Samuel G. Green. *The Bible Hand-Book: An Introduction to the Study of Sacred Scripture.* New York: Fleming H. Revell, 1900.

Bacon, Ernest W. *Spurgeon: Heir of the Puritans.* London: Allen & Unwin, 1967.

Baird, William. *History of New Testament Research: From Deism to Tübingen.* Vol. 1. Minneapolis: Fortress Press, 1992.

———. *History of New Testament Research: From Jonathan Edwards to Rudolf Bultmann.* Vol. 2. Minneapolis: Fortress Press, 2003.

Barbeau, Jeffrey W. "'Songs for My Joy . . . Pleadings for My Shame': Coleridge, Divine Revelation and Confessions of an Inquiring Spirit." PhD diss., Marquette University, 2002.

Bartlett, Edward H. *Mrs. Bartlett and Her Class at the Metropolitan Tabernacle: Being a Brief Account of the Life and Labours of Mrs. Lavinia Strickland Bartlett.* London: Passmore & Alabaster, 1877.

Barton, John. *The Cambridge Companion to Biblical Interpretation.* Cambridge: Cambridge University Press, 2009.

Batalden, Stephen, Kathleen Cann, and John Dean, eds. *Sowing the Word: The Cultural Impact of the British and Foreign Bible Society, 1804–2004.* Sheffield: Sheffield Phoenix Press, 2006.

Bebbington, D. W. *The Dominance of Evangelicalism: The Age of Spurgeon and Moody.* Leicester: Inter-Varsity Press, 2005.

———. *Evangelicalism in Modern Britain: A History from the 1730s to the 1980s.* London: Routledge, 2005.

———. "Spurgeon and British Evangelical Theological Education." In *Theological Education in the Evangelical Tradition,* edited by D. G. Hart and R. Albert Mohler, 217-34. Grand Rapids, MI: Baker Book House, 1996.

———. "Spurgeon and the Common Man." *Baptist Review of Theology* 5, no. 1 (1995): 63-75.

Brastow, Lewis Ormond. *Representative Modern Preachers.* New York: Macmillan, 1904.

Brauer, Jerald C. "Conversion: From Puritanism to Revivalism." *The Journal of Religion* 58, no. 3 (July 1978): 227-43.

Brown, Stewart J. *Providence and Empire : Religion, Politics and Society in the United Kingdom, 1815–1914.* Harlow: Pearson Longman, 2008.

Burridge, Richard A. *What Are the Gospels? A Comparison with Graeco-Roman Biography.* 2nd ed. Grand Rapids: Eerdmans, 2004.

Buss, Martin J. *Biblical Form Criticism in Its Context.* Journal for the Study of the Old Testament Series 274. Sheffield: Sheffield Academic Press, 1999.

Caldwell, Patricia. *The Puritan Conversion Narrative: The Beginnings of American Expression.* Cambridge: Cambridge University Press, 1983.

Carlile, J. C. *C. H. Spurgeon: An Interpretive Biography.* London: Religious Tract Society and the Kingsgate Press, 1934.

Carlsson, Eric. "Eighteenth-Century Neology." In *The Oxford Handbook of Early Modern Theology, 1600–1800,* edited by Ulrich L. Lehner, Richard A. Muller, and A. G. Roeber, 642-48. Oxford: Oxford University Press, 2016.

Carpenter, Mary Wilson. "[Review of] The Victorian Pulpit: Spoken and Written Sermons in Nineteenth-Century Britain." *Victorian Studies* 43, no. 2 (2001): 305-6.

Chadwick, Owen. *The Victorian Church: Part One (1829–1859).* London: A&C Black, 1971.

———. *The Victorian Church: Part Two (1860–1901).* London: SCM Press, 1987.

Coffey, John. "Democracy and Popular Religion: Moody and Sankey's Mission to Britain, 1873–1875." In *Citizenship and Community: Liberals, Radicals, and Collective Identities in the British Isles, 1865–1931,* edited by Eugenio F. Biagini, 93-119. Cambridge: Cambridge University Press, 1996.

Colenso, John William. *The Pentateuch and Book of Joshua Critically Examined.* London: Longman, Green, Longman, Roberts & Green, 1862.

Coleridge, Samuel Taylor. "Confessions of an Inquiring Spirit." In vol. 2 of *The Collected Works of Samuel Taylor Coleridge,* edited by H. J. Jackson and J. R. de J. Jackson. Princeton, NJ: Princeton University Press, 1995.

Collins, John J. "What Is Apocalyptic Literature?" In *The Oxford Handbook of Apocalyptic Literature,* edited by John J. Collins, 1-16. Oxford: Oxford University Press, 2014.

Colquitt, Henry Franklin. "The Soteriology of Charles Haddon Spurgeon Revealed in His Sermons and Controversial Writings." PhD thesis, University of Edinburgh, 1951.

Conwell, Russell H. *Life of Charles Haddon Spurgeon, the World's Great Preacher.* Philadelphia: Edgewood, 1892.

Coon, George Michael. "Recasting Inerrancy: The Doctrine of Scripture in Carl Henry and the Old Princeton School." PhD thesis, University of St. Michael's College, 2009.

Dallimore, Arnold A. *Spurgeon: A New Biography.* Edinburgh: Banner of Truth Trust, 1985.

Daniel, Curt D. "Hyper-Calvinism and John Gill." PhD thesis, University of Edinburgh, 1983.

Dargan, Edwin Charles. *A History of Preaching.* Vol. 2, *From the Close of the Reformation Period to the End of the Nineteenth Century, 1572–1900.* London: Hodder & Stoughton, 1912.

Dickson, J. N. Ian. *Beyond Religious Discourse: Sermons, Preaching and Evangelical Protestants in Nineteenth-Century Irish Society.* Milton Keynes: Paternoster, 2007.

Drummond, Lewis A. *Spurgeon: Prince of Preachers*. Grand Rapids, MI: Kregel, 1992.

Dupré, Louis. *The Enlightenment and the Intellectual Foundations of Modern Culture*. New Haven, CT; London: Yale University Press, 2004.

Edwards, Jr., O. C. *A History of Preaching*. Nashville: Abingdon Press, 2004.

Ellis, Ieuan. *Seven Against Christ: A Study of "Essays and Reviews."* Studies in the History of Christian Thought 23. Leiden: Brill, 1980.

Ellison, Robert H. *A New History of the Sermon: The Nineteenth Century*. Leiden: Brill, 2010.

———. *The Victorian Pulpit: Spoken and Written Sermons in Nineteenth-Century Britain*. Selinsgrove: Susquehanna University Press, 1998.

Epp, Eldon. "Critical Editions and the Development of Text-Critical Methods, Part 2: From Lachmann (1831) to the Present." In *The New Cambridge History of the Bible: From 1750 to the Present*, edited by John Riches, 4:13-48. Cambridge: Cambridge University Press, 2015.

Eswine, Zach. *Spurgeon's Sorrows: Realistic Hope for Those Who Suffer from Depression*. Ross-shire, UK: Christian Focus, 2015.

Eswine, Zachary W. "The Role of the Holy Spirit in the Preaching Theory and Practice of Charles Haddon Spurgeon." PhD diss., Regent University, 2003.

Ferguson, Duncan S. "The Bible and Protestant Orthodoxy: The Hermeneutics of Charles Spurgeon." *Journal of the Evangelical Theological Society* 25, no. 4 (December 1, 1982): 455-66.

Fowl, Stephen E., ed. *The Theological Interpretation of Scripture: Classic and Contemporary Readings*. Blackwell Readings in Modern Theology. Cambridge, MA: Blackwell, 1997.

Francis, Keith A., and William Gibson. *The Oxford Handbook of the British Sermon, 1689–1901*. Oxford: Oxford University Press, 2012.

Frei, Hans W. *The Eclipse of Biblical Narrative: A Study in Eighteenth and Nineteenth Century Hermeneutics*. Rev. ed. New Haven, CT; London: Yale University Press, 1980.

Fullerton, W. Y. *C. H. Spurgeon: A Biography*. London: Williams and Norgate, 1920.

George, Christian. "6 Quotes Spurgeon Didn't Say." The Spurgeon Center, August 8, 2017. Accessed August 14, 2017. www.spurgeon.org/resource-library/blog-entries/6-quotes-spurgeon-didnt-say.

George, Christian T. "Jesus Christ, the 'Prince of Pilgrims': A Critical Analysis of the Ontological, Functional, and Exegetical Christologies in the Sermons, Writings, and Lectures of Charles Haddon Spurgeon (1834–1892)." PhD thesis, University of St. Andrews, 2011.

———, ed. *The Lost Sermons of C. H. Spurgeon*. Vol. 1. Nashville: B&H Academic, 2016.

Gertz, Jan Christian. "Jean Astruc and Source Criticism in the Book of Genesis." In *Sacred Conjectures: The Context and Legacy of Robert Lowth and Jean Astruc*, edited by John Jarick, 190-203. London: T&T Clark, 2007.

Glover, Willis Borders. *Evangelical Nonconformists and Higher Criticism in the Nineteenth Century*. London: Independent Press, 1954.

Goldsworthy, Graeme. *Gospel-Centered Hermeneutics: Foundations and Principles of Evangelical Biblical Interpretation*. Downers Grove, IL: IVP Academic, 2006.

Grass, Tim, and Ian Randall. "C. H. Spurgeon on the Sacraments." In *Baptist Sacramentalism*, edited by Anthony R. Cross and Philip E. Thompson, 55-75. Cumbria, UK: Paternoster Press, 2003.

Greidanus, Sidney. *Preaching Christ from the Old Testament*. Grand Rapids: Eerdmans, 1999.

Gribben, Crawford, and Timothy C. F. Stunt, eds. *Prisoners of Hope? Aspects of Evangelical Millennialism in Britain and Ireland, 1800–1880*. Milton Keynes: Paternoster, 2004.

Harris, Harriet A. *Fundamentalism and Evangelicals*. Oxford: Oxford University Press, 1998.

Harris, Horton. *The Tübingen School*. Oxford: Oxford University Press, 1975.

Harris, Khim. *Evangelicals and Education: Evangelical Anglicans and Middle-Class Education in Nineteenth-Century England*. London: Paternoster Press, 2004.

Harrison, J. F. C. *A History of the Working Men's College, 1854–1954*. London: Routledge & Kegan Paul, 1954.

Helmstadter, R. J. "Spurgeon in Outcast London." In *The View from the Pulpit: Victorian Ministers and Society*, edited by P. T. Phillips, 161-85. Toronto: Macmillan, 1978.

Hevia, James. *The Imperial Security State: British Colonial Knowledge and Empire-Building in Asia*. Cambridge: Cambridge University Press, 2012.

Heyck, T. W. *The Transformation of Intellectual Life in Victorian England*. Croom Helm Studies in Society and History. London: Croom Helm, 1982.

Hinchliff, Peter Bingham. *Benjamin Jowett and the Christian Religion*. Oxford: Oxford University Press, 1987.

Hindmarsh, D. Bruce. *The Evangelical Conversion Narrative: Spiritual Autobiography in Early Modern England*. Oxford: Oxford University Press, 2005.

Hixson, Elijah. "New Testament Textual Criticism in the Ministry of Charles Haddon Spurgeon." *Journal of the Evangelical Theological Society* 57, no. 3 (2014): 555-70.

Hopkins, Mark. "The Down-Grade Controversy: What Caused Spurgeon to Start the Most Bitter Fight of His Life?" *Christian History* 10, no. 29 (1991).

———. *Nonconformity's Romantic Generation: Evangelical and Liberal Theologies in Victorian England*. Carlisle, UK; Waynesboro, GA: Paternoster Press, 2004.

Howsam, Leslie. *Cheap Bibles: Nineteenth-Century Publishing and the British and Foreign Bible Society*. Cambridge Studies in Publishing and Printing History. Cambridge: Cambridge University Press, 1991.

Hsü, Immanuel C. Y. *The Rise of Modern China*. 6th ed. Oxford: Oxford University Press, 2000.

Hurtado, Larry W. "Fashions, Fallacies and Future Prospects in New Testament Studies." *Journal for the Study of the New Testament* 36, no. 4 (2014): 299-324.

Ives, Keith A. *Voices of Nonconformity: William Robertson Nicoll and the British Weekly.* Cambridge: Lutterworth Press, 2011.

Jeanrond, Werner. *Theological Hermeneutics: Development and Significance.* London: SCM Press, 1994.

Johnson, Luke Timothy. "The Sermon on the Mount." In *The Oxford Companion to Christian Thought*, edited by Adrian Hastings. Oxford: Oxford University Press, 2000.

Jones, Peter. *The Christian Socialist Revival, 1877–1914: Religion, Class, and Social Conscience in Late-Victorian England.* Princeton, NJ: Princeton University Press, 1968.

Jones, Tod E. *The Broad Church: A Biography of a Movement.* Lanham, MD: Lexington Books, 2003.

Kidd, Colin. *The Forging of Races: Race and Scripture in the Protestant Atlantic World, 1600–2000.* Cambridge, UK; New York: Cambridge University Press, 2006.

Knight, Mark, and Emma Mason. *Nineteenth-Century Religion and Literature: An Introduction.* Oxford: Oxford University Press, 2006.

Kruppa, Patricia S. *Charles Haddon Spurgeon: A Preacher's Progress.* Vol. 9. Routledge Library Editions: 19th Century Religion. London: Taylor and Francis, 2017.

Landow, George P. *Victorian Types, Victorian Shadows: Biblical Typology in Victorian Literature, Art, and Thought.* Boston: Routledge & Kegan Paul, 1980.

Larsen, Timothy. "Biblical Criticism and the Crisis of Belief: D. F. Strauss's *Leben Jesu* in Britain." In *Contested Christianity: The Political and Social Context of Victorian Theology*, 43-58. Waco, TX: Baylor University Press, 2004.

———. "Biblical Criticism and the Desire for Reform: Bishop Colenso on the Pentateuch." In *Contested Christianity: The Political and Social Context of Victorian Theology*, 59-77. Waco, TX: Baylor University Press, 2004.

———. "Charles Haddon Spurgeon." In *The Sermon on the Mount Through the Centuries*, edited by Jeffrey Greenman, Timothy Larsen, and Stephen R. Spencer, 181-205. Grand Rapids, MI: Brazos Press, 2007.

———. *A People of One Book: The Bible and the Victorians.* Oxford; New York: Oxford University Press, 2011.

Ledger-Lomas, Michael. "Ministers and Ministerial Training." In *The Oxford History of Protestant Dissenting Traditions*, vol. 3, *The Nineteenth Century*, edited by Timothy Larsen and Michael Ledger-Lomas. Oxford: Oxford University Press, 2017.

Luckin, W. "The Final Catastrophe: Cholera in London, 1866." *Medical History* 21 (1977): 32-42.

Magoon, Elias Lyman. *"The Modern Whitfield": Sermons of the Rev. C. H. Spurgeon of London, with an Introduction and Sketch of His Life.* New York: Sheldon, Blakeman, 1856.

Mahoney, Kristin. "Work, Lack, and Longing: Rossetti's 'The Blessed Damozel' and the Working Men's College." *Victorian Studies* 52, no. 2 (January 2010): 219-48.

Mandelbrote, Scott, and Michael Ledger-Lomas, eds. *Dissent and the Bible in Britain, c. 1650–1950*. Oxford: Oxford University Press, 2013.

McCoy, Timothy A. "The Evangelistic Ministry of C. H. Spurgeon: Implications for a Contemporary Model for Pastoral Evangelism." PhD diss., The Southern Baptist Theological Seminary, 1989.

McLachlan, Herbert. *English Education Under the Test Acts: Being the History of the Non-conformist Academics 1662–1820*. Manchester: Manchester University Press, 1931.

Morden, Peter J. "The Bible for the Masses: The Popular Preaching of C. H. Spurgeon." In *Text Message: The Centrality of Scripture in Preaching*, edited by Ian Stackhouse and Oliver Crisp. Cambridge: The Lutterworth Press, 2014.

———. *"Communion with Christ and His People": The Spirituality of C. H. Spurgeon*. Oxford: Regent's Park College, 2010.

Munson, J. E. B. "The Education of Baptist Ministers, 1870–1900." *Baptist Quarterly* 26, no. 7 (1976): 320-27.

Murray, Iain H. *Archibald Brown: Spurgeon's Successor*. Edinburgh: Banner of Truth Trust, 2011.

———. *The Forgotten Spurgeon*. London: Banner of Truth Trust, 1966.

———, ed. *Letters of Charles Haddon Spurgeon*. Edinburgh: Banner of Truth Trust, 1992.

———. *Spurgeon v. Hyper-Calvinism: The Battle for Gospel Preaching*. Edinburgh: Banner of Truth Trust, 2002.

Needham, George C. *The Life and Labors of Charles H. Spurgeon, the Faithful Preacher, the Devoted Pastor, the Noble Philanthropist, the Beloved College President, and the Voluminous Writer, Author, Etc., Etc*. Boston: D. L. Guernsey, 1881.

Neill, Stephen, and N. T. Wright. *The Interpretation of the New Testament, 1861–1986*. 2nd ed. Oxford; New York: Oxford University Press, 1988.

Nettles, Tom. *Living by Revealed Truth: The Life and Pastoral Theology of Charles Haddon Spurgeon*. Ross-shire, UK: Christian Focus, 2013.

Nicholls, Mike. *C. H. Spurgeon: The Pastor Evangelist*. Didcot: Baptist Historical Society, 1992.

———. "Charles Haddon Spurgeon, Educationalist: Part 1—General Education Concerns." *Baptist Quarterly* 31, no. 8 (October 1986): 364-401.

———. "Charles Haddon Spurgeon, Educationalist: Part 2—The Principles and Practice of the Pastor's College." *Baptist Quarterly* 32, no. 2 (April 1987): 73-94.

———. *Lights to the World: A History of Spurgeon's College 1856–1992*. Harpenden: Nuprint, 1994.

Noll, Mark A. *Between Faith and Criticism: Evangelicals, Scholarship, and the Bible in America*. 2nd ed. Vancouver: Regent College Publishing, 2004.

Old, Hughes Oliphant. *The Reading and Preaching of the Scriptures in the Worship of the Christian Church.* Grand Rapids, MI: Eerdmans, 1998.

Parker, Irene. *Dissenting Academies in England: Their Rise and Progress and Their Place Among the Educational Systems of the Country.* Cambridge: Cambridge University Press, 1914.

Parsons, Gerald. "Preaching the Broad Church Gospel: The Natal Sermons of Bishop John William Colenso." In *The Oxford Handbook of the British Sermon 1689–1901*, edited by Keith A Francis. Oxford: Oxford University Press, 2012.

———. "Released from the Thraldom of Mere Bibliolatry: Biblical Criticism in the Sermons of Bishop Colenso." *Modern Believing* 52, no. 2 (2011): 22-29.

Payne, Ernest A. "Gleanings from the Correspondence of George Eliot." *Baptist Quarterly* 27 (1958): 179-81.

Pelikan, Jaroslav. *Divine Rhetoric: The Sermon on the Mount as Message and as Model in Augustine, Chrysostom, and Luther.* Crestwood, NY: St. Vladimir's Seminary Press, 2001.

Phillips, Paul T., ed. *The View from the Pulpit: Victorian Ministers and Society.* Toronto: Macmillan, 1978.

Pike, G. Holden. *The Life and Work of Archibald G. Brown, Preacher and Philanthropist.* London: Passmore & Alabaster, 1892.

———. *The Life and Work of Charles Haddon Spurgeon.* 6 vols. London: Cassell & Company, 1892.

Popov, Alexander. "The Evangelical Christians: Baptists in the Soviet Union as a Hermeneutical Community." PhD thesis, International Baptist Theological Seminary, 2010.

Quiggle, Gregg William. "An Analysis of Dwight Moody's Urban Social Vision." PhD thesis, The Open University, 2009.

Rambo, Lewis R. *Understanding Religious Conversion.* New Haven, CT; London: Yale University Press, 1993.

Randall, Ian M. "C. H. Spurgeon (1834–1892): A Lover of France." *European Journal of Theology* 24, no. 1 (2015): 57-65.

———. "Charles Haddon Spurgeon, the Pastor's College and the Downgrade Controversy." In *Discipline and Diversity*, edited by Kate Cooper and Jeremy Gregory, 43:366-76. Studies in Church History. Suffolk: The Boydell Press, 2007.

———. *A School of the Prophets: 150 Years of Spurgeon's College.* London: Spurgeon's College, 2005.

———. "The World Is Our Parish: Spurgeon's College and World Mission, 1856–1892." In *Baptists and Mission: Papers from the Fourth International Conference on Baptist Studies*, edited by Ian M. Randall and Anthony R. Cross, 64-77. Studies in Baptist History and Thought 29. Carlisle: Paternoster, 2007.

———. "'Ye Men of Plymouth': C. H. Spurgeon and the Brethren." In *Witness in Many Lands*, edited by Tim Grass, 73-90. Troon: Brethren Archivists & Historians Network, 2013.

Reventlow, Henning Graf. *History of Biblical Interpretation: From the Enlightenment to the Twentieth Century*. Translated by Leo G. Perdue. Vol. 4. Atlanta: Society of Biblical Literature, 2010.

———. "The Role of the Old Testament in the German Liberal Protestant Theology of the Nineteenth Century." In *Biblical Studies and the Shifting of Paradigms, 1850–1914*, edited by Henning Graf Reventlow and William Farmer. Journal for the Study of the Old Testament Supplement Series 192. Sheffield: Sheffield Academic Press, 1995.

Rathel, David Mark. "Was John Gill a Hyper-Calvinist? Determining Gill's Theological Identity." *Baptist Quarterly* 48, no. 1 (2017): 47-59.

Rogerson, J. W. *Old Testament Criticism in the Nineteenth Century: England and Germany*. London: SPCK, 1984.

———. *The Bible and Criticism in Victorian Britain: Profiles of F. D. Maurice and William Robertson Smith*. Journal for the Study of the Old Testament Supplement Series 201. Sheffield, England: Sheffield Academic Press, 1995.

———. "History and the Bible." In *World Christianities, c. 1815–c. 1914*, edited by Brian Stanley and Sheridan Gilley, 8:181-96. The Cambridge History of Christianity. Cambridge: Cambridge University Press, 2001.

Rogerson, J. W., Christopher Rowland, and Barnabas Lindars. *The Study and Use of the Bible*. Vol. 2., *The History of Christian Theology*. Basingstoke, Hants, UK: Marshall Pickering, 1988.

Sandeen, Ernest Robert. *The Roots of Fundamentalism: British and American Millenarianism, 1800–1930*. Chicago: University of Chicago Press, 1970.

Sandys-Wunsch, John, and Laurence Eldredge. "J. P. Gabler and the Distinction Between Biblical and Dogmatic Theology: Translation, Commentary, and Discussion of His Originality." *Scottish Journal of Theology* 33 (1980): 133-58.

Serda, Paul. *From Mission to Modernity: Evangelicals, Reformers, and Education in Nineteenth Century Egypt*. New York: I. B. Tauris, 2011.

Shaw, Ian J. *High Calvinists in Action: Calvinism and the City, Manchester and London, c. 1810–1860*. Oxford; New York: Oxford University Press, 2002.

Sheehan, R. J. *C. H. Spurgeon and the Modern Church: Lessons for Today from the "Downgrade" Controversy*. London: Grace Publications Trust, 1985.

Shepherd, Peter. "Spurgeon's Funeral." *Baptist Quarterly* 41, no. 2 (April 2005): 72-79.

Shindler, Robert. *From the Usher's Desk to the Tabernacle Pulpit: The Life and Labors of Charles Haddon Spurgeon*. New York: A. C. Armstrong and Son, 1892.

Smend, Rudolf. *From Astruc to Zimmerli*. Translated by Margaret Kohl. Tübingen: Mohr Siebeck, 2007.

Smith, Donald C. *Passive Obedience and Prophetic Protest: Social Criticism in the Scottish Church 1830–1945.* Vol. 15. American University Studies Series IX, History. New York: Peter Lang, 1987.

Spurgeon, C. H., and Helmut Thielicke. *Encounter with Spurgeon.* London: James Clarke, 1963.

Stanley, Brian. "Christian Responses to the Indian Mutiny of 1857." In *The Church and War, Studies in Church History,* 277-89. Oxford: Blackwell, 1983.

Stanton, Graham N. *A Gospel for New People: Studies in Matthew.* Edinburgh: T&T Clark, 1992.

Stevenson, George J. *Pastor C. H. Spurgeon: His Life and Work to His Forty Third Birthday.* London: Passmore and Alabaster, 1877.

———. *Sketch of the Life and Ministry of the Rev. C. H. Spurgeon: From Original Documents Including Anecdotes and Incidents of Travel, Biographical Notices of Former Pastors, Historical Sketch of Park Street Chapel, and an Outline of Mr. Spurgeon's Articles of Faith.* New York: Sheldon, Blakeman, 1857.

Stewart, Kenneth J. "A Bombshell of a Book: Gaussen's Theopneustia and Its Influence on Subsequent Evangelical Theology." *The Evangelical Quarterly* 75, no. 3 (2003): 215-37.

Stubenrauch, Joseph. "The Evangelical Age of Ingenuity in Industrial Britain." Oxford: Oxford University Press, 2016.

Sugirtharajah, R. S. *The Bible and Empire: Postcolonial Explorations.* Cambridge: Cambridge University Press, 2005.

Sweeney, Douglas A. *Edwards the Exegete: Biblical Interpretation and Anglo-Protestant Culture on the Edge of the Enlightenment.* Oxford: Oxford University Press, 2016.

Talbert, John David. "Charles Haddon Spurgeon's Christological Homiletics: A Critical Evaluation of Selected Sermons from Old Testament Texts." PhD diss., Southwestern Baptist Theological Seminary, 1989.

Tate, Andrew. "Evangelical Certainties: Charles Spurgeon and the Sermon as Crisis Literature." In *Reinventing Christianity: Nineteenth-Century Contexts,* edited by Linda Woodhead, 27-36. Aldershot: Ashgate, 2001.

Thielicke, Helmut. *Encounter with Spurgeon.* Translated by John W. Doberstein. Philadelphia: Fortress Press, 1963.

Thompson, David M. *Cambridge Theology in the Nineteenth Century.* Aldershot: Ashgate, 2008.

Thornton, Jeremy. "The Soteriology of C. H. Spurgeon: Its Biblical and Historical Roots and Its Place in His Preaching." University of Cambridge, 1974.

Treier, Daniel J. *Introducing Theological Interpretation of Scripture: Recovering a Christian Practice.* Grand Rapids: Baker Academic, 2008.

Treloar, Geoffrey R. *Lightfoot the Historian.* Tübingen: Mohr Siebeck, 1998.

Toon, Peter. *The Emergence of Hyper-Calvinism in English Nonconformity, 1689–1765.* London: Olive Tree, 1967.

Twaddle, Michael. "The Oxford and Cambridge Admissions Controversy of 1834." *British Journal of Educational Studies* 14, no. 3 (November 1966): 45-48.

Vanhoozer, Kevin J., ed. *Dictionary for Theological Interpretation of the Bible*. Grand Rapids: Baker Academic, 2005.

Wansbrough, Henry. *The Use and Abuse of the Bible: A Brief History of Biblical Interpretation*. London; New York: T&T Clark, 2010.

Watts, Michael R. *The Dissenters Volume III: The Crisis and Conscience of Nonconformity*. Oxford: Oxford University Press, 2015.

Wayland, Herman Lincoln. *Charles H. Spurgeon: His Faith and Works*. Philadelphia: American Baptist Publication Society, 1892.

Wedgwood, Julia. "Samuel Taylor Coleridge." In *Nineteenth Century Teachers, and Other Essays by Julia Wedgwood*. London: Hodder & Stoughton, 1909.

White, Jonathan. "A Theological and Historical Examination of John Gill's Soteriology in Relation to Eighteenth-Century Hyper-Calvinism." PhD diss., The Southern Baptist Theological Seminary, 2010.

Wright, A. P. M., and C. P. Lewis, eds. "Waterbeach: Introduction." In *A History of the County of Cambridge and the Isle of Ely*, vol. 9, *Chesterton, Northstowe, and Papworth Hundreds*, 237-43. London: Victoria Country History, 1989.

Wyncoll, Hannah, ed. *Wonders of Grace: Original Testimonies of Converts During Spurgeon's Early Years*. London: The Wakeman Trust, 2016.

Zimmermann, Jens. *Recovering Theological Hermeneutics: An Incarnational-Trinitarian Theory of Interpretation*. Grand Rapids: Baker Academic, 2004.

GENERAL INDEX

SCRIPTURE INDEX

Finding the Textbook You Need

The IVP Academic Textbook Selector
is an online tool for instantly finding the IVP books
suitable for over 250 courses across 24 disciplines.

ivpacademic.com